Prisoner Education

Marjorie J. Seashore
Steven Haberfeld
with
John Irwin
Keith Baker

The Praeger Special Studies program —
utilizing the most modern and efficient book
production techniques and a selective
worldwide distribution network—makes
available to the academic, government, and
business communities significant, timely
research in U.S. and international economic, social, and political development.

Prisoner Education
Project NewGate and Other College Programs

Praeger Publishers   New York   Washington   London

Library of Congress Cataloging in Publication Data

Seashore, Marjorie J.
    Prisoner education.

    (Praeger special studies in U.S. economic, social, and
political issues)
    Bibliography: p.
    1. Education of prisoners—United States.   2. Education
of prisoners—Cost effectiveness.   3. Education of prisoners—
United States—Care studies.   I. Haberfeld, Steven, joint author.
II. Title.
HV8875.S32   365'.66   75-23991
ISBN 0-275-56040-6

PRAEGER PUBLISHERS
111 Fourth Avenue, New York, N.Y. 10003, U.S.A.

Published in the United States of America in 1976
by Praeger Publishers, Inc.

Printed in the United States of America

This book is a study of college education in prisons. Under contract with the Office of Economic Opportunity in 1972 and 1973 (no. B2C-5322) the firm of Marshall Kaplan, Gans, and Kahn conducted an extensive study of selected college programs in state and federal prisons throughout the country. The research consisted of on-site observations of program operations as well as the analysis of each program's impact on the postprison "success" of former students. Over 350 former program participants were found and personally interviewed, making the project one of the most ambitious and successful follow-up studies of exprisoners ever undertaken.

The findings of this Office of Economic Opportunity (OEO) study are the primary basis of this book and were first reported in "An Evaluation of 'NewGate' and Other Prisoner Education Programs, April 1973," a publication submitted to the OEO. In addition to presenting the findings of the OEO study, this book reflects the findings and conclusions of a second analysis conducted a year after the first was completed. The second study was funded by the Department of Health, Education, and Welfare, Office of the Secretary (under contract HEW-OS-74-168). The high quality of the statistical data still not yet fully analyzed and the importance of the issues involved (prison reform and prisoner rehabilitation) warranted this second, in-depth analysis. Marshall Kaplan, Gans, and Kahn conducted the HEW study from July 1974 to March 1975 and presented its findings in a separate HEW report, "Additional Data Analysis and Evaluation of 'Project NewGate' and Other Prison College Programs, March 1975."

The authors wish to extend their appreciation to many others who shared in enabling this research. Special thanks certainly must go to Sheldon P. Gans, whose interest went well beyond the contract phases of the study and who generously freed staff time and company resources to prepare this book for publication. Special mention must also be made of the enormous contributions made by Don Leonard as research analyst. From the preparation of the original research design through data collection and analysis, Don's hard work made a lasting impact on both the direction and the final product of the analysis. Due primarily to Don's dogged persistence and ingenuity in ferreting out the often elusive exparticipant, the follow-up phase of the study was able to locate an amazing 96 percent of the sample. The authors also wish to thank David Datz for his help in untangling analytical issues and

and Johanna Sheridan, Julie M. Rothschild, and Lorraine Anne Hilton for their work, patience, and advice in preparing the manuscript.

Many others too numerous to list provided unlimited cooperation and support to the research staff. The prisons and colleges that hosted the prison college programs under study as well as the programs themselves generously provided their records and staff time to assist us. Prison inmates and exprisoners who were interviewed were uniformly willing to answer questions and offer their own opinions and interpretations in response to our own, often still unformulated speculations. Finally, there were countless others—friends and members of exprisoners' families, program and prison staff, probation and parole officers, gas station attendants, bartenders, and traffic cops— who assisted the field staff in finding their way to the doorsteps of their follow-up sample. To these and others, the authors wish to express their heartfelt appreciation. They all contributed to carrying this study to its final conclusion.

CONTENTS

LIST OF TABLES

LIST OF FIGURES

Prisoner Education

BACKGROUND

Within the last twenty years an increasing number and variety of college programs have been established in American prisons. These efforts have ranged from offering correspondence courses to establishing a structured program within the prison walls, to developing some formal relationship with outside academic institutions. Prisons are not the only initiators; academic institutions as well have begun to demonstrate their interest in this area. Either as part of or separate from the prison institution, colleges have begun to offer special opportunities to exprisoners on their own campuses. By 1972, at least California, Colorado, Florida, Illinois, Kentucky, Massachusetts, Minnesota, New Jersey, New Mexico, New York, North Carolina, Oregon, Pennsylvania, Texas, Washington, and Washington, D. C. , had some type of college program operating inside prisons in their states.

In the midst of this activity, the Office of Economic Opportunity (OEO) began to provide funds to a select number of state and federal prisons to set up more elaborate college programs. The first OEO-funded project was introduced in 1967 into the Oregon State Prison on the initiative of Thomas Gaddis, a sociologist long involved in prison reform. As it was first conceived, the project was an adaptation of the OEO Upward Bound concept. Later, it became known in OEO as "Project NewGate" to focus on the program's mission to open a "new gate" out of prison and to honor NewGate Penitentiary in England, considered to be the originator of the idea of prison rehabilitation as well as incarceration for punishment. OEO expanded the NewGate program in 1967 and 1968, funding projects in the Minnesota State

Reformatory in St. Cloud, Minnesota, the New Mexico State Prison in Santa Fe, New Mexico, and later in the Rockview State Correctional Institution in Bellefonte, Pennsylvania, and in the Federal Youth Center in Ashland, Kentucky. In the fall of 1971, a sixth program was started in the Federal Youth Center in Englewood, Colorado.

The NewGate model was much more ambitious and comprehensive than any other prison college program in existence at the time. NewGate essentially intended to establish a self-contained program structure inside the prison that would begin to prepare considerable numbers of inmates for college while they were still in prison by offering quality courses, academic and therapeutic counseling, individual attention from staff members, and such. It was hoped, too, that the program would enrich the atmosphere inside prison. NewGate also consisted of a postrelease program, which would provide financial and other support to a former inmate on a college campus during his transition to life outside. Prior to NewGate, no program conceived of its role as extending into the area of providing extensive follow-up and follow-through assistance after release from prison. To bridge the gap effectively between the prison and outside institutional networks with which the released inmate would come into contact, NewGate insisted on maintaining some structural separateness from the prison system.

All the prison college programs had in common their intent to offer prison inmates an opportunity to obtain college-level education while they were still in confinement. In this sense, all programs had embarked on a rather unusual mission. First, prisons generally are not considered likely settings for a college education. Given their priority on custody and security and their inflexible physical structures, prisons do not easily provide an academic atmosphere. Second, prison inmates are not usually thought of as potential college students. The average prison inmate's past school record is unimpressive. His test scores show that he is usually two to three years behind grade level and he usually has not completed high school. Moreover, it is well-documented that inmates typically come from a socioeconomic background (that is, low income and minority) that is statistically underrepresented on college campuses.

Given these obvious obstacles, the relative effectiveness of those college programs that have operated in the prison context would seem to pose questions of enormous interest: What have been the specific experiences of these "educational-correctional" programs? Have the obstacles of the prison setting and the deficiencies of the inmate student been overcome? What has the program impact been on the host institutions and the participants in terms of educational gain, aspirations, employment, and recidivism over the short and long term? Have some types of programs been more successful than others? Is it ultimately feasible and desirable to offer a college education to prisoners? These questions should be of immediate concern to those who fund and operate educational programs. But they also should be of interest to criminologists involved in correctional reform and professional educators attempting to design effective programs for students from the lower socioeconomic classes.

Despite the fact that many states had had the experience of operating some type of college program in their prisons and thus had the empirical data to answer important questions, there had been no systematic and comparative study of the programs' experiences until 1972, when the OEO initiated such a study. Recognizing the need to assess its own NewGate program and being interested in how the NewGate model compared with other program models, OEO funded a study to evaluate and compare the performance of both NewGate and non-NewGate prison college programs. This OEO study was supplemented by a grant a year later from the Department of Health, Education, and Welfare (HEW) to undertake a second, more intensive look at some of the data still on hand.

NATURE AND SCOPE OF THE STUDY

This book combines the OEO and the HEW analyses. Observations of eight college education programs in federal and state prisons and a nationwide follow-up study of former inmate participants provide the fundamental data base. (Detailed descriptions of all programs are included in the Appendix.) Of these eight programs, five were New-Gate projects operating in the Federal Youth Center in Ashland, Kentucky (Ashland); the Minnesota State Reformatory in St. Cloud, Minnesota (Minnesota); the New Mexico State Prison in Santa Fe, New Mexico (New Mexico); the Oregon State Prison in Salem, Oregon (Oregon); and the Rockview State Correctional Institution in Bellefonte, Pennsylvania (Pennsylvania). By 1972 these programs had been in operation for periods of three to five years, and a considerable number of students who had participated in the prison college programs had been released from prison and were attempting to reestablish themselves in the community. A sixth NewGate program at the Federal Youth Center in Englewood, Colorado, was not included because, as a new program, there were too few released participants at the time the OEO study began. In addition to the five NewGate programs, three other prison college programs, which varied significantly from the NewGate model, were included for purposes of comparison.* These

―――――――――

*A fourth program at California State University at San Diego was included in the study but was dropped from the comparative analysis

programs were located at the Federal Correctional Institution,
Lompoc, California (Lompoc); the Illinois State Penitentiary-Menard
Branch (Illinois); and the Texas Department of Corrections, Eastham
Unit (Texas).

In general terms, each of the eight programs analyzed offered
a standard, if limited, undergraduate liberal arts curriculum, including courses in such traditional areas as English, history, economics, and psychology. All were accredited courses taught by regular instructors from neighboring colleges or universities. The courses
provided both imparted basic knowledge useful in itself and served as
a basis for further study should the participant continue his education
after release from prison.

There were two major areas in which the programs differed from
each other: (1) the provision of supportive services, such as academic
and psychological counseling, and facilities for educational involvement beyond the classroom, and (2) the existence of an outside program for continuing college after release from prison. These differences were principally due to differences in the perceived nature and
purpose of college education for prison inmates.

Among the programs studied, those in Illinois and Texas were the
most limited in scope. Those were restricted to offering college
courses inside the prison with essentially no academic activities or
services outside the classroom. Most students participated only part-
time in addition to holding regular prison work assignments. There
were no formal outside programs after release, although there were
informal arrangements with a few people at Southern Illinois University
(SIU), the sponsoring educational institution in the Illinois program.
These ties benefited some students after their release. On the whole,
however, the Illinois and Texas programs were narrowly conceived.
They were maintained essentially within the prison's administrative
structure and reflected those institutions' primary concerns for custody and security. The classes were available to inmates who took the
initiative to seek them out; no special incentives or accommodations
in the normal prison routine were made.

The Lompoc program was more comprehensive than those of
Illinois and Texas. Not only courses were offered; there was an
attempt to create a college atmosphere: lounge areas were available
for informal contact among students, and opportunities were open for
developing clubs and special interest classes (poetry, transcendental

---

because it lacked certain dimensions (primarily a college program
inside a prison) which were essential to making useful and valid cross-
program comparisons.

meditation, or such). Informal contacts with persons on the University of California campuses at Santa Barbara and Irvine made admission to college after release easier than it would have been otherwise for Lompoc participants, but there was little provision for formal transitional services to support exprisoners through the reentry process.

It should be noted that the greater comprehensiveness of the Lompoc program, compared with the Texas and Illinois programs, was not motivated by a belief that such a structure was necessary to enhance and facilitate the continued education of low income and minority students, as it was in the NewGate programs. The Lompoc program was unique in that it was the only program dominated by a large group of middle class inmates, many of whom had previously attended college. This group of individuals was instrumental in influencing the prison administration to provide additional services, most of which were arranged by the inmates themselves through their own contacts on the university campus.

The Ashland program stood somewhere between the other NewGate programs and the non-NewGate programs in terms of comprehensiveness. It provided outreach, remediation in the basic educational skills, and supportive and extracurricular services outside the classroom. Although the program was committed to providing financial support and personal counseling to its former students on college campuses after release, this support proved to be inconsistent and unsatisfactory. A major deficiency in the Ashland program was the lack of a central university for students continuing after release. In contrast with state prisons, the Federal Youth Center confines persons from a larger geographical area than the host state. Ashland students usually returned to their homes, which were dispersed among 20 eastern states.

The NewGate programs in Minnesota, New Mexico, Oregon, and Pennsylvania offered the most extensive supportive services. Each provided psychological and academic counseling for its students both before and after release. Students whose participation in the inside program had been satisfactory were eligible for postrelease support in obtaining college admission, job placement, and financial assistance. Oregon and Pennsylvania maintained study release centers, where students lived and attended classes on campus prior to formal release from prison. The Minnesota program had a residence at the University of Minnesota in which students continuing in college after formal release were housed for the first two quarters after release. The Minnesota program also differed from the other NewGate programs at the time that the study was conducted in that participation in group counseling activities, both while in prison and while living at the residence house, was mandatory for all program participants. Although counseling services were available in New Mexico, Oregon, and Pennsylvania, participation was optional.

APPROACH AND METHODOLOGY

The basic research design combined a variety of methods for gathering data. The program process was evaluated by visiting the project sites at periodic intervals and conducting extensive interviews with project administrators and teachers, prison guards and administrators, and prison inmates. In addition, observations were made of activities in the classrooms, in the designated project areas, and in the total institution. Questionnaires were administered to all participants currently enrolled in the program inside the prison. In addition, a random sample of 50 former participants who had been released from prison was selected at each project site from a list of all participants released from 1968-71 who had completed a minimum of 12 semester units or the equivalent (15 quarter units) in the inside college program and/or had participated in both the pre- and postrelease educational programs. Background data on each group of 50 were gathered from prison files and program records. Forty persons out of each group of 50 were selected for personal interviews regarding their experiences in the program and after release.

Several departures from this design occurred in the actual execution of the study. The participant sample in Oregon was expanded to 75 persons (60 of whom were interviewed) because of the greater size and longevity of this program. An additional six persons were included from Pennsylvania, which resulted in the inclusion of all eligible participants in the study sample. The samples in Lompoc, Illinois, and Texas were smaller because there were fewer than 50 persons who met the criteria for inclusion and fewer than 40 persons could be located for personal interviews. The study also included control and comparison groups of nonparticipants at Ashland and Minnesota, and comparison groups at New Mexico, Oregon, and Pennsylvania. Data on members of the control groups were obtained in the same way they were for the participant groups: prison files and personal interviews in the community. Data on the comparison groups were obtained exclusively from prison records and available data tapes. Persons in the control group were those whom the program staff had identified as academically qualified for admission to the program but who had not actually participated. The comparison groups consisted of persons selected by the evaluation staff from prison records who were comparable with participants in terms of age, IQ, prior education, tested achievement, level, and time served but who had not applied for admission to the program.

QUESTIONS ADDRESSED

The general topics addressed are the following:

(1) Evaluation of program process: What was the structure and function of these college programs operating inside prisons? How were they set up to achieve their educational goals? What was the comparative quality of their educational services? How were the programs and program components rated by the participants? What impact did the programs have on their host institutions, that is, the prison and the college? Conversely, what impact did these institutions have on the college programs? What strategies were effective in maintaining program quality and in surviving as vital programs?

(2) Evaluation of academic achievement: Perhaps most relevant to a study of education programs in prisons, to what extent could inmate students be seen to achieve academically? How did inmates' academic success correlate with their background characteristics?

(3) Evaluation of postprison performance: What was the nature of the postprison experiences of members of the experimental and control groups? Were there differences between the postprison experiences of NewGate participants, non-NewGate program participants, and nonparticipants? What impact did the various prison college programs have on the former participants' postprison success? Did the life aspiriations, goals, and circumstances of participants improve as a result of their experiences in the programs? Did the college program participants have lower rates of recidivism than nonparticipants? How well did those exprisoners do on dimensions of success other than recidivism, that is, on achieving stability and realizing life goals?

(4) Evaluation of program impact on postprison performance: Were there discernible differences in the contribution to postprison success of various program components: for example, the quality of instruction, academic counseling, therapy, prerelease preparation, postrelease support, quality of the outside sponsoring university, the program's relationship to the prison, and such?

(5) Analysis of cost and benefits: What were the financial costs and benefits of college programs provided to prison inmates? What were the social costs and benefits?

(6) Description of a model program: What were the basic issues facing the planners and administrators of prison college programs inside the prison or at the university? What were the alternative strategies and their implications? On the basis of the study's findings, how were these issues best resolved? What are the basic dimensions of an ideal prison college program?

Serving to sharpen the focus of the analysis that follows, the next chapter describes the historical background and context in which college education has been introduced in prisons. This is followed by six chapters which discuss, in the same order, the six major analytical questions presented above. These are followed by a concluding chapter. Extensive case studies of the eight programs as well as a fuller description of the study methodology are included in the Appendix.

2

FAILURE OF PRISONS AND PRISONERS

It has become increasingly apparent that prisons have not been effective in one of the tasks assigned to them by society—reformation of the criminal. * Incarceration, rather than being the start of a process of reconstructing the individual, appears to constitute only one stage in a cycle from which extrication is extremely difficult. Recidivism studies document consistently that about 40 to 50 percent of an average cohort of released felons will return again to confinement.[1] Making this statistic even more dramatic is the realization that among those who do not return, there could be considerable numbers who, regardless of the prison experience, just happen to be finally at the end of a cycle of previous releases and returns. Moreover, once the end of that cycle is reached, the condition of those persons' lives usually is no less pessimistic. Studies show that

---

*Many studies and surveys in criminology literature have indicated that modern correction techniques have not made any significant difference in the culture of criminal activities of convicts. The reader is referred to two of the best discussions of this issue: Leslie Wilkins, Evolution of Penal Measures (New York: Random House, 1968), and G. Kassebaum, D. Ward, and D. Wilner, Prison Treatment and Parole Survival (New York: J. Wiley and Sons, 1971). See also Robert Martinson, The Effectiveness of Correctional Treatment (New York: Praeger Publishers, 1975).

exprisoners, after extricating themselves from the cycle, usually do
not fulfill their (or society's) conception of a successful life adjustment.*

EFFECTS OF INCARCERATION

The correctional system in the United States is undergoing a
critical examination. Some critics have questioned seriously long-
standing underlying assumptions. For example, the issue of whether
prisoner reformation or rehabilitation should be any concern of the
correctional system has been raised. In many parts of the country
there is a deliberate move toward viewing prisons exclusively as the
means of punishment.

Concurrently, the actual operation of the prisons is being carefully scrutinized to determine whether prison conditions have exacerbated the problems of crime in our society. Many exprisoners
seem to fare worse after confinement rather than coping better with
the obligations and responsibilities of being a law-abiding citizen.
The longer one spends in jail or prison, the greater the difficulty one
appears to have making the necessary adjustment back into society.

One of the most thorough and probing analyses of the country's
criminal justice system was the National Strategy to Reduce Crime
(1971), prepared by the President's Commission on Criminal Justice
Standards and Goals. The commission was a harsh critic of prison
and jail conditions, but the commission merely confirmed much of
what had been observed previously, albeit less comprehensively. For

---

*For instance, a follow-up study of 1,432 youths out for more
than a year from California's youth prisons reported that 37 percent
were unemployed [Joachim P. Seckel, Employment and Employability
Among California Youth Authority Wards, Research Report no. 30
(Sacramento, Calif.: Department of the Youth Authority, August 31,
1962)]. Glaser discovered that the median income of "successful"
parolees after three months was $212 [D. Glasser, Effectiveness of
a Prison and Parole System (New York: Bobbs-Merrill Company,
1964), p. 334]. John Irwin, in tracing the career of the felon, found
that many felons terminated their careers in suicide or dereliction.
See J. Irwin, The Felon (Englewood Cliffs, N.J.: Prentice
Hall, 1970). Jacqueline Wiseman in a study of Skid Row discovered
many exfelons among the skid row population. [J. Wiseman, Stations
of the Lost (Englewood Cliffs, N.J.: Prentice Hall, 1970)].

example, earlier observers had noted that jails and prisons were in effect "schools for crime." Studies had concluded that the effect of being segregated with other criminals to the virtual exclusion of all other contacts can have the effect of deeply immersing a person into criminal (or prison) value and belief systems.[2]

In addition to the problem of prisoners more fully embracing deviant or antisystem values, it also had been noted that most prisoners are maintained in a state of enforced idleness and are thereby made to "unlearn" rather than learn productive behavior. In other words, prisoners often become less technically and socially competent than they were when they entered confinement. In the first place, there are relatively few resources, services, or programs made available that would enable prisoners to make constructive use of their time. Second, what actual work experience is provided is woefully inadequate. Most prisons involve at least some prisoners in work activities necessary to operate and maintain the institution: laundry, bakery, fire department, or such. But because of the nature and structure of this work, it has few benefits to prisoners beyond keeping some busy. When released prisoners seek work on the outside, they find that the equipment and techniques used in the prison are obsolete and that few acquired skills are transferable. Furthermore, their work habits are highly inappropriate. In the prison, where inmate labor is free and economic efficiency is one of the last concerns, prisoners often work only a few hours a day, with three or four persons assigned tasks that normally require one. These handicaps become most obvious when the exprisoner attempts to compete in today's job market, which is highly competitive, especially on the level of unskilled labor, and which is constantly demanding more sophisticated skills.

The emptiness and dullness of the prison experience is debilitating in still other ways. The routines that are established are designed to meet the needs of efficient, (that is, convenient) administration rather than those of its resident population. By deliberate policy, individual decision-making and the assumption of personal responsibility are kept at a minimum through a highly regimented schedule and a system in which authority rests exclusively with the top prison administrators. Living under these conditions (while insuring control) inevitably has an atrophying effect on each prisoner's will and his ability to make personal decisions and to assume responsibility for his life. Once a prisoner is released, he is expected suddenly to be self-reliant and independent in what is, at best, an indifferent world. The lack of skills can have disastrous results. A glimpse of what this means can be seen in the inadequacy of a released prisoner's attempts to accomplish tasks we all perform daily: counting money, cooking, or finding one's way.

Finally, prisoners find, upon release, that ties with family, friends, and community have been seriously weakened, if not completely severed. Without such emotional and social support, exprisoners are completely alone during the initial, critical period of readjustment. For many, this can make the difference between "making it" or returning to prison.

SOCIETAL RESTRAINTS ON THE EXPRISONER

Apart from what correctional institutions do or do not provide the inmate to insure success after release, there are other conditions in civil society that bear independently on an exprisoner's chances. Probably the most serious handicap the exprisoner must confront is his prison record or "convicted felon" status. Society subjects the exprisoner to a variety of disqualifications and disabilities quite apart from the sanction imposed by his sentence.

One of the most important obstacles to satisfactory readjustment has been the obligation to report information about any previous criminal record on job applications. If such information is provided, the chance of employment is minimal; if it is not, it is liable to be uncovered in a job interview, when the applicant must account for large gaps in previous work history. But even should the applicant manage to finesse his way through the hiring stage, he then must live in constant fear that the employer somehow will find out on his own or be told by someone from the many social agencies who follow up on the exinmate.

In addition to the informal discriminatory practices exprisoners face in the private sector, countless federal, state, and municipal laws single out the convicted felon for exclusion from the majority of regulated occupations.[3] Any profession, business, or trade that requires licensing can exclude convicted felons. Finally, the exprisoner can anticipate encountering obstacles to public employment, which are no less formidable than those he encounters in seeking entrance to a licensed occupation.[4]

In addition to employment barriers, convicted felons in many states can be subjected to: (1) the loss of voting rights; (2) the loss of the privilege of residency (if not a U.S. citizen); (3) the loss of the right to hold public office or a position of trust; (4) the loss of testamentary capacity and capacity to serve as a juror; (5) the loss of property rights, contract rights, and the right to court process; (6) the loss of workmen's compensation, pensions, and insurance benefits; and (7) the loss of domestic rights.[5] These civil disabilities confronting the exprisoner upon release not only affect him materially, but they also have a profound psychological effect. They serve to reinforce and perpetuate the degradation that was first imposed by his criminal conviction, legitimizing continued state interference in the exprisoner's life long after his release from prison. [6]

POSTPRISON EXPERIENCES

Given the effects of incarceration and the obstacles confronting exoffenders in society, life after release for many becomes a series of trials or tests which, if failed individually or in some combination, could steer them back into "deviant" lifestyles involving even greater numbers of law violations and the likelihood of return to confinement.

There are essentially two stages along the way toward community reintegration that the exprisoner must successfully negotiate. Initially, he has extreme difficulty achieving equilibrium on the outside. In convict parlance, he has trouble "making it." He might not be able to meet the basic exigencies of coping with outside life; that is, he might not be able to supply himself with an adequate or personally acceptable residence, acquire a job (any job), obtain the necessary clothing, or feed himself adequately.

If he does "make it," he might have difficulty "doing good," or going beyond simply hanging on. He could be unable to achieve any long term stability or to enter a lifestyle that supplies him with some of his desired satisfactions and with some degree of self-respect. He might have difficulty finding a circle of friends with whom he can interact in a "meaningful" and satisfying manner and with whom he shares areas of meaning and interest. This can be very difficult for an exprisoner who has become immersed in criminal or prison worlds and who has had limited access to other worlds. He could also have great difficulty finding a "good" job, one which supplies not only the basic needs but also which earns him some self-respect. Finally, achieving a gratifying relationship with a sexual partner might be a difficult problem. As in other areas, he has lost his skill at meeting and interacting with members of the opposite sex. For some time, he is ill-prepared to compete in those open arenas (such as bars) where strangers of the opposite sex get together. In addition, it will be some time, if it occurs at all, before he becomes immersed in an informal world that can offer opportunities to meet social partners. [7]

The problem of postprison failure is the major target of some of the college education programs in this study. A prison college program is one way of providing the inmate an opportunity to use his time in confinement constructively. It can also shift the focus of the prison itself away from an exclusive concern with custody and security and thereby enrich the atmosphere of the entire prison. And, prison college education programs could provide prisoners with certain skills that will enhance their success after release as well as provide them a viable sequence of transitional steps back to full membership in the community. But before turning to the study of the actual programs, let us briefly examine the development of the concept of education in prisons in general.

HISTORY OF EDUCATION IN PRISONS

One of the most characteristic and persistent attributes of prison inmates in the United States has been their educational deficiency. This is, in large part, due to the "selection process" of the criminal justice system: most inmates are from the lower socioeconomic classes. Rather than being improved, this lower class status has been perpetuated by the lack of adequate educational services in prisons and the lack of programmatic options to incarceration. A survey of correctional education prepared by the Education Commission of the States summarized the educational problems of prison inmates as follows:

> Unofficial estimates by the officials of the Federal Bureau of Prisons reflect that twenty to fifty percent of the approximately half-million adults incarcerated in American federal and state prisons can neither read nor write.
> As many as eight percent of the clients within some of the juvenile facilities are illiterate.
> Up to ninety percent of the adult clients of the penal system are school drop-outs.
> In a majority of prisons, more than fifty percent of the adults incarcerated above eighteen years of age have less than an eighth grade education. [8]

The significance of these observations becomes clearer when one considers the direct relationship between an inmate's failure in the education system and his inability to compete effectively in the job market. Education and employability would seem to be necessary, albeit not always sufficient, to enable exconvicts to extricate themselves eventually from the criminal cycle.

Originally the primary function of education in prison was salvation and moral regeneration. In the early part of the 18th century, the Pennsylvania Quakers built the prison system in the United States

around the goal of reconstructing the criminal through penitence. As
initially conceived, penitence was to consist of Bible study and re-
flection in solitude. The equation of education with religious and
moral training was a dominant orientation of the original colonies.
The first public schools offered the three Rs, the first of them being
religion. The second two, reading and "riting," were taught not for
their separate value, but as means for learning discipline and reading
religious writings.

The practice of prisoners studying the Bible in solitude was
slightly modified when it was discovered that solitary confinement
was too expensive and that many prisoners did not know how to read.
However, the orientation persisted; and illiterate prisoners were
taught basic reading and writing skills so they could carry on with
their Bible studies and fulfill the purpose of their confinement.

In the last half of the 19th century an extensive reform movement
occurred, which began to question some of the basic tenets of contemporary penal philosophy. The conception of the criminal as im-
moral shifted to a more complex view in which he was not simply a
sinner, but deficient in additional ways: intellectually, psychologically,
and vocationally. A more sophisticated penal routine was required
for his reformation. Some of the changes recommended and implemented in penal systems in this period were separation of young and
adult criminals, the establishment of juvenile courts and reformatory
systems, and the introduction of indeterminate sentences. [9]

The new penal philosophy had an impact on the function of the
educational enterprise within the prisons to the extent that educational
and vocational training programs became more formalized and available to larger numbers of inmates. In contrast with preceding periods,
the teaching of educational skills was seen to have some value of its
own. However, its purpose was still the remolding of the criminal,
not through salvation but through almost magical regenerative powers
education presumedly possessed. Zebulon Brockway, who more than
any other person influenced the new penology of his era, supplies us
with an example of the reformation powers of education:

On entering the classroom one summer evening
with Professor Wells, who had picked from the
shrubbery outside a bit of leafy trailing vine and
was playfully twirling it, we observed a pupil
apparently stalled. On the paper before him he
had drawn a six-inch square with bisectional lines,
but now stood puzzled and discouraged. He was a
massive, swarthy, morose man of nearly thirty
years of age; strong of limb, slow of motion and
speech, and apparently of sluggish mind. The

instructor approached and deftly held the vine
within the square, offering a brief suggestion as
to how its form could be incorporated within the
drawing of the square, then passed on to other
pupils. Half an hour afterwards on returning to the
stalled pupil the instructor was surprised and pleased.
at the delicate skill the drawing now displayed, and he
so expressed himself. Some silent evidence of responsive feeling was manifest but the trifling occurrence
was soon eclipsed in the teacher's memory. But
whether by cause or coincidence, from this point the
prisoner progressed well in drawing, in the school of
letters, and in his daily work of iron molding. On his
parole, which was duly issued, I employed him at
regular mechanic's wages to instruct novices in the
molders' trade. He lived in the neighborhood, married
respectably (but not with happy final results), found
steady employment in the city later at his trade, and
ever since, now twenty-four years and more, he has
maintained his liberty and supported himself by means
of legitimate industry. [10]

Around the turn of the 20th century a new force entered the prison
education world. As do most causes of change in the prisons, this
force emanated from upheavals that had been occurring outside the
institutions. Because of the industrial revolution, cities were growing
in number and size; and the level of educational skills required of the
labor force was increasing. The pressure for an extensive public high
school education system mounted. Formerly education above the elementary level was "classical" in nature—college preparatory and, in
effect, reserved for the upper classes. However, with the changes
in the economic and social structure, the concept of a right to education for all, at least through high school, began to emerge. It was not
the high school of the classical tradition with its focus on Latin, Greek,
and the "classics," but progressive education, designed to prepare the
masses for the new industrial society. [11]

Prisoner education was affected by these changes in the general
society's educational system. But it was the notion of a universal right
to a high school education rather than the change in curriculum that
had the most significance. Although the content of the education provided in prisons always had been viewed in essentially pragmatic
terms, rather than in the classical tradition, formal academic education had never been intended for all inmates. Moreover, the "right"
of prison inmates to anything has been a concept that prison officials
and the general society have been slow to acknowledge. Education was
considered to be an amenity and, therefore, a privilege.

The notion of education as a privilege still lingers on in prison administrations, although almost all prisons began to operate some semblance of a high school program around this time. It should be understood, however, that despite the larger number of allocated resources, education never reached all, or even the majority, of inmates. To this day, few prisons have structured their prison routine to allow and facilitate the completion of high school by all inmates. Usually the inmates' work responsibilities and the maintenance and operational needs of the institution preclude full participation in a high school program by all inmates who need it.

The universal right to a free high school education was combined in the prison setting with earlier expectations that education would serve as a reformative tool. Austin MacCormick, who surveyed American prisons in 1927-28, reveals in his statements a mixture of these two perspectives. He reports that he did not discover "a single complete and well-rounded educational program," revealing a concern for the right of the uneducated to a quality education. He writes,

> If we believe in the beneficial effect of education on
> man in general we must believe in it for this particular
> group, which differs less than the layman thinks from
> the ordinary run of humanity. If on no other grounds
> than a general resolve to offer educational opportuni-
> ties to undereducated persons wherever they may be
> found, we recognize that our penal population consti-
> tutes a proper field for educational effort. In brief, we
> are not ready to make its efficacy in turning men from
> crime the only criterion in judging the value of educa-
> tion for prisoners.[12]

From 1927, education in prison expanded rapidly. By 1948 MacCormick commented that the situation had drastically improved since his 1920s survey. Many systems had high schools; and several prisons, such as San Quentin, were offering college courses by correspondence.

After World War II a new concept of prisoner rehabilitation gained a foothold in correctional philosophy. In essence, the remodeling of the criminal was still paramount; but in this new penological era the conception of the criminal had changed. The social sciences, espe-cially psychology, had a profound impact on correctional ideology. The new criminal was no longer a free-willed (although deficient) being but a determined one, propelled by psychopathologies or other personal problems rooted in early childhood or teenage experiences.

Two aspects of the new rehabilitation era are important in under-standing the nature of prison education. First, the criminal was viewed as a person who had psychological problems that had to be "cured." Second, no one pathology was seen as causing all crime. Each criminal "type," therefore, needed a specialized rehabilitative routine. In those prison systems that implemented the new rehabilitative ideology, this philosophy resulted in considerable experimentation with different "programs." Educational programs, including college, [13] were among these.

The first college program within prison walls was conceived by its planners as a rehabilitative device. This is reflected in the following characterization of college education programs by Delyte W. Morris, the president of Southern Illinois University, which introduced that education in 1957:

> Such academic education in prison is supposed to advance rehabilitation. Through improved skill in communication, the offender presumably will be able to reveal and express underlying misunderstandings and conflicts which have caused his deviant behavior. The student prisoner will be able to comprehend more fully his personal problems and his relationships with other persons. His leisure time will be used more constructively during and after his confinement. Through better understanding of government and society, he will be moved toward responsible citizenship. [14]

NEWGATE

In the mid-1960s there emerged still another perspective on criminality and its cure. In brief, the sociological perspective superceded the psychological model. The new philosophy described the criminal as disadvantaged by birth, having been denied access to all social structures through which society's rewards (for example, power, status, and wealth) are distributed. Shut off from legitimate avenues to desired social rewards, it was argued, the lower classes turn to illegitimate, that is, criminal, activities.

From this viewpoint the effective rehabilitative program is one that overcomes deficiencies in preparations and opens up access to the reward-distributing systems of the society. This view is strongly tied to the widespread perspective of several other social movements in the late 1950s and early 1960s, such as the civil rights movement and the War on Poverty. The official mandate of the new federal OEO in 1964 embraced the new doctrine. The Upward Bound program and later the NewGate program were among many OEO programs designed to change the existing opportunity structure.

The Upward Bound program was an attempt to prepare educationally and economically disadvantaged youths from lower economic strata for college entrance by involving them in an accelerated educational enrichment program. These were conducted on college campuses during the summer to ready the youths for fall admission. The basic concept was that some segments of the society, because of their membership in certain classes or ethnic groups, had not had the opportunity to develop the skills and motivation for entrance to higher educational systems and were denied access to educational and occupational structures later in life.

In 1966 Tom Gaddis, who was familiar with the Upward Bound programs and had had a long interest in prison and prisoner issues, decided to transplant the Upward Bound concept into the prison in his home state, Oregon. At the outset the new prison college education program, which at that time (1966) was called "Upward Bound Oregon Prison Project," entailed bringing an Upward Bound, campus-type enrichment program into the prison. The program included "a continuation of seminar and group experiences, individual counseling, and the provision of campus type events and experiences." The original plan included one other component, which initially did not receive the same emphasis as the prison enrichment phase but which became essential later. This was the provision to the participants of postprison college access after release.

This marked the actual birth of NewGate. In 1967 and 1968 OEO was enthusiastic about this new program and made additional funds available. With the name of NewGate, projects were instituted in Rockview, Pennsylvania; St. Cloud, Minnesota; Ashland, Kentucky; Santa Fe, New Mexico; and later in Englewood, Colorado.

It must be emphasized that the sociological view of the criminal as being disadvantaged rather than pathological has been the minority view in correctional circles. To the extent that NewGate programs embodied this perspective, they operated in fairly hostile territory. In addition to these ideological differences, the structural characteristics of the NewGate model were a cause of tension. With very few exceptions, prisons have long been and are still today total systems with highly centralized control. The mere thought of, let alone the actual presence of, a program operating inside the prison walls that is administratively semiautonomous, is a challenge to conventional assumptions about how prisons should operate. Of course, OEO was not totally blind to the potential for conflict, but it firmly believed that some independence was necessary to tap fully the benefits of the independent university system. It was believed that this association would not only benefit the students in providing a higher quality education but also ultimately would benefit the prison as a whole. How this relationship took form and what actually were the benefits are questions the following chapters will address.

To summarize the history of education in prisons, there are, basically, five functions education has been seen to fulfill in the prison context. They are presented below in order of their historical appearance.

1. Uplifting morals through Bible study, hard work and discipline. This is the earliest form of reformation; and, although it sounds outdated, it still exists as a rationale for educational activities in prison.

2. Training in skills. These consist of basic education skills (reading, writing and arithmetic), vocational skills (typing, researching, teaching, counseling, and such), and work-habit skills (meeting schedules, completing assignments, and concentrating).

3. Developing intellectuality and human understanding. This rationale for education was heavily influential in the growth of education as a right of citizens and then prisoners in the United States. The ideal is that, through increased understanding and intellectual capability, the individual becomes a more competent and responsible human being, and thus a better citizen.

4. Changing personality or behavior modes. This objective rises out of the belief that criminal behavior is a product of special types of personalities or personality problems. Education and other subsidiary activities, such as counseling, are aimed primarily at producing changes in the personality or behavior patterns.

5. Increasing opportunity structures. This focus is on education and the involvement of educational institutions as a means to opening access to or removing obstacles from the opportunity structures of the society.

The projects included in this study operated with all these functions in mind, although perhaps some were more dominant than others.

NOTES

1. Daniel Glaser concludes from an examination of a variety of recidivist studies that this rate of approximately 40 percent has held constant from place to place, and time to time. D. Glaser, Effectiveness of a Prison and Parole System (New York: Bobbs-Merrill Company, 1964), p. 24.

2. These studies begin with Donald Clemmer, The Prison Community (New York: Holt, Rinehart and Winston, Inc., 1940). See also Erving Goffman, Asylums (Garden City, N.Y.: Anchor Books, 1961); Donald Cressey, ed., The Prison (New York: Holt, Rinehart and Winston, Inc., 1961); and John Irwin, The Felon (Englewood Cliffs, N.J.: Prentice Hall, 1970).

3. Special Project, "The Collateral Consequences of Criminal Conviction," Vanderbilt Law Review 23, 5 (October 1970): 929, 1241. This article is an excellent compendium of the statutory laws creating disabilities for the convicted offender.

4. Ibid., p. 1013.

5. For a more detailed description of these phenomena and a listing of the states in which these rights are denied, see "Legal Considerations Involved," Appendix II to a concept paper prepared by the Education Commission of the States (Denver, Col.: Correctional Education Project, July 1975).

6. "The Collateral Consequences of Criminal Conviction," op. cit., p. 1231. Also see M.G. Neithercutt, "Consequences of Guilty," Crime and Delinquency 15, 4 (October 1969): 459-462; and E. Sutherland and D. Cressey, Criminology (Philadelphia: J.B. Lippincott, 1974), chap. 14.

7. For further discussion of the processes which serve as obstacles to a convicted felon returning to conventional life, see Irwin, op. cit.

8. Education Commission of the States, op. cit. References cited include President's Commission on Law Enforcement and Administration of Justice, Task Force Report: Corrections (Washington, D.C.: U.S. Government Printing Office, 1967), pp. 2-3; Syracuse University Research Corporation, School Behind Bars (Syracuse, N.Y.: SURC, 1973).

9. See the Proceedings of 1870 Congress of Corrections (New York: American Correctional Association, 1870). At this conference a correctional reform platform, which included these principles, was adopted.

10. Zebulon Brockway, Fifty Years of Prison Service (New York: Charities Publication, 1912), pp. 244-245.

11. For a thorough discussion of the rise of progressive education, see Theodore R. Sizer, Secondary Schools of the Turn of the Century (New Haven, Conn., and London: Yale University Press, 1964); or Lawrence H. Cremin, The Transformation of the School (New York: Vintage Books, 1964).

12. Austin H. MacCormick, The Education of Adult Prisoners (New York: The National Society of Penal Information, 1931), p. 3.

13. See Stuart Adams, "College-Level Instruction in U.S. Prisons," mimeographed (Berkeley: University of California, School of Criminology, 1968).

14. Delyte W. Morris, "The University's Role in Prison Education," Nebraska Law Review 45, no. 3 (May 1966): 546.

3

EVALUATION OF
PROGRAM PROCESS

This study was designed so the quality of the prison college program was evaluated in terms of program process as well as by its
measured impact on released participants.* One reason for going
beyond program impact measures is that there are many intervening
variables that bear significantly on the "success" of exprisoners.
These are often difficult to identify and control with current methodological techniques. It then becomes impossible to draw a direct
causal relationship between the exprisoner's experiences in the program and his success after release. Another problem facing this
analysis in particular was the time lag between the time released
participants went through the programs and when the research staff
made project site visits. Often several years had elapsed, and the
programs had experienced significant changes in the meantime. This
also made it difficult to attribute the experiences of released participants to relative differences in the programs' quality.

Program process was evaluated in terms of the extent to which
the programs contained structural and functional features logically
essential to operating a quality educational enterprise in a prison context. This chapter presents a discussion of the conceptual framework
within which the research staff conducted the process evaluation,
along with the staff's findings.

---

*Program impact on participants is a subject taken up in several
subsequent chapters.

EVALUATION FRAMEWORK

The research staff evaluated the operations of the prison college programs within the framework of the following three questions:

(1) Were the programs effective in fulfilling their educational purposes? It was concluded that the program was effective to the extent it rated high on three important dimensions: challenge, personal social space, and supportive framework.

(2) What was the nature and extent of these programs' impact on their environment? It was concluded that the program had an impact to the extent that it was instrumental in promoting change on the cognitive, procedural, and policy-making levels of the correctional enterprise. It was also measured by the extent to which the program generated participation by program participants and staff and by outside persons, groups, and institutions, for example, the university, in an effort to bring about progressive changes within the correctional system.

(3) Were the programs surviving in the prison context? It was concluded that a program was surviving to the extent that it maintained its internal integrity and vitality and that it performed an increasingly larger role in the prison's educational and "treatment" enterprise.

The evaluation framework used to answer these three questions is elaborated below.

In reviewing the historical development of college education in prisons in Chapter 2, it becomes obvious that college programs can be designed to fulfill different functions simultaneously. In a research effort that calls for an evaluation and comparison of the effectiveness of all programs in the sample, the conceptual framework must be made broad and abstract enough to include each of these different functions.

The conceptual framework used in the evaluation that follows is based on an abstraction from the experiences of colleges in civil society. It is clear that these social institutions have been commissioned to perform the same functions in the general society as prison college programs have on a smaller scale. On a general level, colleges in civil society have always been seen as instruments to train and transform persons into more productive resources for the larger social, economic, and political systems. By design, students who are immersed in the college experience are to be changed fundamentally from the relatively unskilled and uninitiated persons they were when they entered as freshmen.

FUNCTIONS OF EDUCATION

When viewed from the perspective of the larger social system,
the college performs functions that correspond to the five general
functions of education in prison previously described in Chapter 2.

(1) Moral uplifting. Hard work, which is required to meet exacting standards and achieve educational goals at college, is believed
to be good in itself. Although colleges have objectives that are higher
on their list of priorities, one general lesson to be learned is that
life's benefits do not come without some special effort. People must
work hard for what they want.

(2) Training in skills. Colleges are one major instrument to
prepare citizens to meet requirements for available jobs in society
at all levels of sophistication. Certain skills are basic and transferable to all jobs, for example, reading, writing, arithmetic, research, speaking, and organizing ideas. Other skills are designed
for a more specific vocation, such as business and accounting, en-
gineering, scientific research, teaching, or practicing law or medicine. Still other skills learned at college are personal living skills,
which have more general applications. A student learns, among other
things, how to establish realistic life goals and objectives, to establish
routines and manageable schedules, and to develop the self-discipline
and internal organization essential to following them.

(3) Developing intellectuality and human understanding. Persons
are exposed to a wider world through their studies in a variety of
different disciplines—sociology, psychology, history, anthropology,
philosophy, political science, economics, literature, and such. This
exposure is further promoted by their teachers and fellow students in
their social and leisure lives. Through exposure to the nature of
human life and society, the student gains a fuller understanding of
his own life, his past development, and his potential. He also learns
about the nature of his relationship and responsibilities to his fellow
man, his society, and his culture.

(4) Changing personality and behavior modes. In the course of his
experience in the college environment, the student develops a different
and more profound concept of himself. Through contact with new ideas
and new people, his own ideas, perspectives, values, and goals are
challenged, tested, modified, and strengthened. In this context of
differences, he is forced to confront himself and to be aware of and
take responsibility for his own behavior. He learns how to get along
with others, to be tolerant of differences, and to experiment with new
ideas and life styles. Furthermore, he develops a clearer sense of
his own worth and competency by being able to compare himself with

other people and by using the evaluations of relevant others as a reliable measuring rod. He also gains confidence in himself as his own measuring rod.

(5) Increasing opportunity structures. An academic institution in civil society performs two other functions. It develops links with representatives from outside economic sectors and puts them in touch with its graduating students. In this way, the college not only keeps up with society's changing standards and requirements but also provides its students an opportunity to use their skills and to become integrated into meaningful social and economic worlds beyond the college experience. Second, the academic institution has extended the benefits of an education to classes of people who otherwise could not afford to attend college. By providing scholarships and low interest loans to finance their education, colleges have given these students a wider range of life alternatives and, on graduation, the possibility for increases in status and wealth, which represents significant upward social mobility.

The college campus is clearly different from the prison milieu. Certain structural adjustments have to be made to accommodate the difference in setting. Similarly, however, there are logical limits to the amount of change that can be made without destroying the program's capacity to perform its prescribed educational functions. Just exactly what these minimum basic requirements are can be learned from the experience of colleges in civil society and from the structural forms that have evolved in civil society to fulfill their functions.

PROGRAM STRUCTURE

Three major dimensions were abstracted from the college structure and were deemed basic to the internal logic of the educational enterprise. For college programs to perform their educational functions effectively, they must provide (1) supportive framework, (2) personal social space, and (3) challenge. On the assumption that these three dimensions constitute the essential dimensions of any learning context, they were adopted as part of the perspective for assessing the prison college programs. They are discussed below as three basic program variables. Also presented are the specific indicators to which reference was made in rating the programs.

Supportive Framework

The learning program must provide a supportive framework that permits the participants to achieve their goals. In contrast with the variable, personal social space, which measures the degree of choice available to the participant, this variable measures the means that are provided to the students in their efforts to obtain an education. There are two aspects to supportive framework. First, the students must be offered the numerous resources and facilities that constitute the substance of the instructional enterprise—for example, academic courses, special enrichment or remedial classes, tutoring, instructors, materials, counseling, operating funds, student stipends, library facilities, and office and classroom space. These must be of sufficient quality, number, and diversity to accommodate the participants' needs and interests. In addition, the students must be provided a program structure that arranges and coordinates the program's constituent elements into a coherent and intelligent order. A new student who lacks experience in the school setting, especially college, will only have a vague idea of what he wants, what is available or possible, and what is realistic given his own needs and abilities. The program must be structured to assist the student in formulating his objectives and goals and in pursuing a program with a focus. The student must be introduced into a learning process broken down into discrete, understandable parts, arranged in a sequence in which one part leads logically to the next, and the experience at one level develops the information and skills needed to function at each succeeding level. Graduation from one level to the next must be based on standard educational requirements and performance criteria used by accredited institutions. Only in this kind of program will the students have the satisfaction that their accomplishments are not only intrinsically but also extrinsically valuable in that they qualify them for a higher step, are widely respected, and, therefore, transferable to other settings. The supportive structure must include the development of links with other institutional networks to facilitate meaningful transition to areas where newly acquired skills are relevant and in demand.

In this study a program was considered to have a support framework to the extent it contained an academic program including many high quality courses, lower and upper division courses, qualified instructors, and ample instructional materials (books, paper, pencils, and such). A counseling program was also deemed necessary and sufficient if it offered formal academic and vocational counseling, individual and group therapy, more than one therapeutic philosophy, qualified counselors and therapists, and coordination with the academic phase of the program. A college preparation component was considered effective if it had special recruitment and outreach efforts to attract those who previously and otherwise would not consider going to college; special enrichment classes designed to make up deficiencies in math, science, and English; small classes; individual tutoring; programmed learning materials; and coordination with other prison educational efforts, including vocational training, adult basic education (ABE), and General Education Diploma (GED) preparation.

Physical facilities conducive to the development of a college atmosphere were a necessity to this study. The requirements were a college program section that was physically separate from the rest of the prison; classrooms that were numerous, spacious, light, comfortable, and quiet; a social room separate from the study area that was comfortable and spacious; a separate study area; and library facilities easily accessible and containing a large quantity of up-to-date and relevant sources. Library facilities included space in which students could read and study.

Cooperation between the college program and its prison environment was vital. Evidence of that cooperation included a prison administration supportive of program goals, prison guards who respected and encouraged college students, program admission standards that were clear and fair to all inmates, and an atmosphere that discouraged other inmates from regarding program participants as arrogant, hostile, elitist, or exclusivist. Cooperation between the college program and the university was reflected in professors and academic departments actively committed to providing time and resources to the inside academic program; campus students engaged in the inside program, either by attending classes, as practicum students, as tutors, as outside sponsors, or such; a university administration committed to the program as an experiment in higher education; a university involvement that protected the sanctity and standards of a free academic atmosphere in the prison; as well as the necessary university financial or other support to the program.

An extensive after-care program is a basic support component. Included in this category were financial sponsorship at training institutions; academic, vocational, and therapeutic counseling; a mutual spirit of support among outside participants and a qualified outside staff; and an effort at referrals to additional services provided by university and community agencies. Involvement in college academic life through contact with professors and departments in various disciplines and involvement with and acceptance by fellow students in classrooms, student politics, and social activities were both important. Also helpful were comfortable and spacious housing accommodations and assistance in obtaining work-study or other part-time jobs.

Personal Social Space

Once the student has defined the goals he is interested in attaining and has elected to participate in a program designed to move him closer to his goal, he must have the freedom to maneuver, that is, personal social space. This will enable him to pursue his interests and make choices that will tailor his program and schedule so it is designed and paced to fit his individual needs and resources. In any learning situation, there is some sense of personal inadequacy and a fear of failure. Education is a venture into the unknown; it can have high personal stakes. Before a person takes such a risk, he wants to know that he is participating on his own volition and that he has some control over the program's direction and over the amount of time and effort he must allocate. He also wants to know that he is somewhat free from outside commitments and expectations. A person who is given the liberty to make choices and follow his own direction not only is in an optimum position to realize his full potential, but also can learn to mold his own destiny and take responsibility for his own actions.

From the perspective of society as a whole, optimal utilization of available human resources depends ultimately on each individual realizing his full potential. Society must recruit on the basis of strong interests, talents, and motivations. Since each person ultimately knows best where his own talents lie, some measure of independence should be allowed. Personal social space, to find one's own way, is a basic necessity.

The characteristics considered indicative of personal social space demanded some concessions from regular prison routine. The participant had to be able to regulate his schedule, determine his study time and place, take classes at different times, take therapy at different times, vary the number of hours for which he was enrolled, and vary the semester in which a course was taken. These require-ments precluded a participant's choice of alternative courses of action, such as whether to be part-time or full-time student; which among many academic courses at varying degrees of difficulty to take; whether to elect academic, individual, and/or group counseling; and which counselor to choose. The participant also had to have certain possessions and needed to be able to order books easily and own any books, slide rules, or other educational aids normally required for course work.

Next, so the participant could plan a future course of action, he needed to have access to outside persons, groups, and institutions and to have access to information about future job opportunities, training, and financial assistance. Also necessary was a range of release options: such as the choice among different colleges in different locations, the type of training to seek (junior college, four-year college, or a vocational/technical school), and work release or study release programs. The participant also needed a choice of living situations, such as dormitory, private apartment, or program residence house.

The program required that the participant move unencumbered by arbitrary restrictions from the inside situation. For example, he needed a large, uncrowded school area; relaxed behavioral rules; permission for classroom discussions on any subject; and the ability to mix informally with fellow students and to have access to a private study area. Provision for a participant to leave the school area to return to his cell unit or to choose not to attend class or to leave during class was also necessary. Additionally, the participant had to function within the college program unencumbered by outside obligations. If he cared to, he should have the option of becoming a full-time student. His attendance at school should not bring harassment from the prison staff or other inmates, and the privilege to attend school could not be used by the prison administration as a leverage or a means of extortion.

Challenge

There must be some feature(s) in the learning context that stimulate and challenge the student to apply his energies and to take advantage of the program and services offered. Before an individual will be motivated to change his present values, perspectives, ideas, and goals, he must be convinced that there is something better. His interests must be aroused, his imagination must be stirred. He must experience a feeling that there is something he does not have—knowledge, skills, or such—that he feels he wants or should have. Finally, he must be made to feel that these things are possible and within his reach if he expends some reasonable effort. In this study, a program was considered challenging to the extent that it demonstrated that materials were presented and made available in the program (books; assignments; newspapers, magazines, films, records, and laboratories; or lectures, speeches, and debates). The program also should offer activities and expectations of relevant others, such as program instructors, counselors, and therapists; the peers and peer group, and prison personnel. Opportunities anticipated beyond the period of incarceration added to the potential challenge a participant faced. They included a chance for further vocational and academic training, a chance for a respectable job or work assignment, renewed contact with family, and a change in laws and attitudes, which would increase possibilities for exconvicts to "make it" and "do good. "

PROGRAM IMPACT ON THE ENVIRONMENT

In addition to evaluating the college programs in terms of their educational goals, OEO indicated an interest in describing and analyzing the impact of prison college programs on their environments: on the host prison and university; on the inmates who did not participate; and on persons, groups, and institutions in the wider community.

There are a number of different ways college education programs in prison can have an impact on their environments. For the purposes of this study, program impact was considered in terms of (1) cognitive changes, (2) procedural changes, and (3) changes in the policy-making power structure. More explicitly, attention was directed at changes that might have occurred in a person's belief system—in what each knew about and thought about convicts and prisons. Also of interest in this study were changes in policy and procedures that affected convicts inside and outside the prison. Finally, attention was directed at the policy-making function itself, that is, changes in the constellation of interests involved in making authoritative decisions affecting the lives of convict populations.

The initiative and impetus to create these kinds of changes in the prison environment could come from three different organizational levels of the college program. First, the impetus could come from the various persons involved: the students and the program staff. Second, it could come from the program itself and the force generated by the fact that it existed and had needs and priorities that, to varying extents, had to be accommodated by outsiders. Third, the impetus could come from beyond the program. It could be generated through a system of alliances the program had established with persons, groups, and institutions in its environment for the purpose of maintaining and promoting the program.

PROGRAM SURVIVAL

There was an additional function of the college programs beyond fulfillment of educational functions that warranted careful scrutiny by this study. The college programs had an unspoken commitment to survive while maintaining their quality. Experience shows that this is no small matter in the prison context. Prisons have explicit and implicit objectives of their own, which compete with the educational goals of the college programs. Antagonism from a prison staff with different priorities can constitute a formidable threat to an educational program's internal integrity. In fact, it can be expected that precisely those programs promising the greatest success in terms of fulfilling ambitious educational goals will face the greatest threat. A simulated college atmosphere inside a prison would contain philosophic perspectives different from those found in a prison, which is traditionally preoccupied with custody and security matters. Another likely source of friction will be the program staff's encouragement of innovation and experimentation—an area that formerly has been within the exclusive jurisdiction of the top levels of the highly centralized and regimented prison bureaucracy. Finally, ambitious college programs will likely maintain some professional and programmatic ties with outside persons and institutions, for example, the university, specific job markets, and such. This, too, is a logical source of friction since historically prisons have resisted the involvement of outsiders in their internal affairs and have thereby enjoyed a remoteness and insularity that few other institutions in our society have equalled.

Clearly, a college program successful in fulfilling its educational purposes is short-lived if it is unable to make peace with the host prison on favorable terms. Just what pressures were experienced by college programs in prisons and what strategies were effective in guaranteeing program quality and survival were questions under consideration in this study. Some "crisis points" were isolated, which had to be negotiated by the college program along the way. Whether the maintenance of program integrity was enhanced or undermined depended on how these crises were ultimately resolved. The crisis points identified in this study centered on the following issues:

(1) Program direction and operation: Will the prison have exclusive control? If so, will the warden be interested and involved? Will the prison share authority with an outside force, for example, the university or a third force?

(2) Program funding: Will funding come from corrections? Will funding come from outside sources; and, if so, will this be a permanent, dependable funding base?

(3) Staff hiring: Will college program staff be hired by the prison administration or by the university? Or, will it be shared?

(4) Student admissions: Will the prison administration dominate admissions decisions? Will the college program staff determine student admissions? Will there be subjective and informal, or concrete and objective, admissions criteria?

(5) University involvement: Will university involvement be restricted to supplying instructors and academic courses? Will the
university establish curriculum, maintain standards, supply instructional resources, develop administrative links, establish student and
faculty commitment, and such? What kind of university or college
will serve as the host to the program, and to what extent will it be
able to command influence in relation to the corrections establishment?

(6) Program integration with prison staff: Will the college program operate as an enclave and be remote from prison staff and normal prison operations? Will the college program develop functional
links with other prison operations and establish formal and informal
interests and loyalties that cross-cut existing cleavages?

(7) Community integration: Will the program operate as a self-
contained and autonomous enterprise? Will the program develop an
ongoing relationship of exposure and involvement with persons, groups,
and institutions beyond the prison?

FINDINGS

The research staff's ranking of the college programs according
to the three variables—supportive framework, personal social space,
and challenge—is presented in Figure 3.1. The individual program
that ranks "high" on the scale for all three variables is considered
the best program. The reader is cautioned to note that this ranking
is based on the researcher's evaluation of the programs as they existed at the time of the site visits and that there is a possible disparity
between the programs observed by the researchers and the ones actually experienced by earlier participants given the follow-up interview.
For a more elaborate description of individual cases, the reader should
refer to the program case studies in the Appendix.

Supportive Framework

This variable measured the number and variety of instructional
resources, the framework within which they were made available by
the program in the inside, and the outside program component.

Pennsylvania was ranked high on this variable primarily because
of the preciseness and gradualness of its transitional stages through
which the inmate moved from prison with full support to the college
campus. This program enjoyed the immeasurable benefit of having
the Pennsylvania State University seven miles away. Penn State

FIGURE 3.1

Ranking of Program Effectiveness

	High	Medium	Low
Supportive Framework	Pennsylvania Minnesota New Mexico ———▶ ◀——— Oregon	Ashland ———▶	Lompoc Illinois Texas
Personal Social Space	New Mexico Pennsylvania Ashland	Minnesota Oregon Lompoc	Illinois Texas
Challenge	Pennsylvania ◀——— New Mexico Minnesota	Oregon Ashland	Illinois Lompoc Texas

Source: Compiled by the authors.

provided a high quality academic program inside the prison. More-over, the campus is large, diverse, and situated in a university town, where the predominant activities and influences serve to reinforce the inmate's student role once released and on campus. The college pro-gram inside the prison was criticized for not doing more to provide a college atmosphere beyond the classroom and providing comple-mentary support services, such as academic and therapeutic coun-seling, remedial instruction, and extracurricular activities. However, the strong link with the university and the strong outside program already mentioned offset these deficiencies.

The Minnesota program also had an elaborate framework from the time the student entered. It guided and regulated his participation on the inside through to a solid postrelease program on a university campus. It did not, however, measure up to the Pennsylvania program in terms of the strong continuities between the inside and outside ex-periences. This was mostly due to the location of the University of Minnesota, the site of the outside program, 70 miles away. As with the Pennsylvania program, the inside program was faulted for not providing a more extensive inside program. It could have had a greater variety of classes, extracurricular activities, remedial instruction, and academic counseling. Although it had an extensive group therapy program, it could have provided individual therapy as well. In the final analysis, the general ciritcism that was made of this project's supportive framework was that it was well-designed to meet the needs of some inmates inside and outside, but it did not generate additional services and alternatives that were needed to meet the needs of a broad base of participants.

New Mexico ranked high on this variable primarily because of the richness and diversity of its inside program. This program was equipped to attract and support a larger segment of inmates than was any other program. It vigorously recruited inmates, maintained an admissions policy open to everyone, and offered a program in which persons with educational deficiencies were able to perform college work. This was done by offering all the remedial and enrichment services the student needed to perform college work at an acceptable level without lowering academic standards. The program also offered a large variety of college courses, instructors, counselors and tutors, group and individual therapy, and cultural and enrichment activities designed to arouse student interest and tap hidden talents and abilities. Despite these impressive qualities, New Mexico failed to build a firm outside program to which its students could be sent after release. This was a most serious deficiency and was seen as possible grounds for ranking it as medium on this variable. The arrow in the figure indicates the researchers' ambivalence.

The Oregon NewGate project was ranked "medium" on this variable. Its inside program was weak because of its meager instructional resources and services. Other than courses, there was no college atmosphere. Moreover, there was little therapy and no formal academic counseling nor formal remedial instruction provided. The program also had no framework that made program standards and academic requirements explicit and that moved a student's participation along a logical progression of steps. The program would have benefited from students knowing when they could progress to study release and later to parole status, as was done in the Pennsylvania program. Participation in the inside program and on campus was undermined by the students' anxiety over, and preoccupation with, obtaining and later shedding study release status. As it stood, these decisions depended on uncertain criteria used by the prison administration and the parole board. The Oregon program had a fairly strong outside component at the University of Oregon, which is 80 miles from the prison. Even though the distance caused some of the same discontinuities between the inside and outside components as the Minnesota program experienced, this outside program was tremendously important to inmate students in their efforts to obtain a college education and a new lifestyle. The outside program offset many of the inside program's weaknesses and was grounds for ranking Oregon somewhere between "medium" and "high."

Ashland had an inside program that contained many of the deficiencies of Oregon's inside program. Although there was considerable exchange among participants and staff, there was a dearth of activities organized beyond the classroom. Moreover, no therapy or remedial instruction existed; though there was some academic and prerelease counseling. The major deficiency of Ashland's support framework was its inadequate outside program. Trying to support released students in colleges dispersed throughout the eastern states proved to be logistically impossible. There were also problems with insufficient regularity and standardization in paying student tuition and stipends.

The Lompoc program lacked sufficient instructional resources and services and a framework that ordered students' participation in a way that was personally efficient and effective. The prison put greater emphasis on education at the high school and vocational levels. The college courses offered were, for the most part, poorly taught and (as a group) did not meet standard degree requirements. There were no counseling, college preparation, or extracurricular activities. Moreover, there was no formal outside program to which participants could be sent. In making a final judgment about the program, two features, which developed informally, were also considered. A number of courses and activities had been introduced into the prison as a result of the special efforts and personal outside contacts of certain inmates. Also, through one individual at the University of California Irvine campus, many inmate students received special assistance in their efforts to enroll and attend college at Irvine. Both of these developments served to complement the Lompoc program on this variable.

The Illinois program was the lowest quality educational effort in the entire sample. There was almost nothing beyond some college courses offered by instructors from Southern Illinois University (SIU), and these were of average quality. No effort was made to involve and provide for inmates who had educational deficiencies but who had latent college potential. There was little personal contact between students and instructors or among individual students. The program staff (other than SIU instructors) was limited to 30 percent of one man's time. There was no prerelease preparation, and students had no access to information about opportunities after release. The program's one saving grace was an informal liaison with SIU, which enabled some released participants to find their way to its campus to continue their college work.

The Texas program offered a slightly higher quality inside program than Menard did, but only by virtue of the participation of the Lee College professors who offered better instruction and took greater

interest in some individual students. The Texas program was just as
understaffed and meager beyond the classroom. Texas was placed
lower on the scale than Menard only because it was totally lacking in
any outside program. The Texas prison, like Menard, seemed un-
committed to improving its present program and providing a quality
college experience to its inmates.

Personal Social Space

This variable measured the extent to which the college students
were permitted to make choices and participate free from outside
interference. The New Mexico program provided greater personal
social space than any other program in the sample. It was purposely
designed to allow and encourage students to make independent choices.
Within the program framework guidance was provided, but the inmate
was allowed to move according to his own interests and at his own
pace as long as certain minimum performance standards were maintained. Real choices were required to be made among 13 college
courses and instructors, five majors, three different academic and
therapeutic counselors, individual or group counseling, or both, or
none. In addition, program participants received little interference
or harassment from prison staff. The New Mexico NewGate program
was more thoroughly integrated into the prison than any other NewGate
project. The inmate's right to be a student was widely respected.
Finally, the physical facilities were conducive to an atmosphere of
freedom; they were spacious, light, and elaborately decorated. These
facilities produced an atmosphere more like a college than those of
any other program.

The Pennsylvania NewGate program also provided its students
the opportunity to make choices about their curriculum and their own
study routine. The physical facilities included spacious classrooms,
a large and comfortable social room, individual study quarters, which
helped produce a friendly, free, and cooperative atmosphere. The
prison's warden served as the college program director. With his
position he insured that an inmate's right to be a student would be
protected and preserved and that the harassment of students by prison
staff would be limited.

The Ashland NewGate program was much like the Pennsylvania
program with respect to this variable. Students were given the right
to determine their own program and schedule. The program atmosphere was very relaxed, allowing for considerable interaction among
students and staff. Moreover, there was little interference from the
prison staff or formal restrictions on behavior while on the education

floor. The physical facilities were not as extensive as in the New Mexico and Pennsylvania programs, however.

The Minnesota program ranks "medium" on this variable. Its students were as free from interference from prison restrictions and harassment by staff as the students in the programs described above. However, program administrators limited choice by making some important decisions for the students. Personal social space was considerably reduced by making therapy mandatory for all participants. Moreover, the therapy offered was one kind—peer group therapy. Participants could not choose between individual and group, among different therapeutic philosophies, or among different group leaders or groups. The importance of these limitations on choice was accentuated by the fact that therapy played the primary role in the college program and was considered more important than any other part. Another area in which choice was limited was in selecting a college after release. Minnesota was the only program with a formal outside component that would not provide financial support to students who chose to attend a college other than the regular host academic institution.

The Oregon NewGate program provided medium personal social space. Inmates were limited in their freedom of movement by a certain amount of intrusion of restrictive prison rules in the school setting. Moreover, the program was allowed less physical space than any NewGate program in the sample and as little as the non-NewGate programs. Within the program itself, students were also permitted to plan their own programs and schedules. However, their ability to choose among academic alternatives was limited because of the absence of systematic academic counseling and a wide range of course offerings. This was also true for other programs with no academic counseling. Students had to wait to make these choices until they were in the outside program on a college campus.

The Lompoc program was much like the Oregon program on this variable. Although there were fewer restrictions imposed by the prison and prison staff on the inmate while he was on the educational floor, the student's freedom of movement was considerably reduced by a shortage of physical space. The student had no library or study space in which he could enjoy quiet and be free from distraction or interruption. The Lompoc student was able to make choices about his schedule and program. But, though he had this right, choice was again, in effect, reduced by his ignorance about alternatives. The program could have done more to provide such information.

The Illinois and Texas programs offered extremely little personal social space. The inmate was seen first and foremost as a prisoner whose actions had to be carefully guarded and controlled. These prisons made no distinction between the boundaries of the program and the prison routines. The program was dominated by custody and security concerns. The student could not smoke in class, browse in the library, freely converse with fellow students, meet with instructors after class, read an unrestricted list, or gain access to outside publishing houses or library facilities. Students had to be accounted for at all times during the day. When they were not in class, they had to be on their way to, or already somewhere else. Even in class they had to be circumspect in conversation lest they be branded as troublemakers. Instructors were told to avoid certain subjects. As a group, students had little role in influencing the nature of courses to be offered. Since the majority of students in both institutions were part-time and the prison administration did not actively support the program ideals, inmates often had to enter lengthy negotiations with their work supervisors to attend class. Because of this restriction, inmates were limited in being able to attend classes of their choice.

Challenge

This variable measured the extent to which the program stimulated changes in a student's interests, ideas, perspectives, values, and goals. Stimulus could be provided by three different sources: (1) materials presented and made available in the program, (2) activities and expectations of relevant others, and (3) opportunities anticipated beyond prison.

The Pennsylvania program ranked "high" on this variable by virtue of its connection with Penn State. The expectation of attending this university after release was the most powerful motivating force provided by the Pennsylvania program. Another source of challenge was a high quality inside academic program, which offered exciting courses and interesting and approachable instructors, who gave students much personal assistance and encouragement. Program staff could have been more challenging. There also could have been a greater use of activities outside the classroom that tapped additional interests and talents.

The New Mexico program ranked "high" on this variable on the strength of its inside program. This program developed many activities, in addition to an extensive selection of college and college preparatory courses, which were designed to involve the student on many levels. Individual and group therapy were stressed. The approaches differed from one therapist to another, in hopes that students with different cultural backgrounds, temperaments, and levels of sophistication would find a style congenial to them. The program library was the most extensive library found in all the programs. In addition, the project developed a series of weekly presentations by persons outside the prison from the public and private sectors. Topics varied from recent tips on bachelor cooking, current issues in ecology, to a recent report by a person from the state museum on his research on primates. The NewGate staff brought to the program much more than was required for their specific jobs. Several of the counselors taught college courses in the inside program. The area of deficiency was again in the program's limited outside program and the lack of expectation of being able to attend college with full support after release. More than any other program, however, the New Mexico program involved inmates who did not have an interest in continuing college after release.

The Minnesota program ranked "high" on challenge by virtue of its strong outside program, which promised inside participants the opportunity to continue college after release. The inside classes were generally of high quality and, thus, challenged the participants academically. The Minnesota program's peer group therapy was also a source of stimulus. Through vigorous confrontation, it called on students to carefully reevaluate their perspectives, values, interests, and goals. The program did not provide the many sources of challenge that the New Mexico program did, particularly in terms of the breadth of interests of the NewGate program staff, the diversity of therapy, and the range of extracurricular activities.

The Oregon program lacked the stimulation that was provided by the Pennsylvania, New Mexico, and Minnesota programs. There was little intellectual excitement beyond the classroom, either generated by the program staff, by its therapy program, or by the development of extracurricular activities. Some of these deficiencies were compensated for by the existence of the outside program. Inside participants could depend on being able to attend a college campus after release. Once they were there, they were confronted by the same, and perhaps more, challenges than the average college student faces. The Oregon NewGate was ranked lower than the other two programs with a strong outside component because it lacked the same level of excitement and promise of possibility that the others had. Oregon was ranked as "medium" with an arrow pointing to "high" to take into account its outside program and to separate it from the programs that follow.

The Ashland program provided an inside program offering numerous sources of challenge. These consisted of classroom instructors, program staff (some of whom taught courses), interaction with fellow students from a variety of social class backgrounds, and materials presented inside and outside the classroom. The major deficiency was in the program's unsatisfactory outside program, which denied the participants a dependable and realistic way of following up

on new interests and attaining new goals. This dampened the excitement of the inside program.

The Illinois and Lompoc programs offered considerably less
challenge to their participants than did Ashland. Materials were extremely limited. There was no staff with time and commitment to
interact with the student. Instructors had no role beyond the classroom and were not very engaging inside the classroom. The programs
lacked the promise of college after release, which would have served
as an inducement to the efforts of inside students. Both programs,
however, enjoyed the benefit of informal avenues to some college
campuses, which made the prognosis for interested students less
dire than if there had been no college links at all.

Students in the Texas program had no links to outside colleges.
Their participation inside, therefore, usually was intended to use time
profitably or to follow a specific interest. Few had realistic expectations of fulfilling requirements they would need in the pursuit of further
college after release. Serving partially to offset these negative aspects
of the program's isolation and terminal quality, however, was the
quality and commitment of some of the instructors from Lee College.
Some inmates were reached and excited through personal contact with
these instructors.

PROGRAM IMPACT

What was the impact of the college programs on their environment? Did they effect lasting changes on the cognitive, procedural,
and policy making levels of the host institutions (prison and university)
and in the wider community? In the course of the study, it became
apparent that it is possible for college programs to make many changes
on all these levels. It also became apparent that not all programs had
the same potential for creating change. In the first place, because of
their structural relationship to the prison, the room to maneuver in
some programs was narrowly circumscribed. Second, some programs
did not make optimal use of the bargaining resources they had available.

With regard to program impact, the first major distinction among
the programs in the sample is between NewGate and non-NewGate
programs. The Menard, Texas, and Lompoc programs were buried
in the prison's administrative hierarchy; and the innovative initiative
was centralized at the top, in the office of the chief executive—warden
of the prison. Consequently, their impact did not go beyond the students
in the program and the tasks specifically assigned to them to perform.
Moreover, since these programs provided meager resources and

services, their impact even in this narrow sense was not substantial. When compared with the NewGate programs, a smaller proportion of the prison's inmate population was provided a full college experience while inside the prison. Since these programs had no formal outside programs, their impact on inmates' postrelease student careers was inconsequential. The fact that some participants in these programs did continue with their college education after release cannot be construed as a direct effect of the program. Many of these persons were from middle class backgrounds or had college prior to incarceration; thus, they were likely to have gone to college despite a prison college program.

In contrast with these other programs, the NewGate programs represented initially a much greater potential for creating change in the prison and beyond. They came with independent funding and were to bring with them staff members with experiences, perspectives, and expertise quite different from those traditionally found in the prison context. However, just as there was possibility for creative change, there was also the potential for crisis and disaster. Initially, there was great resistance on all levels of the prison to the newcomers, who threatened status quo relationships. Whether this would be overcome eventually and a cooperative arrangement established or whether the early resistance would grow to impossible proportions was dependent on the strategies adopted by the new programs.

The experiences of these programs demonstrated that the impact a new program could achieve in a previously stable institutional environment depended on two factors: (1) the program's external relations policy and (2) the breadth of the influence base from which it operated. More specifically, it was observed that some NewGate programs were more oriented toward influencing the operations of their host institutions, that is, the prison and university, than were others, which were mainly preoccupied with systematizing and protecting their own internal operations. For purposes of the discussion, the strategies of the first group of programs are called "expansionist," and the second group "isolationist." In addition, some programs operated from a narrow influence base, relying predominantly on the staff and program to do its bidding in negotiations with the prison and university. Others developed and operated from a broad influence base, reaching beyond their own boundaries and enlisting persons, groups, and institutions outside the program, thereby structuring their participation on a permanent basis.

The NewGate programs are ranked according to this typology in Figure 3.2. In boxes one to four, they are placed in the order of decreasing effectiveness.

The New Mexico program clearly had the greatest success in establishing itself in the prison on its own terms. From the time its

FIGURE 3.2

Influence Base and External Relations Policy

Influence Base

		Broad	Narrow
External Relations Policy	Expansionist	New Mexico 1	3 Oregon I Pennsylvania I
	Isolationist	2 Minnesota	4 Oregon II Pennsylvania II Ashland

Source: Compiled by the authors.

second director took over, it conceived of its role inside the prison in ambitious terms. It would not serve just a select group of college students, but it would extend the program benefits vigorously to inmates who still had educational deficiencies. In addition, it would weave its services in with other prison services, such as high school training, GED program, vocational training, psychological counseling, educational programs designed for the women's division. Because of these involvements, the program not only had many contact points but also a base inside the prison from which to influence ideas and policy changes on many levels of the correctional enterprise. It also was able to become involved in a number of important decision-making arenas inside the prison.

The New Mexico NewGate program functioned as part of the Eastern New Mexico University, operating as a special project out of its president's office. Though relatively small, this university was actively committed to the success and life of NewGate. It used its offices to influence the state legislature to appropriate funds to New-Gate and worked with persons and groups throughout the state on the program's behalf. It participated on the statewide advisory board of NewGate and attempted to sustain this board's continuous interest in the purposes of the program. The publicity generated by this board and by a project of NewGate funded by the New Mexico State Arts Commission brought to the public a greater awareness of the problems of prisons and prisoners. The involvement of these outsiders not only built their commitment to being involved but also served to strengthen the program's position with the prison and the state legislature.

No other program in the sample had as great an impact on its host prison as New Mexico. The Minnesota program had perhaps the greatest direct impact beyond the prison. It effected change in some attitudes and policies at the University of Minnesota, had some influence in the State Department of Corrections, and in certain legislative committees in the state legislature. NewGate had this impact by virtue of its being an officially recognized program of the university. The Minnesota NewGate program, however, had remarkably little impact on its host prison. Its failure in this regard was due to its reluctance to build links with prison operations and to its preference for remaining isolated and running a self-contained program.

Both the Oregon and Pennsylvania programs in their initial phases were involved in trying to make the force of their innovative experience felt in other parts of the institution. This orientation was a function of the primary tasks set before any new program, which inevitably upsets preexisting institutional arrangements and is ineluctably drawn into a series of efforts to negotiate new commitments. Both of these programs' first directors pursued a strategy they expected would mold new relationships and would promise their program the broadest range of resources and the greatest space in which to maneuver.

Neither of these programs ever realized their ambitions because they could not consolidate their power within the prison. Neither built a broad base of influence outside or inside the prison. The Oregon project eschewed developing a lasting relationship with a university structure. The Pennsylvania project, which began as part of the College of Human Resources at Pennsylvania State, became estranged from its college base and was left to its own devices in a struggle with the prison administration. Neither elaborated strategies designed to build constituencies within the prison. In Oregon, the struggle was resolved by the NewGate director resigning. In Pennsylvania, the prison took full control over the college program.

The policies of the college programs in Oregon and Pennsylvania changed in their second phase. In the aftermath of Phase I, the Oregon project assumed a profile of low visibility and became preoccupied with its own internal administrative problems without trying to effect change in other prison operations or at the University of Oregon, the host of its aftercare program. Oregon continued to function from a narrow influence base, operating as a third force between the prison and university bureaucracies. It did not develop its statewide advisory board nor build commitment of any other group of institutions on which it could have depended for resources and support.

Once the Pennsylvania program came under the authority of the prison, it lost most of its ability to initiate change in or beyond its program. Because of a rather unusual hierarchical relationship to the warden (the program was placed directly under the warden, who

acted as its director) the college program was not buried in the prison
bureaucracy. The warden's continued interest assured the program
that most of the earlier innovations would be retained. However,
since innovation initiative became centralized in the warden's office,
the program's ability to influence greater change in the prison operations effectively was thwarted. The warden defined the program's
role explicitly and expected it not to involve itself in other than academic matters. The staff became almost exclusively involved with
internal program concerns. Moreover, there was no longer any initiative taken by interests at the university or from persons and groups
from the community.

The Ashland program, as the Oregon and Pennsylvania programs,
operated from a narrow base of influence. In the first place, it tried
unsuccessfully to establish involvement and commitment from a university structure. Attempts were made with both the University of
Kentucky and Morehead State University. Second, even if a firm base
had been established, it still might have been difficult for the NewGate
program to make its influence felt in the host prison. It is not enough
in the federal system to establish a friendly working arrangement with
the prison administration. Ultimately, a program such as NewGate
has to deal with the remote and insulated Federal Bureau of Prisons.
In the final analysis, the Ashland program was essentially isolationist,
bidding from a narrow base of influence. It did not succeed in extending its base of influence within the prison by elaborating additional
points of contact with other prison programs. Ultimately, all it had
left to spread its influence was the force of a good record, which
could persuade others of the correctness and desirability of its approach. Apparently, this was not enough to continue to have impact
on the federal bureau's policy, since it took over the college program
itself and eliminated many policies that had been implemented when
NewGate functioned at the Federal Youth Center.

In certain ways the goals of program quality and program survival
work at cross purposes. Many of the features suggested in the report
as enhancing program quality (for example, college atmosphere,
semiautonomy, involvement of outsiders, programmatic links with
the university) serve to exacerbate tensions between the new program
and the prison and ultimately threaten the integrity, if not the actual
survival, of the original program. The non-NewGate programs had
forsaken the goal of quality for survival. Because they were initiated
and endorsed by the prison administration, they were from their inception provided the legitimacy and authority vested in the top executive
of the prison establishment. Moreover, tension was kept at a minimum by making the program follow a format that called for few departures from the established routines. The ideals of the college
program were compromised from the outset.

The NewGate programs' experiences were different. They began with greater ambitions. They intended to realize both goals simultaneously. In reviewing the histories of the NewGate programs, it is obvious that some were more successful than others. The Ashland program was taken over by the prison system and its original design was modified significantly. The Pennsylvania NewGate program (Phase I) was taken over and modified slightly. The Oregon program was not taken over but lost much of its original dynamism and abandoned some of its more effective features in the inside program. The Minnesota program survived the process of institutionalization, preserving its original model and retaining its vitality. Finally, the New Mexico program not only retained its vitality but continued to increase its high quality while also increasing the strength of the prison's commitment to it.

Before completing this discussion, it should be noted that the directors of NewGate programs were continually beset with the unwelcome task of seeking permanent funding sources as an alternative to OEO funding. This all-consuming effort explains in part why some directors neglected some parts of their program essential both to maximum impact and survival. Survival came to be seen as hinging essentially on whether alternative funding could be found. Although it was understood from the beginning that OEO's participation would only be temporary, it was not anticipated that programs would have so much difficulty generating commitments elsewhere. It was unfortunate that federal funds could not have been granted until the idea of providing college education to prison inmates gained greater national acceptance. Eventually, state departments of education might follow the lead this department has taken in the State of Oregon and recognize that the educational enterprise in prisons is but another part of its permanent responsibility.

4

ACADEMIC ACHIEVEMENT
OF RELEASED PRISONERS

The overriding concern of this study was the success of prison college programs. To be successful an educational program must first provide a viable educational experience for participants. As indicated in Chapter 3, each of the programs studied appeared to be sufficiently well designed and managed to do so, although some were superior to others. No matter how well-designed the program, however, the success of an educational program is judged ultimately by the impact of the program on participants. This impact can be measured first by what students achieve educationally in the program and, second, by whether participation results in more productive and satisfying life experiences than students would otherwise have had. In this chapter the subject of academic achievement before and after release is addressed. Subsequent chapters deal with the broader issues of program impact and the underlying assumption of educational programs: that educational achievement is instrumental in facilitating a successful postprison career.

The analysis of academic achievement of released participants focused on three major issues.

(1) The educational achievement of participants in the college program while in prison: how much education participants completed, and how well they performed using standard measures of academic performance.

(2) The impact of the program on the long range educational achievement of participants: to what extent programs provided educational opportunities for persons who would otherwise not pursue a college education, rather than providing courses for persons who might have been expected to find opportunities for college enrollment after release, even if they had not participated in the prison college program.

(3) The relationship between program structure and the impact of the program on participants: how educational achievement of participants varied with the comprehensiveness of program services.

PARTICIPANTS' BACKGROUNDS

Data on academic achievement were obtained from records and interviews with random samples of released participants from each program. As may be seen in Tables 4.1 through 4.3, participants varied considerably with respect to prior experiences and background, both within and between programs.

Social Background

Participants were generally in their early or mid-20s but ranged in age from 17 to 49 at the time they entered the college program. Since the sites included in the study were all institutions for male offenders, few females were included among the participants. The only programs having any female participants were New Mexico and Oregon, which are located in prisons in close proximity to a correctional facility for women. The few female participants included in the study sample (six percent in the New Mexico sample and eight percent in Oregon) had not attended college classes within the program while in prison but received support to continue their college education following release.

Minority group members were underrepresented compared with their proportional representation in the general prison population in Ashland, Minnesota, New Mexico, and particularly Texas. Although proportionately underrepresented in New Mexico, minority group members nevertheless formed a substantial portion of the participant group (about 44 percent). In contrast, Pennsylvania and Illinois each had a larger proportion of minorities in the college program than in the general prison population. Regardless of ethnicity, participants at each site except Lompoc primarily came from either lower or working class backgrounds, as is typical of prison inmate populations. The highest proportions of persons from lower class backgrounds were found in New Mexico, Illinois, and Texas (from 36 to 46 percent).

TABLE 4.1

Social Background Characteristics of Participants

	NewGate Program Sites					Other Program Sites		
	Ashland (N=51)	Minnesota (N=50)	New Mexico (N=50)	Oregon (N=75)	Pennsylvania (N=56)	Lompoc (N=49)	Illinois (N=41)	Texas (N=46)
Age when entered inside program								
Median:	19	22	25	28	23	22	26	26
Range:	17-25	19-29	19-43	20-45	18-39	18-27	18-46	18-49
Sex								
Male	100%	100%	94%	92%	100%	100%	100%	100%
Female	0%	0%	6%	8%	0%	0%	0%	0%
Ethnic background								
White	80%	86%	56%	83%	50%	76%	46%	85%
	68%[a]	76%[a]	37%[a]	84%[a]	69%[a]	—[b]	63%[a]	42%[a]
Black	16%	8%	6%	15%	50%	20%	49%	9%
Hispano	0%	0%	34%	3%	0%	0%	2%	6%
Other	4%	6%	4%	0%	0%	4%	2%	0%
Social class								
Lower	10%	8%	36%	25%	25%	10%	44%	46%
Working	53%	58%	38%	55%	46%	31%	32%	44%
Lower middle	26%	28%	20%	19%	23%	39%	12%	4%
Upper middle	12%	6%	6%	1%	5%	20%	12%	6%

[a]Percentage of whites in general inmate population.
[b]Information not available (percentage of whites in general inmate population).
Source: Compiled by the authors.

48

TABLE 4.2

Criminal Records of Participants

	NewGate Program Sites					Other Program Sites		
	Ashland (N=51)	Minnesota (N=50)	New Mexico (N=50)	Oregon (N=75)	Pennsylvania (N=56)	Lompoc (N=49)	Illinois (N=41)	Texas (N=46)
Prior arrests								
None	24%	10%	22%	8%	38%	33%	34%	0%
One	14%	12%	4%	3%	18%	16%	5%	3%
More than one	62%	78%	74%	89%	45%	51%	61%	97%
Prior felony convictions								
None	80%	56%	66%	24%	70%	82%	49%	13%
One	18%	32%	26%	15%	14%	10%	17%	38%
More than one	2%	12%	8%	61%	16%	8%	34%	49%
Time served this sentence								
Median (years):	1.4	2.0	1.8	2.8	2.4	1.8	2.6	3.2
Range:	0.7– 2.9	1.0– 5.8	0.3– 20.8	0.4– 13.0	0.7– 7.5	0.9– 4.6	0.7– 10.9	1.6– 13.2

Source: Compiled by the authors.

TABLE 4.3

Educational Preparation of Participants When Entering Prison

	NewGate Program Sites					Other Program Sites		
	Ashland (N=51)	Minnesota (N=50)	New Mexico (N=50)	Oregon (N=75)	Pennsylvania (N=56)	Lompoc (N=46)	Illinois (N=41)	Texas (N=46)
Education completed prior to this commitment								
Less than high school graduation	63%	26%	66%	37%	32%	26%	22%	58%
High school graduate	28%	52%	18%	46%	55%	45%	46%	20%
Some college (2 years)	10%	18%	10%	11%	9%	25%	20%	16%
Two or more years of college	0%	4%	6%	6%	4%	4%	12%	7%
Tested grade level								
Median:	9.5	10.8	9.2	10.6	10.6	11.5	—*	9.6
Range:	5.4–12.4	8.6–13.0	6.2–12.6	5.5–15.4	5.1–13.0	5.3–12.9	—*	5.6–12.0

*Information not available.

Source: Compiled by the authors.

Criminal Record

The majority of participants in all programs had more than one prior arrest; although in Ashland, Minnesota, New Mexico, Pennsylvania, and Lompoc fewer than 50 percent had any prior felony convictions (see Table 4.2). Only in Oregon, Illinois, and Texas was there a substantial percentage of persons who had more than one prior felony conviction. Note that persons in these three programs also tended to be somewhat older than those in other programs (Table 4.1) and to serve more time before release from prison (Table 4.2).

Educational Background

To enroll in any of the college level programs, participants must first have received a high school diploma or equivalent certificate (GED). As can be seen in Table 4.3, a substantial number of participants completed this requirement only after participation in lower level educational programs offered by the prison. The percentage of persons who had not yet completed high school at the beginning of their sentences varied from lows of 22 to 26 percent in Illinois, Minnesota, and Lompoc to highs of 58 to 66 percent in Texas, Ashland, and New Mexico. Even with the high school requirement satisfied, special college preparatory classes were necessary for a number of students, particularly in the Ashland and New Mexico programs, before enrolling in college level classes. These classes were provided as part of the college program at NewGate sites, although students did not receive college credit for their participation.

Although the minimum requirement for entrance was completion of high school, some participants at each site had attended college before entering prison, a few having previously completed two or more years of college. Overall, about 20 percent of the participants had previously had some education beyond high school, ranging from 10 percent in Ashland to 32 percent in Illinois. Illinois had the highest proportion of persons (12 percent) with two or more years of college completed before entering the prison college program.

The range in level of preparedness at the time of entry into prison is also indicated by the tested grade level of program participants, which ranged from as low as 5.4 to as high as 15.4, averaging between 9th and 11th grade. Although tested ability is one measure of level of preparation, it should be kept in mind that these tests were administered during the stressful period following conviction, sentencing, and initial entry into the prison setting and, therefore, could underestimate actual level of achievement.

One point that should be stressed is the comparability of the prior educational achievement of the program participants on entering prison with that of the general inmate population when comparing averages for each group. Although many inmates might not be interested in pursuing a college education, it is not the case that only a small number are, or can become, educationally prepared to take advantage of such a program. At each site the mean educational level and tested grade level for the inmate population in general were comparable with those for program participants.

EDUCATIONAL ACHIEVEMENT WHILE IN PRISON

As may be seen in Table 4.4, participants included in the study completed anywhere from three units (one course) to the equivalent of over two years of full-time study while in prison, with 15 to 25 units being typical in most programs. These figures are somewhat higher than would be found if all persons who had participated in the program had been included in the analysis. This is particularly true in the non-NewGate programs. The nature of participation in these programs and the criteria used for inclusion in the study sample resulted in a sample less representative of the total student population than in the NewGate programs. As indicated earlier, the study sample was restricted to those persons who had completed the equivalent of 12 semester units or who had participated in both the inside and outside programs. The 12-unit minimum was imposed both to ensure that participants included in the study had sufficient exposure to college classes to reasonably expect that this experience might have some impact and to make the amount of education received more comparable across programs. The majority of all NewGate program participants met both criteria because the programs were designated for full-time participation. Since the non-NewGate programs did not have formal outside programs, participants were, as a rule, only included if they had completed 12 units. Most students in these other programs, however, took only one or two classes while in prison and thus did not meet the criteria for inclusion in the study sample. Note that because they participated part-time, students in non-NewGate programs progressed at a slower rate and participated in a less intensive college-type experience than NewGate students, even when considering only the extent of on-going class participation.

In the NewGate programs, some participants who were included in the sample had not actually attended college level classes in the inside program. In New Mexico, for example, 44 percent of those included in the sample had participated only in college preparatory

TABLE 4.4

College Level Educational Progress of Participants While in Prison

	NewGate Program Sites					Other Program Sites		
	Ashland	Minnesota	New Mexico	Oregon	Pennsylvania	Lompoc	Illinois	Texas
Number of units completed								
Median	19	25	10	29	17	18	24	21
Range	6–40	11–50	3–32	5–75	4–56	7–54	11–76	12–64
N	39*	50	22*	59*	52*	49	41	46
Number of years in inside program								
Median	0.8	0.9	0.6	1.0	1.3	1.1	1.5	1.2
Range	0.2–1.2	0.3–1.5	0.2–1.6	0.3–3.8	0.3–2.8	0.6–2.4	0.8–6.0	0.6–3.0
N	46*	50	45*	62*	51*	49*	41	46
Grade point average (college classes)								
Median	2.44	2.88	2.99	3.18	3.00	3.32	2.52	2.32
Range	0.50–4.00	1.51–4.00	0.50–4.00	0.50–4.00	1.15–4.00	1.00–4.00	1.33–4.00	1.00–4.00
N	38*	50	11*	56*	52*	41*	41	46

*Information not available for some participants.

Source: Compiled by the authors.

classes offered by the program but were released to attend college
under the auspices of the outside program. Several persons in the
NewGate programs in New Mexico (14 percent), Oregon (12 percent),
and Pennsylvania (2 percent) were supported in the outside program,
although they had not participated in any classes in the inside program.
These persons either had some college prior to entering prison or
had taken college classes outside the NewGate program while in prison
and had been in contact with NewGate staff members prior to release.

The variability in the number of college level semester units completed while inside prison was due primarily to differences in the
length of time spent in the program, which was in turn determined to
a considerable extent by the length of a participant's sentence. For
students who remained in the program more than one year or had had
prior college classes, the number of units completed was somewhat
dependent on the range of classes offered by the program, although
few participants in the study actually were restricted by this potential
limitation.

One standard measure of academic performance is a student's
grade point average. Grades earned by program participants averaged
in the C+ (2.25) to B+ (3.25) range (see Table 4.4). Although students
who did poorly were likely to have dropped out before completing 12
units and thus not be included in these figures, it is clear that the
majority of participants were able to perform well at the college level.
There is no guarantee that instructors used the same standards in
grading these students as they would those on a conventional college
campus, but there is no evidence to indicate that the grading policies
inside were any more or less lenient. In fact, instructors in Pennsylvania had been directed explicitly to apply the same standards they
used on campus so student-inmates would have an accurate assessment of how they could expect to perform when released. One item
of indirect evidence as to the comparability of grading procedures
inside and out is that the grades of persons continuing in college after
release correlated significantly ($p < .05$) with the grades they had
received while in prison at each of the NewGate sites. The correlation coefficients were of the same magnitude (Kendall's tau = .34) in
Lompoc and Texas but were not statistically significant because of the
small sample sizes. Illinois was the only site where there was no
correlation. All indications from observing the programs and looking
at the records of participants as well as talking to instructors and
persons who had been through the program were that the quality of
college education received inside was generally average or about
average insofar as both level of instruction and student performance
were concerned.

Although the focus of this analysis is college education, one
should keep in mind that many of the students who had completed

college classes at the time of release had progressed from the status of high school drop-out to successful college student during imprisonment. The progress of participants was remarkable, given their backgrounds and level of preparation at the time they entered prison.

POSTRELEASE EDUCATIONAL ACHIEVEMENT

A variety of measures were used in evaluating postrelease academic achievement, including achievement of participants' goals, college enrollment, number of semesters completed since release, grades achieved after release, and the total number of semesters completed before and after release. One difficulty in evaluating postrelease performance was the number of factors influencing the extent of progress at the time of data collection. These factors include length of time since release, the timing of release relative to the scheduling of the academic year, and the number of remaining units needed to complete a degree after release.

Educational Goals

Some students had entered the inside college program primarily as a way of making use of their time in prison—an end in itself with no plans to continue in college after release. For others, participation represented entry into a system in which they would be able to find a better job after release and/or to continue on to a college degree after release.

Earning a college degree was identified as being a very important reason for getting into the program by over 40 percent of the interviewed participants in Minnesota, New Mexico, and Pennsylvania, and by over 30 percent in Ashland, Oregon, and Texas. On the other hand, 42 percent of the participants in Ashland, Illinois, and Texas indicated that, for them, getting a college degree had not been an important reason for entering the college program. As would be expected, the same patterns of responses were given in indicating the importance of getting into college after release as a reason for entering the program.

The extent of postrelease progress toward a degree for thos persons indicating that getting a college degree was very important varied considerably between sites (see Table 4.5). Among Texas participants, 62 percent of those who had considered earning a degree very important did not attend college at all after release. This figure was less

TABLE 4.5

Postrelease Educational Progress of Those Participants for Whom Earning a
College Degree Was Very Important

	NewGate Program Sites					Other Program Sites		
	Ashland	Minnesota	New Mexico	Oregon	Pennsylvania	Lompoc	Illinois	Texas
Did not attend	8%	6%	12%	9%	0%	25%	0%	62%
Dropped out before completing 15 units (one full semester)	46%	29%	47%	4%	24%	25%	0%	12%
Completed at least 15 units (one semester)	46%	65%	41%	87%	76%	50%	100%	26%
N*	13	17	17	22	17	8	5	8

*Includes only those persons for whom earning a degree was very important.
Source: Compiled by the authors.

than 15 percent at all other sites except Lompoc, where 25 percent did not attend. Comparing the percentages completing at least one semester after release, the participants in Illinois, Oregon, and Pennsylvania were most successful in progressing toward their goal of eventually obtaining a degree. The extent of progress was not measured beyond one semester in this particular analysis because of the bias introduced by differing lengths of time since release and, hence, differential opportunities for postrelease achievement at the time data were collected. Time since release could not be adequately controlled for given the small sample sizes.

The extent to which college education had become an important value to participants regardless of initial motivation for entering the program can be measured by whether or not they planned to continue in college after release. Their plans and actual behavior following release clearly differentiate between programs with respect to academic achievement following release. At the time of release from prison, a majority of the participants in each program except Texas planned to attend college, most of them on a full-time basis (see Table 4.6). The percentage of persons planning to attend college was much higher among the NewGate participants (at least 90 percent) than among participants in other programs. One reason for this difference between NewGate and other participants is that the NewGate programs had clear channels for continuing education after release in terms of counseling, affiliations with outside universities, and provisions for financial support.

College Enrollment

Virtually all of those planning to attend college after release actually did enroll. Texas program participants constituted the only group in which a number of persons planning to attend college never enrolled (a drop from 44 percent planning to attend to 27 percent actually enrolling). In part this is attributable to the fact that the Texas program provided the fewest channels for entering college after release. As an example of the type of obstacles faced by Texas participants, at least one college located in Huntsville, the central location of the Texas Department of Corrections, would not admit an ex-convict to the school, although the school had a heavy emphasis on penology and made use of the facilities at Huntsville for purposes of on-the-job training and research in corrections. Another factor that differentiates the Texas participants from those at other sites was the high percentage of persons who were discharged directly from prison rather than after serving time on parole under a supervising agency.

TABLE 4.6

Planned and Actual Continuation of College Education Following Release[a]

	NewGate Program Sites					Other Program Sites		
	Ashland (N=41)	Minnesota (N=40)	New Mexico (N=39)	Oregon (N=60)	Pennsylvania (N=46)	Lompoc (N=33)	Illinois (N=31)	Texas (N=26)
Planned to attend college upon release								
Full-time	85%	90%	92%	90%	98%	39%	52%	44%
Part-time	5%	0%	0%	5%	0%	21%	3%	0%
Percentage of students actually enrolling	88%	92%	90%	95%	98%	48%	58%	27%
Percentage completing at least one course after release[b]	54%	70%	51%	85%	88%	42%	52%	27%
Percentage completing at least one semester after release (15 units)[b]	29%	50%	33%	72%	76%	31%	36%	12%
Percentage completing at least one year after release (30 units)[b]	15%	24%	24%	63%	54%	21%	26%	12%
Number of college units completed by those who enrolled after release								
Median	10	14	6	30	24	18	32	12
Range	0-65	0-99	0-95	0-138	0-99	0-90	0-74	3-70
Grade point average of those completing[c] some college work (on a 4-point scale)								
Median	2.48	2.96	2.78	3.00	2.75	3.07	2.88	2.90
Median	2.48	2.96	2.78	3.00	2.75	3.07	2.88	2.90
Range	1.00-3.92	2.00-3.74	1.00-4.00	2.00-3.80	1.25-3.83	2.00-4.00	2.00-3.84	1.20-4.00
N[d]	36	37	35	57	45	16	18	7

[a]Information available only for interviewed sample at each site.

[b]Base number for percentage excludes those still in school who had not reached this stage.

[c]For classes completed since release.

[d]Number of interviewed participants from each site who had completed some college work since release.

Source: Compiled by the authors.

Only 42 percent of the Texas participants left prison on parole, compared with 80 to 90 percent in other programs. Thus the majority of
the Texas participants did not have to answer to a parole agent if they
did not follow through on plans to attend college, nor were they required to have formal plans for the future before release.

College Units Completed Since Release

Although most students planning to attend college did enroll,
many dropped out during the first semester without completing any
courses. This was particularly true in Ashland and New Mexico and,
to a lesser extent, in Minnesota (see Table 4.6). Each of these programs had facilities for transition to an outside program, but they
did not have the extensive study-release program found in Oregon
and Pennsylvania. The study release programs appear to affect the
drop-out rates in two ways. On the one hand, participants on study-
release usually completed at least one semester before being paroled.
If dropping out were merely postponed until formal release, however,
the drop-out rates in Oregon and Pennsylvania should catch up with
those of the other programs after completion of a semester. Since
this was not the case (see Table 4.6), study-release appears to be an
effective means of easing the transition into an outside college program
and reducing the postrelease drop-out rate.

The rate of enrolling but dropping out without completing any
courses outside was lower in the non-NewGate programs than in any
of the NewGate programs. This was in large measure due to the high
drop-out rate in those programs prior to enrolling. Since at the non-
NewGate sites the burden of gaining admission and enrolling was on the
participants with little assistance from the program, those persons
who were not strongly committed to continuing in college did not bother
to enroll in the first place. The differences in early drop-out rates
between programs raise an interesting issue, which will be discussed
further in evaluating the relationship between program structure and
postrelease performance: particularly with reference to the cost
effectiveness of a program, is a little support better than none, or is
extensive support necessary to have a significant impact on performance and return on investment?

Comparing programs, the percentages of persons completing at
least one semester or one year of college following release followed
the same trend as for those completing one course, although the percentages decreased over time for each group. On the average those
participants who enrolled in college from the Oregon, Pennsylvania,
and Illinois programs completed more units since release than

participants in other programs. The median numbers of units completed since release as presented in Table 4.6 do not, however, take
into account differences in length of time since release. To give some
further idea of the progress of participants in each program since
release, data are presented separately for those who were still enrolled at the time of contact (Table 4.7) and those who had dropped
out of school by that time (Table 4.8). The percentage of persons still
enrolled at the time of contact varied from lows of eight percent in
Texas and ten percent in Ashland to a high of 54 percent in Pennsylvania. At least one-third of the participants interviewed were still
enrolled in Minnesota, Oregon, and Lompoc. Although some students
still enrolled had yet to complete a full semester, the majority had
completed at least one year of college since release except in Minnesota. In Minnesota, the drop-out rate was much higher for the first
group of participants enrolled in the program and has since leveled
off. After the data were collected, it was discovered that a disproportionate number of the early participants had, by chance, been included in the randomly selected sample from Minnesota. As a result,
the postrelease achievement of Minnesota participants is probably
greater than the data in this study indicate.

Level of Performance Following Release

Including all participants who had completed at least one course
following release, the median grade point average ranged from 2.48
(C+) for Ashland participants to 3.07 (B+) for Lompoc participants.
Most released participants who had completed some college classes
maintained a grade point average of at least 2.00, with the median for
those still enrolled being 3.00 and that for those having left school
being 2.50. In most colleges a C grade (2.00) is considered average
performance. Considering the fact that the median grades were computed from data including participants who dropped out of college because of poor performance, the grades earned by participants as a
group indicate that they were well prepared at the time of release to
continue successful academic progress. As a further indication of
accomplishment, from 11 to 20 percent of the participants in these
programs who attended college after release made the honor roll at
their respective colleges for their postrelease performance (see
Table 4.9).

Although most participants in this study had not been released
long enough to complete the number of units required for a degree,
this is clearly a realistic goal for some. In Oregon, where participants had been released for the longest period of time, 15 percent had

TABLE 4.7

Postrelease Educational Progress of Participants Still Enrolled in College

	NewGate Program Sites					Other Program Sites		
	Ashland	Minnesota	New Mexico	Oregon	Pennsylvania	Lompoc	Illinois	Texas
Semesters completed[a]								
Less than one (0–14 units)	0%	10%	0%	13%	9%	3%	10%	0%
One semester (15–29 units)	2%	18%	5%	3%	11%	12%	3%	0%
Two or more semesters (30 units)[b]	7%	12%	13%	34%	39%	18%	23%	8%
Semester units completed								
Median	36	20	40	38	40	48	62	—[c]
Range	21–65	5–99	17–95	0–113	10–99	12–90	29–74	52–70
N	4	16	7	26	26	11	8	2

[a]Percentages based on total interviewed participant sample size at each site.
[b]Including those who have completed B. A. degree.
[c]Median not computed due to small sample size (N=2).

Source: Compiled by the authors.

TABLE 4.8

Postrelease Educational Progress of Participants Not in College

	NewGate Program Sites					Other Program Sites		
	Ashland	Minnesota	New Mexico	Oregon	Pennsylvania	Lompoc	Illinois	Texas
Semesters completed[a]								
None—did not attend	12%	8%	10%	5%	2%	52%	42%	73%
Less than one (0–14 units)	59%	38%	56%	20%	20%	15%	16%	15%
One semester (15–29 units)	12%	10%	5%	7%	15%	0%	6%	0%
Two or more semesters (30 units)[b]	7%	5%	10%	18%	4%	0%	0%	4%
Semester units completed[c]								
Median	6	8	0	22	14	4	16	12
Range	0–56	0–57	0–45	0–138	0–53	0–11	0–57	3–31
N	32	21	28	31	19	5	10	5

[a]Percentages based on total interviewed participant sample size at each site.
[b]Not including those who left after completing B.A. degree.
[c]Includes only those who enrolled in school after release.
Source: Compiled by the authors.

TABLE 4.9

Percentage of Participants Receiving Honors and Degrees Since Release

	NewGate Program Sites					Other Program Sites		
	Ashland	Minnesota	New Mexico	Oregon	Pennsylvania	Lompoc	Illinois	Texas
Percentage of persons attending school after release who received honors	11	27	11	18	16	25	11	29
N	36	37	35	57	45	16	18	7
Percentage of all participants who received degrees after release								
A.A. degree (only)	0	20	3	2	2	3	0	0
B.A. degree	0	2	5	15	11	0	16	4
M.A. degree	0	0	0	5	0	0	0	0
N	41	40	39	60	46	33	31	26

Note: Information available only for interviewed sample at each site.
Source: Compiled by the authors.

received a bachelor's degree since release and 5 percent a master's degree. An additional 33 percent of the released participant sample in Oregon were still enrolled, some of whom undoubtedly will complete a degree.

OVERALL ACADEMIC ACHIEVEMENT

Most important in terms of the impact on the individual's future career is the total progress toward a degree. Based on the past records of participants, the projected percentage of students completing a given number of semesters was computed. These percentages are graphed for all sites in Figure 4.1 and presented numerically in Table 4.10. These graphs take into account college classes completed before, during, and after imprisonment. Also included in Table 4.10 are the projected completion rates, excluding those persons who had attended college prior to imprisonment. This second set of percentages is included to control for the advantage gained by some programs that admitted a relatively high percentage of persons who already had some college before entering prison.

It is clear from these projections that Oregon and Pennsylvania had the highest success rates in terms of long range academic achievement of participants, regardless of whether they had previous college experience. If students continue their education at the same rate as in the past, about 45 percent of Oregon and Pennsylvania participants will receive bachelor's degrees. Twenty-six to 28 percent of the participants in Lompoc and Illinois are likely to complete degrees, with lesser percentages continuing to completion at other sites.

Regardless of the postrelease measure used to determine academic achievement, the most successful programs clearly were Pennsylvania and Oregon, followed by Illinois. The least successful were Ashland, New Mexico, and Texas. The achievement rates undoubtedly were somewhat higher for the participants included in the sample than for all persons who had participated in the programs. As indicated earlier this was due in part to the selection criteria used in drawing the original samples. Since postrelease information was by design obtained for only a subsample at each site, an additional element of bias was introduced. Those participants from each site who were attending college were generally among the easiest to locate at all sites because they were most likely to have maintained contact with persons in the inside program and to have remained visible in the community. The possible bias thereby introduced was undoubtedly greater for the non-NewGate programs, where it was impossible to locate the full complement of 40 released participants called for in the study design for personal interviews.

FIGURE 4.1

Projected Academic Achievement of Released Participants at Each Site

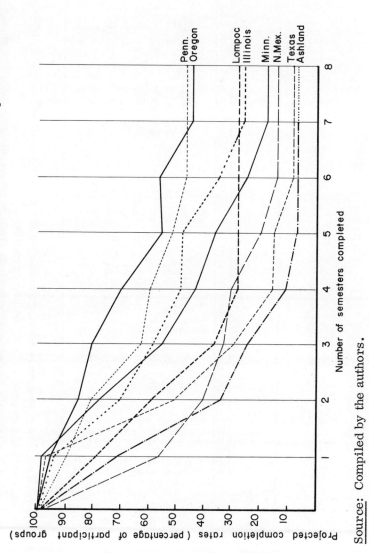

Source: Compiled by the authors.

TABLE 4.10

Projected Academic Achievement of Participants

Number of Semesters	Corresponding Number of Units	NewGate Program Sites					Other Program Sites		
		Ashland	Minnesota	New Mexico	Oregon	Pennsylvania	Lompoc	Illinois	Texas
		(percentages)							
1	15	71 (68)[a]	98 (97)	56 (48)	95 (94)	89 (92)	79 (68)	94 (91)	96 (95)
2	30	34 (27)	78 (74)	41 (30)	85 (86)	80 (81)	58 (36)	71 (59)	50 (32)
3	45	24 (16)	56 (48)	33 (21)	80 (79)	63 (60)	37 (26)	58 (50)	27 (10)
4 (A.A.)	60	11 (8)	43 (36)	30 (18)	70 (67)	60 (57)	28 (13)	48 (34)	15 (0)
5	75	7 (4)	36 (24)	20 (9)	56 (50)	52 (46)	28 (—)	48 (34)	15 (0)
6	90	7 (—)	25 (—)	14 (5)	56 (50)	47 (37)	28 (—)	35 (26)	8 (0)
7	105	7 (—)	17 (—)	14 (—)	45 (43)	47 (37)	28 (—)	26 (17)	8 (0)
8 (B.A.)	120	—[c] (—)	17 (—)	14 (—)	45 (43)	47 (37)	28 (—)	26 (17)	8 (0)

[a]Number in parentheses is projected percentage excluding those who had attended college prior to entering prison.

[b]Insufficient data available to compute a projected percentage.

Note: Percentage of participants projected to complete given numbers of semesters based on data from interview sample (pre- and postrelease).

Source: Compiled by the authors.

PROGRAM IMPACT ON EDUCATIONAL ACHIEVEMENT

An in-college program can be set up to attract persons who would not otherwise attend college as a means of increasing their chances for success after release, and/or it can be set up to provide classes for persons who might be expected to pursue opportunities for college enrollment after release even if the program did not exist. The New-Gate and non-NewGate programs clearly differed in this area in both intent and results. Although none of the programs excluded a person from the program because he had previous college experience, the NewGate programs made greater efforts to attract participants from a variety of backgrounds and to provide compensatory programs for those who were less prepared to pursue a college education than did the non-NewGate programs, which depended on the inmate taking the initiative in seeking information about the program.

One measure of the extent to which the college program serves the more socially disadvantaged participant is the relationship of social class background to academic achievement in each of the programs. One of the consistent findings in research in higher education is that persons from lower and working class families are less likely to attend college and more likely to drop out (particularly during the first semester) if they do attend than those from middle and upper class families.[1] Interestingly enough, the correlations between either social class or father's education and number of units completed for those who enrolled in college after release were not significant in this study at any site except Texas. If, however, we consider not only the length of time a person remains in school but also whether an individual enrolls after release in the first place, some clear differences emerge, as indicated in Table 4.11. Social class background made little difference in the NewGate programs, particularly in Oregon and Pennsylvania. This is clearly not the case, however, in the non-NewGate programs. In these programs the students from middle and upper-middle class backgrounds were the most likely to continue in college after release. This is the group that would have been most likely to go on to college in any case.

There are a number of characteristics differentiating the NewGate programs from the other programs that might account for this: the greater stimulation and support in the inside programs, assistance in academic counseling both before and after release, and assistance in cutting through the red tape involved in both gaining admission to an unfamiliar college or university and securing financial assistance to attend college. The non-NewGate program, which had a relatively high rate of postrelease academic achievement, was Illinois, which, relative to the other non-NewGate programs, had the most extensive

TABLE 4.11

Academic Achievement Since Release by Social Class Background and Level of Education Before Entering Prison

| | NewGate Program Sites | | | | | | | | | | Other Program Sites | | | | | |
| | Ashland | | Minnesota | | New Mexico | | Oregon | | Pennsylvania | | Lompoc | | Illinois | | Texas | |
	Low	High	Low	High	Low	High	Low	High	Low	High	Low	High	Low	High	Low	High
By social class																
Social Class[a]																
None—did not enroll	12%	12%	7%	8%	7%	20%	4%	7%	0%	7%	79%	32%	48%	25%	75%	50%
Less than one semester	58%	59%	41%	31%	62%	40%	24%	14%	19%	21%	0%	26%	17%	12%	17%	0%
One or more semesters	29%	29%	52%	61%	31%	40%	72%	79%	81%	71%	21%	42%	35%	62%	8%	50%
N	24	17	27	13	29	10	46	14	32	14	14	19	23	8	24	2
By level of education																
Prior Education[b]																
None—did not enroll	14%	0%	9%	0%	12%	0%	4%	9%	3%	0%	59%	36%	50%	22%	78%	57%
Less than one semester	62%	25%	42%	22%	61%	33%	22%	18%	20%	14%	18%	9%	9%	33%	22%	0%
One or more semesters	24%	75%	48%	78%	27%	67%	73%	73%	77%	86%	23%	54%	41%	44%	0%	43%
N	37	4	31	9	33	6	49	11	39	7	22	11	22	9	18	7

aSocial class breakdown: "low" = lower or working class; "high" = lower middle or upper middle class.
bPrior education breakdown: "low" = high school education or less; "high" = some college classes.

Note: Information available only for interviewed participant samples.

<u>Source</u>: Compiled by the authors.

provisions for admission and financial aid, although they were not a
formalized part of the prison educational program. Although participation in college classes while in prison can prepare a person academically for continuing in college, this alone is not enough for many
students, particularly for those from more disadvantaged backgrounds.

Generally speaking, those students who had some college prior
to entering the inside program progressed further after release than
did those who had only a high school education or less. The only programs in which participants' postrelease performance was not strongly
related to the extent of preprison education are Oregon, Pennsylvania,
and Illinois. As with social class, the reasons for this differentiation
would appear to be the extent of postrelease support provided.

In a theoretical paper on college drop-outs, Vincent Tinto and
John Cullen (1973) suggest that the probability of dropping out is
affected not only by social class, ability, and commitment to educational goals, but also by the extent of a student's social and academic integration into the college. This proposition is supported by
a number of studies. [2] The NewGate programs would appear to facilitate this integration in two ways: (1) the extent to which the inside
program stimulates a college atmosphere by encouraging peer group
formation among participants and encouraging academic activities;
(2) the extensive postrelease support system provided through group
living arrangements such as study-release centers in Oregon, Pennsylvania, and Minnesota. Both facilitate social integration and provide
peer support for the newly released participant. The existence of a
NewGate "subculture" on campus not only provides for temporary
insulation but eventually eases the transition from lower class convict to middle class student. Subcultural social integration is conducive to academic persistence, however, only insofar as the norms
of the subgroup are consistent with the prevailing norms of the campus,
particularly with reference to academic orientation. This is supported
by the early Ashland experience, where the strength of the NewGate
peer group inadvertently increased rather than lessened social deviance, in part because of the isolation of the NewGate subculture from
the rest of the campus community. One would expect that the greater
the difference between the background of the released participant and
the backgrounds of the general student population, the more important
peer group support and a strong postrelease program would be to the
postrelease experience. The greater educational persistence of participants from lower class backgrounds in NewGate programs as compared with those in non-NewGate programs could be due, in part, to
the support provided through the NewGate postrelease effort.

NOTES

1. See William Sewell, "Community of Residence and College Plans," American Sociological Review, 29, 1 (February 1964): 24-38; and Vincent Tinto and John Cullen, "Dropout in Higher Education: A Review and Theoretical Synthesis of Recent Research," a report for the Office of Planning, Budgeting and Evaluation of the U.S. Office of Education (Washington, D.C.: U.S. Office of Education, 1973).

2. See for example, Irving Rootman, "Voluntary Withdrawal from a Total Adult Socializing Organization: A Model," Sociology of Education 45, 3 (Summer 1972): 258-270; and William G. Spady, "Dropouts from Higher Education: Toward an Empirical Model," Interchange 2, 3 (1971): 38-62.

5

SUCCESS OF
POSTPRISON CAREERS

From the outset of this study the issue of postprison success was approached from a considerably broader perspective than in most studies of exprisoner success, which have generally equated post-release success with nonrecidivism. The customary use of recidivism rates to measure success was avoided because of the serious method-ological and conceptual problems involved and usually ignored. In most studies recidivism, which literally means return to criminal activity, is measured by a single criterion—return to prison or lock-up. Even if one accepts abstention from criminal activity as the most important criterion of success, reincarceration is an inaccurate and easily confounded measure of criminal activity.

Before turning to the serious problems involved in using recidi-vism statistics, however, one should consider whether nonrecidivism taken alone is an appropriate measure of success. If the success of a program is measured by goal achievement, and one of these goals is "rehabilitation," then, following the accepted definition of rehabilita-tion, one should measure the extent to which program participants are engaged in a "useful life" after release. A person's life is not nec-essarily useful simply because he refrains from criminal activity. Conversely, a person could lead his life in a manner that is generally useful to himself and to society and yet be returned to prison for a single transgression, proven or presumed. In studying the impact of a program on postrelease success, reincarceration can only provide an incomplete picture of the exprisoner's experiences and the impact of the independent variable being measured. An exprisoner might be maintaining himself in the community very well (in terms of a job, pocket money, a place to live, clothes to wear, friends to visit and depend on, and such); he could even be achieving long range goals (such as career advancement or raising a family). These experiences

of "success" could be a direct result of participation in the program
being studied, yet a return to lock-up would obfuscate these results.
On the other hand, an exprisoner could have slipped into complete
dereliction or even committed suicide; but because he has not been
returned to prison, he would be considered a "success" if recidivism
were used as an exclusive measure of program impact.

The aim of this study was to measure success as it is conceived
by former inmates and by society in general when measuring the success of members of the society who are not exprisoners. The measure
of success developed in this study takes into account not only staying
out of prison and noninvolvement in criminal activity but also the extent to which a person has achieved a stable and generally acceptable
lifestyle and is realizing life goals in the areas of educational and
occupational accomplishments and personal satisfaction. The measure
was also designed to take into account the extent of accomplishment
given the length of time the individual has had since release to establish his success or failure.

The overall evaluation of success devised for this study was a
weighted composite rating of accomplishments in each of the following
areas: recidivism, achieving stability, and realizing life goals. As
explained below, each participant was initially rated on a scale of 1
(low success—failure) to 5 (high success) in each of these three areas.

MEASURES OF SUCCESS

Recidivism

Despite the methodological problems involved, recidivism as
traditionally measured was included in the determination of success
both for comparative purposes and because the norms of our society
clearly define being sent to prison as an indication of failure. Seven
categories were developed to classify legal status, or recidivism,
based on categories used by the National Council on Crime and Delinquency and by the California Department of Corrections. These
categories and the corresponding scale score assigned are as follows:

    1 = returned to prison with a new felony conviction or in lieu of
        prosecution for a major offense;
    2 = minor or major conviction with 60 days to one year in county
        jail, or returned to prison on technical violation or dry-out
        for three months or longer;

3 = arrest and conviction with 30- to 59-days jail sentence, or
    technical violation or dry-out for less than three months;
4 = minor legal difficulties but less than 30 days jail sentence;
5 = no arrests or violations.

Two residual categories were used for those whose legal status
could not be classified pending further information: awaiting trial for
pending felony, or absconder at large. Because of the nature of these
categories, no scale score was assigned. Persons in these categories
were thus excluded from statistical analyses using scores on recidivism.

Although it is a relatively simple task to rate a person on this
scale given available records (which is undoubtedly the reason such
scales are widely used to measure recidivism), interpreting the
recidivism scale score as indicative of criminal activity involves
three methodological problems. First, the crimes for which persons
can be returned to prison vary in terms of their seriousness. Distinctions should be (but generally are not) made at least among crimes
against statute, property, and person, which represent obvious differences in the extent to which the safety of the community is threatened. Some persons in prison have been incarcerated for acts that
most people in their social milieu would not consider to be serious
or criminal, even though they technically have committed a felony.
An example would be the occasional user of marijuana in some juris-
dictions. Similarly, juveniles can be placed in lock-up for status
offenses such as truancy, running away, disobeying parents, and
curfew violations, all of which are offenses not considered criminal
where adults are concerned. * These distinctions are important to
make despite the fact that they make analysis more complex.

Second, persons being supervised on parole, when compared with
those who are not, are more likely to return to lock-up because conditions imposed on them while in the community are more exacting.
Many persons returned to prison have not committed a new crime.
Parole agencies can return persons under their supervision to jail or
prison for having committed technical violations of their agreement
(for example, association with other exprisoners, drinking, cohabita-
tion, borrowing money without permission from the agent, leaving
the county without permission, not attending school, or such). A

---

*This accounts for at least 40 percent of the children committed
to juvenile hall in California. See George Saleeby, Hidden Closets,
a report to the California Youth Authority (Sacramento, California:
California Youth Authority, March, 1975).

parolee can be returned to the institution for these minor violations without being a "failure" or a criminal by any conventional standards. In addition, with the introduction of many new procedures such as "dry-outs," the parolee can be returned to prison for a short time with no technical violations charged. Persons on work- or school-release also can be returned to prison without a technical violation because in this status the prisoners are not considered officially released. When comparing the postprison careers of exprisoners, one must distinguish between those who have been under close supervision and others who have not. Otherwise, it is unclear whether differences in experience are attributable to the individual in question or to environmental factors, such as agency supervision.

Third, within the category of those on parole or work/study-release, there is wide variation in how persons, rule violations, or new crimes are treated. Rules and practices of parole authorities vary from state to state, region to region, city to city, and agent to agent. First, there is no agreement about either what constitutes a violation or about the degree of seriousness or urgency of various rule infractions. An agent could be aware that the parolee is not adhering strictly to all his parole conditions but will not violate him as long as everything else appears normal. But the mere suspicion that the parolee is involved in illegal activity can induce the agent to write him up for previously ignored rule infractions to get him off the street. Evidence that the parolee actually has committed new crimes can also be dealt with differently for various persons. Some states are harsh on certain offenses and systematically lenient on others. Moreover, certain states have more intense crime surveillance operations, so persons guilty of the same degree or seriousness of criminality will have a different likelihood of being apprehended. Also, within states it has been well documented that certain districts are more sensitive to certain types of offenders, or have different intensities of policing operations. In the case of parole—the type of policing operation most relevant to recidivism—a study in California revealed a great deal of variation between parole districts in violation rates and expressed willingness to reincarcerate for the same offense. These variations were related not only to different locations in the state but also to different district administrative structures.[1]

It is clear that the variations in the practices of parole authorities, both from state to state down and with the individual parole agents, make it extremely difficult to know whether observed differences in postprison experience among a sample of parolees are not significantly a function of differences in parole intervention.

Achieving Stability

The second component of success in this study was the person's success in establishing a relatively stable lifestyle. The exprisoner has extreme difficulty in achieving equilibrium on the outside. Even if he recovers from the initial impact of reentry, he might not be able to meet the basic exigencies of coping with outside life. That is, he may not be able to supply himself with an adequate or personally acceptable residence, acquire a job, obtain the necessary clothing, or feed himself adequately.

"Achieving stability" as conceived in this study measures the person's ability to maintain at least minimal levels of stability and self-sufficiency while refraining from behavior likely to lead to conflict with law enforcement and supervisory agencies. Each person in the study sample was rated on a scale from (1) very unstable to (5) very stable, based on the following items of information:

percentage of time employed or in school;
ability to perform on the job or in school;
self-sufficiency and acceptance of responsibility in maintaining a stable residence;
keeping up with financial obligations;
driving only with a valid driver's license and paying traffic and parking fines;
involvement with drugs or excessive alcohol; and
admitted involvement in illegal activities.

These individual measures reflect the relative ability or willingness of an individual to conform to society's standards of "conventional" behavior. The unstable person is more likely to be returned to prison—either because he returns to criminal activities and/or because he comes under closer scrutiny and is assumed to be likely to return to criminal activities or to be in need of further "rehabilitation."

Realizing Life Goals

The third dimension of success, "realizing life goals," was designed to measure the extent to which a person had established a lifestyle both relatively secure and personally satisfying. Even if a person does succeed in achieving some level of stability, he is often unable to enter a lifestyle that supplies him with some of his desired satisfactions and with some degree of self-respect. He can have

difficulty finding a circle of friends with whom he can interact in a
meaningful and satisfying manner and with whom he shares areas of
interests. This can be difficult for an exprisoner who has become
immersed in criminal or prison worlds and who has limited access
to other worlds. He might also have great difficulty finding a "good"
job, one which not only supplies the basic needs but which also earns
him some feeling of self-worth and respect. Finally, achieving gratifying relationships with sexual partners can be a difficult problem.
As in other areas, he has lost his skill at meeting and interacting
with members of the opposite sex. Typically, he experiences extreme
difficulty both meeting women and, later, establishing more permanent
relationships.

Again, each person was rated on a five-point scale with "5" repre-
senting high success. As indicated below, this rating was based on
objective measures, such as percentage of time employed and prestige and income associated with the job, and on the participant's expressed satisfaction with what he was doing. The following information
was used to arrive at the summary rating: level of educational and
occupational achievement, taking into account the percentage of time
employed or in school and the stability of employment; extent of
savings accumulated; development of strong friendships; and achievement of personal goals.

Composite Summary Score

Initially, each participant and member of the control or comparison groups had been given a score from one to five on each component
of success—recidivism, achieving stability, and realizing life goals.
In developing an overall measure of success, these three items were
weighted, combined, and then adjusted; so possible scores ranged
from 1.0 to 5.0 to correspond with the component scores. The relative weight or importance assigned to each of the three components
for a given person was a function of how long he had remained outside
prison since release. The reason for differential weighting according
to length of time out is that these dimensions vary in relative importance over the different stages of the releasee's life. The changes in
the relative weight of each measure over time are presented in Figure
5.1 and the accompanying Table 5.1. For instance, when a person
is first released achievement of stability and progress toward life
goals are difficult to assess. Initial steps can be evaluated, but these
do not mean too much in themselves. Recidivism, that is, rearrest,
has to be considered as the most important indicator. There are conceptual difficulties in doing this, since arrest at this stage often

FIGURE 5.1

Relative Weights of Each Measure Over Time

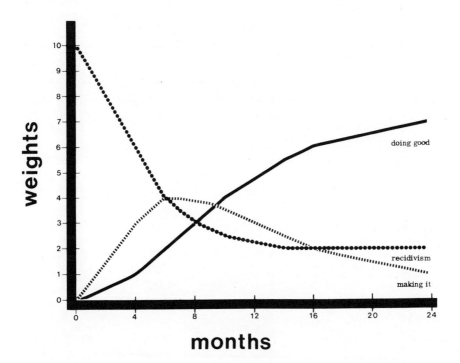

Source: Compiled by the authors.

reflects intense supervision by parole authorities rather than differential criminal activity. But initially this is the most reasonable
measure to use—if a person is rearrested soon after release, his
chances for success on other measures are greatly diminished. Hence,
for persons out for only six months, the recidivism score was weighted
more than either achieving stability or realizing life goals. During
these first six months, the degree to which the person achieves some
stability becomes an important predictor of continued progress toward
life goals and reduced susceptibility to return to criminality. Hence,
the weight given to achieving stability increases steadily until it ex-
ceeds recidivism's weight after the sixth month.

Realizing life goals is initially given little weight because these
accomplishments require time. This component steadily increases in

TABLE 5.1

Weights Applied to Component Sources of Time Outside

Number of Months Outside	Recidivism	Achieving Stability	Realizing Life Goal
0	10.0	0.0	0.0
1	9.0	0.75	0.25
2	8.0	1.5	0.5
3	7.0	2.25	0.75
4	6.0	3.0	1.0
5	5.0	3.5	1.5
6	4.0	4.0	2.0
7	3.5	4.0	2.5
8	3.125	3.875	3.0
9	2.75	3.75	3.5
10	2.5	3.5	4.0
11	2.375	3.25	4.375
12	2.25	3.0	4.75
13	2.125	2.75	5.125
14	2.0	2.50	5.5
15	2.0	2.25	5.75
16	2.0	2.0	6.0
17	2.0	1.875	6.125
18	2.0	1.75	6.25
19	2.0	1.625	6.375
20	2.0	1.50	6.5
21	2.0	1.375	6.625
22	2.0	1.25	6.75
23	2.0	1.125	6.875
24 (or more)	2.0	1.0	7.0

Source: Compiled by the authors.

importance, and after a year of freedom becomes a more important indicator of success than either achieving stability or recidivism. There are two reasons for this. First, if a person continues to accomplish his goals in spite of indicators of instability, then it seems likely that he has achieved a lifestyle that will allow him to continue to progress despite the appearance of instability. Second, if he is rearrested, even for something serious, it again could be due to heavy surveillance by his parole officer and/or because of a momentary lapse into crime. We assume that after he has done well for a relatively long period, it will be easier for him to reachieve success when released again.

Length of time outside prison was computed by summing every month of a period of freedom lasting at least three consecutive months. This allowed the counting of months after a return and subsequent release from jail or prison. When a period outside lasted fewer than three consecutive months, these months were not counted as time outside. The three-month criterion was based on the assumption that it takes approximately three months for an exprisoner to establish a pattern either of staying out—despite brief subsequent returns—or of chronic recidivism. In the case of persons who absconded but later returned, we counted the months outside in the same manner as for persons who had not absconded, since measures of their ability to achieve stability and realize goals were based on total months out, including periods when they were classified as absconders. Those persons in the sample who were still absconders at large or had charges pending were excluded from the analysis of summary scores because of the uncertainty of their current status.

CHARACTERISTICS OF THE STUDY SAMPLE

The total released sample consisted of (1) a group of released participants from each program site who were interviewed directly; (2) an additional group of participants from each NewGate site, except New Mexico, for whom postrelease data were gathered from secondary sources such as parole records; (3) two groups of controls (qualified nonparticipants), one from Ashland and one from Minnesota, including some who were interviewed and some who were followed from records; and (4) a comparison group selected from the general population at each NewGate site, which was followed through parole records. Because of the variability within groups both before and after release, each group and site was considered individually rather than as combined NewGate programs and combined non-NewGate programs.

A breakdown by group of the total sample of 995 persons is presented in Table 5.2. Only those persons for whom both baseline and
postrelease information were available were included in the analyses.
The relatively high number of persons in Ashland and Minnesota for
whom sufficient information was not available is due to the fact that
the computerized information provided by the Federal Bureau of
Prisons and the Minnesota Department of Corrections did not include
all persons released by January 1, 1972. A summary description of
selected characteristics of persons in each group is presented in
Tables 5.3 through 5.6. Characteristics included in the tables were
selected because they indicated differences between groups that might
be related to differences in postprison careers. Although there is
considerable variability within as well as between groups, the sam-
ple(s) from each site can be characterized in general.

Ashland: Young, white offenders who had served relatively short
    terms, primarily for crimes against property, with numerous
    prior arrests but few (if any) prior felony convictions and little
    history of use of opiates or excessive alcohol. Most participants
    had at least some high school; 10 percent had some college before
    entering prison.
Minnesota: Young, white offenders who had served one and one-half
    to two years for a variety of crimes. Most had more than one
    prior arrest and either no, or only one, prior felony convictions;
    many had a history of drug or excessive alcohol use, except in the
    general comparison group. Participants were primarily high
    school graduates; 18 percent had some college experience before
    entering prison.
New Mexico: Older, white, and Hispanic offenders who had served one
    and one-half to two years for a variety of crimes, most with more
    than one prior arrest, about 40 percent with one or more prior
    felony convictions. The majority of participants had less than a
    high school education before entering prison, and 18 percent had
    less than a ninth grade education.
Oregon: Older, white offenders convicted a variety of crimes. Almost
    all had more than one prior arrest, about half had records of drug
    or excessive alcohol use, and most had completed a high school
    education. Participants had more prior felony convictions than
    those in the comparison sample (53 percent versus 24 percent
    with more than one conviction). In the participant group, 15 per-
    cent had some college before entering prison.
Pennsylvania: Young, white, and black offenders with some prior
    arrests, but the majority had no prior felony convictions. The
    general comparison sample had more prior arrests than the par-
    ticipants, 35 percent of whom had no prior arrests. The majority

TABLE 5.2

Number of Persons Included in Released Follow-Up Samples

Sites	Interviewed N	Secondary Sources of Information N	Total N	No Information available (in selected sample) N
NewGate Program				
Ashland				
Participant	41	39	80	22
Control	23	32	55	0
Comparison	0	95	95	0
Minnesota				
Participant	40	19	59	20
Control	25	18	43	0
Comparison	0	189	189	0
New Mexico				
Participant	39	11	50	0
Comparison	0	50	50	0
Oregon				
Participant	60	33	93	6
Comparison	0	50	50	0
Pennsylvania				
Participant	40	16	56	0
Comparison	0	49	49	0
Other Program				
Lompoc				
Participant	33	13	46	3
Illinois				
Participant	31	10	41	0
Texas				
Participant	26	13	39	7
All Groups	358	637	995	58

Source: Compiled by the authors.

TABLE 5.3

Background Characteristics of Released Follow-Up Sample: Current Commitment

| | NewGate Program Sites | | | | | | | | | | | | | Other Program Sites | | |
| | Ashland | | | Minnesota | | | New Mexico | | Oregon | | Pennsylvania | | Lompoc | Illinois | Texas |
	Partic-ipant	Control	Com-parison	Partic-ipant	Control	Com-parison	Partic-ipant	Com-parison	Partic-ipant	Com-parison	Partic-ipant	Com-parison	Participant	Participant	Participant
Age at release:															
Median	20.0	20.1	20.7	22.1	22.3	21.0	25.5	27.0	29.1	27.2	24.2	23.6	23.0	28.5	28.9
Range	18-25	16-24	17-24	19-29	18-26	17-26	19-43	18-40	20-45	16-47	19-40	19-36	19-26	20-48	19-52
N	80	55	95	59	43	189	50	50	93	50	56	49	46	41	39
Time served this sentence (years):															
Median	1.3	1.3	1.2	1.9	1.6	1.8	1.8	1.8	2.4	0.9	2.4	1.6	1.8	2.5	3.1
Range	0.4- 2.9	0.2- 2.4	0.1- 3.2	0.9- 5.8	0.6- 4.6	0.2- 7.4	0.3- 20.8	0.3- 8.1	0.4- 13.0	0.2- 2.9	0.7- 7.5	0.5- 4.0	0.9- 4.1	0.7- 10.9	1.6- 13.2
N	80	55	90	59	43	189	50	50	93	50	56	49	46	41	39
Present offense															
violent crime against person	0%	2%	2%	22%	12%	1%	28%	24%	23%	10%	41%	16%	4%	20%	28%
nonviolent crime against person	11	2	3	17	9	27	12	8	22	14	25	26	20	15	10
crime against property	71	89	74	42	65	63	42	52	41	56	27	47	17	44	49
crime against statute	6	0	15	0	5	2	0	4	6	10	2	0	6	5	10
possession of drugs, alcohol	9	7	6	17	5	4	12	6	4	8	4	8	39	12	3
sales of drugs, alcohol	1	0	0	2	2	1	6	6	3	2	2	2	13	5	0
parole violation	1	0	0	0	0	0	0	0	1	0	0	0	0	0	0
N	80	55	95	59	43	189	50	50	93	50	56	49	46	41	39

Source: Compiled by the authors.

TABLE 5.4

Background Characteristics of Released Follow-Up Sample: Prior Record

| | NewGate Program Sites | | | | | | | | | | | | Other Program Sites | | |
| | Ashland | | | Minnesota | | | New Mexico | | Oregon | | Pennsylvania | | Lompoc | Illinois | Texas |
	Partic-ipant	Control	Com-parison	Partic-ipant	Control	Com-parison	Partic-ipant	Com-parison	Partic-ipant	Com-parison	Partic-ipant	Com-parison	Participant	Participant	Participant
Prior arrests															
None	21%	16%	21%	10%	9%	—	22%	14%	9%	12%	38%	10%	33%	34%	0%
One	18	24	22	12	9	—	4	14	2	10	18	22	17	5	3
More than one	61	60	57	78	82	—[b]	74	72	89	78	45	67	50	61	97
N	80	55	95	50[a]	33[a]	189	50	50	93	50	56	49	46	41	39
Prior felony convictions															
None	80	88	—	59	70	90	66	54	24	52	70	63	80	49	13
One	18	12	—	29	21	10[c]	26	30	24	24	14	22	11	17	38
More than one	2	0	—[b]	12	9		8	16	53	24	16	14	9	34	49
N	51[a]	32[a]		59	43	189	50	50	93	50	56	49	46	41	39
Record of drugs, excessive alcohol															
No use of drugs, alcohol	68	84	62	30	49	80	60	78	42	52	57	53	46	63	38
Alcohol only	4	6	6	34	37	11	14	10	30	26	4	24	4	7	31
Opiates only	6	4	5	17	9	7	18	10	16	16	18	20	28	20	10
Alcohol and opiates	1	2	0	5	2	2	0	0	6	6	4	0	0	5	0
Nonopiates (only)	12	2	14	14	2	0	8	2	4	0	18	2	15	0	5
(Missing information)	9	4	13	0	0	0	0	0	1	0	0	0	6	5	15
N	80	55	95	59	43	189	50	50	93	50	56	49	46	41	39

[a]Information available for original sample only.
[b]Information not available from records.
[c]No differentiation between one or more in records.
Source: Compiled by the authors.

TABLE 5.5

Background Characteristics of Released Follow-Up Sample: Educational Preparation

	NewGate Program Sites												Other Program Sites		
	Ashland			Minnesota			New Mexico		Oregon		Pennsylvania		Lompoc	Illinois	Texas
	Participant	Control	Comparison	Participant	Control	Comparison	Participant	Comparison	Participant	Comparison	Participant	Comparison	Participant	Participant	Participant
Education completed prior to present committment															
less than 9th grade	4%	12%	—	0%	5%	0%	18%	8%	5%	8%	2%	12%	0%	5%	18%
some high school	59	72	—	25	56	67	48	56	32	42	30	47	26	17	41
high school graduate	28	16	—	56	30	32	18	26	47	48	55	37	44	46	13
some college (<2 years)	10	0	—	15	9	1	10	8	11	0	9	2	26	20	18
two or more years college	0	0	—[b]	3	0	0	6	2	4	2	4	2	4	12	8
N	51[a]	32[a]	—[b]	59	43	189	50	50	93	50	56	49	46	41	39
Tested grade level															
Median	10.1	9.0	9.1	10.8	9.7	—	9.2	8.7	10.5	10.2	10.6	9.0	11.5	—	9.6
Range	5.4–12.4	4.2–12.1	7.0–12.8	8.6–13.0	7.2–12.4	—	6.2–12.6	6.7–12.0	5.5–15.4	8.3–12.1	5.1–13.0	8.1–11.8	5.3–12.9	—	5.6–12.0
N	76	52	95	38[a]	31[a]	—[b]	48	50	93	50	56	49	43	—[b]	39

[a] Information available for original sample only.
[b] Information not available from records.
Source: Compiled by the authors.

TABLE 5.6

Background Characteristics of Released Follow-Up Sample: Social Background

| | NewGate Program Sites | | | | | | | | | | | | | Other Program Sites | | |
| | Ashland | | | Minnesota | | | New Mexico | | Oregon | | Pennsylvania | | Lompoc | Illinois | Texas |
	Partic-ipant	Control	Com-parison	Partic-ipant	Control	Com-parison	Partic-ipant	Com-parison	Partic-ipant	Com-parison	Partic-ipant	Com-parison	Participant	Participant	Participant
Social Class															
Lower	10%	28%	—	8%	12%	—	36%	16%	18%	6%	25%	12%	11%	44%	46%
Working	53	47	—	58	74	—	38	72	64	86	46	76	33	32	43
Lower middle	26	22	—	28	9	—	20	10	16	6	23	8	35	12	5
Upper middle	12	3	—	6	6	—	6	2	1	2	5	4	22	12	5
N	51ᵃ	32ᵃ	—ᵇ	50ᵃ	34ᵃ	—ᵇ	50	50	93	50	56	49	46	41	39
Race															
White	86%	84%	97%	85%	93%	81%	56%	60%	83%	96%	50%	61%	74%	46%	90%
Black	12	16	3	10	2	9	6	8	14	2	50	39	22	49	5
Hispano	0	0	0	0	0	0	34	32	2	0	0	0	0	2	5
Native American	0	0	0	5	5	10	4	0	1	2	0	0	0	2	0
Other	1	0	0	0	0	0	0	0	0	0	0	0	4	0	0
N	80	55	95	59	43	189	50	50	93	50	56	49	46	41	39

ᵃInformation available for original sample only.
ᵇInformation not available from records.
Source: Compiled by the authors.

85

of participants had been convicted of crimes against person rather than property and had at least a high school education; 13 percent had some college.

Lompoc: Young, white offenders, over 50 percent of whom had been convicted of possession or sale of drugs or alcohol; some with prior arrests; 80 percent had no prior felony convictions. Thirty percent had some college, 35 percent were from lower middle class families, and 22 percent from upper middle class families.

Illinois: Older, white, and black offenders who had served terms over two years for a variety of crimes, the majority having had more than one prior arrest and at least one prior felony conviction. Thirty-two percent had some college education before entering prison.

Texas: Older, white offenders who had served about three years, primarily for crimes against property. Ninety-seven percent had more than one prior arrest; 49 percent more than one prior felony conviction. Twenty-six percent had some college before entering prison.

These summaries are intended only as a general description of each group. As may be seen in Tables 5.3 to 5.6, there is a wide representation of characteristics in each group.

Inspection of the data indicates there is no consistent difference between the NewGate project samples and their respective comparison groups except that the NewGate participants had a somewhat higher level of educational achievement prior to incarceration. In view of the generally small magnitude of this difference and the comparability of the samples on the other variables, we concluded that the comparison groups provided an unbiased control for the NewGate projects.

Participants in the NewGate programs could differ from those in other programs on another possibly significant variable—the extent of self-motivation required to join the program and to continue long enough to satisfy the definition of participant used in this study. NewGate participants had many more external incentives to participate in the college program than did those in non-NewGate programs. As indicated in the discussion of academic achievement, the only way a student at a non-NewGate site could meet the definition of a participant was by completing a minimum of 12 semester units in the inside program. Most students in non-NewGate programs attended school on a part-time basis in addition to a regular prison job assignment. The non-NewGate student thus required several semesters to accumulate 12 units. He also had additional demands on his time and energy. Many took only one or two courses and then dropped out of the program. These students were not defined as participants. As a result, the number of "participants" included in the study sample was much lower than the actual number of students who had taken part in these programs. This was not the case for the NewGate programs. Most persons entering the NewGate programs enrolled as full-time students, program participation serving as their prison job assignment. Most completed 12 units in one semester. In addition, students with fewer than 12 units qualified as participants by continuing in the outside program. Unlike the sample for the non-NewGate programs, the sample of NewGate participants included most of the students enrolled in the programs who had been released by January 1, 1972.

Lacking the incentives available to NewGate students, particularly the possibility of support after release, the non-NewGate student had to generate his own incentives for continuing. This is not to say the NewGate student was not motivated, but that he had more to lose by dropping out. High self-motivation, if carried over into other aspects of the person's life, might indicate a greater determination to succeed following release. Self-motivation is difficult to measure and data to substantiate or refute this line of reasoning are not available. This argument, however, should be considered in interpreting group differences in success after release.

FINDINGS

The purpose of these analyses was to determine the relative success of the exprisoners in this study, comparing participants in different programs with each other and with the comparison and control groups of nonparticipants. Comparisons were made using the composite summary scores, the three components of the summary score (recidivism, achieving stability, and realizing life goals), and on individual items that were used in arriving at the component ratings. In addition to comparing groups as a means of measuring overall program effectiveness, the influence of background characteristics on participants' success and the relationship between program characteristics and success were examined.

Overall Success

The data on overall success for each group are presented as percentage distributions in Table 5.7 and as mean scores in Table 5.8. Comparisons using the weighted composite success scores indicate (1) that the most successful groups were the NewGate participants in Pennsylvania and Oregon and the comparison group in Pennsylvania,

TABLE 5.7

Distributions on Overall Success Measure
(in percent)

Sites	Highly successful (4-5)*	Moderately successful (3-3.9)	Unsuccessful (1-2.9)	N
NewGate Program				
Ashland				
Participant	33	38	29	42
Control	39	30	30	23
Minnesota				
Participant	42	18	40	50
Control	50	13	37	30
New Mexico				
Participant	33	31	36	48
Control	52	16	32	43
Oregon				
Participant	54	18	28	90
Control	49	6	45	49
Pennsylvania				
Participant	57	21	23	53
Control	63	12	25	41
Other Program				
Lompoc				
Participant	49	18	33	45
Illinois				
Participant	43	30	27	37
Texas				
Participant	39	22	39	36

*Range of scores included in category (weighted sum divided by ten).

Source: Compiled by the authors.

TABLE 5.8

Mean Scores on Measures of Postrelease Accomplishment

Sites	Legal status	Stability	Goal accomplish- ment	Success* (summary measure)	N
NewGate Program					
Ashland					
Participant	3.7	3.5	3.2	3.4	46
Control	4.1	3.4	3.2	3.4	23
Minnesota					
Participant	3.7	3.4	3.3	3.4	50
Control	4.1	3.5	3.0	3.4	33
New Mexico					
Participant	3.5	3.3	3.4	3.3	50
Comparison	3.7	3.3	3.3	3.5	50
Oregon					
Participant	3.8	3.6	3.6	3.7	93
Comparison	3.5	3.5	3.2	3.3	50
Pennsylvania					
Participant	4.3	4.2	3.5	3.8	54
Comparison	4.1	3.7	3.4	3.8	49
Other Program					
Lompoc					
Participant	4.1	3.4	3.4	3.5	46
Illinois					
Participant	4.2	3.4	3.3	3.6	41
Texas					
Participant	3.7	3.4	3.1	3.3	38

*Weighted sum divided by ten.
Source: Compiled by the authors.

but (2) that the differences among groups are only slight. Overall, these summary data provide no evidence that program participation leads to a significantly more successful postprison career. To evaluate further whether programs had any apparent impact on success after release, groups were compared on each of the three component scores of success.

Recidivism

To give as accurate a description of recidivism as possible, several different methods of computation were used. These did not avoid the problem of differential treatment by law enforcement and supervisory agencies but did make the statistics between groups more comparable. The limitations of each method are discussed below.

Legal Status at the Last Time of Information

Although using legal status at the last time for which information was available has the advantage of utilizing the maximum amount of information, one major difficulty is introduced: controlling for the variability in length of time since release. Since recidivism is distributed over time, the rate of recidivism within a group is likely to increase over time. In general, the longer a group of persons has been released, the greater the cumulative number of persons who will have recidivated. In the study sample some groups had been out for as long as 28 months on the average (the New Mexico comparison sample), but other groups had been out for as short as 11 months on the average (the Minnesota general comparison sample). Differences in the rates of recidivism using this method thus could be attributable, at least in part, to differences in length of time released. Moreover, these data give no indication as to whether persons in one group recidivate sooner after release than those in another group. It is possible that the effect of program participation is to delay recidivist behavior rather than to reduce the percentage of persons who ultimately recidivate.

As may be seen in Table 5.9, there is no consistent relationship between program participation and the recidivism rate comparing NewGate participant groups, non-NewGate participant groups, and comparison groups. In the Oregon and Pennsylvania NewGate participant groups, the percentage of persons returned for a felony was lower than that of the comparison group at each site. In the Ashland and Minnesota NewGate participant groups, however, the percentage of persons returned for a new felony was higher than in the comparison

TABLE 5.9

Legal Status of Released Sample at Last Time of Information
(percentage distribution)

| | NewGate Program Sites | | | | | | | | | | | | Other Program Sites | | |
| | Ashland | | | Minnesota | | | New Mexico | | Oregon | | Pennsylvania | | Lompoc | Illinois | Texas |
	Partic-ipant	Control	Com-parison	Partic-ipant	Control	Com-parison	Partic-ipant	Com-parison	Partic-ipant	Com-parison	Partic-ipant	Com-parison	Participant	Participant	Participant
No arrests	48	47	63				40	50	59	56	71	59	65	54	49
Some arrests, < 30 days in jail	12	18	5	68*	77*	80*	12	8	4	0	5	6	11	22	15
< 60 days jail; < 3 months technical violation	2	4	3	3	2	1	12	4	3	6	4	2	2	5	3
< 1 year jail; 3 months parole violation	11	18	16	12	5	7	18	10	17	12	7	4	11	0	5
Returned to prison, new felony	16	13	12	17	9	11	14	14	14	24	7	14	9	12	20
Charges pending	6	0	1	0	7	0	4	6	2	0	2	8	2	0	5
Absconded, not returned	4	0	0	0	0	0	0	8	0	2	4	6	0	7	3
N	80	55	95	59	43	189	50	50	93	50	56	49	46	41	39

*Insufficient reliable information distinguishing between the top two categories.
Source: Compiled by the authors.

group at each site. The only evidence that program participation might
have an impact on recidivism is the success of the Pennsylvania New-
Gate participants relative to other participant and comparison groups.
The Pennsylvania participants had both the lowest percentage of persons returned for a new felony and the highest percentage of persons
who had had no arrests or convictions since release. It could be recalled from Chapter 3 that the Pennsylvania NewGate program had a
particularly strong transitional and postrelease program, which may
in part account for this success.

Recidivism Rates at Three-Month Intervals Following Release

Because of the problem of variation in time since release, legal
status was also evaluated at three-month intervals using only those
persons in each group who had been released for at least that long
(see Table 5.10). This method limited the length of time to which
the analysis could be extended since the number of persons for whom
information is available decreases rapidly after six months.

In analyzing recidivism over time, the recidivism categories
were further collapsed, dropping from analysis those whose status
was uncertain because of pending charges or having absconded and
not returned. The first three categories in Table 5.9 were considered
"favorable" outcomes, although some persons in these categories had
minor legal difficulties. Those persons in the favorable category who
were returned to prison were included because they were returned on
technical violations, usually for a short dry-out period. The fourth
and fifth categories were considered unfavorable outcomes. This
dichotomy and the definitions of favorable and unfavorable outcomes
are consistent with those used by the California Department of Corrections. In the following tables only the dichotomized measurement
of favorable-unfavorable outcome is presented. Although this is an
oversimplification of a complex problem, the small size of the samples in each group made it necessary to do this to carry out successfully more involved analyses.

The data in Table 5.10 illustrate changes in recidivism rate over
time. Three groups emerge as having consistently high percentages
of persons with favorable outcomes: Pennsylvania NewGate participants, Lompoc participants, and Ashland controls. In each of these
three groups, 85 percent or more of the persons in the sample still
had favorable outcomes by the end of 18 months. The percentage of
those with favorable outcomes at the last time of information (using
the dichotomized categories) is also included in Table 5.10 for comparison. Note that this is an upper limit to the percentage of persons
in this sample with favorable outcomes. This is due to the fact that
conventional recidivism analysis makes no allowance for reentry as a

TABLE 5.10

Percent of Those Released for N Months with Favorable Legal Outcomes at N Months

| | NewGate Program Sites | | | | | | | | | | | | Other Program Sites | | |
| | Ashland | | | Minnesota | | | New Mexico | | Oregon | | Pennsylvania | | Lompoc | Illinois | Texas |
	Partic-ipant	Control	Com-parison	Control	Partic-ipant	Com-parison	Partic-ipant	Com-parison	Partic-ipant	Com-parison	Partic-ipant	Com-parison	Participant	Participant	Participant
Length of time since release															
N = 3 months	98; 78/80	98; 53/54	94; 88/94	100; 42/42	97; 57/59	97; 181/187	92; 46/50	94; 46/49	94; 86/92	96; 48/50	96; 53/55	100; 48/48	96; 43/45	100; 41/41	97; 38/39
6 months	97; 74/76	94; 50/53	90; 78/87	98; 39/40	82; 45/55	91; 166/182	76; 38/50	90; 44/49	85; 74/87	90; 45/50	94; 51/54	100; 48/48	93; 40/43	98; 40/41	92; 35/38
9 months	93; 65/70	93; 42/45	—*	88; 30/34	70; 33/47	84; 123/146	74; 35/47	84; 41/49	80; 66/82	86; 42/49	90; 43/48	96; 44/46	88; 37/42	90; 35/39	90; 33/37
12 months	88; 51/58	91; 39/43	—	88; 21/24	61; 22/36	76; 70/92	63; 22/35	80; 39/49	76; 57/75	80; 39/49	92; 34/37	91; 42/46	80; 32/40	85; 28/33	91; 32/35
15 months	85; 34/40	95; 35/37	—	80; 16/20	58; 17/30	65; 40/62	56; 15/27	78; 38/49	75; 50/67	74; 35/47	93; 27/29	82; 36/44	85; 29/34	82; 22/27	86; 25/29
18 months	79; 27/34	95; 35/37	—	82; 14/17	58; 15/26	44; 12/27	53; 10/19	75; 36/48	74; 46/62	67; 28/42	91; 21/23	79; 34/43	86; 25/29	77; 17/22	80; 16/20
At time of last information	69; 50/72	69; 38/55	72; 68/94	85; 34/40	71; 42/59	82; 154/189	67; 32/48	72; 31/43	68; 62/91	63; 31/49	85; 45/53	79; 33/42	80; 36/45	87; 33/38	72; 26/36
Number of months since released when last information obtained															
Median	16.5	23.9	11.6	14.2	15.0	11.3	15.2	28.1	24.8	22.5	15.5	25.2	19.2	18.4	17.8
Range	3–36	2–43	2–36	3–31	5–36	2–21	6–34	21–35	5–59	14–59	5–34	13–40	5–36	7–38	8–42
N	72	55	94	40	59	189	48	43	91	49	53	42	45	38	36

*Reliable information not available by month after 6 months.

Source: Compiled by the authors.

"favorable" statistic once a person has fallen into the category of unfavorable outcome or "failure." Once a person has failed, he is there-
after counted as a failure in the data regardless of subsequent accomplishments.

Using the dichotomized categorization of favorable versus unfavorable outcomes at the last time of information, the Pennsylvania
participant group again has a high percentage of persons with favorable
outcomes (85 percent). The Illinois participant group and the Minnesota
control group also have high percentages of persons with favorable
outcomes (85 and 87 percent), although they compared somewhat less
favorably with other groups in the analysis broken down by three-
month intervals.

One limitation of analyzing these data at specified intervals is
the assumption that persons with ultimately favorable outcomes are
distributed proportionately by time of release. In the Minnesota
NewGate participant group, the assumption of proportional distribution was not justified. A high proportion of persons in the first group
of participants released from Minnesota returned to prison soon after
release. This group of recidivists is thus overrepresented in the data
after nine months since the many nonrecidivists in later groups had
not been out as long when the data were gathered.

Projected Recidivism Rates Based on Present Information

In a further attempt to equalize groups with respect to length of
time since release and to predict future performance of the groups as
a whole, month-by-month projection of recidivism rates was made
based on the success rate of participants who already had been released as long as or longer than each given month. The data from this
projection are presented in Table 5.11.

The projected percentage of persons with favorable outcomes at
18 months varies from 67 percent (the Oregon comparison group) to
86 percent (the Illinois participant group). Among participant groups,
the Illinois and Pennsylvania NewGate programs have the highest projected percentages of persons with favorable outcomes at 18 months.
Only Oregon and Pennsylvania have higher projected percentages of
favorable outcomes than do their respective comparison groups. (In
Minnesota the projected percentage of persons with favorable outcomes
is higher for the NewGate participants than for the comparison group
but lower than that for the control group.)

It should be noted that the reliability of the projection decreases
as the time since release increases, the projected percentage being
based on decreasing numbers of persons. The percentage figures are
an accurate prediction of the future percentage of persons with favorable outcomes only if those participants in each sample who have been

TABLE 5.11

Projection of Expected Percentage of Persons with Favorable Legal Outcomes

	NewGate Program Sites												Other Program Sites		
	Ashland			Minnesota			New Mexico		Oregon		Pennsylvania		Lompoc	Illinois	Texas
Length of time since release	Partic- ipant	Control	Com- parison	Partic- ipant	Control	Com- parison	Partic- ipant	Com- parison	Partic- ipant	Com- parison	Partic- ipant	Com- parison	Participant	Participant	Participant
3 months	97	96	92	97	100	97	92	93	93	96	96	100	96	100	97
6 months	93	91	82	83	98	89	75	88	87	90	94	100	93	97	91
9 months	88	87	79	73	86	85	73	84	81	86	88	95	89	89	88
12 months	79	81	74	73	83	82	68	79	77	80	88	90	81	86	88
15 months	72	81	70	73	78	76	68	77	74	76	85	81	81	86	81
18 months	68	81	68	73	78	76	68	74	72	67	85	78	81	86	76

Source: Compiled by the authors.

released for relatively short periods of time continue to be arrested and reincarcerated at the same rate as did earlier participants. These rates could change if such factors as program selection procedures, programs, or reactions of law enforcement and supervisory agencies have changed over time.

Achieving Stability

Comparisons between groups on the extent to which persons in each group were successful in achieving a stable lifestyle indicated no consistent differences between NewGate participants and other groups (see Tables 5.8 and 5.12). By far the most successful group on this measure of success was the Pennsylvania NewGate participant group. This high degree of success is apparent both in the total sample and in the subsample of persons with favorable legal outcomes. As demonstrated earlier, the Pennsylvania NewGate, Lompoc participant, and Minnesota control groups had the lowest rates of recidivism of any groups in this study. Of these three, only the Pennsylvania NewGate participant group is impressive in the extent to which persons had achieved a relatively stable lifestyle. This could be attributed to the high degree of support provided by the Pennsylvania NewGate program before and after release, which better equips participants for taking care of routine business.

Three principal factors in determining a person's rating on stability were (1) the percentage of time employed and/or in school, (2) drug and/or alcohol problems, and (3) admitted criminal activity. The percentage distrubutions on these individual measures are presented in Tables 5.13 through 5.15.

Employment Status

Considering full-time study as an occupation, an impressive percentage (70-80 percent) of NewGate and Lompoc participants were fully employed since release.* At each site except Minnesota there was a difference of 20 percent between NewGate participants and their respective control and comparison groups in the percentage of persons fully employed. In Minnesota, the lesser difference between the participants and controls is due to the success of the controls rather than

---

*For those persons who were returned to prison, the percentage of time employed was based only on the time between release and reincarceration.

TABLE 5. 12

Percentage Distributions on Summary Ratings of Achieving Stability

	Ashland			NewGate Program Sites Minnesota			New Mexico		Oregon		Pennsylvania		Other Program Sites		
	Partic- ipant	Control	Com- parison*	Partic- ipant	Control	Com- parison*	Partic- ipant	Com- parison	Partic- ipant	Com- parison	Partic- ipant	Com- parison	Lompoc Participant	Illinois Participant	Texas Participant
Ratings for total sample															
Stable	30	30	—	32	42	—	22	32	36	38	63	41	28	34	26
Minor instability	23	26	—	22	15	—	28	16	26	14	15	16	26	20	26
On the line	21	9	—	14	12	—	22	20	11	10	9	14	17	15	21
Unstable	19	26	—	16	18	—	16	18	18	30	9	26	15	10	16
Highly unstable	6	9	—	16	12	—	12	14	9	8	4	2	13	22	10
N	47	23	—	50	33	—	50	50	92	50	54	49	46	41	38
Ratings for those with favorable legal outcomes															
Stable	38	39	—	39	52	—	32	42	47	61	70	50	35	39	31
Minor instability	26	22	—	27	15	—	30	21	23	19	15	20	32	20	24
On the Line	18	11	—	18	15	—	30	21	11	10	7	12	14	17	21
Unstable	18	17	—	9	15	—	6	8	15	10	7	18	16	11	14
Highly unstable	0	11	—	6	4	—	3	8	5	0	2	0	3	14	10
N	34	18	—	33	27	—	34	38	66	31	46	40	37	36	29

*Information not available.

Source: Compiled by the authors.

TABLE 5.13

Time Employed and/or in School Since Release
(in percent)

Sites	90–100	75–89	40–74	0–39	N
NewGate Program					
Ashland					
Participant[a]	76	10	7	7	41
Control[a]	56	22	13	9	23
Comparison[b]	—	—	—	—	—
Minnesota					
Participant[a]	80	5	8	8	40
Control[a]	72	4	8	16	25
Comparison[b]	—	—	—	—	—
New Mexico					
Participant[a]	72	13	13	3	39
Comparison	52	14	16	18	50
Oregon					
Participant	73	5	7	15	84
Comparison	50	10	20	20	50
Pennsylvania					
Participant	70	0	12	18	40
Comparison	49	22	12	16	49
Other Program					
Lompoc					
Participant[a]	73	3	12	12	33
Illinois					
Participant[a]	64	6	10	19	31
Texas					
Participant[a]	65	12	4	19	26

[a]Information available only for those persons interviewed.
[b]No information available.
Source: Compiled by the authors.

TABLE 5.14

Percentage of Persons With Drinking or Drug Problems
Pre- and Postprison

Sites	Pre-prison	Post-prison	Net change	N
NewGate Program				
Ashland				
Participant	27	10	−17	41
Control	4	9	+5	23
Minnesota				
Participant	82	25	−57	40
Control	56	24	−32	25
New Mexico				
Participant	41	28	−13	39
Control	22	46	+24	50
Oregon				
Participant	60	19	−41	60
Control	48	42	−6	50
Pennsylvania				
Participant	40	5	−35	40
Control	47	35	−12	49
Other Program				
Lompoc				
Participant	64	12	−52	33
Illinois				
Participant	39	19	−20	31
Texas				
Participant	54	4	−50	26

Source: Compiled by the authors.

TABLE 5.15

Admission of Involvement in Illegal Activity by Interviewed Releases
Who Were Not Returned to Prison or Jail
(in percent)

| | NewGate Program Sites | | | | | | | Other Program Sites | | |
| | Ashland | | Minnesota | | New Mexico | Oregon | Pennsylvania | Lompoc | Illinois | Texas |
Admitted involvement in illegal activity	Participant	Control	Participant	Control	Participant	Participant	Participant	Participant	Participant	Participant
None	37	35	46	56	38	37	75	45	58	40
Minor	29	22	19	16	23	17	3	32	10	12
Major	0	14	3	12	0	7	3	6	13	4
Not relevant— returned to prison or jail	34	30	33	16	38	38	18	16	19	44
N	40	22	39	24	38	57	37	31	31	25

Source: Compiled by the authors.

100

the failure of the participants. In fact, the Minnesota NewGate participants had a higher percentage of persons fully employed than any
other group.

Problems with Drugs and/or Alcohol

All participant groups scored favorably on freedom from drug and
alcohol problems after release. Clearly, the percentage of persons
in each participant group with drinking or drug problems following
release was lower than the corresponding percentages with prior
drinking or drug problems. The comparison groups in New Mexico,
Oregon, and Pennsylvania showed less success on this measure despite
the fact that, compared with participant groups at their respective
sites, the comparison groups had as low or lower percentages of persons with a prior history of drug or alcohol problems. Moreover,
there was a greater drop in the percentage of persons with such problems for each NewGate participant group than for the comparison
group at the same site.

From these data it appears that the benefits of participation in a
college education program go beyond educational and occupational
preparation. Regardless of occupational skill, the person with drinking
or drug problems is likely to have difficulty in maintaining employment.
Two groups—Pennsylvania NewGate participants and Texas participants and Texas participants—stand out as remarkably successful in
this area. In each group 95 to 96 percent had no postrelease drinking
or drug problems. This in itself is impressive, but even more impressive when compared with the past history of persons in these two
groups. Prior to their most recent prison commitment, 43 percent
of the Pennsylvania NewGate participants and 46 percent of the Texas
participants had records of drinking or drug problems.

Admitted Criminal Involvement

A third critical factor in assessing how well a person succeeded
in achieving a stable lifestyle was the extent of admitted involvement
in criminal activities. As discussed earlier, rearrest and reimprison-
ment are inaccurate measures of criminal activity. Criminal activity
can escape detection or be ignored. On the other hand, a person could
be returned to prison for infractions of supervision rules rather than
illegal activity. Information on admitted criminal activity obtained
from those persons who were interviewed is presented in Table 5.15.
These data suggest varying degrees of bias in the classification of
recidivism using conventional measures. Three groups—Illinois participants and Ashland and Minnesota controls—which had relatively low
percentages of persons returned to prison had comparatively high

percentages of persons who were not returned but who admitted to involvement in major criminal activities (12 to 14 percent). The comparable percentages for other groups with higher recidivism rates are from zero to seven percent.

Realizing Life Goals

A comparison of summary scores between groups indicated a slight superiority of NewGate participants compared with others in realizing life goals (see Tables 5.9 and 5.16). The NewGate participants in Minnesota were more successful on this measure than were the controls from Minnesota. The only other clear difference that emerged was, as indicated in Chapter 4, that more participants in NewGate programs continued in college after release than did participants in other programs.

Further comparisons of success in realizing life goals focused on three areas of achievement, which were components of this measure: self-assessment of goal achievement to date, confidence in future goal achievement, and occupational achievement.

Goal Achievement

Interviewed released participants and controls completed a questionnaire on current and projected goal achievement; the following goals were indicated:

hold down a good job;
get along well with other people;
succeed at whatever I set out to do;
face situations of uncertainty with confidence;
develop strong friendships;
make a good life for myself;
stay on top of things;
have dignity in the eyes of others;
make enough money to get by without having to work too hard;
stay out of prison;
have self-respect;
get a lot of money;
develop a way of living that has meaning for me;
achieve gratifying relationships with a sexual partner; and
have relationships with many sexual partners.

TABLE 5.16

Percentage Distributions on Summary Ratings of Relating Life Goals

	NewGate Program Sites											Other Program Sites		
	Ashland			Minnesota			New Mexico		Oregon		Pennsylvania		Lompoc	Illinois	Texas
	Participant	Control[a]	Comparison[b]	Participant	Control	Comparison[b]	Participant	Comparison	Participant	Comparison	Participant	Comparison	Participant	Participant	Participant
Ratings for total sample															
High	35	44	—	54	39	—	48	46	59	54	57	55	52	44	40
Medium	47	30	—	20	29	—	32	30	19	0	20	14	22	17	26
Low	19	26	—	26	32	—	20	24	21	46	22	31	26	39	34
N	46	23	—	50	34	—	50	50	93	50	54	49	46	41	38
Ratings for those with favorable legal outcomes															
High	42	45	—	76	48	—	59	60	71	84	65	66	64	47	45
Medium	42	33	—	9	33	—	29	26	14	0	22	12	19	19	24
Low	15	22	—	15	18	—	12	13	15	16	13	23	17	33	31
N	33	18	—	33	27	—	34	38	65	31	54	40	36	36	29

[a]Sample sizes reduced due to inadequate information from hearsay data for some persons.
[b]Information not available from records.
Source: Compiled by the authors.

Each person was asked to indicate (1) how important each of fifteen goals was to him, (2) how much progress he felt he had made on each, and (3) how well he thought he would do in achieving each in the near future. To arrive at summary measures of perceived goal accomplishment and confidence in future goal achievement, responses were weighted and multiplied by weighted scores on importance of the item to the individual. A goal identified as "very" important was given a weight of 2; one "fairly" important was given a weight of 1. Goals that were not important were excluded from the computations. If a person felt he had made a "great deal" of progress, his responses were given a weight of 2; "quite a bit" was given a weight of 1; "not very much" a weight of 0; and "none at all" a weight of -1. For each goal named as very or fairly important, the weight assigned to the goal was multiplied by the weight assigned to the accomplishment category. The resulting numbers were then summed and divided by the number of goals named as either very or fairly important. The resulting mean scores had a possible range of -2 (equivalent to no progress at all on very important goals) to +4 (equivalent to a great deal of progress on very important goals).

The mean scores for each group on perceived goal accomplishment are presented in Table 5.17 along with the correlations of perceived goal achievement and the summary success score. The released participants in Oregon, Pennsylvania, and Lompoc perceived themselves as more successful in attaining their goals than did other groups, although these differences are not statistically significant. Perceived goal achievement correlated significantly with the summary success measure for all groups except the Ashland controls (p < .05, using Spearman's rank-order correlation coefficient).

With respect to confidence in future goal accomplishment, the Lompoc and Illinois participant groups were the most confident, the Texas participants and Ashland and Minnesota controls the least confident. Although this reveals a difference in level of confidence between released felons who participated in a prison college program and those who did not have this opportunity, the evidence that this is attributable to program impact is only suggestive. It will be recalled that the Lompoc and Illinois projects were ranked among the least substantial and would not be expected to "build" confidence as much as the NewGate programs. On the other hand, Lompoc and Illinois participants could have had self-confidence despite the program. Whereas no pre- and post-data were collected to reveal change in self-confidence over time, there is evidence that the participants in these two programs were comparatively well situated when they entered the program, thus providing a basis for high self-confidence. Thirty-two percent of the Illinois participants and 30 percent of the Lompoc participants had some previous education beyond high school (Table

TABLE 5.17

Mean Scores on Goal Achievement and Correlation
with Summary Success Score

Sites	Goal achievement to date		Confidence in future goal achievement	
	$\bar{X}$	r	$\bar{X}$	r
NewGate Program				
Ashland				
Participant	1.9	.37*	2.6	.10
Control	1.8	.29	2.3	.36
Minnesota				
Participant	1.6	.48*	2.7	-.08
Control	1.9	.49*	2.2	.43*
New Mexico				
Participant	1.6	.52*	2.4	.23
Oregon				
Participant	2.1	.33*	2.6	.09
Pennsylvania				
Participant	2.1	.31*	2.6	-.11
Other Program				
Lompoc				
Participant	2.1	.57*	2.8	.27
Illinois				
Participant	1.9	.61*	2.8	.49*
Texas				
Participant	1.6	.49*	2.8	.43*

Note: Correlation uses Spearman rank-order method.
* $p < .05$
Source: Compiled by the authors.

5.5). Lompoc had the highest median grade level tested (11.5). The
Illinois sample also had the highest percent previously employed in
white collar jobs (Table 5.18).

Persons in all groups expected higher levels of accomplishment
in the future than they had already attained. Note that scores on this
measure correlate with the summary success scores only for the
Illinois and Texas participants and Minnesota controls. The reasons
for this are not clear. The data suggest that NewGate participants
were less tied to their current level of accomplishment in predicting
future accomplishments than were persons in other groups. To the
extent that this is true, it carries both positive and negative implications. On the one hand, self-confidence can be instrumental to continued and/or future achievement. On the other hand, overconfidence
can signify self-delusion or unrealistic expectations and can increase
dissappointment and perceived failure in the future. Without knowing
the subsequent progress of participants, it is impossible to choose
between these two alternative explanations or predictions.

In addition to comparing the summary scores for each group,
responses for each individual goal were studied. There were no consistent patterns of differences between groups on these measures.

Occupational Goals and Achievement

One specific area of goal achievement that was of major importance to participants, and which is instrumental to ultimate success, is occupational achievement. Information was obtained from
participants on their previous occupation, their occupational goals
before and after entering the program, and their occupation after
release.

Although a college education could be valued in itself, it also
provides access to new and higher occupational levels. As shown in
Table 5.18, participants in all programs raised their occupational
aspirations after entering the program. Although this information is
retrospective and thus subject to some bias, the magnitude of the
shift in aspirations toward higher level white collar jobs suggests
that the programs did have considerable impact in this area. The data
show that there was a larger increase in occupational aspirations
among NewGate than non-NewGate participants. It is also interesting
to note that the order of rank of the programs on this dimension follows closely the order in which the programs were ranked on "challenge" (Chapter 3, Figure 3.1).

It is not clear what are the ultimate consequences of this obvious
increase in occupational aspiration. It is commonly observed that
exconvicts often have low expectations of themselves, which is self-
defeating. It also has been said that exconvicts have narrow life

TABLE 5.18

Occupational Goals After Entering College Program and in Comparison with Goals Prior to Entering the Program

	NewGate Program Sites										Other Program Sites					
	Ashland		Minnesota		New Mexico		Oregon		Pennsylvania		Lompoc		Illinois		Texas	
	Participant		Participant		Participant		Participant		Participant		Participant		Participant		Participant	
	Percent	Change	Percent	Change	Percent	Change	Percent	Change	Percent	Change	Percent	Change	Percent	Change	Percent	Change
High white collar	73	+41	75	+42	51	+28	64	+39	65	+32	39	+ 6	52	+23	50	+31
Low white collar	5	- 2	8	0	18	- 8	15	+13	28	+12	9	- 3	19	0	4	0
Skilled labor	15	-14	0	- 2	8	-10	5	-12	2	-18	6	- 9	3	0	19	0
Unskilled labor	7	- 5	2	- 8	3	- 2	0	-12	2	-12	0	- 3	10	- 9	12	- 4
Menial	0	0	0	0	0	- 3	0	0	0	- 2	0	0	0	0	0	0
None/didn't think about it	0	-17	8	-30	5	-18	12	-25	2	-10	18	- 9	13	-16	12	-26
Student	0	- 2	8	- 2	15	+12	3	- 4	0	- 2	27	+18	3	+ 3	4	0
N =	41		40		39		60		40		33		31		26	

Source: Compiled by the authors.

experiences and meaning worlds; it is the lack of recognized alternatives that helps to perpetuate criminal careers. An increase in aspiration well could lead exprisoners to take advantage of a wider range of
opportunities. On the other hand, increased aspirations easily could
lead to increased frustration and bitterness. This is particularly true
when dealing with a population such as prison inmates, given the
liability of their convicted felon status in finding employment after
release. This is not to suggest that their aspirations should not be
raised, but such a rise will only be effective in proportion to the
extent that high aspirations are combined with adequate training and
with a change in the existing attitudes of the public toward employing
exprisoners.

Data on occupational achievement relative to goals are presented
in Table 5.19 for those persons who were employed after release
(excluding students and those who were unemployed). The data on
occupational achievement must be interpreted cautionsly because of
the limited nature of the samples on which these data are based.
Students were not included in measures of occupational achievement
because it is not clear what their relative occupational level was or
would be at the completion of their studies. Persons who were unemployed were not included in the tables because of the nature of the
data gathered. Some persons had not been employed for the three
months necessary for occupation to be classified. Some had not been
released long enough to fulfill this requirement; others had been returned to prison or had attended school but dropped out and had not
yet been otherwise employed for three months. A further complica-
tion is the inclusion of persons in the Oregon and Pennsylvania samples who were on study release and, therefore, not eligible for employment.

Within the limitations imposed by the data, some trends are clear.
From 46 to 61 percent of the employed participants in the Oregon,
Pennsylvania, Illinois, and Texas samples were able to find (and
hold down) a job that met or surpassed their aspirations. For the
NewGate participants in particular, these data probably underestimate
goal achievement because of the sizable percentage of persons still
attending college after release. In the future, these students should
be in a better position to achieve their occupational goals than the
persons included in these analyses. On the other hand, the higher
the percentage of eligible persons unemployed in the samples, the
greater the extent to which these data overestimate goal accomplishment.

Changes in occupational level by group are included in Table 5.20.
From these data, it is clear that the actual occupational level as well
as aspirations increased after participation in the program. Again,
the NewGate programs show a greater increase than the non-NewGate

TABLE 5.19

Occupational Level After Release Compared
with Occupational Goals
(in percent)

Sites	Occupational level met goals	Occupational level lower than goals	N
NewGate Program			
Ashland			
Participant	36	64	28
Minnesota			
Participant	17	83	12
New Mexico			
Participant	6	94	16
Oregon			
Participant	46	54	13
Pennslyvania			
Participant	58	42	12
Other Program			
Lompoc			
Participant	23	77	13
Illinois			
Participant	61	39	18
Texas			
Participant	50	50	20

Source: Compiled by the authors.

TABLE 5.20

Percentage Distributions for Occupational Level Before and After Prison

	NewGate Program Sites													Other Program Sites					
	Ashland				Minnesota				New Mexico		Oregon		Pennsylvania		Lompoc		Illinois		Texas	
	Participant		Control		Participant		Control		Participant		Participant		Participant		Participant		Participant		Participant	
	Before	After	Before	After	Before	After	Before	After	Before	After	Before	After	Before	After	Before	After	Before	After	Before	After
High white collar	0	3	0	9	13	0	4	9	0	0	12	35	11	22	4	4	13	22	12	24
Low white collar	3	17	5	14	13	20	9	9	9	22	19	8	6	17	8	29	30	22	16	8
Skilled labor	14	28	5	23	0	13	13	13	13	26	12	8	11	22	21	33	0	0	12	16
Unskilled labor	62	41	64	45	47	53	61	43	61	30	35	15	56	11	29	21	43	43	48	44
Menial	3	0	5	0	13	0	4	0	13	9	4	0	6	0	4	4	0	4	0	0
Unemployed	17	10	23	9	13	13	9	26	4	13	19	35	11	28	33	8	13	9	12	8
N =	29		22		15		23		23		26		18		24		23		25	
Student	10	25	4	0	12	62	0	8	8	18	4	53	10	55	6	24	3	26	0	0
N =	41		23		40		25		39		55		40		33		31		25	

Source: Compiled by the authors.

TABLE 5.21

Postrelease Occupation Level Compared with
Prior Occupational Level
(in percent)

Sites	Changes in occupational level*			
	Upward	Same	Downward	N
NewGate Program				
Ashland				
Participant	54	27	18	22
Control	53	40	7	15
Minnesota				
Participant	33	50	17	12
Control	29	59	12	17
New Mexico				
Participant	42	37	21	19
Oregon				
Participant	47	27	27	15
Pennsylvania				
Participant	62	31	8	13
Other Program				
Lompoc				
Participant	33	47	20	15
Illinois				
Participant	11	83	6	18
Texas				
Participant	24	67	10	21

*Excluding students and unemployed.
Source: compiled by the authors.

programs. The direction of changes in occupational level are summarized in Table 5.21, again excluding those persons who were unemployed or students.

BACKGROUND CHARACTERISTICS OF PARTICIPANTS
AND THEIR SUCCESS

If programs are to be evaluated on the basis of the success of
their released participants, more factors must be considered than
participation in one program. Regardless of whether one participates
in a college education program, some persons are more likely to
succeed than others. Several types of analyses were performed to
determine the relationship between participant characteristics and
success. Two questions were addressed in these analyses: (1) Are
differences in success between groups attributable to differences in
the characteristics of the persons included in these groups? and
(2) Within participant groups, is the program more effective (as
measured by participants' success after release) with some types of
persons than with others?

These analyses initially focused on the relationship between background characteristics and recidivism as a measure of success. Predicting recidivism by identifying differential characteristics of those
with favorable versus unfavorable outcomes has been the subject of
intensive study. [2] To identify characteristics related to recidivism
in the present study, individual items found to be significant in prior
studies were cross-tabulated with legal status at (1) six months,
(2) nine months, (3) twelve months, and (4) the last time of information. Several additional characteristics felt to be related logically
to recidivism also were included. Only the results of the cross-
tabulations using last known legal status are reported here. These
analyses showed the strongest relationship (primarily because of the
greater number of persons included) and were consistent with trends
in the analyses restricted to specific times since release

The percentages of persons within each category of the dichotomized (in a few cases, trichotomized) characteristics who had favorable legal outcomes are presented in Table 5.22. The significance
levels (using chi square) for the differences in distribution of favorable versus unfavorable outcomes are presented in Table 5.23.

The results of these relational analyses were not especially
productive in demonstrating relationships with recidivism. Although
those variables included in Table 5.22 all had a statistically significant relationship to recidivism for the total combined sample; this is
to a considerable degree due to the large number of persons on whom

the statistics are based. The fact that a relationship is statistically
significant does not necessarily mean that the finding is useful. For
example, commitment for a crime against property was significantly
related to unfavorable outcome in the total combined sample (p < .05),
but 72 percent of those convicted of a crime against property had
favorable outcomes (as compared with 79 percent with favorable outcomes among those convicted of other types of crimes). Furthermore, in within-group analyses this relationship was significant only
for Lompoc participants and was, in fact, reversed (although not
significantly so) in three other groups. No characteristic consistently
showed a significant relationship with recidivism within sites, nor
even within a majority of sites. Given the inconsistency of relationships across groups, group differences in recidivism rates cannot
be explained by differences in characteristics of group members.

These findings are not inconsistent with those of other studies
attempting to identify variables related to recidivism. In the present
study, as well as in others, significant correlates of recidivism can
be identified using a sufficiently large sample of releasees. What
this "significance" means, however, is that if one tried to predict
whether or not a person would be successful after release, the prediction would be correct more often if one knew some characteristics
of the individual than if one had no information at all. Nevertheless,
the prediction would be wrong in a significant number of cases.

Although it did not appear fruitful to pursue development of a
base expectancy scale using the study sample, a further relational
analysis was carried out using the base expectancy scale developed
by NCCD.[3] The NCCD scale was used rather than those of the California Department of Corrections or the configuration developed by
Daniel Glaser for two reasons. Unlike the California scale, the
NCCD scale was developed using a nationwide sample. The Glaser
configuration, unlike the NCCD scale, includes information not
available for this study sample.*

The items included in the NCCD scale are presented in Figure
5.2, along with the points assigned for each characteristic. The
percentage of persons with favorable outcomes in each of the NCCD
categories is presented in Table 5.24 for each group in this study
along with the data from the NCCD study. These data indicate, in
general, that the more favorable the NCCD category, the higher the

---

*Although the information used in the NCCD scale was available
for most groups, the analysis for the Ashland and Minnesota groups
had to be limited to those persons in the original sample due to insufficient information in the computerized records.

TABLE 5.22

Percentage of Persons with Favorable Legal Outcomes at Last Time of Information
Within Classifications of Selected Background Variables

| | NewGate Program Sites | | | | | | | | | | Other Program Sites | | | All Groups |
| | Ashland | | Minnesota | | New Mexico | | Oregon | | Pennsylvania | | Lompoc | Illinois | Texas | |
	Participant	Control parison[a]	Participant	Control parison[a]	Participant	Comparison	Participant	Comparison	Participant	Comparison	Participant	Participant	Participant	
Current Commitment														
Current offense (general category) not crime vs. property[b]	76 34/51	50 3/6	74 25/34	82 9/11	71 20/28	71 15/21	67 36/54	68 15/22	87 34/39	86 18/21	89 33/37	91 21/23	80 16/20	79 336/426
Crime vs. property	67 34/51	71 35/49	68 17/25	86 24/28	60 12/20	73 16/22	70 26/37	59 16/27	79 11/14	71 15/21	38 3/8	80 12/15	62 10/16	72 374/521
Current offense (specific categories) not burglary, theft, forgery, auto theft, checks[b]	78 18/23	50 3/6	74 26/35	83 10/12	70 21/30	76 16/21	70 35/50	76 19/25	91 32/35	81 17/21	89 33/37	92 23/25	71 10/14	80 339/423
theft, checks, forgery, auto theft	65 31/48	70 32/46	64 7/11	94 15/16	64 7/11	58 7/12	70 14/20	57 8/14	80 4/5	73 11/15	38 3/8	100 5/5	75 9/12	72 296/412
burglary	100 1/1	100 3/3	69 9/13	73 8/11	57 4/7	80 8/10	62 13/21	40 4/10	69 9/13	83 5/6	0 0/0	62 5/8	70 7/10	68 77/114

Postcriminal Record

Number of prior arrests																
0–1[b]	80 12/15	64 9/14	80 32/40	91 10/11	83 5/6	75 9/12	—	92 12/13	90 9/10	80 8/10	93 28/30	69 11/16	91 21/23	94 15/16	100 1/1	85 150/177
2–8	54 12/22	87 13/15	70 33/47	61 19/31	79 15/19	61 19/31	—	81 13/16	69 31/45	69 20/29	83 15/18	83 20/24	75 12/16	75 12/16	75 18/24	72 219/306
9 or more	100 6/6	100 3/3	43 3/7	50 4/8	80 4/5	80 4/5	—	43 6/14	61 22/36	30 3/10	40 2/5	100 2/2	50 3/6	100 6/6	64 7/11	62 72/117
Number of prior felony convictions																
none[b]	73 47/64	71 36/51	—	85 29/34	89 25/28	82 139/170	62 20/32	96 24/25	73 16/22	84 21/25	90 34/38	77 20/26	83 30/36	85 17/20	80 4/5	79 530/670
one or more	38 3/8	50 2/4	—	52 13/25	75 9/12	79 15/19	75 12/16	39 7/18	67 46/69	42 10/24	73 11/15	81 13/16	67 6/9	89 16/18	71 22/31	65 185/284
Prior institutional commitments for illegal activity																
none[b]	81 34/42	70 19/27	94 47/50	100 13/13	78 7/9	83 20/24	74 17/23	90 17/19	76 13/17	76 13/17	91 29/32	76 16/21	88 23/26	90 18/20	100 3/3	84 289/343
one or more	53 16/30	68 19/28	48 21/44	64 28/44	87 27/31	81 134/165	60 15/25	58 14/24	66 49/74	56 18/32	75 15/20	81 17/21	67 12/18	83 15/18	70 23/33	70 423/607

(continued)

(Table 5.22 continued)

| | NewGate Program Sites | | | | | | | | | | | | Other Program Sites | | | |
| | Ashland | | | Minnesota | | | New Mexico | | Oregon | | Pennsylvania | | Lompoc | Illinois | Texas | |
	Partic-ipant	Control parison^a	Com-parison^a	Partic-ipant	Control parison^a	Com-parison^a	Partic-ipant	Com-parison	Partic-ipant	Com-parison	Partic-ipant	Com-parison	Partic-ipant	Partic-ipant	Partic-ipant	All Groups
Number of jail commitments																
none[b]	69 25/36	78 21/27	—	71 22/31	81 13/16	—	69 25/36	86 18/21	80 31/39	79 19/24	86 37/43	76 22/29	88 29/33	89 24/27	71 10/14	79 296/376
one or more	71 5/7	80 4/5	—	58 11/19	79 11/14	—	58 7/12	59 13/22	60 31/52	48 12/25	80 8/10	85 11/13	58 7/12	82 9/11	73 16/22	65 145/224
Age at first arrest																
18 or older[b]	73 19/26	64 9/14	89 24/27	89 8/9	75 6/8	—	65 15/23	76 22/29	74 37/50	70 21/30	91 29/32	83 19/23	88 23/26	81 21/26	88 14/16	79 267/339
under 18	70 31/44	71 29/41	66 42/64	62 24/39	82 18/22	—	68 17/25	64 9/14	64 25/39	53 10/19	75 15/20	74 14/19	68 13/19	100 12/12	60 12/20	68 271/397
Longest period between arrests																
3 or more years (or first arrest)[b]	100 15/15	70 7/10	—	100 10/10	100 7/7	—	74 17/23	84 16/19	78 25/32	59 10/17	88 22/25	83 19/23	85 23/27	95 18/19	70 7/10	83 196/237
less than 3 years	52 14/27	82 18/22	—	57 21/37	74 17/23	—	60 15/25	62 15/24	62 36/58	66 21/32	82 22/27	74 14/19	71 12/17	79 15/19	73 19/26	67 239/356
Alias																
never used alias[b]	67 26/39	82 22/27	—	70 30/43	82 23/28	—	69 27/39	74 31/42	69 49/71	69 29/42	85 44/52	—	85 35/41	85 29/34	80 20/25	76 398/525
has used alias	100 4/4	60 3/5	—	43 3/7	50 1/2	—	56 5/9	0 0/1	65 13/20	29 2/7	100 1/1	—	25 1/4	100 4/4	54 6/11	57 43/75

116

Opiate, excessive alcohol use																
neither[b]	72 41/57	74 35/47	75 53/71	73 19/26	95 20/21	79 120/152	69 22/32	75 27/36	77 33/43	76 19/25	88 35/40	87 20/23	86 24/28	92 23/25	75 12/16	78 503/645
alcohol	75 3/4	50 2/4	50 3/6	83 19/23	73 11/15	92 22/24	86 6/7	40 2/5	62 20/32	38 6/16	100 4/4	80 8/10	0 0/2	80 4/5	82 9/11	71 119/168
opiates	67 4/6	33 1/3	60 3/5	46 6/13	75 3/4	94 16/17	44 4/9	100 2/2	53 10/19	54 6/11	73 8/11	56 5/9	85 11/13	88 7/8	33 1/3	65 87/134
Work History																
Longest period working for one employer																
6 months or more[b]	81 13/16	67 8/12	—	81 17/21	100 10/10	—	68 23/34	83 20/24	72 33/46	60 12/20	85 28/33	87 20/23	86 18/21	96 21/22	75 12/16	79 235/297
less than 6 months	67 16/24	89 16/18	—	54 15/28	70 14/20	—	64 9/14	58 11/19	64 29/45	66 19/29	84 16/19	76 13/17	75 18/24	73 11/15	72 13/18	69 200/290
Percent time employed in preceding two years (while eligible for employment)																
more than 50 percent[b]	79 11/14	56 5/9	—	90 9/10	100 8/8	—	83 10/12	83 20/24	80 12/15	78 7/9	85 22/26	94 15/16	81 13/16	100 14/14	100 7/7	85 153/180
50 percent or less	69 18/26	90 19/21	—	59 23/39	73 16/22	—	61 22/36	58 11/19	66 50/76	60 24/40	85 22/26	72 18/25	79 23/29	78 18/23	67 18/27	69 282/409

[a]Dash indicates information not available.
[b]Classification presumed to be associated with more favorable outcomes.
Source: Compiled by the authors.

TABLE 5.23

Significance of Relationships Between Selected Background Variables
and Favorable–Unfavorable Legal Outcome

| | NewGate Program Sites | | | | | | | | | | | | Other Program Sites | | | |
| | Ashland | | | Minnesota | | | New Mexico | | Oregon | | Pennsylvania | | Lompoc | Illinois | Texas | All Groups |
	Participant	Control	Comparison	Participant	Control	Comparison	Participant	Comparison	Participant	Comparison	Participant	Comparison	Participant	Participant	Participant	
Present commitment																
Not crime against property	—	R	—	—	R	—	—	R	R	—	—	—	.01	—	—	.05
Not burglary, theft, checks, forgery, auto theft	—	—	—	—	R	—	—	—	—	—	—	—	.01	R	R	.01
Past criminal record																
0–1 prior arrests	—	R	—	.01	—	—	—	—	—	—	—	R	—	—	—	.001
No prior felony convictions	.10	—	—	.05	—	—	R	.001	—	—	—	R	—	R	—	.001
No prior institutional (penal) commitments	.05	.001	—	.05	R	—	—	.10	—	—	—	R	—	—	—	.001
No prior jail commitments	R	R	—	—	R	—	—	—	.10	—	—	R	.10	—	R	.001
18 or older at first arrest	—	R	.05	—	R	—	R	—	—	.05	—	—	—	R	—	.01
3 or more years between arrests or no prior arrests	.01	R	—	.05	—	—	—	—	—	R	—	—	—	—	R	.001
Never used an alias	R	—	—	—	—	—	—	—	—	—	—	—	.05	R	—	.001
No use of opiates, excessive alcohol	R	—	R	—	—	—	—	—	—	—	R	—	—	—	—	.01
Work History																
6 or more months for one employer	—	R	—	.10	—	—	—	—	—	R	—	—	—	—	—	.01
Percent time employed or in school in preceding 2 years (when employable)	—	R	—	—	—	—	—	—	—	—	—	—	—	—	—	.01

Note: This table uses chi-square with df = 1; dash represents no significant relationship; R = relationship revealed.
Source: Compiled by the authors.

TABLE 5.24

Percentage of Persons With Favorable Legal Outcomes at Last Time of Information Within Categories of NCCD Base Expectancy Scale

NCCD category	NCCD Test	Ashland Partic-ipant	Ashland Control	Ashland Com-parison	Minnesota Partic-ipant	Minnesota Control	Minnesota Com-parison	New Mexico Partic-ipant	New Mexico Com-parison	Oregon Partic-ipant	Oregon Com-parison	Pennsylvania Partic-ipant	Pennsylvania Com-parison	Lompoc Partic-ipant	Illinois Partic-ipant	Texas Partic-ipant	All Groups
					NewGate Program Sites										Other Program Sites		
1. Most favorable	89 158/177	86 12/14	100 3/3	—	85 11/13	80 4/5	—	70 14/20	90 9/10	85 11/13	89 8/9	93 27/29	83 14/15	89 25/28	100 12/12	75 3/4	88 153/175
2.	81 282/350	71 12/17	76 16/21	—	70 14/20	75 6/8	—	68 13/19	92 11/12	70 14/20	75 12/16	85 11/13	53 9/17	78 7/9	73 11/15	100 10/10	74 146/197
3.	71 399/559	50 6/12	75 6/8	—	31 4/13	93 13/14	—	50 3/6	58 7/12	63 24/38	53 9/17	56 5/9	100 10/10	50 3/6	88 7/8	50 4/8	63 101/161
4.	57 86/152	—	—	—	100 3/3	33 1/3	—	50 1/2	40 2/5	89 8/9	50 2/4	100 2/2	—	50 1/2	100 2/2	62 5/8	68 27/40
5.	61 132/217	—	—	—	100 1/1	—	—	—	50 2/4	50 5/10	0 0/2	—	—	—	100 1/1	75 3/4	55 12/22
6. Least favorable	50 32/64	—	—	—	—	—	—	100 1/1	—	0 0/1	0 0/1	—	—	—	—	50 1/2	40 2/5
N	1519	43a	32a	—b	50a	30a	—b	48	43	91	49	53	42	45	38	36	600

aSufficient information available only for original sample.
bInsufficient information available to categorize.
cUsing parole outcome at 12 months.
Source: Compiled by the authors.

FIGURE 5.2

Calculation of Base Expectancy Scores

BASE EXPECTANCY SCORE CALCULATION

ADD

16   if property offense (burglary, theft,
      vehicle theft, forgery, or other
      fraud)   _____

12   times the number of prior prison
      commitments (count 9 or more as
      9)   _____

10   times the number of prior sentences
      other than prison (count 9 or more
      as 9)   _____

7   if any history of drug use   _____

                    TOTAL

SUBTRACT

              above sum from 114:   114

                                            - _____

      BASE EXPECTANCY SCORE =

Source: From Don M. Gottfredson et al., A National Uniform
Parole Reporting System (Davis California: National Council on Crime
and Delinquency, December 1970), p. 95.

percentage of persons with favorable outcomes. Comparisons between
groups, however, are difficult to evaluate. In Pennsylvania, for
example, it is clear that within the two most favorable categories
more NewGate participants have favorable outcomes than do persons
in the comparison sample, although this difference would not be
statistically significant given the small number of persons included.
Fewer Pennsylvania NewGate participants than general comparison
persons, however, have favorable outcomes in the middle category.
Comparing these two groups, there is no clear-cut indication that
one group is more successful than another when background characteristics are taken into consideration. In general, these results
give us little information beyond the comparison of recidivism rates
disregarding background characteristics, except perhaps that the
particular characteristics and weightings included in the NCCD base
expectancy scale do not account for differences in recidivism between
groups in this study. Although the Pennsylvania NewGate and Lompoc
participant groups both had a high percentage of persons in the most
favorable NCCD scale category and a high percentage of persons with
favorable outcomes, the Minnesota control and Illinois participant
groups had an average percentage of persons in the most favorable
NCCD scale category relative to other groups, but a high percentage
of persons with favorable outcomes.

 Although these analyses of the relationship between background
characteristics and recidivism offered little encouragement that differential success could be explained by differences in background or
prior criminal involvement, one further set of analyses was performed
using multiple regression analysis. In addition to recidivism, these
analyses included achieving stability, realizing life goals, and the
combined success measure as dependent variables. The independent
variables are identified in Table 5.25. These variables were selected
on the basis of prior studies and the preliminary analyses discussed
above, which indicated that they, and not other background variables,
bore some relation to success. Although the results of these analyses
were no more fruitful in "explaining" differences in success than had
been the earlier analyses, a summary of the results is indicative of
the problems involved with this common approach to analyzing and
predicting success.

 In the first set of regression analyses all participants and comparisons were combined. These analyses were helpful in identifying
those characteristics most strongly related to success for the total
sample: regularity of employment pattern before prison, number of
prior arrests, number of prison terms served, and, to a lesser extent, imprisonment for a crime involving drugs or alcohol. In these
analyses, being a participant in the Oregon NewGate program was
related positively to success. Beyond this relationship, group

TABLE 5.25

Regression Analysis

	Summary Success		Realizing Life Goals		Achieving Stability		Legal Status	
	F Value	r	F Value	r	F Value	r	F Value	r
Stability of employment	13.76[d]	.28	13.55[d]	.27	10.32[c]	.26	8.53[c]	.22
Number of prior arrests	5.16[b]	-.24	3.73	-.19	5.04[a]	-.25	4.91[a]	-.24
Time since release	3.89	-.05	<1	.02	—	.00	16.47[d]	-.15
Father's occupation	3.63	.12	3.28	.12	4.42[a]	.11	2.39	.11
Not imprisoned for auto theft, theft, checks, forgery, or burglary	3.01	.13	1.76	.11	3.42	.08	5.20[b]	.14
Number of prior prison terms	6.03[b]	-.19	4.38[a]	-.15	<1	-.18	4.62[a]	-.20
Not ethnic minority	<1	.05	<1	.04	<1	.04	1.54	.05
Salary level	3.63	.17	6.11[b]	.20	<1	.12	1.39	.09
Age as of 1/72	1.41	.02	1.60	.06	1.20	.01	<1	-.05
Crime not related to drinking or drugs	4.77[a]	.08	3.91	.06	5.04[a]	.09	2.21	.06
Age at first institutional commitment	<1	.20	—	.19	<1	.19	<1	.16
No prior parole violations	<1	.14	<1	.12	1.30	.15	<1	.15
No alias	1.22	.13	<1	.09	4.77[a]	.16	2.10	.16
Former occupation	<1	.14	<1	.15	<1	.14	2.32	.06
Group Membership								
Ashland participant	<1	-.03	—	-.03	—	.01	<1	-.01
Minnesota participant	<1	-.03	1.12	-.01	—	-.04	—	-.02
New Mexico participant	<1	-.06	<1	-.01	1.05	-.07	3.74[b]	-.08
Oregon participant	14.97[d]	.06	11.31[d]	.09	4.08[a]	.03	5.49[b]	-.01
Pennsylvania participant	<1	-.07	<1	.00	2.37	.13	<1	.08
Lompoc participant	—	.00	—	.00	1.77	-.04	—	.04
Illinois participant	<1	.00	<1	-.01	<1	-.03	1.76	-.02
Texas participant	4.80[a]	-.01	3.31	-.02	2.47	.00	1.57	.01
Ashland control	<1	-.01	<1	-.01	—	-.01	2.83	.05
Minnesota control	1.04	-.03	—	-.08	<1	-.01	—	-.03
New Mexico comparison	—	-.02	<1	.00	1.25	-.04	<1	-.08
Oregon comparison	<1	-.06	<1	-.05	<1	-.03	1.30	.07
Pennsylvania comparison	3.03	.08	1.91	.08	<1	.08		
N = 547 Degrees of freedom =	25/522		23/524		23/524		24/523	
Percent variance accounted for	19%		16%		17%		18%	

[a] p < .05. [c] p < .01.
[b] p < .025. [d] p < .001.
Source: Compiled by the authors.

membership showed no significant effect on success. Despite the fact that a few variables emerged as significantly correlated with success, only 16 to 19 percent of the variability in success was accounted for by all these variables combined.

A second step involved applying multiple regression analysis to the data for persons from each NewGate site individually, combining participants and comparisons at each site. In these analyses, being an Oregon participant was again shown to be related to success: when controlling for differences in background, Oregon participants were more successful than persons in the Oregon comparison group. The only other finding was that a somewhat higher percentage of the total variance was accounted for than in the analysis including all groups (ranging from 20 to 30 percent). There were, however, no consistently strong relationships between background variables and success evidenced in these analyses.

A still finer analysis involved using multiple regression analysis within each individual group (treating participants and comparisons as different groups at each site). In these analyses, the relationships between background characteristics and success were further diminished, even when taking into account the reduced degrees of freedom resulting from the smaller sample size. Generally speaking, however, the combined characteristics accounted for a substantially higher percentage of the variance in success (averaging close to 50 percent).

Dividing the total sample into participants from strong NewGate programs, those from weaker NewGate programs, those from other (non-NewGate) programs, and those from control and comparison groups did not contribute further to explaining success. Differences in background again accounted for a relatively small percentage of the variance (from 12 to 15 percent). The only clear result of these regression analyses is the inadequacy of using past experience to predict success.

NOTES

1. See Paul Takagi, "Evaluation and Adaptations in a Formal Organization," unpublished manuscript (Berkeley: University of California, School of Criminology, 1965).

2. Three of the most widely cited base expectancy studies are those conducted by NCCD [see Don M. Gottfredson et al., A National Uniform Parole Reporting System (Davis, Calif.: National Council on Crime and Delinquency, December 1970), pp. 130-132], Daniel Glaser [see D. Glaser, Effectiveness of a Prison and Parole System

(New York: Bobbs-Merrill, 1964)]; and the California Department of Corrections [see Don M. Gottfredson and J. Bonds, A Manual for Intake Base Expectancy Scoring (Form CDC-BE-61A) (Sacramento, Calif.: Research Division, California Department of Corrections, 1961)].

3. Gottfredson et al., op. cit.

6

POSTRELEASE SUCCESS
AND PROGRAM QUALITY

The preceding discussions of program quality and postrelease performance of participants leave unanswered the question of the relationship between the various program components and the success of participants. In Chapter 3 the eight college programs were rated on the variables of challenge, support, and space. These ratings were based primarily on the quality of the programs at the time of the evaluation. Several programs, most notably those in Pennsylvania, Oregon, and Ashland, had changed significantly over time. In analyzing the postprison careers of released participants, it became clear that analysis of the relationship between program quality and outcome for participants necessitated compiling evaluations of the programs as they existed when the released participants had been in the programs. In this subsequent analysis, we have specified a more detailed set of variables and have evaluated the programs on each for the time period covered by the experiences of the released participants.

MEASURES OF QUALITY OF PROGRAM
CHARACTERISTICS

Based on our experience with the programs, the following variables were identified as important measures of program quality:

(1) Quality of entering students: This measures the preparedness, academic ability, motivation, and other qualities related to the academic achievement potential of the students when they entered the program.

(2) Quality of instruction in the inside program: This variable is related to those aspects of the instruction, such as capabilities of the instructors, teaching techniques, and facilities, that increase the quality of the educational experience.

(3) Quality of inside program staff: This dimension is a measure of the staff's ability to coordinate activities in the program (and between the program and the prison) and to lead, counsel, and motivate the participants.

(4) Quality of therapy available to the inside program participants: This item measures the availability, intensity, regularity, and appropriateness of the therapy routines in which the participants engaged.

(5) The adaptability of the inside program to students' academic needs: This measures the degree to which the college programs could administer to the range of academic needs, interests, and capabilities of the students.

(6) Quality of academic counseling in the inside program: This variable should indicate the quality of all counseling other than "psychological" counseling. This includes career, academic, and vocational counseling.

(7) The degree to which a college atmosphere was approximated in the inside program: This measures the complex of routines, characteristics, and resources—such as availability of books, outside speakers, academic journals, library resources, free time, and comfortable lounging areas—which typically exist in the outside college context.

(8) The degree to which the students learned from each other: This measures the amount of classroom participation, seminars, and peer tutoring that the students themselves initiated and practiced.

(9) The degree of integration of the program into the prison: This refers to the absence of conflict between program staff and participants on one side and the prison staff and administration on the other.

(10) Amount of positive impact of the program on the prison: This variable measures the degree to which the existence of the program improved the prison routine, the attitudes and motivation of the general prisoner population, and the quality of service delivery in the prison as a whole.

(11) Amount and quality of feedback from the outside to the inside program: This variable indicates how much valid information about the outside program and the progress of released participants regularly flowed from persons attached to the outside program to participants on the inside.

(12) Quality of prerelease orientation: This measure is directed at the adequacy of the total range of activities and resources designed to prepare the participant for the transition to the outside program.

(13) Strength of affiliation between the outside sponsoring university and the inside program: This is intended to measure the extent of interest, resources, advocacy, and help that the outside sponsoring institution provided the inside programs.

(14) Quality of the outside sponsoring university: This measure is aimed at the quality of the sponsoring university as a university. This includes the quality of its academic offerings, its professors, its library, its physical facilities, its location and its prestige in the academic world. For those programs without a sponsoring university, the university to which most participants were released was evaluated.

(15) Quality of the outside program staff: As in the case of the quality of the inside staff, this measures the staff's ability to coordinate activities and to lead, counsel, and motivate the released participants.

(16) Strength of the affiliation between the outside sponsoring university and the outside program: This is intended to measure the university's support for, and concrete involvement with, the outside program.

(17) Quality of financial supportive services available to outside participants: This measures the amount of financial support provided through the program and the efficiency, ease, and convenience of its delivery.

(18) Quality of other outside supportive services: This measure includes all supportive services other than financial aid—for example, tutorial, medical, and counseling services—available to released program participants and provided by the outside program or the university.

Programs were rated on a scale from 1 (high) to 10 (low) for each variable by the three staff members who had had the most knowledge about the programs and contact with former participants. Initially the programs were rated independently by each of the three persons. The three persons then met as a group and arrived at consensus ratings for each program and variable, refining categories as necessary.

This procedure served to clarify the variables, resulting in the addition of several new variables, and to correct for differences in ratings attributable to differential knowledge of the programs. The differences in knowledge were due to the variability among the staff members in the type and extent of their experiences with each program. A summary of the consensus ratings is presented in Table 6.1.

A summary rating based on the mean scores received by each program across the 18 individual variables follows:

TABLE 6.1

Evaluation Staff Ratings of Program Quality on 18 Selected Variables

	Pennsylvania	Minnesota	New Mexico	Oregon	Ashland	Illinois	Lompoc	Texas
Quality of students	2	3	7	4	4	3	2	8
Quality of instruction	2	3	2	4	3	6	9	3
Quality of inside program staff	3	4	1	4	4	9	8	10
Quality of therapy in inside program	7	3	3	2	7	10	8	10
The adaptability of inside program to students' academic needs	2	4	1	5	3	10	7	10
Quality of academic counseling in inside program	2	3	1	4	3	10	8	10
Degree to which a college atmosphere was approximated	1	2	1	3	3	10	6	10
Degree to which students learned from each other	2	3	2	3	3	10	4	10
Degree of integration of program into prison	5	4	1	6	8	3	3	3
Amount of positive impact of the program on prison	3	5	1	4	5	10	6	10
Amount and quality of feedback from outside to the inside program	1	1	4	1	7	9	8	10
Quality of pre release orientation	1	1	2	2	3	9	8	10
Strength of affiliation between outside sponsoring university and inside program	2	3	2	7	10	8	10	10
Quality of sponsoring university	2	1	6	2	9	5	7	10
Quality of program staff	1	3	4	1	6	10	10	10
Strength of affiliation between outside sponsoring university and outside program	1	1	5	2	8	7	7	10
Quality of financial supportive services available to outside participants	1	1	3	1	5	10	9	10
Quality of other outside supportive services	1	1	4	2	6	9	10	10

Note: Ratings based on 10-point scale with 1 = high, 10 = low; programs are listed in order of overall quality from high to low based on mean score across all variables.

Source: Compiled by the authors.

128

Program	Mean Score on Past Program Quality
Pennsylvania	2.17
Minnesota	2.56
New Mexico	2.77
Oregon	3.17
Ashland	5.49
Lompoc	7.30
Illinois	8.18
Texas	9.17

In previous research, the programs were classified into high, medium, or low groups on the three broad program dimensions of supportive framework, personal social space, and challenge. To compare this previous classification with our new rankings, point scores were assigned to each program in each of the three areas: 3 for high, 2 for medium, and 1 for low. When a program fell between categories, it received the average point score of the two. Summing these three scores results in the ordering shown below.

Program	Mean Score on Present Program Quality
Pennsylvania	3.0
New Mexico	3.5
Minnesota	4.0
Oregon	5.0
Ashland	5.5
Lompoc	8.0
Illinois	9.0
Texas	9.0

The Spearman rank correlation coefficient between these two ratings is .90, indicating that despite changes in come of the programs, the quality of the programs relative to each other changed little. The New Mexico program represents the only shift in relative position.

PROGRAM CHARACTERISTICS AND SUCCESS OF
RELEASED PARTICIPANTS

In Chapter 5 the manner in which overall success scores were assigned to former participants was described. After deriving scores for individuals, the mean success score for all participants in each program was determined.

Program	Mean Score on Success of Released Participants
Pennsylvania	3.8
Oregon	3.7
Illinois	3.6
Lompoc	3.5
Minnesota	3.4
Ashland	3.4
New Mexico	3.3
Texas	3.3

The Pearson correlation coefficients between mean score on success and scores on the 18 program variables are displayed in Table 6.2. Few of these coefficients are large enough to imply a strong relationship between the program variables and success. Most striking is that, with the exception of quality of entering students, the higher correlations involve aspects of the outside programs. Even variable 11—the amount of quality and feedback from the outside program—relates to the outside, although it was designed as a measure of quality of the inside program. The clear implication is that a high quality outside program, providing opportunity, encouragement, and help to former inmates, is crucial if the benefits of the inside program are to have a lasting effect.

One other result deserving mention is the negative correlation between program variable 9—integration of the program into the prison—and success. An explanation of this is that programs such as those in Illinois and Texas, which were well integrated into the rest of the prison and had little conflict with it, tended also to be overwhelmed by it. Consequently, the prison administration's concern with security and routine tended to dominate, and to an extent stifle, concerns for educating the inmates. Moreover, participants' interest in education was aroused when the program had more of the atmosphere of a real college and less the atmosphere of a prison. The prison atmosphere tended to prevail in those programs that were more integrated into the rest of the correctional institution.

One factor that might mitigate this tendency of integration with the rest of the prison to stifle a college program is variable 10—the amount of positive impact of the program on the prison. A program that works closely with the prison administration can be a good one if it manages to influence the rest of the prison to move in its direction, rather than the other way around. The New Mexico program is the most notable example of combining integration into the prison with positive impact.

TABLE 6.2

Relationship Between Program Variables and
Success of Released Participants

Program Variables	Correlation with Success Scores*
Quality of entering students	.69
Quality of instruction in the inside program	-.13
Quality of inside program staff	.10
Quality of therapy available to inside program participants	.02
The adaptability of the inside program to students' academic needs	.07
Quality of academic counseling in the inside program	.08
Degree to which a college atmosphere was approximated in the inside program	.16
Degree to which students learned from each other	.18
Degree of integration of the program into the prison	-.36
Amount of positive impact of the program on the prison	.12
Amount and quality of feedback from outside program	.44
Quality of prerelease orientation	.24
Strength of affiliation between the outside sponsoring university and the inside program	.19
Quality of the outside sponsoring university	.62
Quality of outside program staff	.43
Strength of the affiliation between the sponsoring university and the outside program	.56
Quality of financial supportive services available to outside participants	.32
Quality of other outside supportive services	.37

*Pearson correlation coefficients (signs corrected so a positive value indicates that the higher the quality of the program, the more successful the participants).

Source: Compiled by the authors.

131

PROGRAM CHARACTERISTICS AND RECIDIVISM

Recidivism is a negative measure of success, that is, the higher the recidivism rate the less successful the participants. To maintain consistency, high scores were given for nonrecidivism. The programs are listed below run most to least successful as measured by mean scores on recidivism (the higher the score, the lower the recidivism).

Program	Mean Score on Nonrecidivism
Pennsylvania	4.3
Illinois	4.2
Lompoc	4.1
Oregon	3.8
Ashland	3.7
Texas	3.7
Minnesota	3.7
New Mexico	3.5

The Pearson correlation coefficients between the scores on the 18 program variables and mean nonrecidivism scores are presented in Table 6.3.

At first glance, these relationships are disturbing. Most of the variables that were positively, if weakly, correlated with success as measured by the combined success measure are negatively correlated with success as measured by nonrecidivism. Only the quality of students shows a strong positive relationship to nonrecidivism. As with the overall success scores, the quality of the outside sponsoring university and the strength of the affiliation between the university and the outside program are the principal program variables related to success as measured by nonrecidivism, although these correlations are low. This suggests that persons participating in a high quality outside program are more successful than others in achieving general goals, but not necessarily less likely to recidivate.

Two factors must be considered in interpreting these relationships. The first is that scores on the summary success measure, but not scores on recidivism, take into account the length of time a person has been released. Using nonrecidivism as a measure, a person who has been released for three months without detected illegal activity receives the same score as someone who has been out for two years with no detected illegal activity. Conversely, for persons returned to prison the scores on recidivism do not differentiate between those who return in the first month from those who return after

TABLE 6.3

Relationship Between Program Variables and
Nonrecidivism of Released Participants

Program Variables	Correlation with Nonrecidivism*
Quality of entering students	.73
Quality of instruction in the inside program	-.46
Quality of inside program staff	-.34
Quality of therapy available for the inside program participants	-.51
Adaptability of the inside program to students' academic needs	-.28
Quality of academic counseling in the inside program	-.33
Degree to which a college atmosphere was approximated in the inside program	-.24
Degree to which students learned from each other	-.18
Degree of integration of the program into the prison	-.08
Amount of positive impact of the program on the prison	-.27
Amount and quality of feedback from outside program	-.06
Quality of prerelease orientation	-.24
Strength of affiliation between the outside sponsoring university and the inside program	-.06
Quality of the outside sponsoring university	.27
Quality of outside program staff	-.13
Strength of the affiliation between the sponsoring university and the outside program	.16
Quality of financial supportive services available to outside participants	-.21
Quality of other outside supportive services	-.12

*Pearson correclation coefficients (signs corrected so a positive value indicates that the higher the quality of the program, the more successful the participants in not recidivating).

Source: Compiled by the authors.

two years of relative success. As may be recalled, the problem of controlling for time was one of the considerations in developing a summary success measure.

The second important consideration in interpreting the relationship between program quality and recidivism is that although recidivism is equated generally with return to criminal activity, a principal determinant of recidivism is the closeness of surveillance by the parole authorities and other social control agents. Recall that, although when compared with the NewGate participants members of the control groups admitted to more involvement in serious criminal activities, they had a lower overall recidivism rate than did participants. Using individual scores, the correlation between self-admitted criminal activity and recidivism for all interviewed participants was .38. Although this correlation indicates that persons who by their own admission were involved in criminal activity were more likely than others to receive legal sanction, recidivism is not an accurate measure of criminal involvement. This conclusion has been reached in many studies prior to the NewGate evaluation.[1]

It was earlier suggested that the closer surveillance of participants of some programs could, in part, account for the observed differences in their recidivism rates. This possible relationship was tested by having the evaluation staff rate each program on the relative intensity of surveillance of its participants. The ratings took into account program participants' observations of the intensity of surveillance by program staff, local police, and parole agents.

Program	Score on Intensity of Surveillance
Minnesota	1.0
Pennsylvania	2.0
Oregon	3.0
New Mexico	3.0
Illinois	7.0
Ashland	8.0
Lompoc	9.0
Texas	10.0

As a check on these ratings, the programs were ranked on the basis of the percentage of participants who responded that the parole agent supervised them closely. The correlation between this ranking and the staff ratings was .86.

Using the evaluation staff's ratings, the correlation between overall quality (using the mean scores across all 18 variables) and intensity of surveillance is .93 (Pearson correlation coefficient).

This means that persons who participated in the highest quality programs experienced the closest surveillance. These relationships suggest that program participants might be more likely to be returned to prison than nonparticipants who have engaged in the same, or even more serious, criminal activities. This would lower the overall success scores of participants from the highly ranked programs, not only because recidivism is one of the three components of the success measure but also because return to prison makes it difficult, if not impossible, for a person to score well on achieving stability and realizing life goals.

The likelihood that persons in the outside program were watched more closely leads to speculation on how highly some of the programs would have been scored on success if this process were not operating. Participants in the Pennsylvania program, for instance, who reported the second most intense surveillance and still had the second lowest recidivist rate, probably would have had a still lower recidivist rate and been even more successful overall (compared with other programs) had surveillance been less intense.

The implications for future research using recidivism as a measure of program effectiveness are clear. Valid comparisons of recidivism rates between different programs or between program participants and control groups of nonparticipants must take into account the intensity of surveillance by all control agents, the parole agents' exercise of discretionary powers in returning persons for parole violations, and, when possible, the individual's admission of illegal activity.

NOTE

1. For instance, see Paul Takagi, "Evaluation and Adaptations in a Formal Organization," unpublished manuscript (Berkeley: University of California, School of Criminology, 1965); and "Work Unit Evaluation," California Department of Corrections Report, December 27, 1965.

7

Increasingly, cost-benefit arguments have begun to appear in correctional planning and analysis. The effort is made to calculate the cost of a particular program and then balance this against the benefits in dollar value that are derived as a result of the program. For instance, Stuart Adams, one of the major proponents of cost-benefit analysis in corrections, suggests that

> . . . the criterion of monetary return seems much
> more powerful analytically than recidivism rates, or
> psychological adjustment scores, or social values.
> Consequently, this technique should prove a welcome
> addition to the array of instruments or methods avail-
> able to the correctional researcher, the correctional
> administrator, and the public official interested in
> the field of correction.[1]

There are, however, many dissenters to the idea that cost-benefit analysis can be accomplished in corrections or that it should be important in establishing agency policy.[2] Many of the assumptions underlying cost-benefit analysis in prisons appear questionable. Although the reduced cost of crime and correctional administration, which stems from lower rates of recidivism, has been the most popular cost-benefit analysis in corrections, this approach was not adopted in this study for two reasons. The first reason is the conviction that recidivism is not a valid measure of return to criminality, since it reflects variation in agency policy and visibility to agents of control more than differential criminal activity. This conviction was supported by the interview data gathered in this study. It would be misleading, therefore, to calculate a program's benefits using a variable affected

more by factors outside the program than by changes in behavior that
might result from participation in the program. The second reason
is that calculation of the dollar benefit of reduced recidivism depends
on the dollar values of some unknown variables. David Hentzel[3]
argues that the following variables must be included in a recidivism-
based analysis: (1) the cost of crime in terms of damage, loss of
property, or harm to persons; (2) the cost of incarceration; (3) the
cost of new rehabilitative efforts after reincarceration; (4) the costs
of parole; (5) the costs of the loss of production as a result of incarceration; and (6) the costs in terms of unemployment, public assistance expenses, and perhaps new crime ventures because of increased
damage done to the individual during the period of reincarceration.
Only (2), (3), and (4) can be estimated, given the present level of
knowledge. In the case of (1), estimates of the costs of crime are
available at a macro level; but these are unreliable because they are
based on reported crime, which grossly underestimates true crime
and ignores some categories, such as white collar crime. Even if
these estimates were accurate, the proportion of these costs due to
recidivists still would be unknown. Variables (5) and (6) cannot be
estimated with accuracy either; the costs to society from the loss of
production of the incarcerated introduces another set of unknowns.
For instance, we cannot calculate how the person would have been
employed, how much he would have produced, or other such unknowns
because information about the employment patterns of exfelons is too
incomplete to permit such estimates. Likewise, the cost of postprison
increases in unemployment, dependence on public assistance, or
criminal activity because of reincarceration cannot be estimated.

Because of these weaknesses, increases in tax dollars resulting
from increased educational level were chosen over recidivism as the
basis for calculating program benefits. This was considered an appropriate measure for three reasons: (1) education has been used extensively in calculating dollar returns; (2) the return to society (that
is, increased taxes paid by persons whose incomes have increased)
is a direct return and a form of paying back costs in kind; and (3) this
method emphasizes the tangible aspect of the program—the delivery
of education—which is more amenable to evaluation and planning than
is the more intangible dimension of "rehabilitation."

The question addressed in this chapter, then, is whether the
prison college education programs, and particularly Project NewGate,
returned the public's investment in the programs through increases
in the payment of federal taxes.

METHOD OF CALCULATION

The overall logic and the general techniques employed in calculating costs and benefits were based on those used by W. L. Hansen
and B. A. Weisbrod[4] in studying public higher education in California.
First, financial data for the 1971-72 fiscal year were collected from
each program. To estimate the cost effectiveness of the programs,
the total cost of each program was established; then a unit cost for
each person participating in the program was calculated. Defining
what to include or exclude as costs across the programs was difficult
because there were many services and facilities related both to the
program and to the operation of the prison. For instance, each program occupied space in the prison. Should the college program be
charged rent, maintenance, and utilities in these borrowed facilities?
Some institutions remodeled their facilities wholly or partially for the
college program. Should this capital investment be charged against
the program? Some prisons involve all inmates in work assignments,
which produce one or more commodities that the prison sells. Should
this lost income be charged to the program?

It was decided to charge only direct costs to the program, ones
clearly incurred by the program operation. This excluded items the
prison would have to supply even if there were no college program—
such as the items mentioned above. If the inmates were not in the
college rooms during the day, they would be in some other location
provided by the institution. Prisons are engaged constantly in building
new facilities or remodeling for a variety of purposes; so this was not
considered a direct cost of the program. Direct costs include items
such as salaries of special staff, the costs of instruction, books,
special supplies, special costs for maintaining the program, telephone,
and, where applicable, the costs of the aftercare program.

Calculating unit costs was difficult. What was sought was the
average cost of offering "rehabilitative" services to an individual
through the educational program. This would have been an easy task
if the programs had been in steady operation for many years, thereby
providing a large base from which to calculate the average yearly
output. But programs have not been in operation long enough to have
attained a steady-state, so a base could not yet be established. Consequently, the total cost of operations, including the aftercare program, was divided by the total number of semester equivalent college
units earned in each program during fiscal year 1971-72. This figure
represented the price of supplying a person with one unit of the program's services, including not only college courses but also counseling
and aftercare services as well. To derive the total cost of program
services per student, the price of offering one unit to an individual was

TABLE 7.1

Program Costs
(in dollars)

Program	Total Cost of Program 1971-72	Cost per Unit	Average Cost per Participant
NewGate			
Ashland	196,000	192	3648
Minnesota	245,189	126	3276
New Mexico	150,884	62	868
Oregon	290,547	70	2170
Pennsylvania	293,481	211	4009
Non-NewGate			
Lompoc	26,319	11	209
Illinois	33,884	11	339
Texas	71,498	21	533

Source: Compiled by the authors.

multiplied by the average number of semester credits earned by participants in each program (see Table 7.1).

Studies consistently have revealed significant increases in income due to education. In 1972 the average annual income for American men between the ages of 25 and 64 was $10,700 for those with a high school education and $16,600 for those with four years of college. [5] This increase of $5,900 for the general population is probably not valid for a released felon population, since they experience special problems and restrictions in finding employment. Income estimates must come from the exfelons' own occupational experiences. To establish income increments by education, the salaries of all respondents who either had not attended school after release or had left school and worked full-time for at least three months were classified by years of college education. The annual federal income tax for the mean salary level within each classification was calculated using 1972 federal income tax tables for persons with three exemptions, averaging across the subcategories of single not head of household, head of household, and married filing joint return. To establish an income tax increment, the tax paid by those who had completed one year, two years, three years, or four or more years was compared with the tax paid by those who had completed less than one year of college. This produced an estimate of increases in taxes paid by

exfelons of different educational levels (see Table 7.2). The present
value of the increased taxes over a presumed lifetime earning period
of 40 years was then determined using a five percent discount factor
(see Table 7.3). In performing these calculations recidivists were
defined as program failures and were assigned to the base category
regardless of their actual level of educational attainment. ·Thus,
recidivists contributed nothing to program benefits but were fully
charged to program costs. No correction was made for increases
in income over time, nor for unemployment. Data gathered in the
study indicate that the resulting projection is more likely to underestimate than overestimate taxes paid.

The dollar benefits of the program were determined from the
present value of projected tax increments and program costs. The
total program costs, the cost per unit of credit earned, and the cost
of the program per participant are presented in Table 7.1. Because
of the variability in length of time since release both within and among
groups, the actual proportions of students completing successive
semesters were not used. Instead, the ratio of the number of students
dropping out after each semester to the number continuing on to the
following semester was used to project the proportion of participants
completing various levels of higher education (see Table 7.4).

Since some students entered the prison college program having
already completed some college, it was necessary to adjust the benefit
data so only that part of the total educational tax increment due to
program participation was reflected. The available data for prior
education were trichotomous—no college, less than two years of
college, or two to three years of college completed before enrollment
in a prison college education program. Consequently, it was not
possible to remove the effect of prior education using the same metric
(semesters or units completed) as was available from the postrelease
interviews. Therefore, Table 7.3 includes a range for the benefit
measures, based on the most and least favorable possible distributions of the prior education data. For the most favorable case, all
participants with less than two years prior college were assigned
less than one year prior college completed. Then, $0, the base figure
for the educational tax increment (see Table 7.2), was subtracted
from their total postprogram educational level tax increment. All
students falling in the category of two or more years of prior college
education were assigned to the two-year category and the corresponding amount ($188) from Table 7.2 was subtracted from their total tax
increment due to college education.

In the least favorable case, all students having completed less
than two years were assigned the maximum possible value for this
category (one year), and all students having completed two or more
years were assigned three years, which is the maximum possible

TABLE 7.2

Mean Income and Federal Tax Increment by Education
for Employed Exconvict Population
(in dollars)

College Level	N	Mean Annual Wage	Annual Federal Income Tax*	Annual Increment Over Base Tax
Less than one year (base)	107	6348	437	0
One year	44	6624	490	53
Two years	13	7385	625	188
Three years	8	7350	616	179
Four years	10	9120	953	516

*Based on average of 1972 federal tax rates for single not head
of household, head of household, and married filing joint return, each
with three exemptions.

Source: Compiled by the authors.

value for this category since project admission criteria required
participants to have at least one year of college education left to
complete. The corresponding amounts ($53 and $179, respectively)
were subtracted from the tax increments for this computation. The
actual differences in the benefits under the best and worst cases are
actually quite small, as may be seen in Table 7.3.

Although the three non-NewGate projects were never funded
entirely by the federal government, for the purposes of this paper
they will be treated as if all were federal projects so the advantages
to the taxpayer of different program models can be considered.

RELATIVE COSTS AND BENEFITS

The most important finding to emerge was that, in general,
taxpayers can reasonably expect to more than recover their investment in prison college education programs through the higher taxes
program participants pay as a result of their increased education

TABLE 7.3

Cost-Benefit Analysis by Program

	Program Cost per Participant	Mean Annual Increase in Federal Taxes		Present Value of Future Increased Taxes		Present Value Minus Cost		Percent Increase of Present Value Over Cost		Pay Back Period In Years	
		High	Low	High	Low	High	Low	High	Low	High	Low
NewGate											
Ashland	$3648	$ 29	$ 28	$ 498	$ 480	-$3150	-$3168	-86	-87	60	60
Minnesota	$3276	$141	$139	$2419	$2385	-$ 857	-$ 891	-26	-27	60	60
New Mexico	$ 868	$ 91	$ 89	$1561	$1527	$ 693	$ 659	80	76	14	14
Oregon	$2170	$223	$221	$3826	$3792	$1656	$1622	76	75	14	14
Pennsylvania	$4009	$248	$246	$4255	$4221	$ 246	$ 212	6	5	35	35
Non-NewGate											
Lompoc	$ 209	$154	$151	$2642	$2591	$2433	$2382	1164	1140	2	2
Illinois	$ 339	$166	$163	$2848	$2797	$2509	$2458	740	725	3	3
Texas	$ 533	$ 61	$ 60	$1047	$1030	$ 514	$ 497	96	93	12	13

Note: "High" estimates are those based on most favorable distribution of those with prior college; "low" estimates are those based on least favorable distribution of those with prior college.

Source: Compiled by the authors.

TABLE 7.4

Percentage of Program Participants Completing
Different Levels of College
(in percent)

	<1 Year*	1 Year	2 Years	3 Years	4 Years
NewGate					
Ashland	78	15	3	0	3
Minnesota	40	20	19	5	17
New Mexico	67	11	9	0	14
Oregon	40	8	12	3	38
Pennsylvania	28	16	14	0	42
Non-NewGate					
Lompoc	46	26	0	0	28
Illinois	42	17	14	1	26
Texas	62	27	4	0	8

*Persons who were returned to prison after release were
assigned to the base year (less than one year) regardless of actual
educational attainment.
Source: Compiled by the authors.

(see Table 7.3). Only the Ashland and Minnesota projects were
economic failures.

Important lessons for establishing successful programs can be
learned from the Ashland experience. The Ashland program's great
operational failure was its inability to develop a successful postrelease program. Although this was due in part to the relative youth
of the Ashland inmates and to the wider geographical area served by
that institution, the failure of the program to establish an adequately
supervised postrelease program contributed to the high recidivism
rate and low completion of education for Ashland participants. All
other programs exceeded Ashland's proportion of persons completing
four years of college by a factor of three to 14 (see Table 7.4). The
economic failure of Minnesota is much less severe than that of the
Ashland program. It is also more difficult to explain in terms of
operational failure. As indicated earlier, a disproportionate number
of recidivists from the early stages of the program apparently were
included in the study sample. It was not possible to correct this bias
when discovered because of insufficient information about the total
participant population in Minnesota. The expectation is that, if

information had been available, the Minnesota program would be
shown to pay for itself over the long run but would still rank fourth
among the NewGate programs using economic criteria. A caution
must be noted at this point. This chapter considers the success of
prison college programs in the very narrow, economic sense. Other
criteria well could lead to the decision that taxpayer subsidies are
indeed worthwhile to achieve the noneconomic goals of these programs

The cost data alone indicate that NewGate type projects are the
most expensive to operate. Again, however, the limits of purely
economic criteria to evaluate these programs are reached. The
greater investment in NewGate results in more participants getting
more education as a result of participation in the program than in the
non-NewGate programs (see Chapter 4). The noneconomic and intangible benefits of more education well could justify the added dollar
costs of the NewGate projects. On the other hand, as long as non-
NewGate programs are willing to accept more limited program goals
and their relative lack of success in producing a completed college
education, they can point with pride to the dollar returns they generate for the taxpayer.

Although most of the greater costs of the NewGate projects were
due to the broader range of services they provided, some were also
due to the fact that the NewGate project students were initially less
college-ready than the non-NewGate students. The non-NewGate
students tended to be older, more mature, and to have had a higher
level of educational achievement on entering the program. In addition,
self-selection in program admission and continuation in the non-
NewGate programs leads to a biased evaluation in favor of these programs, given the inclusion criteria of this study. The non-NewGate
programs were able to purchase instruction at a lower cost per unit
than were the NewGate programs, possibly due to their being older,
established programs rather than experimental projects. In short,
the NewGate type projects, although more expensive to operate than
some less encompassing college prison programs, are more successful in getting convicts through a college education once they enroll.

When viewed as taxpayer investments, the prison college programs are impressive. A caution must be added, however, for the
most impressive performers—Lompoc and Illinois. Since the New-
Gate programs made little use of volunteers, volunteer time was not
included in the cost analysis. Lompoc, however, placed heavy reliance on volunteer efforts to operate its program. Not including
these efforts as a cost inflated the return for the Lompoc program.
On the other hand, if the programs are examined strictly from the
perspective of alternative models of tax investment, which is what
is shown in Table 7.3, the conclusion is obvious that the taxpayers
will get a higher return if some of the total program cost is shifted
from the taxpayer to volunteers.

The Illinois statistics might be misleading. Earning estimates
were based on released program participants whose program experience actually occurred 12 to 38 months prior to data collection.
In the authors' judgment, program stability was great enough that
fiscal year 1971-72 cost data reasonably can be taken as representative of program costs at the time the interviewed exparticipants were
in the program, except for the Illinois program, which in the interim
had a change of administration leading to a drastic curtailment of the
scope of the Illinois program. Thus participants from the Illinois
program who were interviewed generally had been through a more
expensive project than that which was operating at the time of the
interviews.

CONCLUSIONS

In addition to increasing the participants' educational level,
developing a more stable and socially acceptable lifestyle, and perhaps reducing recidivist behavior, prison college education programs
can be shown to pay their own way. In seven of the nine programs
studied, the costs to the taxpayers in providing the program are more
than repaid through higher future tax payments from participants due
to their higher incomes as a result of their college education. Although NewGate type programs are more expensive to operate and
yield a lower rate of return on the tax dollars invested than do programs only operating courses inside the prison, NewGate programs
have a lower drop-out rate and are more successful in extending
college education to disadvantaged populations.

The relative economic failure of the Ashland program serves to
point out important program features, such as a structure to keep the
student in school if he is doing successful work, which are necessary
to the development of an economically sound program. Once such a
program is established, the economic payoff is spectacular. A prison
college program completely paid for from federal taxes reasonably
can be expected to repay its cost within 15 years. A program making
extensive use of volunteer efforts could repay the taxpayers in as
little as two years.

NOTES

1. Stuart Adams, "Is Corrections Ready for Cost-Benefit Analysis?" revised version of paper presented at the 98th Congress of
Corrections (San Francisco), August 1968, p. 22.

2. See, for example, Victor A. Thompson, "How Scientific Management Thwarts Innovation," Trans-Action 5, 7 (June 1968): 51-55.

3. David Hentzel, "The Cost of Crime: An Alternative Model," unpublished manuscript (University of Missouri: Department of Economics, 1972).

4. W. Lee Hansen and Burton A. Weisbrod, Benefits, Costs and Finance of Public Higher Education (Chicago: Markham Publishing Co., 1969).

5. U.S. Bureau of the Census, Statistical Abstracts of the United States (Washington, D.C.: U.S. Government Printing Office, 1974), p. 120.

8

A MODEL PROGRAM—
ISSUES AND
RECOMMENDED SOLUTIONS

In the course of the study it became apparent that college programs in prison have to negotiate a series of critical issues that arise as a function of the peculiarities of the prison context. What these critical issues are, their alternatives and implications, and how they are best resolved in the interest of their educational purposes are subjects of this section. The college program itself begins the discussion, which moves from the more general problems to the more specific, considering a program's major objectives and the nature of its participants, staff, and specific features (both inside the prison and in the aftercare phase). This discussion is followed by the consideration of issues that concern the college program's relationship to elements in its environment, such as the prison administration and staff, the nonparticipating inmates, the parole board, and, beyond the prison, the university and the larger community.

To facilitate the description and analysis a fourfold typology is offered which highlights the important differences among college programs in prisons. Which of the four basic types is to be adopted is considered as the first issue.

ESTABLISHING OBJECTIVES AND PRIORITIES OF THE COLLEGE PROGRAM

In the programs studied, there were four different program formats. The programs are described and ordered (from A to D) according to the increasing intensity of involvement they offer students (see Figure 8.1).

FIGURE 8.1

Program Formats

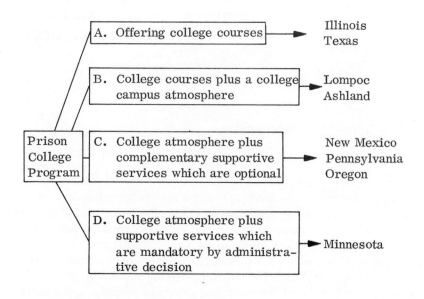

Source: Compiled by the authors.

Each has its advantages and disadvantages. Type A, which consists of no more than offering college courses, provides its participants a very limited college program. Although this has negative implications for the students in the program, it has certain advantages in the prison setting. By providing no extra benefits to participants than are available to other inmates in the prison, it is more egalitarian from the perspective of the prison as a whole. It precludes the development of an inmate elite and thus averts the resentment of nonparticipating inmates. It also avoids creating a new source of resentment for the prison staff, who favor treating all inmates the same when the alternative means extra work for the prison staff.

Programs following the Type B format conceive of the educational experience as being a function of much more than course work. This type of program is modeled more after the structure of colleges in civil society, where the student world is constructed, by design, to be a more comprehensive and all-encompassing experience. A student in college in the free society is not only provided a prescribed set of college courses but also is presented a variety of alternative areas of concentration and vocational majors, different teachers and fellow students, and extensive libraries and research materials. Activities outside the classrooms are just as important. Provided are student newspapers, student government, debating and other clubs, visiting lecturers, academic seminars and symposiums, concerts, art shows, movies, organized recreation, and social events. These diverse experiences are designed to stimulate and supplement the student's learning, to tap previously undiscovered interests and talents, and to enrich the life of the entire student body.

A college program can generate a college type atmosphere inside the prison by offering a wide variety of courses, including cultural and enrichment courses, an extensive library with a wide assortment of books and periodicals, research and study facilities, major university involvement, informal and personal contact with college professors, extensive association with other students, lectures, debates, seminars, outside speakers, and such. In this way, Type B programs will provide a richer, more absorbing educational experience. This means a greater likelihood that these inmates (though perhaps a select segment of the prison population) are given an experience that will enhance new life chances after release.

Type B will have negative implications in the prison context as well. There will be extra privileges granted the participants because of the exigencies of the more extensive college program: for example, study time in cells, uncensored book lists, freedom of movement and association, relief from work duty, less cell time, or day passes to campus. This could cause resentment among nonparticipants. Moreover, as responses from participants in the more comprehensive programs in the study sample document, this resentment can be markedly greater among the prison staff. Many prison personnel initially object because they see it as "giving the inmate too much." They are accustomed to believing that no experience during incarceration should be made enjoyable. They also fear that the inmates might get more of an education than they themselves have and that, as a consequence, the staff will lose some of its authority.

Type C programs supplement the academic program with supportive services for the student. Special recruitment, counseling (academic, therapeutic, and vocational), and college preparation courses (remedial work) are provided in the inside program. In addition, an outside postrelease program is provided with support in obtaining college admission, job placement, and financial assistance. The motivation for providing these additional services is the belief that without them the learning process is severely hampered and the full benefit from the academic program will not be derived. Colleges in civil society provide these services because their experiences have shown them to be necessary. However, based on the kind of students prison programs serve and the difficulties exconvicts have in their postrelease lives, the need is expected to be even greater. The vast majority of persons in American prisons today are from lower or working class families. Many of them are minority group members. Moreover, the majority are high school drop-outs. What this means for a college program in a prison setting is that, despite their innate endowment, most exprisoners will have a greater than average fear of academic failure and a belief that college is reserved for people from a higher socioeconomic class who possess some rare and undefinably superior qualities, which they themselves do not possess. Their educational preparation in the basic skills will be deficient. Moreover, their knowledge of the opportunities and alternatives provided by academic institutions will be limited; so the inmates' disadvantages will continue after release. What ability they had to "make it" on the outside prior to going to prison will have atrophied through disuse. In addition, they will now have the "ex-con" stigma, which will limit their marketability when job hunting. These problems, coupled with their low skill level, their lower class, and the minority background of some, will make it highly unlikely that any employer will hire them right out of prison. Unless the program can introduce its participants into meaningful worlds beyond prison, their college experience inside might just raise their expectations and thereby create the basis for greater frustration. This describes, in part, the experience of the Ashland NewGate program, which provided a rich college atmosphere in the inside program but was not successful in providing needed emotional and financial support on the outside.

The administrators of Type C college programs maintain that, in the prison context, they must go beyond the level of effort of most American colleges in civil society and provide a program geared to the needs of other than middle class students. This means supplementing the regular college academic program in the inside program with support services and developing links and continuities with external institutional networks in the prerelease phase to help the inmates generate opportunities beyond their inside program experience. It also means developing an aftercare program in the postrelease phase to compensate for the inadequacies of universities in providing the support structure necessary to accommodate students with inmate backgrounds.

The problem with this more comprehensive program (C) is that it requires greater commitment on the part of the prison administration than Types A or B. First, it most likely will mean an obligation of more funds and, at the very minimum, a larger program staff. Second, if resentment among nonparticipant inmates is to be avoided, the prison will have to develop other inside programs, such as vocational training, high school, or drug therapy, and transitional programs, such as work-release, furlough, study-release, and community treatment, which offer noncollege inmates comparable opportunities to those offered to the college students. Third, the prison will not be obliged merely to enlarge its treatment opportunities; it will have to accept greater involvement by outsiders. With more extensive programming, prisons will be moving automatically into areas in which they have no expertise. They will have to call on people with this expertise (for example, industry for sophisticated vocational training, colleges for academic training, the medical and psychiatric community for therapy programs) and involve them in a sustained and systematic way. This ultimately will mean sharing in decision making, at least on matters that pertain to the program. This will mark a dramatic departure from how the typical prison operates today.

Both Type C and Type D programs supplement the academic program with supportive services. However, there is a difference in the degree of emphasis that is put on a student's participation in these additional activities. A Type C program puts primary emphasis on the academic program and offers the support services essentially as additional opportunities, which the participants can use of their own volition. They are designed to compensate for deficiencies that result from an inadequate opportunity structure available before prison and to exprisoners in postrelease life. In contrast, the program planners of Type D have a strong commitment to "changing the individual." They see their contribution as going beyond skill training and providing additional opportunities to compel the involvement of the total individual. In these programs there will be various ways in which the participants are pinned down and forced to confront themselves and others. In Type C the participant is allowed to pick and choose his experience (which includes therapy if he wants it), but the participant in Type D is programmed according to what is judged by the administration to be "most suitable" for him. The implications of Type D program for the inmate and the prison will be spelled out more fully in a later section dealing with the question of mandatory therapy.

Given the nature of the average inmate-participant, his limited backgrounds, and his limited opportunities in the future, Type C and D programs with their supplementary support services appear to be the most effective in fulfilling the educational goals of a prison college program. The programs of these two types appeared better able to draw, involve, and advance inmates who had educational deficiencies. The participants were better able to capitalize on what they gained from the inside program by continuing with their college education after release. They made a smoother, easier transition to life on the streets during the initial period after release; and they were able to get better, higher paying jobs. They developed greater self-awareness and gained personal confidence from their successes and contacts inside the programs. Finally, more participants of these programs indicated that the programs met their educational needs. Given these benefits, it is important that the quality of the college program not be sacrificed to accommodate other interests; the negative repercussions an effective college program has inside the prison on prison staff and on nonparticipants should be offset with other strategies.

NATURE OF PARTICIPANTS

One of the first decisions that must be made about the college program is who the participants should be. Basically, should the program be designed to accommodate inmates with demonstrated college ability, perhaps with previous college experience and a high degree of demonstrated motivation to enter a college program? Or, should the program be designed also to accommodate persons with the potential for college work who may not yet be aware of that potential?

Some programs are designed for the most highly motivated. The result is that these programs induce the most extensive involvement among inmates who have had previous college experience, and/or have come from upper and middle class backgrounds, with parents, family, or friends who went to college and had set that example for the inmate. Those inmates without those experiences are more reluctant to attend college in prison. The college programs in Lompoc, Texas, and Illinois all revealed this close relationship between socioeconomic class and participation in the college program. Lompoc, because of its unusually high number of middle class offenders in the general population, showed this most dramatically. The ratio of middle and upper class to lower class inmates in the college program was much higher than the ratio in the general population.

Illinois and Texas revealed the relationship also, but in a different way. In both programs, though a large number of inmates were taking some courses, there were barely enough inmates who had completed a minimum of twelve units in the inside program to qualify to be included in the study sample. Among the participants in the final sample, those who accumulated their credits over a short interval, that is, those with the fullest participation, were from higher socioeconomic classes than the participants who took one or two classes per semester and required long periods of time to accumulate the needed twelve units.

There are prison college programs that have been designed to also serve inmates with latent college potential; the NewGate programs were cases in point. As a result, larger numbers of convicts with lower and working class backgrounds are encouraged to participate fully. Under these conditions the college program is, by necessity, a more ambitious undertaking. There is need for a special recruiting or outreach effort and for a remedial section to help students make up their deficiencies in basic educational skills. Moreover, fewer participants will excel without motivation and support from the staff; and fewer will continue with college after release without the program providing continued assistance. It is logical that a program composed mostly of persons with demonstrated ability and motivation at the time of entry into the program (there is no such program in the sample) would show a higher proportion of success (that is, number of college graduates) than one which saw part of its function as motivating people with latent ability. However, the more ambitious program will possess the potential for fundamentally changing a larger segment of the inmate population.

A prison college program should be addressed to the needs of those inmates with latent potential as well as those with demonstrated capability and motivation. It is mainly the former segment of the inmate population that otherwise would not obtain a college education in the free world and that has the greatest potential for being changed in terms of life chances and lifestyles by the college experience. And this rehabilitative function is one of the primary tasks assigned to the college program.

SELECTION OF PARTICIPANTS

A decision related to whom the participants should be is how they are to be selected. A program has two alternatives: either to make admissions selective according to certain predetermined ascriptive criteria or to keep admissions open to everyone meeting certain minimum academic performance standards. The Minnesota, Ashland, Oregon, and Pennsylvania programs applied special selection criteria. The Texas, Illinois, Lompoc, and New Mexico programs maintained open admissions policies.

Programs which choose to keep admissions selective do so precisely because they want to select out, for administrative purposes, all inmates in certain ascriptive categories. They might want to control for participants' length of sentence, type of crime, custody, age, or race. Most NewGate programs fall into this category. The most prominent reason for their keeping admissions selective was that the

inside program had not been seen as a terminal effort but as preparation for college education after release. For this reason these programs were not prepared to expand the course offerings in the inside
program to meet the needs of long termers who became "saturated"
with the more limited programs.

In addition, certain programs have excluded inmates convicted
of certain kinds of crimes (Oregon Phase I and Pennsylvania Phase I
and Ashland during its initial period). This has sometimes been
motivated by a realization that the local community would resist
allowing certain inmates (for example, those convicted of murder,
rape, or child molesting) to come out on study-release. It has also
been based on the rationale that persons convicted of certain crimes
have more serious psychological problems than the college program
alone is equipped to deal with (for example, drug addiction) and that
the lack of essential facilities would prevent these students from
deriving any benefit from the college program. In the initial Ashland
group, conscientious objectors were excluded on the grounds that they
did not need the special college program. Special selection procedures
also have been used by programs to limit the number of participants
when more apply than can be accommodated (Oregon, Pennsylvania,
Minnesota, Ashland). Lastly, the programs have used these procedures to create a racial balance that would not have occurred automatically (Pennsylvania).

Though controlling selection can be seen to serve certain administrative purposes, the explicit procedures raise questions of fairness
among inmates. Why should inmates convicted of certain crimes,
who can gain as much as anyone else from the program, be excluded
just because they have a greater social stigma? Perhaps the "hard
criminals" could benefit even more than other inmates? If college
is a productive way of doing time, then should not people with still
considerable time to serve also be provided such benefits? Might it
not be good for the program's coherence and continuity if some of
the participants had been involved for several years? Could the more
recent entrants gain from the experience of the older students? If
the selection of participants depends on the subjective judgments of
the interviewers (Oregon, Pennsylvania, and Minnesota), those who
are not selected will be suspicious of the procedure and of the entire
program. In a prison setting the program will be suspected of being
controlled by the prison administration and thereby contaminated—
even if it is not.

A college program that has an open admissions policy has the
potential for having a heterogeneous student body, including inmates
who still have long prison terms to serve. This will have implications for the program. In the first place, the presence of persons
with long sentences (who cannot qualify for resident work on a college

campus) can help the college program play a different role than one
that exports all its trained people to the outside campus. Such a college program can enrich the entire educational enterprise inside the
prison by using the long term college students to tutor and to teach
the less educated inmates in the other prison education programs,
such as GED, Adult Basic Education, or high school. The New Mexico
NewGate program demonstrated how a college program could have
such a "multiplier effect" on the entire educational enterprise in the
prison. Because it saw its obligation as going beyond just those inmates close to their release dates, the New Mexico program was
more thoroughly integrated, that is, accepted, in the prison setting
than any other NewGate or non-NewGate program in the entire study
sample.

An open admissions policy also serves to enhance the college
program itself. Long termers appear to add immeasurably to the
quality and continuity of the inside program. This was most note-
worthy in the Pennsylvania program, which included a number of
inmates serving life sentences. They take the program more seriously
because they view it as an end in itself and not solely as a means
toward release. They help to set the tone of seriousness and can
remind the program administrator of the need to maintain the quality
of the inside program. The presence of persons without the expectation of early release in the Oregon program could have prevented its
staff from neglecting the quality of the inside program and from fo-
cusing on it as just a way station before study-release.

There are distinct disadvantages, too, in having an open admissions policy. What can a program do if the number of applicants is
greater than can be accommodated given the current space and resources? A program based on a "first come first served" principle
(Lompoc) will lead to considerable "wheeling and dealing" by inmates
and will heighten feelings of injustice among those excluded, who will
suspect that unprincipled actions were taken by the decision makers.
This pressure, coupled with the pressure from students who already
have been in the program long enough to have taken all the basic
sourses, will require the program to enlarge its facilities and to
expand its offerings. It will have to become more like a college campus inside the prison. There could be a need to offer a four-year
Bachelor of Arts degree, independent study assignments, tutorials
with college professors, and even advanced work.

An open admissions policy presents yet another problem. Although an admissions program is, on the surface, more democratic
because it appears to allow everyone to take advantage of the college
opportunity, a class of persons needing the program as much or more
might exclude themselves if there is no special outreach effort to
give extra encouragement. Unless this is done, these programs will

play a smaller role than they could in changing inmates' goals, values, interests, and perspectives. Those socioeconomic classes who ordinarily do not have the opportunity for higher education will once again be excluded. Justice considerations will require that the program go beyond "equal opportunity" (open admissions) and institute policies of "affirmative action" (active recruitment).

In the interest of justice and also of making the greatest possible strides toward fulfilling its educational goals, a college education program operating inside a prison should be open to all inmates who can meet certain objective performance standards. This policy should be accompanied by a vigorous outreach effort, to acquaint all inmates of the facilities and opportunities of the college program, and by a college preparation component, which helps applicants make up deficiencies that might prevent them from meeting the minimum admissions standards. Also, all inmates should be permitted to have full time student status (full time high school students also) if they so choose. To obviate the necessity of establishing selection procedures because of a shortage of space, the program should be enlarged to accommodate the increasing numbers of inmates interested. Upper division as well as lower division courses should be developed. A study-release plan, which permits "saturated" students to attend classes on campus, should also be developed gradually for students who have fulfilled certain inside program requirements and are eligible for release in minimum custody.

SOCIAL AND OCCUPATIONAL BACKGROUND OF STAFF

Another dilemma facing the college program is whether the staff should be chosen from outside the prison structure or from within? If they are chosen from within, there will be an assurance that they are acquainted with prison routines and therefore more likely to be harmonious partners in a joint enterprise. The program can be integrated more effectively into the prison structure by making staff appointments consistent with an already established career ladder (Lompoc, Texas, Illinois). On the other hand, by selecting staff from outside the corrections system (Oregon, Minnesota, Pennsylvania, New Mexico, and Ashland), the program builds in the ability to recruit persons with different experiences and perspectives from persons with whom convicts are usually in contact.

By hiring persons from the academic sectors to work inside prisons, there is a greater risk of friction between regular prison personnel and outsiders. Those coming from the academic community initially could be regarded as effete intellectuals who have no understanding of the "mentality" of convicts or, for that matter, of the practical working class world from which most of the prison personnel come. For their part, the academic types may be contemptuous of the prison personnel whom they see as not-too-bright, unsophisticated, and unenlightened. Clearly, two different worlds will be in conflict, at least in the initial organizational phases.

In the interest of a college program's educational goals, it is believed that persons composing its staff should be drawn mainly from and maintain roots in the academic community. Their chief commitment must be to academic education; their continuing link with it will enable them to keep open channels of communication between the college and prison communities. It will also facilitate periodic staff rotation from the prison to the college and the opportunity for a lateral transfer back to the academic world without loss of security or status once a staff member is ready to change jobs. No staff member should work more than three years in any prison college program. Such work is so thoroughly taxing that no person can possibly remain vital and innovative after a three-year period.

THERAPY IN COLLEGE PROGRAMS

One of the more controversial issues considered in this study concerns psychotherapy as part of the college program. The considerable intensity of the debate that has been generated is due both to the marked differences of emphasis placed on therapy in the various programs and to the different philosophical orientations of the proponents of opposing views. The constituent issues of the debate can be broken down into the following questions: Should psychotherapy be provided as part of the prison college program? If it is decided that it should, then should it be: (a) mandatory or voluntary or (b) group or individual, or (c) confidential or nonconfidential?

Therapy should be offered to inmates as part of the academic program. The choice between therapy or no therapy has been covered sufficiently in the more general discussion, which dealt with the advantages of a college program with complementary supportive components. The learning process potentially can be enhanced for at least some students if the program staff establishes a symbiotic relationship between the classroom and the therapeutic session. A therapy program established as part of the academic program can, under certain circumstances, offer the added advantage of being seen as essentially a learning experience, unencumbered by other uses to which it typically is put in prisons.

Mandatory or Voluntary

Persons who advocate mandatory therapy justify it with a stereotype they have of the average prison inmate: an emotionally immature,
irresponsible, manipulative, and self-centered person. Therapy is
designed to break the inmate out of his unrealistic world and make
him deal with the exigencies of a society of others. The Minnesota
NewGate staff, for example, argues that each NewGate participant
must be made to realize that he is in the program not only to serve
his own needs but also to understand his obligations to and responsibility for the needs of others. Certain social values and norms, which
guide interactions among people living side by side, are to be instilled
in the participants as part of the college experience; the peer group
operating as a whole is the educator and the enforcer of these values.

Proponents of mandatory therapy argue that persons needing help
are not always in the best position to decide what is best for them.
This fact, coupled with the prevailing norm in prisons of "doing your
own time," necessarily could lead convicts to steer away from therapy
programs, which are designed to engage and challenge them. According
to this justification, the delinquent mind conceives of himself and his
relationship to others in terms of his being right and they wrong.[1]
Because of the peculiarities of his family background and the harshness
of his parents, this person has withdrawn into himself as the only
source of life and security and has ruled out any obligation to, or contact with others. He has no "conscience." He is unable to be objective
about his own "complicity" in what happens to him. It is always someone else's fault. He goes through life refusing to look inward. Since
this person has no anxiety about the correctness of his orientation, he
rarely volunteers to enter therapy. The proponents argue that real
freedom can be gained only from therapy. According to them, freedom
of choice exists in the freedom to change at will, to change the responses to recurring and new stimuli. In this sense, the freedom that
results from the benefits of good therapy can be seen as more than
compensating for the initial lack of freedom the participant had in not
being able to choose for or against therapy.

Inmates must be compelled, then, to put themselves in a structure
in which attitudes and behavior will be different from their own and
those encouraged by the prevailing inmate culture. Once in this structure, the inmates will be encouraged, and also given new tools, to
reassess their attitudes and goals and to adopt more productive—that
is, constructive—behavior.

The critics respond to the proponents of mandatory therapy on
both philosophical and pragmatic grounds.[2] Philosophically, they feel
inmates are coerced into a particular treatment routine. They argue

that this is a violation of an inmate's constitutionally protected freedom of choice. Moreover, the fact that it is psychotherapy that is being imposed on the inmate means that his right to personal privacy and his right to refrain from invading the privacy of others are also being disregarded. The critics urge that the preservation of these basic human and civil rights are particularly important in a prison context in which inmates are already stripped of most of their individual identity and rights of self-determination.

Basically, the philosophical or ethical issue over mandatory therapy revolves around the more general issue concerning the proper role of correctional authorities in relation to their prisoners. With regard to the issue of choice, proponents of mandatory therapy reserve the rights of program and prison staff to decide what is in the "best interests" of the inmates. Opponents argue that to permit this discretionary authority is to invite tyranny over the weak and helpless. They argue that it must be assumed in prison, as in free society, that individuals are in the best position to decide what is best for them. Even if exceptions can be conceived, there can be found no better, more consistently reliable mechanism for making these decisions.

With regard to the issue of privacy, the proponents of mandatory therapy argue that prison officials have a right to transform inmates' attitudes and behavior and to put them in a setting (the group session) in which their "problems" will be exposed and resolved. Opponents argue, on the other hand, that inmates are punished by having to serve time in prison. They must be protected from further punishment, which can come in the form of being forced to subject themselves to "treatment" they do not want. Opponents argue that there is nothing so sacred about openness and introspection that it outweighs the importance of the right of an individual to self-protection. Self-protection includes being able to refuse, without fear of negative sanction, to be forced to accept a new morality, that is, a prescribed set of new attitudes, which is not better in any objective sense but closer to the values of the therapist. Deviant lifestyles might be abhorrent to the people in positions of authority, but they must be tolerated until the adherents actually commit violations of the law. Then they must be punished for their transgression and not for being different.

The second level of debate takes place on the level of effectiveness. Opponents of mandatory therapy argue that inmates who enlist in a therapy program of their own volition will be more receptive to treatment than those who are forced into one. They will participate because they are sincerely interested in gaining new insights into their own attitudes and behavior, as will all other participants. Only under these conditions will group therapy be conducive to productive change.

Another argument made in connection with ensuring the quality of the therapeutic experience is that there must be a way of evaluating the quality of the therapist. Under free market conditions, the quality of the professional is determined by the size of his clientele. Clients are permitted to solicit or not solicit his services according to whether they judge them to be meeting their needs and standards. When participation in therapy is mandatory, this yardstick is lost and inmates effectively are removed from the evaluation process.

Therapy should be made voluntary in the prison context. This study revealed no evidence that mandatory therapy is individually more effective or collectively "reaching" larger numbers. What the study did reveal was that therapy under voluntary conditions (Oregon and New Mexico) is significantly more popular among the participants than therapy under mandatory conditions (Minnesota NewGate). Inside participants rated the program's group counseling in the following way: 10.5 percent and 20.0 percent of the participants in Oregon and New Mexico, respectively, rated group counseling as less than adequate; 53.8 percent rated it less than adequate in the Minnesota program. The study indicates that no single approach will be able to accommodate the needs of everyone. Programs are better advised to develop numerous alternatives from which participants can choose according to their own needs and preferences than design one routine and force everyone to conform to it.

Individual Versus Group Therapy

The benefit of individual therapy is that it allows the therapist to tailor the program to the individual's needs. It can offer him the privacy and confidentiality that he might require before he dares explore some of his more personal and threatening problems. The drawback is that it is economically unfeasible to provide extensive therapy to all individuals in a college program. At most, individual attention can be provided for short term crisis periods.

Group therapy not only requires that the therapist provide less time to the program but it also removes him from the center of action. It plays down tension between the convict and someone who is perhaps older and who has more authority and emphasizes the peer group as a source of authority. The group consists of other persons who are similarly situated. The individual in this setting begins to discover that his problems and fears are not as unique as he once believed, and he thereby learns how others resolve or cope with those difficulties.

Therefore, both individual and group therapy should be offered. Many persons who were interviewed indicated that there were special problems they were unable to discuss with the group, but they were

comfortable talking about them with someone with professional experience, who could be trusted not to use it against them. Some administrators who stress the group approach, especially those in the
Minnesota program, argue that "someone who is not an inmate has
nothing to tell another inmate," therefore individual therapy serves
no purpose. There appears to be little basis for this. Inmates who
had the benefit of individual therapy with a staff member with a non-
inmate background stated it differently. They said that although there
were things that the therapist could not tell them about life in prison
as an inmate, there were just as many other things that they could
not have learned from another inmate who had a "narrower" life experience in the outside world. If one of the primary purposes of college education in prison is to introduce inmates to alternative lifestyles
and opportunities, they should be provided extensive contact with
persons most familiar with these new worlds, even if they are not
former inmates, and even if they are older and in positions of authority.

Confidential Versus Nonconfidential Therapy

Confidentiality is generally respected in relationships between
therapists and their patients in the free world. In prisons this contract is often violated. Violation is justified by the prison administration on the grounds that inmates do not have the rights of free men and
that the prison must know about the man in their control to make in-
formed decisions concerning his stay in prison. Moreover, many
prison systems and parole authorities have taken on the responsibility
of deciding when a person is "ready" to be released. Thus, these
prisons argue, it is important to know what the inmate is thinking and
doing to make the correct decision about his release.
    Those arguing for confidentiality maintain that unless this is re-
spected in therapy (what the inmate does and says is not held against
him), the potential for personal development will be undermined.
Furthermore, they argue, projections of expected behavior on the
outside based on inmates' attitudes and behavior on the inside are
often unrealistic. People do not act in a vacuum; they respond to
pressures emerging within a social context. Prison environments are
different from those to which inmates are accustomed and from those
they can expect once they are released. Each inmate's behavior will
be unique. Just as a "poor adjustment" to prison life cannot be a reliable indicator of poor chances for success in the real world, so a
"good adjustment" cannot be a reliable indicator of good chances for
success once a man is released from prison. The proponents of

confidentiality argue that since nothing of real value is gained by
sharing information about the inmate with the prison authorities, the
inmate should be promised privacy so he can risk opening up and engaging in introspection without fear that he is causing himself irre-
versible damage.

Therapy should be offered in prison with the acknowledged purpose of expanding self-awareness and stimulating personal problem
solving, and the authors believe this must be the private affair of the
inmate. Information revealed in therapy sessions must not be used
for the purpose of inmate evaluation, surveillance, fact-finding, or
interrogation. This means that staff persons in the college program
who are involved in the counseling and therapy phase of the program
must not perform student evaluations when such evaluations have a
bearing on release decisions.

SELECTING STUDENTS FOR PARTICIPATION IN
OUTSIDE PROGRAM

Programs that have a postrelease program must decide whether
all participants automatically should receive financial assistance to
attend college on the outside, or whether they should be selected on
the basis of certain criteria.

The implicit assumption underlying the choice to make assistance
automatic is that no distinction should be made between inside and
outside programs and that once an individual has been admitted into
the program inside the prison, no further decision is necessary. The
Pennsylvania and Oregon programs made this kind of assumption. The
decision to provide financial assistance to all students who are released established a policy whereby all are treated without distinction.

The New Mexico and Minnesota NewGate programs did not support
all their participants on the outside. They regarded the inside and
outside programs separately. Participants had to prove that they were
interested and able to perform well on campus while they were still in
prison. Program administrators in these two programs argued that
this forced the student to use his time profitably while inside the
prison. It not only impressed on students the fact that the program
had certain standards that had to be met but also engendered a sense
that the program was a privilege that must be earned rather than taken
for granted.

There is one subsidiary issue. The criteria used in these financial
support decisions can be either objective or subjective. In the New
Mexico program, certain objective requirements were established
that had to be met: certain minimum number of class hours completed,

a minimum grade point average (GPA), one semester of therapy, or such. The program thereby established a stepwise procedure, which all participants had the option to work through if they wished to qualify for advancement to the outside program.

The Minnesota NewGate program made these decisions by conducting subjective evaluations of its students' progress. The rationale for this practice was to control for persons who perform well academically and meet all the objective requirements but who, in the judgment of the administrators, did not respond to other facets of the college program such as counseling and therapy. These students, in the opinion of the administrators, would not use the outside program constructively and would be destructive to the program effort.

There are obvious dangers in making decisions (instead of automatic procedures) about whether to provide financial support to released students. The question takes on special significance in case the prison's decision to release inmates from prison depends on whether the program will provide support. Such is the case where there is a study-release program in which inmates can live and study in the community under limited custody conditions prior to parole. Such is also the case where the parole board requires the inmate to set up a "release plan" for his parole. Here a decision not to support a student on the outside automatically would postpone his release from prison.

If the basis for a decision that can so acutely affect a student's future is not clear to the student and he does not have explicit requirements set in advance that he knows he must meet, there can be (1) suspicion of favoritism and arbitrariness, (2) participants who are preoccupied with winning the personal favor of the instrumental decision makers, (3) conformity to what is believed to be the preferred posture, and (4) a program that leans in its decision making toward the more even-keeled and "sure" successes and avoids the "high risk but high gain" students.

In contrast, objective criteria, of which the participant is made aware when he enters the program, present him with a challenge and a reward toward which he can work. He is thereby given a way of testing himself, rallying and directing his energies and resources, and ultimately having the satisfaction of experiencing his own effectiveness. Rather than being made to feel as a hapless "victim" of forces beyond his control, he will be given the choice to exist as an "agent" with some control over his destiny. Of course, the student must be given the supportive framework he needs to fulfill successfully the standards used by the decision makers in their financial support decisions; otherwise the right to choose is purely illusionary.

Decisions to provide financial support to students in the post-release phase of a college program should be made on the basis of objective predetermined standards of performance, which all students have an equal chance to meet. This should give students maximum control over their lives and futures and a program that provides the framework within which they can learn to make choices and assume individual responsibility for the consequences. This type of selection process to the outside program should be coupled with an open admissions policy inside the prison, which permits all interested inmates an equal chance to try to meet the minimum requirements. This appears to be most consistent with the educational goals of the prison college program.

THE PROBLEM OF CHOOSING THE HOST
ACADEMIC INSTITUTION

In selecting the academic institution to host the outside phase of the college program, two major dilemmas must be confronted: (a) Is it better to send exconvicts recently released from prison as a group to one central location or to disperse them among numerous institutions? (b) If it is decided to send the inmates to one central location, should the institution be large/urban or small/rural, or large/rural or small/urban? Because of the relative isolation of some prisons, some inside college programs will not have many options when selecting an affiliated college; they will have to make do with what is available. Nonetheless, it is important to understand the implications of the possible choices.

One Central Location or Numerous Locations?

Two arguments can be made for selecting one college site. First, it is better for the participants. A large number of friends and associates can constitute a necessary socioemotional support base during the initial transition, in which the problems of fear and isolation are typically great. Freshmen entering college who come from stable and secure middle class families are usually apprehensive and disoriented when they first arrive on campus. Logically, it would seem to be even more true for persons who do not come from stable family backgrounds, who have just left highly structured and regimented prisons in which personal choice was extremely limited, and who are suddenly confronted by the prospects of an academic career for which they are not yet convinced they are wholly suited.

Second, the selection of one site enables the program to provide a more comprehensive postrelease support component. It is more economically efficient to centralize these facilities. Furthermore, because it wields more muscle by virtue of the larger number of participants on campus and the larger supply of program resources at its disposal, (tuition, student fees, paid program staff, high visibility, and such), the outside program potentially can wield greater influence in the institution's administrative circles. The program could be in a position to encourage the college to take steps to accommodate the special needs of exconvicts and other disadvantaged groups on campus.

There are also positive consequences of having more than one affiliated college. Being able to choose from among numerous academic institutions enables a participant to select an institution that most closely fits his personal needs and career plan. Moreover, it provides him an opportunity for anonymity if he wishes to no longer be identified with his convict past. Alone, a participant could become immersed in a student identity and achieve his goals on his own merits. As part of a group of exconvicts on campus, he might have to resist pressure from other members to preserve his exconvict identity; this could separate him from regular student life. Moreover, his higher visibility could make him a target of hostile persons and groups in the community. Another benefit of having numerous academic institutions from which to choose is geographical. Some programs will be composed of participants who come from diverse geographical areas and have intentions to return there after release. They should have as many options as possible.

College program participants should be concentrated on one or two nearby campuses and supported by an aftercare office. The experiences of the New Mexico and Ashland NewGate program participants demonstrated that students who are sent on their own to dispersed college campuses tend to drop out of school prematurely. In contrast, participants in the Oregon, Minnesota, and Pennsylvania NewGate programs, which had the benefit of a highly structured aftercare office on campus, on the average stayed in college longer and dealt with initial problems of adjustment more effectively.

Should the Host Institution be Large/Urban or Small/Rural, or Large/Rural or Small/Urban?

A large university provides a wide range of possible majors and career programs. It can therefore accommodate a group of exconvicts with a diverse set of interests. Moreover, if it is situated in an urban area, the student body presumably will be diversified with representation from low-income and minority groups. This will benefit the exconvict participants in that there will be other students with lifestyles with which they can identify. Also, there likely will be a number of special programs for the disadvantaged student in which the institution will be involved, such as the Educational Opportunity Plan (EOP), work-study, black studies, or Chicano studies. A program of exconvict education would appear to be integrated easily into this ongoing effort on campus.

There are at least two drawbacks in selecting a large/urban institution to host the outside phase of the program. The exconvict student could be overwhelmed by the vastness and impersonality of a large campus. In addition, if his search for companionship leads him to people from his former neighborhood, he is liable to come under old influences and fall into his former criminal routines.

Whereas a small/rural academic institution will isolate exconvict participants from previous sources of temptation and thus facilitate immersion into new student lifestyles, it can contain pressures which are equally debilitating. A large group of exconvicts will not be welcomed in a rural community. Parochial values are not congenial to persons who are different from local inhabitants or who have a history of deviance from society's prevailing norms. The heterogeneity of urban society has made its people much more accepting of differences; rural areas have not had to make these adjustments. Therefore exconvicts in the rural setting could be stigmatized and made targets for attack. Moreover, the small institution will not serve as a countervailing power base to the state correction system as effectively as a large academic institution. The only exception to this general rule might be a small college that is administratively tied into a statewide college system with great resources at its command.

Logically, in selecting a host academic institution, there are two other options: a large institution situated in a rural area or a small institution in an urban area. The large/rural institution combines the virtues of the large institution (which provides a diversity of resources and opportunities and serves as an effective countervailing power base in negotiations with the prison) with those of a rural setting, which isolates exconvicts from urban neighborhoods. Serving, however, to offset these advantages will be the aforementioned consequences of high visibility of exconvicts in a rural setting. In contrast with the small/rural institution though, the large/rural institution might enjoy some immunity from local pressure by virtue of its greater resources and its importance to the economic well-being of the area.

A small/urban college choice offers the typical benefits and liabilities of the urban setting. However, its small size will mean a scarcity of alternatives provided and thus rather specialized opportunities for a concentrated group of exconvict students. On the other hand, it will offer a campus atmosphere, which is more intimate and manageable than one on a larger campus.

Ideally, a prison college program should situate its outside program on a large/urban or large/rural campus, while also providing the option to its students of attending a small college nearby. The aftercare office could be set up to provide services to students on both campuses. The Oregon NewGate program did this satisfactorily by setting its main program near the University of Oregon campus (urban) and by having it also serve students who chose to attend Laney Junior College, also in Eugene. For those programs with limited options, the preferred order of desirability is as follows: (1) large/urban or large/rural, (2) small/urban, (3) small/rural.

WORK OBLIGATIONS OF RELEASED PARTICIPANTS

Should outside participants be expected to fulfill work obligations while they are attending school? The argument in favor states that exconvicts who appear to be "working themselves through college" will project a more favorable public image than those who appear to be "getting a free ride." This will help to develop external constituencies with a commitment to the program. Just as important, work obligations will bolster a participant's self-image. He will be helping to earn his own keep and will have some tangible proof of his own effectiveness. This will be essential to persons who have been kept in a dependent state in prison for a long time. Moreover, if his work obligation is on campus, under a work-study program, the participant will be provided an additional avenue for immersing himself in yet another facet of university life.

The argument against obligating exconvict students to work states that the student already has more pressures than he can handle effectively. He not only must make the personal adjustment to being a free individual just released from prison and the social adjustment of meeting and relating to other students with backgrounds and experiences vastly different from his own, but he also must negotiate the pressures of his academic studies, reading, taking tests, writing papers, laboratory reports, solving problems, and such. To require the student also to work for a certain period each week might make it impossible for him to succeed in school.

A related issue, if it is decided to require a student to work part-time, is whether this obligation should be imposed immediately or gradually. Those arguing for immediate assumption of responsibility minimize the seriousness of the other pressures right after release from prison and emphasize the importance of giving exconvicts a way to earn extra money to afford some luxuries, which program stipends do not provide. Those favoring a more gradual approach emphasize the other pressures and would rather see the program providing a larger budget for incidentals during the first period on campus.

Students in the program should have part-time jobs after a minimum period of adjustment on campus. These jobs should be related to the students' studies, such as teaching, tutoring, counseling, or research, thereby providing the participant relevant work experience and an opportunity to pursue his interests as other than a passive student. Released participants who were interviewed in the course of the study reported consistently that they had time for a part-time job after the initial period of adjustment, that the job provided them with money to cover essential incidental expenses, especially for social dating, and that some money in their pockets helped remove a barrier to a life on campus similar to that of other students.

CAMPUS HOUSING

Should program participants be required to reside in program housing for a stipulated time period after release? Participants on study-release are required by law to be under a minimum form of custody control until their parole dates. This is most realistically managed under some group housing arrangement. For persons released from prison on parole or as discharges, this is a different question.

Those arguing against such a requirement state that a parolee or dischargee should be rightfully on his own. Possibly one of his strongest desires is to not be part of any group living scene, especially with other exconvicts. In the outside phase, emphasis should be on the provision of supportive services to those in the program who, on their own volition, want to take advantage of them.

Proponents of the requirement feel that it is not asking too much of a participant to require him to stay in a residence house for a limited time. They emphasize the difficulties of transition, especially for persons who have been locked up for a long time. Many persons leaving prison have an inflated picture of life on the streets and an exaggerated notion of their own ability to cope with everyday problems. In addition, having never been to college, they have no understanding of the pressures with which the average student must deal. Proponents argue that the program's primary goal must be to build a structure around the released participant that will support him through a gradual transition to the real world. They add that a common problem is that many exconvicts have become dependent on the prison to provide them with their needs and thus are reluctant to leave the security of the program residence. These persons will benefit from the presence of other exconvicts who are anxious to get out on their own once their period of required residence is expired. The more independent thereby will provide a useful service to their more reluctant compatriots.

Released students on outside support should be required to live in a program residence house for a minumum period. The recommendation is based on the demonstrated need for a graduated transition from prison to life on the streets. However, the length of time required to stay in one transitionary stage, whether it be program resident house, study release status, parole, or such, must be made short and explicit to enable participants to calculate exactly how and when they can qualify to move to the next stage. There is evidence that unless the transition is so defined, the resulting indeterminacy will undermine whatever positive effects are derived from the gradual reentry into the rapid and demanding life on the streets. The experience of NewGate students in the Oregon residence house provides a case in point. Those released on study release were required by law to remain in the residence house until they received parole. The granting of parole could occur at any time in Oregon, leaving some NewGate participants in the study-release status for more than two years. Administrators, professors, and students alike on the University of Oregon campus maintained that study release served to separate exconvicts from the regular students on campus and over a long period of time prevented them from taking on a college student identity. Instead of smoothing their transition, it erected a definite barrier to their success. This is also true for parole if it is too long and/or indeterminate.

EXTERNAL PROGRAM RELATIONSHIPS

Up to this point the issues discussed have been concerned primarily with the structuring of the inside and outside college programs. Issues remain that concern the college program's relationships to the prison and to the university.

Program Staff's Hierarchical Relationship to
Prison Administration

The basic question is whether the college program staff should
be part of the prison authority hierarchy or in a semiautonomous
relationship as part of a parallel authority hierarchy. As part of the
prison authority hierarchy, the program staff is paid, supervised,
and evaluated by the prison administrators in superordinate positions
(Texas, Lompoc, Illinois, and Pennsylvania New View). In the typical
case the college program director is answerable to the superintendent
of education, the deputy warden of treatment, and the chief prison
warden. Under this structure the program's relationship to custody
concerns depends on the prison's internal balance of power and how
heavily it is weighted in the direction of the custody power block. In
every prison there is that tension between the custody and treatment
sections.

Wherever college programs are part of the prison hierarchy, the
extent to which they are allowed to retain the flexibility needed to
experiment and innovate and to run an education program without custody concerns obtruding is heavily dependent on the individual warden.
If the warden is committed fully to the ideals of the program, the
successful experiments in the college program (either teaching techniques, counseling, therapy, prerelease preparation, early release,
or postrelease opportunity and support) can be transmitted and transplanted to other phases of the prison operation with the endorsement
of the prison's top executive. This is a major advantage, which college programs that are part of the prison hierarchy enjoy over college
programs that are not. On the other hand, if the warden is hostile or
indifferent to the college program and there is no parallel to offset
the weight of the warden's office, the college program gradually will
be watered down and made to conform to custody concerns. The program, not the prison, will make the accommodations.

Even if the warden is fully supportive, there could be problems.
First, he can be subjected to the pressure from the powerful custody
interest group and will have to concede at least some of their demands.
Second, in the absence of institutionalized structural restraints, the
program will always be precarious at the time of succession when one
warden is replaced by another. This is what happened in the Illinois
college program when Warden Ross Randolph left and was replaced by
a man with no interest in the college program (see the Illinois case
study in the Appendix).

As part of a parallel hierarchy not directly answerable to the
prison administration, the college program is receiving part or all its
funds from an outside source (federal or state, public or private). It

is also supervised and evaluated by this outside source. The prime advantage of this structure is to enable the program to reach beyond the prison's limited resources allocated for education and to tap those institutions that have the resources and expertise: the university. This structure also offers the program a potential for generating and pyramiding a base of outside influence as a counterweight to the power and ideology of the corrections system.

But, there are clear disadvantages. Operating semiautonomously in a prison bureaucracy, which is perhaps one of the most rigid and all-inclusive establishments in our society, tensions are inevitable. Feelings of distrust and antagonism will be generated automatically among prison personnel who will be afraid, and rightfully so, that when the college program is run by outsiders, the prison's internal balance of power is threatened to be altered. In this kind of atmosphere of apprehension and antagonism, it will be difficult for the college program to provide an impetus for changes in other parts of the prison. There will be a lack of receptivity. Moreover, it could be difficult to survive without eventually being taken over. This is true especially where the program functioning as a parallel hierarchy operates with funds that are not permanently reliable, such as OEO support.

A college program in prison must have as its first priority developing its capacity to provide its inmate-students a quality education. To do so it must be part of a parallel authority hierarchy that has links with a university system, which lends its resources and expertise to the educational efforts inside the prison. The programs in the sample which were part of a parallel authority hierarchy and maintained close ties with the university were more successful in achieving their educational goals (according to the evaluative criteria of the study and the opinions of a comparative sample of participants) than programs that were from their inception part of the prison authority hierarchy. The repercussions inside the prison that follow from the program being part of a parallel rather than the prison hierarchy must be dealt with by other strategies. The educational goals of the program, however, must not be sacrificed.

The existence of parallel authority hierarchies will present problems inside the prison. A division of roles will have to be defined as well as outlining points of coordination that facilitate peaceful integration of efforts inside the prison. In the course of this study it was observed that it is not easy for a college program with outside ties to define its role to other aspects of the prison operation. One dilemma is the extent to which the program should insulate itself from the rest of the prison. Another is the extent to which the program participants should be separated from the nonparticipant inmate population. Both are discussed below.

Insularity or Fusion

Should the college program operations be insulated from or fused
with the prison routine? In colleges in civil society, the student world
is constructed by design to be relatively isolated from distracting influences and temptations in the outside world. Almost every activity
in which the student is involved during this time represents a break
with the familiar past and reinforces the new student role. This is
consistent with other institutions that attempt to change or resocialize
a recruit. Total immersion in a new lifestyle is regarded as an effective strategy, whether the recruit is entering the monastery, a mental
institution, a prison, the army, a revolutionary political party, or
any other enterprise attempting to inculcate a new way of life. The
degree of impact college programs in prison will have on their students
will also vary with their ability to cut students off from past commitments and from interests and loyalties outside the program.

Program insularity is justified on another level. It enables program directors to organize internal relationships exclusively in the
interests of the program's own goals and priorities. Such autonomy
provides the program the opportunity to innovate and experiment at
its own pace free from constant scrutiny and interference from outside
interests. Again, programs and institutions other than the prison
college programs recognize and pursue this need for insulation, albeit
at certain times more than at others. Because the college program is
attempting to operate within the context of a total institution, which
has historically been in total control over the activities inside its
walls, the program must expect an abnormal amount of external pressure. The prison will attempt to impose both its authority and operating ideology onto the new program. Strategies of insulation are
highly desirable to protect program integrity.

Building insularity is motivated in the prison context by still
another reason: to preserve a separate identity. Convicts have a basic
distrust of persons working for the prison, a deep-seated suspicion of
bureaucratic practice, and a cynicism about treatment programs that
are part of the prison rehabilitative process. The college program
inside the prison walls will, from the outset, be suspect. It will be
run by persons who have authority over convicts and who may be
working for the prison. It will, to varying extents, elaborate its own
bureaucratic systems and necessarily will be enmeshed in the bureaucracy of the prison administration. Moreover, it will be a treatment
program inasmuch as one of its more explicit goals is to change the
convict participants. Its very existence in the prison will render it a
more or less recognized part of the prison's rehabilitative process.
Insulation is one strategy that will encourage the participants to

distinguish the program and its personnel from the usual prison routine and prison staff and, thus, prevent automatic "contamination by association."

As tempting as it is to try to insulate the college program, there are definite risks involved when operating in the prison context. It is clear that although a move toward insulation is effective in the short run, it creates problems that threaten to undermine the program's long run effectiveness. In the first place, it denies the prison the full benefit of its services, especially with respect to the prison's other educational programs. Second, by shutting itself off from external relationships, the program will shroud itself in an aura of mystery. The unknown will cause alienation and fear among other prison personnel. Once the college program staff encounters the suspicion of the others they, too, will retreat from closer relationships. This will encourage a deepening of the chasm between the "good guys" and the "bad guys," which will result in intensifying the resentment and competition between two clearly defined camps. Because there has been no self-conscious attempt to establish personal and program links with other facets of the prison, there will be an absence of cross-cutting loyalties, which work to mute conflict. Under these conditions the prison will not develop a commitment to supporting the college program.

Complete fusion between the college program and the rest of the prison operations is no solution either. Experience shows that a program that has no separate identity or autonomy in decision making offers no hope for the development of a vital college atmosphere. Inmates will neither be given a real college education nor an opportunity to experiment with a new identity and lifestyle. Clearly, this type of college program will eliminate the possibility of serious conflict inside the prison, which undoubtedly helps to ensure the program's survival. However, the college program allowed to exist unchallenged and unthreatened might be of little worth. It might have reached a point where it is questionable whether some program is any better than no program at all.

A semiautonomous college program should be developed as a way out of the dilemma between the extremes of complete fusion and complete insularity. Of course, this program will not eliminate the source of friction within the prison. However, this is not bad in itself. Most prisons have stagnated precisely because over the years they have eliminated all sources of internal disagreement. In the course of the study it appeared that certain college programs can help rejuvenate some of these tired and unimaginative institutions. Friction need not spell imminent disaster. On the contrary, with imagination and foresight on the part of all concerned, it can spell exciting opportunity for constructive change.

There are definite areas of autonomy that must be extended to the college program. However, the resulting disruption can be minimized by pursuing two separate strategies. First, areas of potential conflict can be narrowed by agreement. Second, the prison administration can be compensated for its losses in delegated authority to a semi-autonomous program by providing it with new unexpected benefits: a richer, fuller college program for its inmates.

The areas of autonomy that should be preserved are the following:

(1) The college program should have the freedom to innovate within the realm of the program's educational enterprise. The program personnel must have and must be recognized as having authoritative expertise in their professional areas, and they must be immune from interference from those who do not.

(2) Custody and security staff cannot be permitted unobstructed entry into the college program. They must clear their intended interventions with the college program staff. Certain ground rules have to be established, which at once preserve internal security and at the same time eliminate unnecessary restrictions, which only deny the inmate the opportunity of immersing himself in a meaningful college experience.

(3) The college program should be given a degree of visible structural separation from the rest of the prison. This will prevent the close identification with the prison that contaminates the education program in the eyes of the inmates. This separation may be achieved by (a) separate funding, (b) ongoing university ties, or (c) separate physical facilities.

(4) The college program should have the freedom to relate to and mobilize the assistance of cultural, social, political, and economic resources and facilities outside the prison, for example, the university, volunteers, private foundations, additional funding agencies, art commissions, or such. With these on tap, the college program will be able to expand and diversify the program as well as involve the community in a social problem they have heretofore avoided.

Some ways in which the possible range of conflict can be narrowed by agreement are as follows:

(1) The college program staff should agree to refrain from interfering with custody matters when they do not directly involve the inmate's life as a student. This should be made in exchange for the promise that custody and security personnel respect the bailiwick of the college program staff by clearing their concerns over such matters with it before dealing directly with the students.

(2) The indeterminacy of release to the outside college program should be eliminated to prevent the political machinations between prison and program staff that serve to exacerbate tensions and cause bad feeling. This would also reduce tension within the program that would enhance the program.

Some ways of offsetting losses by extending unexpected benefits are as follows:

(1) Involve the college program in the total educational enterprise of the prison: including GED, Adult Basic Education (ABE), or vocational training. College students can serve as instructors and/or tutors and thereby increase the resources available to inmates at lower educational levels. This will enrich the academic atmosphere in the entire prison by extending interest and involvement beyond the college elites.

(2) Create an open admissions policy to a college education program, coupled with outreach and college preparatory components. The program must develop the capacity to accommodate everyone who potentially can meet the requirements. This will provide a program fit for more than just the cream of the inmate population and capable of stimulating significant changes in people's goals, values, interests, and perspectives.

(3) Create academic courses and programs designed for prison staff to advance them in knowledge, skills, and job and pay classifications. In mobilizing these kinds of external educational resources, the program can "turn on" the prison staff to education and further legitimize the new emphasis on educating inmates. It will also contribute to muting the valid criticisms by custody staff that free college education is given to prison inmates, while it is not free for them and their families. Expanded opportunities at the university should also be made available.

(4) Activities generated by the college program initially to benefit its students should be extended to benefit nonparticipating students, for example, art and drama programs, outside speakers and lectures, and field trips.

(5) Program staff should be involved in trying to develop external contacts, which would be capable of generating different but comparable programs for inmates not interested in college. The prison must be encouraged to take advantage of outside contacts beyond the college program. If no further effort is made, the college program, which benefits a relatively small segment of the population, will continue as a source of inequity and injustice in connection with those not involved.

(6) Staff should become involved in other prison activities as well. Insights and experiments in the counseling efforts should be shared

and exchanged with the prison counseling activities. Efforts at job
development and job placement must also be coordinated with other
offices that maintain an ongoing interest.

(7) College program staff must develop personal and informal
ties with the prison staff. Both staffs, if they establish a basis of
trust and understanding, can learn from one another and thereby take
a more positive step in correctional reform than either staff would
be in isolation.

Elitism versus Egalitarianism

How should college program participants relate to nonparticipants
in the general prison population? Should they be treated differently
or similarly? By separating program participants from nonparticipants, the college program will remove the new recruit from the
pressures of the convict code and subculture and will have maximum
impact on him as a student. Separation can be physical, as in housing
all college students in separate facilities; or it can be in the form of
special privileges afforded a distinct status group.

Separation will provide greater opportunity to develop the consciousness of a common identity and a group esprit de corps. Rather
than as an aggregate of separate individuals, college students will
confront and negotiate the new challenges offered by the program as
a cohesive group. Each individual will be stronger and more effective
with the emotional and technical support of the group behing him.

As a negative consequence, separation can lead to elitism and
exclusivism. The extra privileges provided inmates attending school
inside the program can be interpreted by the participants as evidence
of their superiority, innate or earned. From their more privileged
vantage point, they well might see inmates who are differently situated
as less endowed and less deserving. This sense of superiority will
cause the division between college participants and nonparticipants,
which will prevent the program from reaching and extending its benefits beyond the current participant group. Nonparticipants will not be
receptive to people who think they are superior; and they will be reluctant to apply for the program, either because they do not want to
separate themselves from fellow inmates in the prison yard, who might
not be equipped or interested in going to college, or because they feel
different from the dominant student group in the program and anticipate
being rejected by it. The homogeneity of the student group, which
results from such a self-selective process, will not be good for the
program. Diversity and contrast are needed to shake complacency
and to promote a full examination of a wide range of alternatives.

Homogeneity also will jeopardize the program's position in the prison
context. It is almost inevitable that it will represent and, thereby,
reinforce a division along class and ethnic lines. Race and class
privilege are already highly sensitive issues among prison populations,
and a college program that provides evidence of this will become a
source of discord.

A program that grants the college student no special privileges
will be more egalitarian and, as a result, will cause less resentment
on the part of other inmates or prison personnel. Yet because some
privileges generally accorded the participants are functional to the
student role (for example, exceptions to lights out in cells, library
privileges, or contact with outsiders), their absence will constitute
obstacles and, thus, sources of discouragement. As a result, attending the inside college program might be seen by inmates as an undesirable way of doing time in prison. The pool of potential recruits
will, in this case, be small; and, thus, the potential impact of the
college program is slight.

Division and resentment between program participants and nonparticipating inmates can be broken down partially if (1) extra privileges granted inmate-students are only those that are functionally
required by the student role, (2) inmate-students are assigned a regular formal role providing education and perhaps other services to
nonparticipants, (3) the college program adheres to a deliberate and
highly visible policy of recruiting persons from all class and ethnic
backgrounds, (4) if necessary, the program contrives a balance by
making special provisions to assist persons who do not meet all qual-
ifications at the outset, and (5) the prison develops comparable opportunities for nonparticipants.

Program's Involvement in Release Decisions

The basic question is whether the college program should be
involved in the decision to release the inmate from prison. Proponents of program involvement in these decisions argue that the college program staff, by advocating on behalf of the inmate participants,
can help to protect interests that have no power or legitimacy of their
own in the prison context. In this sense the program, in associating
with the inmate students, introduces a countervailing power source
into correctional decision making—making it more pluralistic and
thus more democratic. The substance of the program staff's input is
based on information recorded by persons who have seen the convict
in question from an entirely different perspective (in the school setting),
which is different from the typical prison setting in which he necessarily

acts differently. Thus, it is argued, the program helps by providing more complete information, which will instruct more adequately the ultimate decision makers.

The program staff sees on a daily basis persons who in its judgment should not be kept in prison any longer. If there is any way to secure a shorter time to serve, such as in states that give indeterminate sentencing and/or offer transitional programs, which provide for community release prior to parole date, the program staff feels morally obliged to make sure those who warrant it secure an early release. When they are successful they feel that they are reducing, at least for some, the regressive and stultifying effects of incarceration, which work as obstacles to successful transition to life in the free society. These debilitating forces have less time to take effect when these inmates are able to serve what is, in effect, a shorter sentence.

Those who argue against a program getting involved in these judicial decisions argue on four different levels. In the first place, the college program staff is perpetuating the practice of keeping an inmate's length of sentence indeterminate. Indeterminacy is objectionable because it places the prison administration, the parole board, and now the college program staff in the same role as the judge who determines the initial sentence. The basic difference is that the prisoner has no due process rights or opportunities to contest decisions he believes made arbitrarily or on the basis of personal grudges or dislikes. This is totally unjust.

Second, these decisions will be invalid and unreliable, even if the decisions are based on considered projections of the possibilities for an inmate's "successful adjustment" after release. They are stabs in the dark. No one has demonstrated to anyone's satisfaction that there is a valid and reliable formula for projecting which inmates will be "successful" or "unsuccessful."

The third basic issue concerning the college program's involvement in release decisions is the effect their intervention has on the inmates who are not recommended. By advocating for certain program participants, only the favored will enjoy the advantages of greater leverage. Others who do not impress the program staff, especially those who do not even participate in the college program, are, in effect, discriminated against and could serve longer for the same offense, or even for a less serious one.

The fourth argument against involvement by the college program in release decisions is that it does harm to the inmate student and to the college program itself. Inmate students are denied the freedom to enter the college program with sincerity. "Posturing" becomes more important to the inmate than does an honest personal assessment of his own progress. Participants cannot afford to avoid "shuck and jive;" that is, display behavior and motives intended to influence program staff and ultimately to manipulate decisions in release and disciplinary matters. If the inmate does not posture, he risks being overlooked; someone equally qualified will be given a release before he is.

Preoccupation with release functions will interfere with progress in both areas of academic performance and personal development. The anxiety that results from the "indeterminacy" in the length of his sentence will interfere with his making and sticking to a realistic study schedule. Also, achievement will be valued as an extrinsic means of moving closer to release, rather than as a source of personal gratification and a measure of intrinsic worth. Moreover, since early release depends on "every man for himself," learning will not be an enterprise in which all students are cooperative and supportive. This invaluable learning device also could be lost.

The program staff members inadvertently could ignore their responsibilities toward the academic and counseling phases of the program if they are involved deeply in the release function. Furthermore, because of the inevitable frustration that results from engaging in political machinations in the prison bureaucracy, especially when operating from a relatively powerless position, the program staff is likely to become disillusioned and dissatisfied. This negative spirit would pervade the college program and distract it from its primary purpose. This was strikingly evident in the Oregon NewGate program. Individual staff members became apologetic for their impotence in the face of the prison administration and, thereby, put themselves in a position to be manipulated even more effectively than before by the students eager to secure early release.

A program involved in the release function will try to make a case before the prison authorities for giving their recommendations increasingly greater weight. As a result, the program will develop a heavy emphasis on "success" measured in terms of low recidivism rates. This will lead to tailoring the program to favor sure successes, thereby narrowing the scope of the program to control for uncertainty and to avoid taking risks. This insures disaster for the quality of the program.

The program's relationship with other facets of the prison also will be hurt by its involvement in release decisions. In the first place, tension will emerge between program staff and prison functionaries over contradictory recommendations regarding inmates' release plans. Second, because the program staff makes recommendations, their critics will hold them personally responsible for the program's "failures." The latter will be used to evaluate the worth of the college program. Thirdly, the credibility of the college program will suffer from what appears to outsiders as a preoccupation on the part of the program staff and participants to get inmates a quicker release from prison. Insiders will see it as unwarranted interference by persons who are neophytes to the correctional enterprise, who are being "conned" by insincere inmates looking for a quick way out.

College programs should not intervene in release decisions. Prison terms should be set at the time of sentencing by the courts when persons affected can appeal. If the growing feeling is that prison terms should be shorter, then they should be shorter for all inmates and not just for some in the college program. Inmates should all qualify automatically for some type of transitional release when they have served a previously agreed period (work- or study-release) without the need for program staff intervention. In prison systems where this is not a matter of policy, the college programs should exert their influence to change procedure rather than to approach the problem on a piecemeal basis, serving special people special advantages.

The Nature of the Program's Structural Relationship to the University

Should the university be tapped only as an educational resource, or one integrally involved in the planning, administering, and governing functions of the prison college program? The programs in the study sample fall into three categories. They are either part of (1) the prison hierarchy (Texas, Illinois, Lompoc, and Pennsylvania New View), (2) a third-force parallel hierarchy with only some functional ties with the university (Oregon and Ashland NewGates), or (3) a parallel hierarchy as an integral part of the university's administrative structure (New Mexico, Minnesota, and Pennsylvania's Phase I NewGates).

Programs operating as part of the prison hierarchy have argued that the universities should be tapped mainly as sources of instructors and courses. In effect, they have chosen to discourage active involvement by instructors and the universities and trade the consequent loss in vitality for the greater security and less disruption in routine that results from circumscribing the activities of outsiders.

Programs that pursue the third force strategy defend their ability to enlist the involvement of instructors and educational materials of their choice. Within the confines of the program's quarters their autonomy in decision making is respected without being buried either in the prison or the university bureaucracies. They can bring the best of both worlds together in a combination that proves through experimentation to be the best under the circumstances. While these third-force programs have provided an educational experience superior to that provided by the programs in the first category (according to both the participants in the respective programs and the criteria used in the study), they have not developed an ongoing and lasting commitment from university systems. What involvement the university has had is a result of the initiative taken by the college program directors. The university's structural relationship to the program gives it no authority or responsibility to even take the initiative on its own. One result has been the failure of these programs (Ashland and Oregon) to get the university to provide program funding once OEO funds dry up.

The third possible strategy for involving the university is to make it a permanent part of the planning, administrative, and governing structure of the college program. It already has been suggested that the university has resources that are essential to the quality and survival of a college program operating in the prison context. Proponents of the third strategy go further by arguing that prison college programs must be the prime responsibility of a university because they are immediately relevant to its doctrinal purpose. The university's involvement is essential to its fulfilling its obligation to all persons interested in obtaining a college education. Bringing higher education to persons beyond the college campus is an increasingly acknowledged commitment of universities. There have been recent efforts to enlarge the scope of departments of continuing education in many states throughout the country. Second, universities must acknowledge their responsibilities to grapple with contemporary social problems and, to do so, build links with new institutions, social groups, and individuals in society. Prisons and correctional reform are relevant subjects for university concern, not just for departments of law enforcement and corrections but also for the full spectrum of academic disciplines.

Universities should share with the prison in the planning, administrative, and governing functions of the prison college program. This is required before its sense of commitment and responsibility can be secured permanently. Only the programs in the third category were able to build a comparatively high quality education program while also showing a promise of generating the support needed to continue to function. The only exception to this rule was the Pennsylvania program, which was taken over by the prison but continued to preserve its ability to achieve its educational goals. However, there was evidence that even this program was losing its vitality, with the resulting decrease in quality. Furthermore, its fine record was largely due to the warden's commitment to the college program and the fact that the program was directly under his leadership. But this is a precarious situation. As the case of the Menard program so dramatically shows, heavy reliance on the individual who is warden leaves it unprotected when the warden is succeeded by a new man. Reliance on personalities is no substitute for instituting a mechanism that ensures responsibility will continue to be taken by the university no matter who the individuals involved are, either at the prison or the university.

One mechanism that can perform these tasks is a governing board of directors, on which the various parties have a division of well-defined individual responsibilities but together share the joint responsibility for the success of the whole enterprise. This board should be composed of persons from the prison and from various parts of the university. A typical board might consist of

> the prison superintendent;
> the director of treatment;
> a representative from the parole department;
> the university president;
> a representative from the office of dean of students, the office
>   of admissions and financial aid, or other such office;
> a representative from the academic faculty;
> an elected representative of the university student body; and
> an elected representative of the program's participant group.

Ideally, the prison superintendent and the university president would be cochairmen, and the board would meet at least once a month. The board as a whole would have the responsibility of hiring and, once a year, evaluating the program director. It would decide all major policy questions. The university's responsibilities would consist of

> putting together the curriculum,
> obtaining instructors,
> establishing and enforcing admission standards,
> maintaining performance standards,
> issuing credits and recording grades,
> organizing extracurricular and cultural activities for inside
>   students and other prison inmates,
> recruiting the program director, and
> supplying books and instructional materials.

The prison officials' responsibilities would consist of

> providing all qualified inmates access to the program,
> making whatever release decisions have to be made,
> establishing necessary security precautions, and
> integrating the college program with the entire educational
>   enterprise inside the program.

In this chapter we have identified and discussed the most critical issues confronting those who develop and operate college programs in prisons. Although these observations were based specifically on college programs, the lessons have much broader applicability. Most are directly relevant to the proper structuring of all types of education programs that operate in the prison context—elementary, secondary, vocational, technical, or baccalaureate.

NOTES

1. The conceptualization presented here is taken from Thomas A. Harris, I'm Okay, You're Okay: A Practical Guide to Transactional Analysis (New York: Harper and Row, 1967). Though he does not deal with the issue of mandatory versus voluntary therapy, he indirectly offers a rationale for making it mandatory.

2. For an interesting and thorough elaboration of the position against mandatory therapy see Nicholas N. Kittrie, "The Right To Be Different: Deviance and Enforced Therapy" (Baltimore: Penguin Books, Inc., 1973).

9

The study of Project NewGate and other prison college programs attempted to determine the nature and extent of the impact of program participation on postprison experience. Some of the analytical operations did not produce findings that were definitive. The lack of decisiveness was a result of both the great complexity of the phenomena that were being studied and some methodological problems inherent in the original research design. Despite these difficulties and the fact that many questions must remain unanswered, this study reveals some clear and positive relationships between prison college programs and success among participants after release from prison. Also revealed are very definite conclusions about what type of prison college programs are most appropriate to the needs of prison inmates and have the greatest impact on participants' postprison success. Not surprisingly, these clearer relationships are discernible, where it is possible to minimize the complexity of the relationships being tested, that is, by reducing the influence of intervening variables and where comparable data are available at successive time intervals allowing for measurement of change. The findings and their implications for a model prison college program are briefly summarized here.

Though the study began with a conception of postprison success broader than recidivism (operationally defined as return to lock-up), there was, nevertheless, an attempt to measure the exprisoners in the study samples on this dimension. The results of this part of the analysis are unsatisfying, however. No consistent differentiations among groups on relative scores appear that would suggest relationships either to the participants' program experiences or their background characteristics. At first glance some may interpret these data as indicating that participation in a prison college program has no bearing on whether a participant will recidivate. However, this would be a hasty conclusion and one too often made in studies of this kind. Although it may be valid to say that no relationship has been demonstrated one way or another, one must keep in mind that participation in prison college programs could have an impact on its participants' behavior and attitudes, but one which either is not measured or is being offset or obscured by the impact of other yet unidentified variables.

Clearly one problem in the analysis of program impact on recidivism is a lack of sufficient methodological sophistication. This is a problem this study has in common with other studies of human behavior, brought on by the obvious intricacies of human response and the enormous difficulties of identifying and controlling for intervening environmental variables. However, there is an additional problem inherent in the current analytical task. The causal links, which must be hypothesized between college program participation and the ultimate decision to return or not to return an exprisoner to lock-up, are numerous. As a general proposition, the longer this sequence of links is, the more difficult it is to make a strong causal argument. This was demonstrated by the finding that the Minnesota NewGate participants had a higher recidivism rate than the Minnesota control group, despite the fact that the latter had reported to the research staff a higher rate of involvement in criminal activity. Why did the Minnesota NewGate group show a higher rate of return to lock-up? Was it because, as a group, the members were more easily identifiable? Did the parole department's policy toward the group determine differential detection and reporting, or was there greater and more effective law enforcement in the areas in which NewGate participants resided? These possible factors are not suggested to imply that any one is more important than another in accounting for different rates of recidivism. Neither are they suggested to imply that external forces are more important than the actions of the individual exoffenders, that is, that the latter are hapless victims of the vagaries of circumstance. What should be clear is that a group's "success" is dependent on both its members' actions and different environmental factors beyond their control. What defies the researcher in measuring program impact is being able to identify and assign the relative importance of all the variables impinging on the outcome of the exprisoners' experiences. And this is a most difficult undertaking.

Two additional outcome measures, other than recidivism, were defined in this study in the attempt to measure the impact of prison college programs. "Achieving stability" and "realizing life goals" were defined in hopes that possible gains made in other aspects of the exprisoner's life could be isolated. However, again a comparison of programs did not reveal a consistent differentiation among participants on relative success. Of course, there was no way of separating

and controlling for recidivism in conducting the analysis of these two
additional dimensions. An exprisoner's ability to score well depended
on his life not being interrupted by a return to lock-up. In addition,
the analysis was encumbered by the fact that persons in the sample
had been out of prison for different lengths of time when they were
interviewed. Persons out just a matter of months realistically could
not be compared with persons who had been out for years on how
successful they were in "achieving stability" and "realizing life goals."
In the recidivism analysis the different times out also presented a
similar methodological problem. No distinctions were made about
the participants' relative success: between a person who was returned
to lock-up, for example, after three months out and a person who was
returned after three years of not being locked up.

One of the accomplishments of the analysis was the combining of
the three separate dimensions—recidivism, achieving stability, and
realizing life goals—into one composite score, which was weighted to
reflect the differences in time out of prison. Recidivism was defined
as a greater failure, that is, assigned a lower score, the sooner after
release a man was returned to lock-up. In contrast, a man was scored
higher on realizing life goals the longer the period he had remained
in the community. However, despite the fact that this was a more
refined measure than the component scores, the relative success of
each group on the combined measure showed no greater differentiation
than did the scores taken individually. If relationships exist, they were
obscured by the complexity of the methodological enterprise. It should
be recalled that the new composite score still contained recidivism
data, and all the problems that they imply.

In an effort to reduce the methodological complexities we began
to look at hypothetical relationships, which implied shorter causal
sequences and for which good pre- and postdata existed. Note that the
data we used to measure recidivism, achieving stability, and realizing
life goals were outcome data; no account was taken of comparable information for time periods prior to contact with the prison college
program. Actually, our ability to measure change over time was always limited by the original structure of the study. Instead of implementing a longitudinal study, which would have permitted measurement
of student performance at regular intervals, we had to form a snapshot
at a fixed point in time.* In a few instances, useful historical data
could be retrieved from past records; but for the most part such data
had to be gathered from participants, retrospectively.

---

*Recall that even the inside participant and follow-up samples were
composed of entirely different persons, instead of studying one group
at two different points in time.

Certain aspects of the participants' experiences, which had been computed as part of the different success dimensions, were separated out and analyzed discretely. Here advantage was taken of some of the few areas in which good pre- and postdata existed. The results of these analytical operations revealed consistent relationships between program participation and postprison experience.

One area in which there was a significant change among participants that logically can be attributed to program impact is in the decreasing use of drugs and alcohol. The percentage of persons in each participant group with drinking or drug problems following release was lower than the corresponding percentages with prior drinking or drug problems. And, there was a greater drop for each NewGate participant group than for the comparison group at the same site.

Another area in which we obtained pre- and postinformation was in regard to changes in occupational goals. Participants in all programs raised their occupational aspirations after entering the program, and there was a larger increase in occupational aspirations among NewGate than among non-NewGate participants.

Data on occupational achievement were also analyzed by comparing jobs prior to prison to ones those persons had after prison. Excluding from the analysis those persons who were students or unemployed at the time of the interview, the data showed an increase in occupational level after participation in the college program. Again, the NewGate programs showed a greater increase than the non-NewGate programs, demonstrating a greater impact.

The analysis of the prison college programs on the dimension of academic achievement revealed perhaps the most dramatic findings. Academic achievement was measured on five dimensions: (1) change in educational goals, (2) college enrollment, (3) number of semesters completed since release from prison, (4) grades achieved since release, and (5) overall academic achievement. The data showed that the NewGate programs especially made an impact on their participants' academic success. There is no question that these programs proved to be highly effective vehicles for facilitating academic achievement among high school drop-outs from socially and economically disadvantaged backgrounds. The NewGate program participants at the time they entered the program were not the "cream" of the prison population. Few had previous involvement in college, and the mean educational level and tested grade level for the program participants was comparable with that for the general prison population. The Oregon and Pennslyvania groups are, for example, attending college and obtaining postsecondary degrees at a rate comparable with that of an average segment of the population in civil society. This ability of NewGate programs to overcome class disadvantage is most dramatic and has implications for educating the disadvantaged that go well beyond the realm of prison education.

The data are remarkably clear about what constitutes the best and most effective prison college program. In the first place, the research staff as well as the program participants themselves indicated consistently the superiority of the NewGate model in their evaluations of college programs. Second, the impact data revealed that NewGate programs have the greatest potential to change the program participants. Even though the Lompoc and Illinois participant groups ranked high on certain aspects of success, it appears that these outcomes often were not attributable to program participation. These programs were more passive, and there is reason to believe that the participants would have achieved similar outcomes with or without the benefit of the prison college programs of which they were a part.

Four features of a prison college program must be implemented to offer quality education and to make an impact on prison inmates: (1) active outreach and remedial components, which will attract and support prisoners who would not otherwise attend college; (2) the existence of activities and services outside the classroom offered as part of the college program; (3) a sequence of transitional components, which continue to provide support, financial and other, to participants after they leave prison; and (4) integral involvement in program activities of a strongly committed and independent college or university, which also provides a congenial campus for students after release. These features clearly differentiate between more or less effective programs. Their importance in providing prison inmates a real opportunity to choose an alternative lifestyle cannot be overplayed. The data show that once inmates receive this initial assistance, they are more likely to continue with their higher education and achieve a greater return on the financial investment made in them.

PROJECT CASE STUDIES

The case studies of the eight programs in the sample as they were operating at the time of the study are presented here. Primary attention is focused on the most important issues in prison college education programs. An attempt also has been made to discuss the changes that have occurred over time, although these historical references are brief and general. Many programs were in existence for four or five years but were observed for only nine months. The record of changes that took place outside this period were based on restrospective observations of interviewees and were often sketchy and impressionistic. A second reason for keeping historical references general was to be consistent with the purposes of the analysis, which was interested only in documenting major changes, which made a significant change in emphasis and effect on the overall program. In this way, programmatic changes were isolated, and the factors that appeared to account for them were described.

Each case study concludes with a discussion of the extent to which the program was successful in three dimensions: (1) Did it provide a college program that enabled the participants to achieve their educational goals? (2) Did the program have a significant impact on its environment? (3) Did the program survive without losing its essential features? The case histories of the NewGate Projects are presented first, followed by the non-NewGate programs.

NEWGATE

Oregon

The Oregon NewGate program's inside component was in the Oregon State Penitentiary, the principal of three correctional facilities in the state; it received most male convicted felons. The other facilities were the Oregon State Correctional Institution, a medium-security prison, which confined about 475 younger first offenders, and the Oregon Women's Correctional Center, which received all

females in the state and some women from the federal prison system
and the state of Idaho under special arrangement. All three facilities
are located in Salem, the state capital.

The physical facilities of the Oregon State Penitentiary are old
and awesome, originally constructed in 1866 and relatively unaltered
since then. Following a traditional maximum security design, the
23-acre site is surrounded by a 25-foot high reinforced concrete wall
marked with numerous gun-towers.

The institution's functional capacity is 1,250 inmates, but the
usual population is about 1,000. The penitentiary historically has
emphasized industrial work as opposed to agriculture. About 30
percent of the inmate population was involved in industry, with most
of the others assigned jobs required to maintain and operate the institution. Until recently, there was no significant commitment to formal
training or education. Vocational-technical programs have been minimal. What leisure time or educational programs have existed relied
mainly on volunteers from outside.[1]

Recent history of the Oregon State Penitentiary is dated as "prior
to" or "since" the riot. On March 9, 1968, the most serious incident
in the more than 100-year history of the institution took place. There
was a "rampage of arson, theft, vandalism and general destruction
of property which enveloped the housing units, culinary department,
canteen, hospital and shop area."[2] The riot lasted 15 hours, hostages
were taken, and hundreds of inmates became involved. The riot had
a profound effect on the operation of the Oregon corrections system.
By coincidence, a new warden was appointed during the riot. His
predecessor, whose reign had been characterized by stringent rules
and tight discipline with emphasis on punishment and control, had
retired a few days before the riot. The new warden began a more enlightened course in tune with changes occurring elsewhere in the country. Among the changes instituted after the 1968 riot were the development of a wider variety of programs directed toward self-improvement
and leisure; a systematic replacement of many of the "old guard" by
younger and better trained persons; a reorganization of the administrative staff designed to reduce the former custody-treatment schism;
a remodeling of the facilities, including rebuilding many structures
that had been destroyed by the fire; the construction of a more elaborate vocational training facility; and the implementation of a more
relaxed policy on visiting and correspondence. The number of corre-
spondents is now unlimited and outgoing mail is randomly censored.

Aside from attempting to make the penitentiary more responsive
to inmate needs, the other major change since the riot in 1968 has
been a shift toward community-based transitional programs, consisting of graduated opportunities while in prison for assignment to
work details outside the walls, for participation in group activities in

the outside community, and for obtaining short term home furloughs. Finally there are transfers to facilities outside the walls (the Annex, or farm dormitory, and the Forestry Camp), work- or study-release under minimal custody, and, ultimately, parole and discharge.

NewGate: Phase I

The NewGate college program has been operating in the Oregon State Penitentiary for almost six years. During this time it has gone through many changes. To capture the most significant ones, the description below is divided into two parts (Phase I and Phase II), corresponding to the incumbencies of the project's two directors. Phase I illustrates the problems and possibilities a new program experiences in the initial period of experimentation and innovation. Phase II illustrates what happens as a program becomes institutionalized.

The Oregon NewGate Program began as the Upward Bound Oregon Prison Project (UBOPP) on March 17, 1967. It was a novel approach to providing college education to convicts and became the model for NewGate programs implemented in other parts of the country. As originally conceived by Thomas E. Gaddis,* the first project director in Oregon, a college program for convicts had to simulate a college atmosphere as much as possible, while taking into account the nature of the participating individuals. He saw convict students as similar to high school dropouts in OEO Upward Bound programs. Upward Bound was intended to provide a highly intense and accelerated curriculum on a college campus during the summer months with the purpose of making its students ready for regular college in the fall. UBOPP, as Upward Bound programs elsewhere, was designed to provide financial and other support on a college campus to students who successfully completed the precampus program. The UBOPP was to operate with federal funds administered from outside the prison according to the OEO guidelines.

The program was introduced seven months before the riot of March 1968 and was not an entirely novel idea to the Oregon correctional system. The Upward Bound concept fit in with a shift in orientation that could already be seen within the state's Department of Corrections. During the 1967–68 fiscal year, a new leadership began to convert the system's other facility, the Oregon State Correctional Institution (OSCI), from a security-oriented facility to one emphasizing training and treatment.[3] Second, the concept of college education for

---

*Gaddis is a prison reformer of national renown, perhaps best known as the author of <u>Birdman of Alcatraz</u>, which stimulated reform at Alcatraz.

convicts was not new to the Oregon State Penitentiary (OSP) administration. Since September 1965, college courses had been offered at the prison through the Division of Continuing Education, Oregon State System of Higher Education. In 1967 there were 24 volunteer faculty members from nearby colleges teaching tuition-free college courses in the evenings. At that time there were also 176 college correspondence courses offered free to qualified students through the Division of Continuing Education.

Perhaps the most important aspect of the Upward Bound program introduced by Gaddis was the role convicts would have in forming the program before operations began. Gaddis formed a Convict Advisory Committee to assist in planning the program. The committee included inmates who had been teaching elementary and secondary classes in the prison, inmates who had indicated an interest in college, and inmates who were considered influential in the prison yard. By involving "heavyweights" in the program, Gaddis hoped to build credibility and an inmate support base. The advisory committee saw its role as one of sensitizing the outside academic types to the problems and pressures of the prison and to the themes of convict culture. They felt this was necessary to establish a program that would be sensitive to inmates and would survive in the prison bureaucracy. After the program was established, the participants were to have an ongoing part in the decision-making process.

The first Upward Bound group consisted of 50 inmates who were selected to eliminate sex offenders and hard-core heroin addicts. There was to be an even distribution of other kinds of offenses and lengths of prison terms. Special effort was made to attract convicts with a record of multiple offenses or ones who had done a lot of time. Gaddis wanted to demonstrate that the program was open to even the "hardest criminal." He could have no better evidence of the program's merit than to show it worked for "incorrigibles."

Program Content. The original proposal submitted to OEO indicated it was UBOPP's intention to structure the program loosely to provide the flexibility necessary for experimentation and to avoid creating a preconceived structure to which all participants had to conform. Instead, UBOPP was designed to provide a framework within which each participant could tailor a program to his own needs.

The program followed a definite philosophy of education. Classes were seminars, in which participants could channel the discussions into their areas of interest and could learn to appreciate the free exchange of ideas. Teachers (from nearby colleges) were to avoid dominating the time with lectures; they functioned to engage the individual students in dialogue, not only with the teacher but also with one another. Emphasis was placed on involving the inmates in the excitement of the learning process, encouraging them to articulate their thoughts, to share them with others, and to expose them to the scrutiny of others with different perspectives. Emphasis was put not on the collection of information but on concept formation.

Outside the classroom the program staff also challenged students to think and take responsibility for their actions. Often, according to some of the participants, the staff deliberately contrived situations which served to frustrate the students, to force students to make choices, and to deal directly with an immediate problem.

The program tried to develop interest in learning about the outside world on an informal basis as well as in the classroom. Newspapers and magazines were readily available, as were books on a wide range of subjects. Informal discussions about literature and current events were encouraged as an additional way of stimulating participants and of generating interest in the world beyond the prison walls.

The UBOPP also provided group therapy to participants who wanted it. The therapist maintained a private practice in Eugene and worked several days each week for the college program. According to many of the former participants who were interviewed, therapy was the most important part of their college program experience. They said it brought them out of their isolation, taught them to share and to trust, and to learn a new definition of "manhood" and "strength." It broke down their identity as "criminal" or "hood," and they began to see themselves as more complex and interesting than the role they were playing.

Although the University of Portland (a private Catholic college) served as the administrative center for the entire UBOPP program, administering the OEO funds, issuing credits for classes taken inside prison, and maintaining student transcripts, NewGate did not become part of this university. The program set up its outside office in Portland near Portland State University because that was the college most of its students were attending. In addition, UBOPP students and program staff established working ties with individuals in some of the departments and administrative offices of Portland State. However, there no formal links were established, as was true for the inside program. Most of the persons teaching in the inside program came from the Salem area. UBOPP planned the curriculum and selected the teachers and program staff. The program began and continued to operate as a "third force," separate from both the prison and academic institution. When OEO created the NewGate program, UBOPP became the first NewGate project; and project administration was shifted to the University of Oregon in Eugene.

The Outside Program. During the early phases of the UBOPP, the postrelease program was poorly organized. A number of inside participants were released from prison either as parolees or dischargees before the outside program was set up and were dispersed among several institutions throughout the state without much follow-up. After an outside office was established in Portland, most releasees from then on were sent to colleges in the Portland area. The program office in Portland issued outside support checks and served as a medium through which participants could keep in close contact with and provide emotional support to one another.

Summary. Most exconvicts interviewed found the UBOPP to have been exciting and beneficial. Some emphasized the academic curriculum and the joy of learning about the world beyond. Others were impressed by having close personal contact for the first time in their lives with persons of professional status who took an interest in them and who believed in their intrinsic worth. Others were excited about the dramatic personal changes they went through in psychotherapy and in the classroom. Still others emphasized the group spirit that existed among the participants and a hope that, through joint personal struggle, there would come something worthwhile.

The novelty of the enterprise contributed to the enthusiasm of the initial period. There was an atmosphere of hope and expectation. However, there was also considerable conflict between the prison and the college program. Because the program staff fought vigorously for the convicts, the latter believed they had found new allies against the prison. The resulting program solidarity contributed to polarization between the program and the outside enemy, the prison, which led to neglect and deterioration of the educational program during the height of the struggle.

The prison staff was suspicious of the program from the beginning. They felt that the college program staff acted as though it had all the answers about how to run a prison. They also were critical of the kinds of convicts admitted into the college program. They saw those who had been around a long time as hardened criminals, as "shuckers and jivers," who were not "deserving," and on whom time should not be spent. Prison personnel on every level were critical of the relaxed atmosphere in the Upward Bound classrooms. They opposed smoking in the classrooms, feet on the desks, and loud arguments in the hall. From their viewpoint, topics were discussed that had little relevance to education and that had been brought up deliberately by convicts trying to sidetrack naive instructors into internal prison matters. The warden, partly in response to pressures from the prison staff, began to put restrictions on the program. One restriction, which particularly infuriated the NewGate staff and students, was the confiscation of some reading materials, especially those dealing with politics and social change.

The college program staff saw themselves as significantly different in style and philosophy from others working in the prison. They were not committed to just running an education program but ultimately to changing prisons. One vehicle for accomplishing the latter goal was to involve convicts in the program who, after obtaining an education and credentials, would turn around and direct their efforts toward penal reform. Part of the reason this had not happened in the past was the lack of opportunity for the underprivileged to obtain a higher education. NewGate in a sense would be compensating for the class biases of the social and educational systems. Its graduates would have the skills and awareness needed to make them effective spokesmen for all convicts. In addition to preparing students to be instruments for social change, the program staff was not adverse to getting involved in disputes with the prison administration. Certain staff members, especially Gaddis, took their case to the public. Gaddis appeared on talk shows and was openly critical of certain practices at the Oregon penitentiary, contending that the prison staff was against rehabilitation.

Tension between the prison and its new college program became great and finally focused on Gaddis. One congressional representative from Oregon, a frequent critic of NewGate and most OEO programs, joined in a personal attack against Gaddis, who resigned in the spring of 1969 to save the program.

As a result of his reluctance to establish ongoing links with outside institutions, Gaddis and his staff fought alone against the prison establishment. If an academic institution had had greater involvement with the program, there might have been a more equal distribution of power in the dispute. There might have been other potential sources of countervailing power. At one time the state legislature appeared ready to consider matching federal funds with a yearly appropriation. Gaddis, however, was reluctant to be hamstrung during the initial period of experimentation by interfering legislators. In retrospect, the increased flexibility gained from keeping NewGate autonomous might not have been worth the costs of failing to broaden the program's support base.

Phase II

The program was so different under its second director that it can be treated as a separate entity. Below is a description of the Oregon NewGate program in its second phase, followed by an analysis of its accomplishments.

Inside Program

Students. The first step in the selection process was for inmates to
contact a NewGate staff member on their own initiative. Students had
to have no less than six months and no more than three years left to
serve before parole. If they qualified they were interviewed by a committee of NewGate staff to judge their motivation, sincerity, and
potential for college work. According to staff members and students,
applicants understood the first three requirements, but not the standards used in the interview. Fifty-eight percent of the inside participants felt the selection process did not use clear standards. The only
program where a higher proportion of students felt the selection procedure was not clear was Pennsylvania, another program that put
heavy reliance on a personal interview. There were more applicants
than spaces available. The NewGate staff estimated a maximum capacity for 60 to 65 inside and 60 outside, given the staff and space
available. The level of participation was maintained near the maximum.

As of the fall of 1971, inside participants were expected to carry
a minimum of 15 semester units and maintain at least 2.5 grade point
average (C+). Those who did not meet the minimum requirements were
put on academic probation; high achievers got a letter of commenda-
tion from the NewGate director.

Staff. Under the second director, the staff had two inside and two
outside counselors, one deputy director, one administrative assistant,
one secretary, and one therapist, none of whom had a background in
corrections.

The instructors who taught the inside NewGate classes were
mostly from colleges around Salem. Teachers were paid $425 per
three-hour class. On the average they were young, competent, and
responsive to the needs of inmates as students. A few held private
sessions with individual students to discuss their progress. Instructors
never met together as a group to discuss matters of common concern
and never met formally with other NewGate staff to coordinate efforts.
Some instructors complained they did not understand NewGate's goals
or programmatic emphasis. Joint meetings, they felt, would have
made these clearer to the instructors and also could have acquainted
new instructors with the problems of teaching in the prison. Another
result might have been that academic standards would have been more
uniform and consistently applied.

Program Content. Ten to 12 courses were offered each term. Most
were first- and second-year general liberal arts courses: psychology,
art, mathematics, sociology, English, economics, political science,

biology, geology, and literature. Grading varied with the instructor. Some were as strict as they would be on a college campus; others were reputed to "go easy" and make allowances for convicts. The teachers interviewed felt the interest and motivation of inmates was equal to that of students on campus. However, interest in class dropped off when inmates were close to release. Two of the instructors interviewed felt it was necessary to do more to prepare inside students for campus. They taught useful techniques in their classes such as how to write clearly and succinctly, how to take an exam, and how to read a book quickly and still extract the essential meaning. Inside teachers rarely maintained contact with students once they left the penitentiary, primarily because the students left the Salem area.

Therapy. Although group therapy was a central part of the Gaddis NewGate program, it received decreasing emphasis after that. The original psychiatrist left NewGate because of financial disagreement and the doctor's unwillingness to share information with NewGate about the individual's "readiness for release." After he left, participants were less enthusiastic about group therapy. There were long periods when no trained group therapists were on the staff. Therapy generally became informal "counseling" sessions with staff counselors, consisting mostly of friendly chats and establishing buddy relationships. There was also some informal and irregular academic counseling.

Facilities. The NewGate physical facilities were limited. Having to share classroom space with the prison education department gave NewGate relatively little space of its own. There were a social room; a library, which was also used as a classroom; one small counseling office; another small room for staff office space; and one classroom where NewGate had priority use. Compared with the other programs in the study, the Oregon NewGate program had the least space for its activities. Unlike other NewGate programs, the Oregon program had no self-contained area physically separate from the rest of the prison. There were no quiet reading rooms or individual study carrels available, both contributing to an atmosphere not conducive to academic enterprise. The decor in the NewGate area was drab. Nothing indicated there was anything interesting or exciting happening. There were no prints or paintings on the walls, no carpets or comfortable furniture. No effort had been made by the prison to create a happier atmosphere. It looked and felt like prison.

Outside Contacts. Contact with the outside college community was not extensive. Occasionally, former inside participants returned to visit

with information about the outside campus. These discussions helped
acquaint those about to be released with what to expect on the outside.
Outside counselors also visited the prison once a week. However,
contact with the academic world was slight.

From time to time, NewGate made video tapes of television programs to show the inside students. Infrequently, college students
from nearby colleges visited for discussions with the inmates. Little
else was done in the way of bringing in outside speakers, staging debates, organizing seminars or debates among inmates and outside
groups, or other activities designed to stimulate thought and encourage
extracurricular reading and research.

Relationship of the Program to the Prison Administration and Staff.
The program's relationship to the prison administration appeared
extremely congenial. The warden indicated satisfaction with the program and that he and the staff maintained an effective working relationship. The NewGate staff claimed friends throughout the administration and had privileged access to the warden's office without always
having to go through channels. The NewGate staff's informal network
of associations developed over time in the course of program operations, especially through negotiations for study-release.

NewGate's relationship with the guards and the lower echelon
prison staff was just cordial. It appeared that they cooperated because they had to in the course of the workday. After almost six years,
the program had been accepted as part of the regular operation. Nonetheless, except for the guards directly involved with inmates on the
college floor, guards had serious reservations about the program.
Many were dubious about the sincerity of convicts and their ability to
stay out of prison; others were resentful that convicts were getting
free college education while they had to struggle to pay for similar
opportunities for their children. The inside participants confirmed
this tension. Thirty-five percent of the inside participants reported
that they felt the guards were negative toward them since joining the
program. The only programs where inside participants reported
greater hostility were Pennsylvania and Illinois, where 46 percent
and 41 percent reported negative reactions from the guards. The
lowest were Lompoc and New Mexico, with 3 percent and 9 percent,
respectively.

Relationship of the Program to the Inmate Population. There appeared
to be tension between the NewGate participants and inmates in the
general population. This was not a result of physical separation, since
NewGate students did not have separate living or dining quarters. Nor
did they have special privileges, such as easier access to the library
or exceptions to the lights-out rule or to hair and dress regulations.

Most prison regulations applied to students on the NewGate floor.
Classrooms and offices were locked unless a supervisor was present.
Smoking was not allowed in class. Inmates did not have access to
telephones, nor were they allowed to make calls to outside contacts
on campus in preparation for their release.

Two major sources of tension between the participants and nonparticipants were identified. First, inmates in the general population
thought NewGate chose to play it "safe" instead of going after the
hard core. In the second place, inmates in the general population
asserted that inmates who got into NewGate were not serious students
but were thinking only about themselves. The program was seen as
a quick way out; participants were believed to serve shorter sentences because they were in the program.

NewGate was deeply involved in release decisions, largely because of the procedures to qualify for study-release. As a general
rule, a student must have completed at least two terms inside and
have been recommended for study-release by the NewGate program
staff. The recommendation then was passed on to the prison's classification board for final decision.

The NewGate staff also made recommendations to the parole
board. Positive recommendations were said to help, neutral ones
did not hurt, and though negative comments were not given, the absence of recommendation from NewGate hurt.

Much NewGate staff time was spent on study-release and parole
decisions. The staff complained that this responsibility was too time
consuming, leaving increasingly less time to spend with the men in
the program. The staff acknowledged that the indeterminacy of study-
release caused anxiety among students, which interfered with other
program goals and also prevented students from settling down with
their work and cooperating with fellow students. The staff was not
overly concerned with how the special release procedure for students
affected inmates not in the college program. The staff felt that if
there was a chance to help some to get a speedier release, it had the
responsibility to do everything possible to help those whom it could.

Outside Program. In 1969 the host institution for NewGate changed
from the University of Portland to the University of Oregon due to
the University of Portland's lack of interest in the project and the
fact that most releasees were attending the University of Oregon. The
university is located in Eugene, the second largest city in Oregon
(population 76,346).

The university's School of Community Service and Public Affairs
administered the federal funds. For administrative purposes all professional staff members of NewGate had academic appointments at
the university. However, the Oregon NewGate program operated from

its office in Salem with almost complete autonomy in policy-making and administrative matters.

Most NewGate students who continued their college education attended the University of Oregon, about 80 miles from the penitentiary. All students who participated in the inside program were given full financial support on campus for at least the first term. Persons in school-release status were required to live in the program residence house, a former fraternity house near the campus, and were given full support as long as they were on school-release. Full support included tuition, room and board, a $40 stipend each month, and up to $50 for books each term. When study-release students were paroled or discharged, they were given the same support as students who entered the outside program as parolees or dischargees. The first term on parole provided full tuition, a $40 stipend, $75 for rent, $60 for food per month, and a $50 book allowance. Students had to provide their own room and board and incidental expenses. The fourth term carried no financial support.

Counseling. The 25 to 30 study-release participants were divided between the two NewGate counselors, who provided both psychological and academic counseling. This effort appeared more competent and systematic than the counseling in the inside program. Most of the students saw it as very useful, especially during the initial period of transition. NewGate counselors also advised their students about resources in Eugene and helped establish links to civic or church groups interested in NewGate.

The Residence House. The two outside NewGate counselors had offices in the residence house as did an employee of the department of corrections who was responsible for custody in the house. Four graduate students provided 24-hour supervision, making sure school release participants signed in and out and were in the house by 10 p.m., except the weekend when they were permitted to stay out until midnight.

Physical Facilities. The program residence house, as the one used by the Minnesota NewGate program, was a former fraternity house near campus with two floors of single student rooms and a maximum capacity of 30 students. A large recreation room on the ground floor contained a pool table and an unused kitchen (students took all their meals on campus). There was no common study hall or self-contained social room.

There was little community spirit among the house residents. The house functioned more as a dormitory than a fraternity with mutual obligations and responsibilities. This was reflected in the poor way the house was maintained and in the residents' reluctance

to become involved with others or to protect the interests of the program. There were at least three reasons for the lack of cohesion.
First, the program did not encourage it philosophically, nor did the
program encourage group interaction by structure. The use of the
kitchen to prepare meals to be eaten in common, or the development
of a common study area, or the assignment of house maintenance
responsibilities to the group as a whole would have considerably
broken down individual isolation. The second reason was the heterogeneity of the student group both in terms of age and race. The peer
group emphasis as found in Minnesota probably could not have been
transplanted to the Oregon program without considerable modification.
Older persons are generally more individualistic and more reluctant
to take direction from a peer group. The third reason for the lack of
cohesion was that many residents disliked living in the house and were
anxious to move out, a result of the indeterminacy of study-release
status. Some NewGate participants remained in this status for over
two years before they were granted parole and were free to live where
they pleased. Unable to make definite plans about the future and compelled to live under conditions that separated them from full-fledged
university students, they inevitably began to regard their stay in the
residence house as an unwelcome burden rather than as an advantage.

Integration of the Outside Program with the University Structure.
NewGate had no structural links to any academic departments or
student body groups. For that matter no contacts were maintained
with public service agencies (such as the Department of Employment
or the Department of Public Health) in the community. This lack of
contact ensured the NewGate program administrative autonomy, but
it was isolated from much university life. Another consequence was
that NewGate students had little help securing a greater share of
system benefits, such as health care, psychological counseling, work-
study slots, access to academic advisors, or student housing. As
individuals, they were at a disadvantage with other university students,
who were more familiar with the system. Where services were not
sufficiently available, as for example, work-study slots, individuals
were less effective than organizations in getting the university to
recognize the need for more. But as individuals, NewGate students
developed a contact in the Office of Student Services, who helped program participants.

The NewGate program had inadequate facilities for drug addicts;
and as a university town, Eugene could supply heroin, barbiturates,
amphetamines, and marijuana. The temptation to users was great
and, according to many released participants, rarely resisted. Eugene
had no treatment programs to which NewGate counselors could refer
participants.

According to the respondents, the NewGate program was ineffective in assisting participants to get part-time jobs as their financial support was cut back. Many complained that even full support was insufficient, and a part-time job would have been helpful. The policy was not to allow students receiving full support to work part-time. Another complaint sometimes voiced was that some school release students discovered that college was not for them once on campus, but dropping out of school meant returning to prison, since there were no transfers to the work-release program or other alternatives available.

Analysis

Did the program offer support structure, personal social space, and challenge sufficient to promote the educational goals of the Oregon NewGate students?

Support Structure. In Phase I, support was principally in the form of a wealth of educational resources, which included written materials, exciting classes, high quality and experienced teachers, an ample supply of tutors for every subject, an academic atmosphere, a substantial psychotherapy component, and NewGate staff who were personally engaging and interesting inside and outside the class.

Support did not come from a framework that organized the program around a defined course of action designed to move the participants toward their goals. Classes were not arranged to complement one another either in academic content or scheduling, individual teachers' efforts were not coordinated, and academic counseling was not systematic. Many released participants involved in the inside program during the first phase, while enthusiastic about an exciting experience, remembered it as lacking structure and direction. They did not know what the inside experience prepared them for. More aggressive students took the initiative and learned, but the less assertive found some of their experiences bewildering.

In contrast with Phase I, Phase II provided fewer educational resources but slightly more of an organized framework in the inside program. On the other hand, the outside program of Phase II was superior to the one in Phase I, both in terms of the number and diversity of resources and the framework provided released students. It was on the same level as the outside components at Pennsylvania and Minnesota.

During the site visits, little college atmosphere was observed in the inside program. Part of the reason was the lack of physical facilities, which were cramped and provided little room for different activities. Sixty-three percent of the released participants regarded the physical facilities as inadequate, higher than any other NewGate program. In comparison, Lompoc was 67 percent, Illinois was 71 percent, and Texas was 81 percent. Of course, the physical facilities were not significantly different during Phase I of the program. Therefore, the investigation must look beyond simple lack of room to explain the decrease in the quality of the inside program.

One area where the program clearly failed during Phase II was in neglecting to organize activities beyond the classroom. There were no organized debates, no outside discussion groups, no visiting lectures, and no cultural or extracurricular events to supplement a student's regular course material. These are important aspects of a college experience. Their absence in a college program operating inside a prison is a serious deficiency.

Second, no formal academic counseling was provided. This is an essential part of any college program intending to go beyond exposing a person to a few college courses. The need for counseling is especially great for students with a prior history of school failure. They are not only ignorant of the programs and possibilities of higher education, but their commitment to schooling can be tenuous. The Oregon NewGate program made no systematic effort to determine the academic strengths and weaknesses of its students and to plan their programs accordingly.

Third, there was no coordination between instructional and informal counseling efforts. The NewGate counselors had little idea of what happened in the classroom. Nor did the instructors know about program operations outside the classroom. In the Phase II inside college program, staff taught college level courses in addition to their counseling responsibilities. This bridged the gap, sensitizing the counselor to a student's difficulties in class, providing a useful support source outside the classroom, and keeping him tuned to the central aims of the college program. Counselors with no involvement in the academic life of the program lacked a clear sense of purpose, since they were not fully involved with the program.

Fourth, there was no college preparation component, resulting perhaps from the program's failure to determine the educational deficiencies of its students. Had the inside program staff provided formal counseling to all incoming students and had it coordinated efforts with its instructors, there would have been greater awareness of each student's educational problems, how many were affected by the same problem, and what special enrichment courses were needed. During the site visits only the instructors seemed aware of these needs, and they took it upon themselves, time permitting, to help those in their classes by developing special skill training sessions.

The fifth area of deficiency of the inside program was in psychotherapeutic counseling. Many persons in prison for a long time could use therapy to help them come to terms with their problems and their apprehensions about release. Confidential therapy was one of the strong points observed in the NewGate college programs; therapy can be an important complement to academics. The Oregon NewGate program deemphasized therapy in Phase II and there was no therapist for a long time. The counseling staff attempted informally to fill in, but to neither staff nor the student satisfaction. The staff counselors had no private office space nor scheduled office hours.

Another major cause of the inside program's decline in quality in Phase II was the vague way study-release status was granted. Just exactly who, when, and according to what criteria participants would be advanced to study-release status was unclear, leading to great anxiety among students. Students became preoccupied with trying to manipulate the program to secure their release, which all but destroyed their interest in the academics. The staff also became preoccupied with study-release decisions and how to manipulate the system on the inmate's behalf. Everyone came to see the inside program as a temporary way-station to the outside for the students, and its educational role became of secondary importance.

A much better arrangement for the students, the program staff, and the program would have been for the prison to agree on a set of explicit requirements that all students were expected to meet before study-release was granted. Once the participants were in the program, they would have known exactly what they had to do. In this context, the kind of help students would have sought from the program would have been that which it was qualified to provide. The other result would have been greater mutual assistance and cooperation among students. Under the Phase II arrangements, there was little mutual assistance among the students since everyone was trying to work his own deal to get an early study-release.

At one time there was an attempt to establish minimum standards, which all inside and outside students would have had to maintain. Inasmuch as it provides the student objective feedback about his standing in the program, this can be supportive. But unless it is accompanied by services that enable the student to achieve the standards (high quality instructors, academic counseling, college preparatory courses, individual attention, varied courses, tutoring, and therapy), the effect will be to frustrate slower learners, thus leading to a program favoring those more gifted or previously better prepared for college work.

The Phase II outside program provided a great deal more support than during Phase I, with more extensive and consistent services: housing was provided; education was financed; a large group of students were concentrated on one campus, providing a social support base to the individual; responsible counseling was provided on a regular basis; and supervision was well defined and systematic. Lastly, the program was situated on a campus offering a wide range of alternatives in a congenial community.

Personal Social Space. In Phase I, the initial disagreement between the NewGate program and the prison administration was over the issue of letting inmates make significant choices. NewGate was determined to establish a free college atmosphere similar to that on the college campus. Gaddis felt an inmate had to be treated as a student before he would think and act as one. He was determined to allow the inmate-student to make choices, to pursue his own interests, to make new discoveries, and, most of all, to experiment with the idea of attending college and adopting a student identity. Gaddis resisted interference by prison staff in the internal affairs of the program. The type of program that was established was bound to frighten the administration. Convicts were allowed to do what they wanted. There was arguing, shouting, laughing, and often verbal confrontation with the program staff and one another. There was little of the kind of order to which prisons are accustomed.

In Phase II, the inmate was still allowed to function as a student even though there was less in the program to make him feel like one. The inmate was given a full-time student assignment. He could pick and choose from a variety of well-taught courses. He could choose to participate in therapy, and he could participate inside the classroom without fear. Academic freedom was not restricted in topics of discussions or in available reading materials. Once he was ready for parole, he could choose from colleges throughout the state with the promise that the NewGate program would provide financial support.

Despite these freedoms, the personal social space provided by the Oregon program was only medium, compared with the other programs. There were three limiting factors. First was the practice of having guards lock every room in which no staff supervisor was present, a prison policy not observed in any other NewGate program. This restricted the ability of the student to utilize fully the education facility. Second, the rather frequent checking by the floor guard was a constant reminder to the student that he was a prison inmate with limited freedom. Finally, the student's freedom to design a program to fit his needs was constrained by his limited role in influencing program policy. This was not a problem during Phase I but during Phase II it was. Students attributed their inability to influence the program to a lack of responsiveness by the second program director, whose office was outside the prison and who had a particular temperament that prevented him from establishing an easy rapport with the inmates.

Challenge. During Phase I the NewGate program was very high on challenge—probably its most dramatic feature. Gaddis designed the program to reach the "hardest criminal" to turn them on to something so exciting that they would never consider returning to crime. He was determined to show inmates a new dimension of themselves and the world, to open their minds to possibilities of which they had been unaware. This was done through personal confrontation, by bringing in outside speakers and materials of interest, by introducing students to books and to newspapers, and by dialogue with one another. Interviews with participants who went through NewGate at this time emphasized that it was a rich and exciting program. Five years later, they remembered with relish class discussions and other experiences. There was case after case of "losers" leaving prison and making something meaningful of their lives.

In Phase II, the excitement wore off. Following a volatile period, a special effort was made to show the prison there was nothing subversive about NewGate. Partly out of a need for caution and partly due to his temperament, the new director adopted a posture of low visibility. A new staff was hired. The new employees were not as enthusiastic as were their predecessors.

There were other reasons for the leveling off of excitement. Many students remained loyal to Gaddis after his forced resignation and were suspicious of the new director, who was quickly approved by the prison administration. It was hard to convince them that he would not sell out to the prison. Instead of being excited about future possibilities, they lamented what they had lost from the past.

Another reason for decreasing enthusiasm was the natural wearing off of the novelty of a new program. Once a program gets under way and begins to move toward institutionalization, administrators become more preoccupied with standard operating procedures. They discourage innovation and its uncertainty. Phase II of the Oregon NewGate followed such a sequence. The second director was an administrator who was primarily concerned about improving the internal management of the program. His predecessor had been an innovator and an inadequate administrator. Judging from observations of other programs, especially in New Mexico, leveling off of excitement is not inevitable. There is a built-in tendency, but it can be offset by deliberate strategies.

Our position is not that Oregon NewGate became devoid of challenge. Any college program in prison is in a unique position to challenge inmates in a way that they have never been before. By insisting that inmates are capable of doing college level work the program offers an intriguing test. Although the Oregon program could have done more to draw those with less motivation into the program and to provide the preparatory facilities needed to meet their deficiencies, the Oregon program attracted some students who would not otherwise have gone to college. The program's strongest source of challenge was its strong, comprehensive postrelease program. College after release with full support is a strong stimulus to change values and perspectives. The main criticism is that the program relied principally on the outside program to stimulate the participants, rather than beginning the job while still in prison. Not only would more students be reached, but also introducing them to a college atmosphere while still inside would reduce the cultural shock most students experienced when they first hit the campus.

Institutional Change. Since its inception, NewGate brought about positive changes in the institution. Prison personnel began to see the convict differently—as someone with the potential to learn academic subjects. They saw men whom they had viewed as hopeless undergo dramatic change. They saw former students stay out of prison when everyone believed they would be back quickly. Though these observers always did not understand how the college program brought about constructive change, they associated the progress they observed with NewGate.

The NewGate program had an impact on the prison education program on lower levels. Many prisoners lacking high school diplomas began to show an interest in acquiring a diploma or a GED so they could enroll in the college program. It was evident that NewGate had shown inmates they were not only capable of college work but also that there was a payoff for getting an education, starting with an earlier release, financial assistance, a muting of the exconvict stigma, possibly a college degree, and, finally, a better job and higher income.

Persons in the outside community, as a result of publicity about the NewGate program, came to see exconvicts in a more human and personal way. The negative effects of incarceration have become better understood, as have exconvicts' needs during their transition to life in free society. The Oregon NewGate outside students had more exposure in classroom discussion, on panels, before community groups, and in the media than any other group in the study. And they have been effective in raising many issues about prison reform.

The Oregon penitentiary began developing transitional programs, such as work-release. Although this was independent of NewGate, the relative success of the college program strengthened the resolve of prison officials to expand other efforts. A work-release center containing many of the features of the study-release house, including individual counseling, was established in Eugene.

Little institutional change occurred in the university community. The University of Oregon was receptive to exconvicts from the outset,

an attitude that was strengthened by the success of the program participants on campus. However, the institution made few adjustments
to facilitate program operations. No money, for example, was appro-
priated for the program. Moreover, provisions for a new type of
student with special needs were not developed. The work-study program was not expanded, and the university did not increase its involvement in corrections. The university was not involved in the
college program inside the prison, although this was an area in which
it possessed unquestionable expertise. Lack of university involvement
was partially the result of NewGate's decision to operate autonomously,
yet one would expect some initiative in this area from the university.

NewGate had an advisory board with representatives from a
cross section of the community. This board could have been an instrument to initiate community involvement with NewGate to advance correctional reform. It could have brought to bear resources from different sectors of society. However, the board did not take any
initiative in this direction. The NewGate director was partly to blame
because he did not involve the board in program planning or operations
on an ongoing basis.

Program Survival and Vitality. The Oregon NewGate program survived, but it lost some of its essential features. The program administrators had the potential to recreate a higher quality program:
one which would have fulfilled its goals of enhancing participants'
life chances while creating constructive institutional change. This
could have been done without alienating the prison system or threatening the goals of custody and security.

There were strategies that could have been adopted to restore
the inside program. NewGate provided personal social space to participants in which they "wallowed" rather than discovered their potential. The academic and counseling effort should have been coordinated
to offer the student real alternatives and assistance. The inside academic program should have been more closely associated with a university. The staff failed to create a college atmosphere. Professors
from the University of Oregon should have been encouraged to teach
in the inside program and to take part in developing the inside program. This would not only have improved the quality of the academic
program but also would have provided additional support to students
proceeding to the outside program by developing prior personal contacts among the faculty on campus. None of these improvements
necessarily would have been rejected by the prison.

An additional change should have been considered in the interest
of improving the quality of the college experience inside the prison.
Study-release is an invaluable tool in making an inmate's transition
to life back on the streets. However, as set up in the Oregon prison,

it was a source of unnecessary anxiety. Passing to study-release status should be automatic after satisfactory accomplishment of specified objective requirements. Second, study-release should not be indeterminate. Parole, too, should be automatic after the inmate has demonstrated an ability to fulfill specific requirements. If all students know what has to be done and can anticipate exactly when they will move to the next status, they will have the freedom to participate in the program in earnest and the peace of mind to settle in and take full opportunity of the services available.

The long run survival of the NewGate program rests on its ability to involve outside institutions, such as the university, in supporting it and, if necessary, in protecting it. This is a necessary counterweight against the custody interests in the prison.

Ultimately, NewGate must progress beyond the point of having to hustle funds on a year-to-year basis. A permanent funding source must be developed. The university has some responsibility in this area, but first a commitment must be developed to the NewGate idea. One way of creating that commitment is involving as many sectors of the university community as possible in the program operations. A broader group of people will thereby begin to assume responsibility for the program's continued existence.

Minnesota

The Minnesota NewGate program had its inside component in the St. Cloud Reformatory, one of the most forbidding prison structures in the United States. Built of large granite blocks from a quarry which the prison now surrounds, it has an outer wall that local people claim is the second longest stone wall in the world. This monument to the "classical" age of American prison architecture stands in a relatively open space on the outskirts of St. Cloud (35,000 population), approximately 70 miles north of the twin cities of St. Paul and Minneapolis. The correctional enterprise indise the walls does not reflect the prison's antiquated exterior. The inmates' routine was humane and moderately relaxed. Although there were bars, cellblocks, gates, and stone walls on the inside, the facilities were clean, well lighted, and spacious. Helping maintain this atmosphere was a recent remodeling, which included building a colorful and comfortable visiting room, a large education wing, and several new shop buildings.

At the time of the study (1972) the Minnesota correctional system was undergoing considerable changes. There was an emphasis on reducing the length of sentences and the size of the inmate population. Along with it was a shift to community-based operations as alternatives to incarceration. St. Cloud Reformatory was affected directly by the reduction of inmate populations. Though it served as the maximum facility for younger offenders in the past, many older inmates were being transferred to the state's other maximum facility, Stillwater, which historically had accommodated only older felons. With a capacity for more than 800, St. Cloud maintained an average of less than 500 inmates during 1972.

The Minnesota NewGate program was the second college program funded by the Office of Economic Opportunity; it started operation in 1968. The initial interest and initiative came from a professor at the University of Minnesota who had been involved in developing experimental and demonstration projects addressed to the needs of young offenders. In his view, NewGate was to be both an instrument to change inmate attitudes and behavior and to offer participants otherwise unobtainable educational opportunities. The program was to further these joined purposes in two ways. First, it placed heavy emphasis on group therapy, that is, guided group interaction. Second, the Minnesota NewGate project was integrated closely with the University of Minnesota in Minneapolis. These two characteristics of the Minnesota NewGate program distinguished it from most other programs in the sample.

Inside Program

Staff. The inside program had four staff members: the inside assistant director, two counselors, and a secretary. Over the assistant director was the program director, who oversaw both the inside and outside program components. The director's office was on the University of Minnesota campus, but he visited the prison about once a week. The inside program functioned independently from the campus program.

The assistant director and his two counselors were experienced group leaders in juvenile correctional programs. Two of them worked with Harry Vorath in Minnesota, who had a reputation for his skill in the use of "guided group interaction," a technique of group behavior modification developed by William Glaser, a southern California psychiatrist.

Students.

In determining an applicant's qualification for entrance into Project NewGate, four general criteria were used:
1. Does the individual have the intellectual ability to complete a two or four year college training program?
2. Does the applicant have the motivation and attitude necessary to make the sacrifices required to finish

a college program or does he have the potential
to develop this attitude and this motivation
through the first phase of the NewGate program?
3. Will the individual be reasonably assured of release
within the six months to fifteen months required for
entrance into Project NewGate?
4. Will the individual be able to obtain a financial plan
that will assure him of the means to carry out his
college training program?

Initial referrals to Project NewGate came from a variety of sources—
from the caseworker, the interested individual himself, teachers,
vocational instructors, and other staff.

Once an individual was referred to Project NewGate, the NewGate
staff first contacted the caseworker involved to determine whether
NewGate should proceed with the initial screening process. If the
caseworker approved, the applicant's file was checked to determine
his probable length of stay in the institution, his intelligence and
achievement scores, and also any past indication of a desire for higher
education. The referred individual was then called in for an individual
or group interview with the NewGate staff plus one or more of the
presently enrolled NewGate students. The purpose of this interview
was to be certain the applicant was fully aware of all aspects of the
program and of what his responsibilities would be on entering it. The
applicant was called in for further interviews if necessary.

If the NewGate staff and the caseworker agreed that the applicant
was a good candidate for the NewGate program and if the applicant
indicated that he wished to be considered for Project NewGate, he
was scheduled to take the Minnesota Entrance Examination, which
tests achievement and aptitude in five areas: vocabulary recognition,
reading comprehension, critical thinking, organizational ability, and
quantitative thinking. The results were recorded in percentiles against
the norm of all college freshmen at the University of Minnesota and
were used by the selection committee in determining an individual's
ability to do college level work.

Following the interview and testing, the applicant was given a
preliminary screening by the NewGate selection committee, which
consisted of representatives of the NewGate staff, the Department of
Education, the individual's caseworker, the Social Services supervisor
or coordinator, custody officials, and the Division of Vocational Rehabilitation (DVR). The individual's case was presented by his caseworker with additional information supplied by the members of the
committee. The selection committee decided whether to deny his
application, defer it to a later selection committee meeting, or
approve him for further consideration for entrance in Project NewGate.

If the individual was accepted for further consideration, he was referred to the DVR, where he was put through their standard intake procedure and a determination was made as to whether he qualified as a DVR client. If the applicant was accepted, the DVR would provide financial assistance for his college program, contingent upon adequate performance in the inside phase of the program.

Following DVR approval, the individual was referred back to the Project NewGate Selection Committee for final acceptance. If an applicant received final approval, he was referred to either the Adult Corrections Commission or the Youth Conservation Commission for approval of the individual's entrance into NewGate and their determination as to whether they would be willing to consider the release of the individual at his next review, or within fifteen months of entering the program. In the case of the Youth Conservation Commission, the selection committee recommended a minimum number of quarters they felt the student should spend in the inside phase of Project New-Gate.

Several consequences of this selection process must be examined. In the first place, the selection procedures were involved in the release process. NewGate had to obtain approval from the parole authorities to accept a prisoner. This approval included a tentative agreement for parole after a certain number of semesters were completed. This could pose a problem if the program were seen as an avenue for early release. However, only 52 percent of the students stated that getting an early parole was an important reason for entering the program, a smaller percentage than in all other programs except Texas. Parole concerns did not dominate inmate motivation because most inmates served short sentences. Some even chose to serve additional time to become involved with NewGate. Sentences were extended to permit completion of a semester.

Another problem with the selection process at St. Cloud was that the program rejected inmates who potentially could have benefited from it. These were persons who failed to demonstrate intellectual ability, either in the initial intelligence and achievement test scores or on the Minnesota Entrance Examination, or who did not reveal the appropriate attitudes or motivation to the staff. There was also a built-in class and racial bias in a selection process employing these criteria. The effects of this bias can be seen in the fact that the proportion of blacks and native Americans in the program was lower than their proportions in the general population.

Another selection bias resulted from the positive peer culture approach. The program selected persons who were amenable to intense group interaction, which was so important in the program. Many persons who were judged to be unsuited for the group process were excluded from the program. Furthermore, those who did not "fit in" might have selected themselves out. In short, the strong emphasis on the peer group culture made it unclear whether the program selected participants for their suitability for college work or for their suitability to participate in the group therapy program.

Program Content. The NewGate project had a large room, which served as an office, lounge, library, and study room. Two classrooms adjoined this room. The room had tables, bookshelves, a desk, filing cabinets, some study carrels, and a row of lounge chairs. In the fall of 1972 there were 35 NewGate students who were assigned to the project full-time and spent their entire day on the education floor. There were also 11 part-time students. Activity in the NewGate room between classes was intense. Some men were studying by themselves; others were studying in groups; still others were engaged in discussion. Moreover, the four staff members were in the room most of the time. Although the room was too small for all the activities which took place in it, what was lost in distraction was perhaps gained in vitality. The NewGate room at Minnesota was among the most vital settings encountered in the study.

The program's library contained some current topical and reference books in addition to those required in the courses being given. However, it was far from adequate for college students. The prison itself maintained a small library on the floor below, which was open in the afternoon and evenings. However, as in most prisons, that library was also inadequate. Serving partially to alleviate these shortcomings was an arrangement whereby books could be ordered from the University of Minnesota library or from St. Cloud State College. However, this option was seldom used since considerable waiting periods and paperwork were involved. The major sources of outside reading material were the instructors, who lent books to students.

The courses in the inside phase were all taught by full-time instructors from nearby St. Cloud State College, who taught part-time at the prison for extra pay. Instructors were selected by the inside NewGate director. Some teachers had been in the program for several semesters and enjoyed this type of teaching. The quality of the teaching was very high, as shown by the fact that over 95 percent of outside participants at Minnesota, a higher proportion than at any other program, agreed with statements such as: "The courses offered were challenging enough to stimulate my interest in education"; "Instructors did a good job teaching"; "Instructors were sensitive to the problems and capabilities of the convict as a student"; "The instructors showed a personal interest in the participants."

The course selection was directed toward the completion of an associate degree through St. Cloud State College and toward the student who would be moved to the outside phase at the University of Minnesota.

Approximately six courses were taught each quarter. The spring 1972 quarter offered two courses in English, one each in math, economics, psychology, and biology. The course selection was not very broad, but it was appropriate for most of the students. However, some part-time students (not admitted as full-time because of long sentences to serve) soon ran out of courses to take.

Interviews with teachers indicated that instruction was rewarding. The instructors stated that the NewGate students were more prone to questioning ideas and entering into discussions on issues than were their outside students, which made prison teaching enjoyable. Some instructors indicated that one source of this interest in questioning was generated by the program's emphasis on challenging interaction in group therapy. There was more convict tutoring convict here than in most of the other programs, also a likely outgrowth of the positive peer culture approach.

Therapy. Every man in the program had to attend "group" four times a week. Each session lasted one and a half hours. Group activities and much of the unstructured interaction between staff and the participants aimed at three objectives: (1) developing insight into one's own character, personality, and problems; (2) developing a sense of reality; and (3) generating a cohesive "cohort" whose members will continue to support and sanction each other while in prison, working to reconstruct their values and plans, and in reentering the outside society.

The group discussed the problems, attitudes, and activities of the members. Usually, they focused on one person at a time to "pull off his covers," expose his "game," or otherwise try to reach a more honest or "real" level of his personality. The group leader played a passive role, only intervening when he thought it necessary to prevent the group from dealing too severely with an individual or to move the group in more productive directions.

One aim of the positive peer group method was the development of a cohesive group whose members had a great deal of knowledge and compassion for each other. The emergence of such a group inside the prison was intended to maximize the potential for change by opening up the individual to new views of himself and new courses of action, and to give him support in striking out in new directions. Moreover, if a cohesive group was sent to the outside, its members could aid each other in the transition to life outside.

Did the peer group approach work as well as in practice as it did in theory? This question warrants attention because of the tremendous emphasis placed on the approach in the Minnesota program. Also it represents one of the common treatment strategies in youth corrections in America, and the Minnesota program was the only one in the study sample that provided an opportunity to examine it closely.

Another reason for the careful consideration of the consequences of this group approach in the Minnesota program was that staff's unusual reluctance to consider its problems.

The effectiveness of the peer group therapy was evaluated primarily through the opinions expressed by staff and participants. The evaluation staff was not permitted, during any site visits, to observe the structured group sessions. The inside program staff spoke highly of the positive effects of the group therapy. In fact, their interest in the NewGate program did not appear to go much beyond the therapy component and their role as group leaders. The participants, however, had greater reservations about the emphasis on therapy. They consistently felt that the inclusion of persons who were in therapy against their will interfered with the progress of those who sincerely wanted to participate. The participants also complained that one group leader was sarcastic and arrogant, and that being in his group was "a complete waste of time."

The second reservation about the Minnesota NewGate therapy program was that it could have harmful effects on participants. Persons have been known to suffer profoundly from having had their "inner selves" bared before a group and from being viciously (if often subtly) dealt with by amateurs, who had no sensitivity to the nature or extent of one person's problem and who had serious psychological problems themselves. Instead of building a personality more capable of dealing with the world, the personality might be destroyed in this context and left with no resources for rebuilding. Because of these dangers, it seems essential that an individual be allowed to withdraw from the therapy program when in his judgment it is destructive to him.

The mandatory aspect of peer group therapy raised problems for many inside participants. If they found that it was not for them, dropping out meant having to leave the NewGate program entirely. This would not only mean missing an opportunity to go to college, but would be interpreted negatively by the prison and paroling authorities. There were inmates who excluded themselves from NewGate because of the requirement to participate in the peer group therapy, and there were others who dropped out because of it. In the Minnesota program, these problems were most noticeable among native Americans. Because of mandatory therapy, some refused to enter NewGate, and others left the program after they had failed to adjust to it. Only one remained, still uncomfortable but reconciled to play the game rather than drop out and spoil his chances to get a college education. In conversations with native Americans at the reformatory, it was revealed that personal privacy was among their most highly cherished cultural values. It was considered a common obligation to respect another's independence and separateness. No man was to question another's value system or force his own unto him.

Inside participants in general indicated concern about their privacy, that it was not being respected. In response to the question: Is the staff sensitive to your need to be left alone, 42 percent said that it was not, more than twice as high as any other NewGate program. However, it was still lower than Lompoc (60 percent), Illinois (75 percent), and Texas (47 percent). Furthermore, 23 percent of the inside participants felt that the Minnesota NewGate staff did not treat participants with dignity. This was more than three times higher than any other NewGate program, though it was still considerably better than Lompoc (37 percent), Illinois (55 percent), and Texas (19 percent).

Other negative aspects of the intense group counseling activities showed up. For instance, of the 40 persons interviewed who had passed through the program, 17 named the mandatory groups as an objectionable aspect of the program. Even more dramatic was their overall rating of the group counseling in comparison with the participants in other programs. Fifty-four percent of the Minnesota inside participants rated it as "less than adequate," as opposed to 21 percent for all programs combined.

Relationship to the Prison and Other Inmates. The general impression of the evaluation team was that NewGate was relatively isolated from the rest of the prison. This did not, however, appear to affect the program's relationship with the administration. The associate warden, with the most direct jurisdiction over the program, stated that New-Gate was a positive benefit to the prison. Thw lower echelon staff, however, were reluctant to give NewGate such a strong endorsement. This attitude was reflected in the participant interviews. Sixty-two percent of the released participants interviewed characterized the guards' attitudes as hostile, cynical, or suspicious (about the same as the average for all programs). In comparison, the Oregon and Pennsylvania programs reported considerably more hostility; the Ashland and New Mexico programs showed considerably less than Minnesota.

The Minnesota program staff appeared to make little effort to relate NewGate to the lower echelon prison staff. There was little mixing or friendly exchange during the workday, during the midday meal, or after work. Neither the NewGate staff nor the prison staff considered NewGate a part of the larger prison operation. Because of this orientation, it seemed understandable that the relationship had never gone beyond suspiciousness and remoteness on both sides.

Program's Relationship to Other Inmates. The program's relationship to other inmates was not good. Thirty percent of those interviewed after they had been released (and who, therefore, had passed through

the program at an earlier stage) indicated that the other inmates
viewed the program negatively. Among the participants in the program
during the summer of 1972, 35 percent indicated a negative attitude.
This was the highest for any program in the sample. The closest was
New Mexico with 16 percent.

A major source of tension between NewGate participants and
nonparticipants was the program's extreme "ingroupness." Tight-
knit groups can be very supportive. On the other hand, they also
tend to become elitist and exclusive. The Minnesota NewGate attempted to involve the person totally in the group and to build up the
prestige of the group, while ignoring the development of social relationships between participants and other inmates. It was interesting
that the Minnesota NewGate program was the only one in the entire
study in which the inside participants reported a slight increase in
negative feelings toward other inmates after joining the program. All
other programs showed a decrease in negative feelings toward nonparticipants by students after they were in the program.

Relationship to the Outside College. The University of Minnesota, the
host institution for the outside program, was an excellent base for
inmate-students after release. First, the university administration
was interested in and fully supportive of NewGate's objectives. Second,
the campus facilities were diversified and large (44,000 students) and,
therefore, offered the participants a wide range of different academic
programs and many different social milieus in which they could participate. Over half the convicts at St. Cloud came from the Minnea-
polis-St. Paul area. As a result, the released participants found they
were not isolated totally from their families and familiar surroundings
while attending the university on study-release.

The University of Minnesota, on the other hand, was not so con-
veniently situated for the inside program. The major drawback was
that it was about 70 miles away from the St. Cloud Reformatory. This
restricted interchange and continuity between the prison phase and
the postrelease phase. For instance, instructors could not come
from the University of Minnesota to teach courses on the inside as
they did in Pennslyvania. Released participants in Minnesota were
strangers to the campus, the other students, and the faculty.

The NewGate program attempted to compensate for the lack of
continuity between the prison and university phases through several
strategies. Both the project director and others from the outside
program visited the inside program weekly. A man from the admissions office at the university visited inside participants periodically
to acquaint them with procedures and requirements and to assist
them in making application. Also, the inside director was put in
charge of the peer group therapy component in the outside program,

which required his being on campus twice a week. In addition, there
had always been an effort to structure the inside program as an ex-
tension of the university campus. Over the door of the NewGate room
was a sign reading, "The University of Minnesota." Also, on the
walls in the NewGate room were photographs of scenes in the outside
halfway houses. These helped to create a feeling of oneness with the
outside program.

Outside Program

The Minnesota NewGate project offered its released participants
one of the more elaborate and comprehensive outside programs of
those studied. It was built around a series of consecutive steps along
which a participant moved in a gradual transition to the outside world.
On release, if he wished NewGate's financial support, he had to move
into the NewGate residence house for two terms and take part in the
house activities. The house was a converted fraternity house located
on "fraternity row" within easy walking distance of the campus. During
these first two terms he received free room and board from NewGate
and free tuition from the university. During his third and fourth
terms, he moved out of the program residence house and was responsible for his own food and lodging. The university continued to
provide free tuition and student fees for the third and fourth quarter.
NewGate paid for books and other materials for the first four quarters.
After the fourth quarter the student no longer received NewGate's
financial assistance. Some students were able to get the DVR to pick
up the cost of tuition and books and provide, on the average, $80 per
month (maximum $140) for maintenance after NewGate funds ran out.
Originally, students were not permitted to obtain jobs until after the
first quarter, but a later change allowed them to begin work six to
eight weeks after arriving on campus.

At the beginning of the January 1973 winter quarter 32 NewGate
students were on campus: nine were on their own and working, three
were receiving some help from DVR, and 20 were NewGate students
in their first four quarters, receiving free tuition from the university.
Eleven of the 20 were living in the NewGate house with free room and
board.

The NewGate staff considered the residence house and its activities to be the essence of the outside program. Living in the house
was considered so necessary in transition to the streets that it was
a mandatory prerequisite to receiving support during the first two
quarters. Even persons on parole had to live in the house. This was
very different from the Oregon NewGate residence house, which was
primarily for study-release participants who were required by law
to be under supervision. Parolees in Oregon could live wherever they

pleased and received NewGate support. There was no work- or study-release program in Minnesota at that time. There were only three study-release participants in the Minnesota NewGate house; they were under 24-hour supervision and had to be in the house by 5:00 p. m. on weekdays and sign in and out whenever they entered or left.

Physical Facilities. The three-story residence house was spacious, clean, attractive, and comfortable. The upper floors had about 20 single rooms and common bathroom facilities. The street level floor consisted of a large social room with fireplace; a long rectangular study hall with tables, book shelves, and good lighting; and office space for the staff of the residence house. The house was big enough for both quiet study and socializing. The basement had a large kitchen and dining room. A full-time cook was assisted by residents who worked rotating shifts. The food was reported by all to be excellent. Also in the basement was a game room, including a pool table.

Staff. There were two full-time persons at the residence house, a counselor who functioned as the group leader, and the outside director whose responsibilities included directing and supervising the residence house and integrating the NewGate program and its students into the university. The new NewGate director, hired in January 1973, re-organized the project's administration so the inside assistant director supervised the outside group therapy and was on campus two days a week. The outside assistant director devoted half-time to the resi-dence house and half to developing a Felony Diversion Project, where young felons would be assigned to the NewGate house in lieu of incar-ceration, one of Minnesota's newest efforts in community treatment.

NewGate hired eight counselors, six of whom were past or present NewGate participants. Three were resident counselors to provide in-formation and advice to the new campus students. Three were on call during the night to provide the supervision required by state law for the work-release program. The remaining two counselors filled in when the other six were not scheduled to work. Most counselors re-ceived $1. 90 an hour. Three were on work-study assignments where NewGate only paid 20 percent of the cost. The hiring of participants was intended to give them actual work experience and an opportunity to make some money while attending school. It also gave participants a larger share in running the program to reinforce the idea that it was their program. The Minnesota program was one of two programs in the sample with exconvicts on its staff.

Therapy. In the words of one of the outside NewGate staff, group counseling was "the meat and potatoes" of the outside NewGate pro-gram. Three days a week all the participants living in the residence

house met in "group" from 5:00 to 6:30 p.m. The group consisted of
students who had met as a group in the inside program at the prison
and who were released together as a cohort. Maintaining the group
was intended to maximize the benefits of a tight-knit and mature group
in the transition period. The members were expected to "make it"
on the outside through mutual assistance.

Participants were expected to devote much of their time to the
group, including not only sharing the work in the house (for which
they were paid $1.90 an hour) but also discussing in group problems
and individuals who were not meeting their responsibilities. For
example, a group meeting might deal with a student who was not
keeping his grades up, one who was using or dealing dope, or one
who treated his girlfriend unfairly. The members of the group, after
indicating their "care and concern," would ask the individual under
question to respond. The matter could be resolved by the individual
promising to make an effort to behave more responsibly, or the group
could impose restrictions, which were believed to be constructive in
developing more responsible behavior. As an example, a student was
spending too much time with his girlfriend, failing to attend class,
and was not fulfilling his work obligations in the house. The group
decided that he must be in the house by 10 p.m. each night until he
could show he could handle both his relationship and his other responsibilities. Some groups have been known to use the threat of
returning an individual to the prison (violating him), as a form of
discipline. This was usually done in the spirit of trying to impress
on the individual the seriousness of what he was doing and to encourage him to change his ways before he got into serious trouble with
the police.

The evaluation of the therapy component in the outside program
revealed strengths and weaknesses similar to those seen in the program in St. Cloud. Peer group counseling had certain benefits. One
was its emphasis on assuming responsibility. On visiting the New-
Gate house in Minnesota, one was immediately impressed with the
cleanliness and order of the facility. Not only were individuals' rooms
clean but so were the common facilities, such as bathrooms, halls,
stairwells, and study and social rooms. Part of the motivation for
tending to these matters was payment for work tasks. However, other
important factors were the feelings of pride in and responsibility for
maintaining the program's image. There was also a feeling that participation in NewGate was a privilege to be earned and not something
to be taken for granted. This was different from the attitudes of the
Oregon participants. The group approach also seemed to help develop
spirit among its members. Many participants found warmth and
emotional support from their friends in the NewGate house. The
house became a home, and the difficulties of adjustment to the free

society and to academic life were significantly reduced. In addition, the house continued to serve former participants. Many of those who no longer lived in the house often visited to maintain their ties with the staff and other participants. One of the most popular occasions for these visits was mealtime.

Many participants felt that this quasi-family provided a feeling of security and belongingness that gave them strength. Perhaps the encouragement in the group to open up, to communicate, and to care about fellow human beings promoted good feelings about fellow participants and the program. On the other hand, there were other factors. One of the most important was the homogeneity of the group. All the participants were roughly the same age, and from the same socioeconomic background and geographical areas. Members of minorities were even more rare in the outside program than in the inside program. Another force contributing to the cohesiveness of the social unit was the vastness of the University of Minnesota. The New-Gate students could have stayed with what was familiar and where they had friends to counter the impersonality of campus life. Consequently, it was the lack of viable alternatives on the outside, as well as the appeal of the group, that contributed to its importance to the participants.

During visits to the house and in discussions with individuals in various phases of released status, it became obvious that the peer group presented serious problems. The emphasis on the group enabled a "bad" group to encourage irresponsibility as well as to allow a "good" group to encourage responsibility. When participant leaders were prepared to take responsibility the group became, in the staff's words, a "good" group. If the leaders did not take control, a more laissez-faire group would develop. Weaker, more dependent members take courage from the fact that "everyone else is doing it" without having to deal with their own complicity. Were there not such a heavy emphasis on the group, these weaker individuals might have had to learn how to make decisions on their own rather than going along with the "crowd."

Not only can the group establish a poor frame of reference to which the members are pressured to conform, but also "bad" groups might treat members differently. In group meetings, some members were left alone or confronted only superficially, especially if they were powerful, while the activities of others were scrutinized more carefully. This is probably common to all therapy groups and not always undesirable. But because the peer group in Minnesota NewGate also had governing authority, it could make decisions that acutely affected an individual's life. Because the group was mandatory, an individual participant could not walk away from the group, as is possible in voluntary group therapy. Failure to please the majority of the group members could lead to being ostracized, isolated, picked on, and, ultimately, to run the risk of being kicked out of the house before he was financially ready to go it alone, or even of being sent back to prison if the group took a particular dislike to him. Some persons reported feeling picked on or ostracized because they did not fit in. This, of course, happens in other contexts. However, their alienation and isolation was accentuated by the emphasis put on being part of the group and by the staff's contention that any problem, no matter how personal, was the responsibility of the group. This left the isolated individual without even staff members to talk to about his problems.

Another problem observed in the Minnesota NewGate was a lack of sensitivity to the problems of differential opportunity in the larger society. Participants argued against having the program make a special effort to encourage more minority inmates to join. They did not see race as an advantage they had over the minorities by virtue of the fact that minorities were more reluctant to try NewGate than were whites. The ingroupness and the "pull myself up by my own bootstraps" attitude generated by the Minnesota program helped inspire aloofness and an exclusivism toward people who did not "fit in." The homogeneity of the in-group in effect denied them the opportunity to learn how to deal with real diversity in backgrounds, lifestyles, and attitudes.

Integration of the Outside Program with the University. The NewGate director had his headquarters on the University of Minnesota campus in the Delinquency Control Institute, which is part of the law school. The director of the institute was instrumental in setting up the Minnesota NewGate program, as well as other projects designed to develop innovative approaches in criminal justice and corrections. He set up a program that utilized third-year law students and two attorneys to provide Legal Assistance to Minnesota Prisoners (LAMP); a Correctional Ombudsman Program developed in Minnesota; and a Felony Diversion Program (mentioned earlier), which was originally funded by the Ford Foundation but came to be supported by the governor's Crime Commission and Law Enforcement Assistance Administration (LEAA) funds. The institute was also the home of an Indian NewGate project, the Anishinabe-Waki-Igan, Inc., for Indians incarcerated in the county workhouse, which provided GED preparation inside the county jail and established a residence house in Minneapolis to aid transition to the streets.

NewGate's link to the university was through the institute's administrative ties to the law school. Although the Minnesota NewGate was more thoroughly integrated into the university structure than any other programs in the study, it was seen by the university more as an experiment in correctional reform in higher education. This image of NewGate was reinforced by its attachment to an institute involved in corrections work and by the makeup of the institute's policy-making board, the All-University Advisory Board, which lacked representation from the fields of higher academics and sciences.

Academic departments were not involved in NewGate at the program level, partly because the prison was located so far away and the inside instructors were drawn from St. Cloud State College. If a NewGate program is developed at the other state prison, as seemed likely, university professors would be able to drive the thirty miles to the prison, which should generate greater involvement with the NewGate program on the campus.

Analysis

Did the program offer support structure, personal social space, and challenge sufficient to promote the educational goals of the Minnesota NewGate program? The Minnesota program ranked "high" on supportive framework and challenge and "medium" on personal social space when compared with the other programs in the sample.

Support Structure. The Minnesota program offered an extensive support structure. It took inmates who most likely were not college-bound, provided an intensive therapy program along with a high quality collegiate academic program inside the prison, prepared them for release to a specific campus, situated them as bona fide students with full tuition and materials essential to their studies, housed them in a resident house close to campus, fed them well, continued to provide them with formal group counseling, and slowly integrated them into university life. In other words, Minnesota NewGate provided an elaborate, self-contained, and logical sequence of steps along which an individual could make meaningful progress toward his academic goals.

The major criticism of this structure is that it was tailored to meet the interests and needs of only a special group of inmates. Inmates who needed additional services or who were uncomfortable with those provided by NewGate had no alternatives. The academic program was a case in point. All full-time NewGate participants were expected to follow a basic junior college curriculum. The classes that were provided were of high quality and well taught, but they were too few and insufficiently varied. Advanced students complained that there were no upper division courses. Others complained that there were no music, art, or ethnic culture courses (only during one term was an Indian history course offered). If not expanding the offerings was due to a lack of funding, an attempt could have been made to enlist

the involvement of volunteer instructors. The only program seriously
to attempt this approach, the New Mexico NewGate, was amazingly
successful in enriching its inside program. The three NewGate staff
persons also could have become involved in tutoring and teaching—
at no extra cost to the program. This would not only have helped
bridge the gap between the academic and therapy efforts, but also
would have involved the NewGate staff with the students on a more
active basis than they were in their passive role as group leaders.

The Minnesota NewGate staff could respond to this criticism of
the narrow course offerings by pointing out that the inside program
was never intended to be a comprehensive college program. Its students had relatively short terms left to serve before release to the
outside phase, where alternatives were almost limitless. It follows,
then, that the limited number of inside courses were not a problem.
One can, however, argue that this view of the program's obligations
is too narrow. Inmates who were not close to release were prevented
from becoming full-time students by the narrow set of course offerings, which were quickly exhausted. The program thereby shirked
its responsibility to enrich the lives of a broader group of inmates,
those who could have participated more fully if the offerings had been
greater.

The NewGate academic program lacked two other support facilities that seem to be important in an education program for those with
a previous history of failure in school: a formal academic counseling
unit and a structured college preparatory component. Inside participants revealed, on the one hand, an impatience on the part of some
instructors with students who were slow or inadequately prepared
and, on the other hand, a demand for courses in how to study, read,
take notes and exams, type, and such, as well as for general re-
fresher courses in basic education. The therapy program was also
structured narrowly. Though peer group therapy was provided to
every one, no alternative therapeutic or counseling strategies were
offered.

Personal Social Space. In terms of the lack of restrictions on the
NewGate floor, personal space was great. Once on the NewGate floor,
students were given only general parameters to guide their personal
behavior in school. (Fifty-eight percent of the Minnesota inside participants reported "relaxed" rule enforcement in the school setting.
The New Mexico program was next closest with 49 percent.) The
full-time student was insulated from petty security and custody concerns, which remind the inmate that he has no control over his life
and which rob him of that personal satisfaction derived from doing
something constructive with his time while incarcerated. He could
smoke, sit on tables, hang around without having to account for

himself, read anything he wanted, and such. In this atmosphere the individual could shed his inmate status and begin to experiment with a different identity—that of a college student. This showed up clearly in the academic setting, where there was considerable excitement, uninhibited questioning, and deliberation. Students demonstrated a vitality and enthusiasm equal to that in classrooms on college campuses in the free society.

On the other hand, the Minnesota NewGate program offered the student little chance to develop a program based on his interests and needs. The student could not weigh program alternatives and future opportunities systematically because he was never provided formal academic counseling. Instead these decisions were coopted by the program: everyone received what everyone else received. In the postrelease phase the participant had limited choice. The program would not finance a released student's education at any institution other than the University of Minnesota. Consequently, he had to go to school in Minneapolis, he had to follow a program available at the university, and he had to live in the NewGate house during the first two terms. Although this routine probably fit the needs of most students, it did not suit all students.

The major area in which the participant had no choice was therapy; it was mandatory for all. An inmate who just wanted to participate in the college program for the academics did not have this option. Nor could he choose among different types of therapy. There were no substitutes or supplementary programs for an individual who also desired individual therapy. Moreover, the individual had no choice as to which group and which group leader with whom he underwent therapy. These decisions were all made by the group leaders. Many inside participants complained about one group leader and stated that they derived no benefit from his group. Many had requested transfer to the other group, but all were denied. They were unable to indicate their dissatisfaction by withdrawing from a group. If a person "chose" to drop out of group therapy, he was kicked out of the program. This was not the end of the matter, however, since a person removed from the program surely would be judged negatively by the prison authorities and parole board.

Challenge. Basically, there were three different dimensions along which a student might be challenged in the program: (1) from interaction with other students and staff; (2) from ideas, informal discussions, classroom, or group counseling sessions; or (3) from learning of future opportunities beyond the program.

Probably the major source of challenge in the Minnesota program was the classroom. Students interviewed, past and present participants alike, indicated that the instructors in the inside program

introduced them to the excitement of new ideas and demanded that they
come to grips with their own ideas and values when dealing with the
course materials. Class discussions were popular and honest; logical
consistency was demanded.

Another source of challenge was the important fact that once they
were in the NewGate program, the students generally could expect to
become full-time college students after release from the prison. This
was something to think about. It was a break for most inmates who
otherwise probably would not have gone to college because of financial
difficulties. While attending college with financial support from New-
Gate was a matter of course in Oregon, it was a privilege in Minnesota,
and not something taken for granted. Students were expected to earn
outside support in the inside program. They were watched to see if
they were serious, if they attended classes, did their work, and kept
up their grades.

Another source of challenge in the Minnesota program was the
peer group wherein the participant was encouraged to open up, to
care for other people, to let others into his life, and to develop a new,
more positive self-concept. The peer group was emphasized more
by the project staff than by participants interviewed. Some participants felt the group was helpful, but just as many felt it was a waste
of time and that most people were posturing. There was no opportunity
to observe a group firsthand because the staff did not permit outsiders
to sit in on group sessions.

Institutional Change. As most NewGate programs, the Minnesota
program successfully conveyed to the general public that there was
a significant segment of the prison population that had the ability to
do college level work if given the opportunity. The Minnesota program
engaged in deliberate promotional work from its office on the university campus to make the NewGate experiment publicly visible. It ran
a series of feature stories about NewGate in a number of newspapers
throughout the state, held an open house for statewide officials at the
NewGate house, involved professional people from a variety of different areas on campus in its All University Advisory Board, maintained close contact with the state legislature, and participated in
designing, planning, and implementing new experiments in correctional reform.

Although the central NewGate office on campus was effective in
establishing statewide credibility, it was not as successful inside the
St. Cloud Reformatory. The inside NewGate staff, because of its remoteness, had not changed many prison staff persons' minds about
inmates or the usefulness of college. Most prison guards contended
that NewGate just selected the cream of the inmate population, a
general accusation often made against such programs. Logically,

such doubts can be dispelled only if the program deliberately demon-
strates that it is open to everyone. This could be done by a completely
open admission policy based on uniform objective standards and by
establishing an active outreach program to those not yet qualified to
do college work, including minority people and persons with serious
discipline problems. The New Mexico NewGate program was the
only program to do this effectively and was the only prison in which
many prison staff remarked on how the "hard-core" were being
reached by the college program.

Another area in which NewGate had not made much progress inside St. Cloud was in influencing policy and procedure. NewGate was
not included in the orientation of new inmates. NewGate was reluctant
to recruit inmates actively into the program, according to the inside
staff, lest it increase the jealousy and competition from the prison
industries, who had production quotas to fill and consequently competed for hard-working inmates. Applicants to NewGate were drawn
mainly by informal feedback from participants and by referrals from
the prison case worker staff. The lack of a more deliberate effort on
the part of the inside staff to establish relations with other parts of the
prison was due to at least three factors: (1) The NewGate director
had his office in Minneapolis, making him remote from the prison.
(2) There was a belief that the program's political (that is, external)
relations should be left to the people in the campus office, while the
staff inside the prison was to be concerned with program operations.
(3) The personalities of the inside staff were not those of outgoing or
engaging people.

When NewGate did become engaged actively in changing policy
and procedure, its success was impressive. The former NewGate
director was instrumental in getting a state law passed permitting
inmates to be released from prison prior to parole on work- and
study-release. NewGate managed to get the university to make an
important exception for NewGate students by waiving their tuition and
student fees for the first four quarters. Individual program staff also
were engaged actively in some of the other programs the institute had
developed and sponsored. Its role in the Felony Diversion Project
and in the Indian NewGate project was central. The NewGate staff
and a few select NewGate participants were involved since this study
in a pilot project in the twin cities high schools. Peer group counseling was introduced as a way of helping high schools develop a better
atmosphere and as a way of breaking down racial prejudice among the
students.

Program Survival and Vitality. One might assume from the experiences of the other programs in the sample that because the Minnesota
program allowed itself to become isolated from the rest of the prison

it eventually would be terminated, reduced to ineffectiveness or taken over by the prison. None of these happened, and the program appeared to be able to maintain its quality for at least two reasons. In the first place the program was not aggressive or expansionist but was content to operate as an enclave within the prison on behalf of a special group of inmates. Due to the pending reorganization of the state's corrections system, the prison administration was forced into a bureaucratic holding pattern, and, not knowing which way the wind would blow, was reluctant to undertake any major changes in ongoing programs.

Second, if the prison administration were to attack NewGate, it would encounter two formidable foes: the State Corrections Department and the University of Minnesota. The State Corrections Department had taken a progressive direction under the leadership of its controversial commissioner. To take on NewGate might risk a confrontation with the state office. The logic of the changes instituted by the commissioner was that large prisons were outdated and at least some should be put out of business. The prison administration then had a vested interest in not causing tension between the prison and the state office. Whether the State Department of Corrections would have intervened on behalf of NewGate in a struggle with the prison administration, the university undoubtedly would have done so. The university community was firmly behind the NewGate program and would have, if the need arose, mobilized considerable political pressure to protect NewGate.

Though NewGate's future was not put in question by any struggle between the program and the host prison, its continued existence at St. Cloud was nonetheless in doubt. If the St. Cloud facility closed down, the NewGate program at the institution would end. Two different contingency plans were being pursued. First, the NewGate staff was exploring the possibility of setting up a NewGate program at Stillwater, which would continue as the state's main facility. Second, an effort was made to enlarge the outside program and to anticipate the new directions the state was going with its reforms. Work was undertaken to use the NewGate residence house to accommodate young offenders being diverted from prison to community treatment facilities—the Felony Diversion Project. This new project would pay for itself since the county was reimbursed in full by the state. NewGate would provide the same services to felons diverted from prison as it did to study-release participants attending the university. In the final analysis, though the Minnesota NewGate might not continue to exist as it did in 1972, it will remain in one form or another.

New Mexico

The NewGate program in New Mexico operated in the state penitentiary situated 11 miles outside Santa Fe. The prison, completed in 1958, was modern and spacious with up to date training facilities for both academic and vocational instruction. A series of two-story, medium-sized rectangular buildings were arranged parallel, connected at the middle. The compound was surrounded by a high chain link fence, overlooking a barren desert and, on the horizon, New Mexico's majestic blue mountains.

The institution had a planned capacity for 1,000 but the population in 1972 was less than 700. Chicanos made up 46 percent of the population, whites, 37 percent, blacks, 12 percent, and native Americans, 3 percent. The inmates came from predominantly rural backgrounds. The educational and achievement test grade levels of the population were lower than in the institutions, which drew more heavily from urban areas. Of 104 guards, 82 were Chicano. Most of the administrative staff, including the warden, were Chicano.

Project NewGate in the New Mexico penitentiary was associated with two academic institutions. Eastern New Mexico University in Portales was the grantee for OEO funds and had the responsibility for administering NewGate. Eastern selected the NewGate director and oversaw program operations. Since Eastern was about 250 miles from Santa Fe, its involvement in the inside program was limited.

A private Catholic college in Santa Fe, the College of Santa Fe, had offered a few college courses inside the institution before NewGate was established. This program was merged with NewGate; and the College of Santa Fe provided the inside college academic program, issuing credits, offering courses, arranging the course schedule, and providing instructors. NewGate recruited, tested, and selected the students, provided psychotherapy and a college preparation curriculum, and developed the cultural and extracurricular component of the inside program. In addition, NewGate had exclusive jurisdiction over the outside program, which sponsored some of the students on a university campus after their release from prison.

The original proposal to OEO for NewGate funding in 1968 grew out of Eastern's Upward Bound project. The first NewGate director was appointed because of pressure from the warden at the time. According to all accounts, the initial program was regarded as a project of limited goals, emphasizing primarily adult basic education and GED preparation. It duplicated the prison's ABE program. The students did not see NewGate as anything particularly novel in prison education and distrusted the director's close contact with the warden. The first director resigned after one year under pressure from her fellow staff members.

The second director was appointed by Eastern New Mexico University and approved by a new prison administration in July 1970. Many felt the new director was ideal for the job; he had ideas, vitality, and the respect and trust of both inmates and prison officials. The second director believed college education should be offered to prison inmates because justice required that everyone, wherever they were, have an equal opportunity to go to college. Equally important to him was a belief in the efficacy of college as a rehabilitative device in prisons. Through a college program inmates could make new discoveries about the world and break out of the "loser" syndrome. Toward these ends, he set out to create a program that would resemble a college campus and that would adjust to the inmate student and to the prison as much as possible without sacrificing educational goals.

The second director appreciated the difficulty of accomplishing rehabilitation in the prison environment. However, he felt a start could be made if certain ideas were kept in mind. In his view, prisons necessarily provide an atmosphere of fear, suspicion, and hate. Prison administrators expect the worst of convicts, and convicts expect the worst of prison officials. These negative prejudgments reinforce negative self-images and lead to negative behavior, which is neither conducive to learning nor to positive and lasting behavioral change. The college program, to effectively promote positive change, had to develop a different atmosphere, one in which there were feelings of trust, respect, and self-worth. One of the primary ways this could be done was by hiring sound, sensitive staff members who had no custodial responsibilities; people who could maintain an idealistic position toward their task in the program. A change in the kind of people working in the prison was one of the few ways a prisoner's environment could be altered.

The other strategy adopted to develop a proper college atmosphere was to give the physical facilities a separate identification. Under the first director, NewGate was housed in a tightly controlled area of the prison. Guards were always present, and the student group was locked in the program area while school was in session. The College of Santa Fe program was in a separate building elsewhere in the prison complex. The second director was instrumental in getting the prison administration to house all the educational programs—vocational, ABE, GED, and college—in the same building. On his insistence, there were no locked doors in the education area. The walls were brightly painted, the floors were carpeted, and comfortable furniture was purchased. Inmate students were free to move around as they wished in the NewGate area. Furthermore, they could leave the area whenever they wanted, without escort, to return to their cells to study. There was considerable resistance from the prison administration to implementing this plan. The prison personnel, from the warden to the guards, felt NewGate was giving the students more than they deserved. The program director was also concerned about how the program fit into the prison environment. He felt the guards and prison officials had to be convinced that college program would not undermine prison security. To do this, he felt it important to hire staff members who had their eyes open, who were not easily conned. It was important that the prison see the program as a serious enterprise with clear-cut expectations of its participants. It was also important that nonparticipating inmates view NewGate as a serious, albeit special, program. It was thought that the future of the program depended on this kind of reputation.

The final objective was the development of opportunities to continue college studies after release. Those inside participants demonstrating competence in their work and an interest in continuing their studies were provided financial and counseling support after they were paroled or discharged from the prison.

The program's second director proceeded gradually and systematically in developing a program structure whose success was due, in part, to his approach to the prison administration. There were moments of tension and disagreement, but always in a context of trust and respect between persons who recognized the other's differences in priorities but who were determined to work together.

The second director resigned in June 1971. For three months the assistant director functioned as the interim director until September 1971, when NewGate's third director was appointed. While his administration was as innovative and vigorous as his predecessor's, the thrust was in different areas. His predecessor's accomplishments were in creating the basic framework of NewGate and in establishing it as a permanent program. This necessitated selling the NewGate model to the public, the prison administration, and the state legislature to ensure its survival. At the time the third director took over, the NewGate program lacked internal coherence. He began systematizing procedures, defining expectations of students and staff, and improving the quality of the program. He consolidated NewGate's position in the prison, coordinating its operations with other prison programs (the College of Santa Fe, the ABE, DVR training programs, the prison guards, the women's division, the prison case workers, and Psychological Services). His efforts also were directed toward improving the quality of NewGate's outside program by developing new strategies to provide more effective support to released participants on campus. The following is a description and analysis of the New Mexico NewGate project under the third Director.

Inside Program

Students. As of the fall of 1972 there were 80 inmates in the NewGate program, 50 of whom were full-time college students. Twenty were full-time students but divided their time between college classes and classes in preparation for college work. Only 10 of the 80 were taking less than a 12-credit hour work load. A few inmates enrolled in the DVR's vocational training program were involved for half a day in the NewGate program.

The selection process changed over the years, and NewGate gained an increasing role in decision making. Originally, the primary means of entry into NewGate was recommendation by the case worker to the prison's Classification Board. During its first year, NewGate had no representation on the Classification Board. The board did not send NewGate many qualified inmates because the prison administration was not capable of identifying them and because of the administration's distrust of the program. One month after the first director was replaced, the new director requested and was granted a seat on the Classification Board. NewGate was also included in the general orientation sessions for incoming inmates and was able to acquaint a larger audience with the aims of the program.

In addition, an informal means of gaining access to NewGate developed. Inmates who had appeared already before the Classification Board and later developed an interest in NewGate began requesting interviews with NewGate staff members. In the interview, a counselor would describe the program, its goals, and the student's responsibilities. Any testing needed beyond that received on entering the prison was scheduled. If it was felt he qualified for NewGate, the inmate was referred to the NewGate director, who requested the prison administration to assign the inmate to the program.

Under the third director, all interested inmates contacted the NewGate office directly. The program was described to them, and they were told when the required admission tests were going to be given. A high school diploma or GED was the only prerequisite to taking the tests. All prison units were notified when tests were to be given. NewGate also made a special effort to announce testing dates to persons who were enrolled in the prison GED program and to all incoming inmates during orientation. The following tests were administered: The American College Test (ACT), the Diagnostic Reading Examination, the Group Personality Projective Test, and the Edwards Personality Preference Test. The first two were to determine the inmate's present academic level, whether NewGate could design a program for him, and as an aid to the new student's academic counselor. The second two tests were used to provide psychological counseling information. The tests were gone over with the participant and used as a starting point in the therapy program.

After the tests were given, borderline cases were interviewed. Then a selection committee, consisting of the NewGate staff plus three or four inmates who worked in the program met to review the results. No one had been rejected for bad behavior records, according to the program director. The committee recommended that some be admitted to take college preparatory courses prior to college courses, that others "prep" in special areas (for example, in reading) while taking some college courses. The majority were approved to take a full college load. Anyone not accepted could take the entrance tests again each time they were administered. The recommendations of the NewGate selection committee were submitted to the prison's classification committee for approval. In practice, the prison officials increasingly came to accept NewGate as the most qualified to determine who should be allowed in the program, although the Classification Board did not accept the entire recommended list in the fall of 1971 when two inmates applied who were considered disciplinary risks and were deemed unable to handle the freedom on the NewGate floor.

Continued participation in the college program depended almost entirely on the student's academic performance. He was expected to maintain the same grade point average (GPA) as a student on the College of Santa Fe campus. Unless a 2.0 was maintained and 12 semester hours taken, he was placed on academic probation. If a student "cut" a class four times or more, he was dropped from the course. A student's counselor discussed the matter with him before a fourth absence. If a student was dropped from the program for academic reasons, he could reapply after one semester.

Staff. The staff structure was reorganized under the third director. There had formerly been an associate director in charge of operations directly under the program director; this responsibility was divided between two positions—an academic coordinator and a counseling coordinator, who were to coordinate their efforts. Under each new coordinator were two staff members, that is two full-time teachers and two counselors. The third director had a B.A. in physical education, an M.A. in school administration, and a Ph.D. in student personnel administration. His doctoral program was designed as preparation for a position as dean of students, with emphasis on admissions, personnel services, financing, job placement, and counseling. He had had seven years experience in the public schools as a teacher and as an administrator. The new coordinator of counseling had an M.A. in guidance and counseling and a B.A. in political science, with a minor in psychology. He had worked in programs dealing with juvenile delinquency and drug abuse. He was young, well trained, bright, and had a rich imagination.

In addition to the director, two coordinators, two counselors, and an office manager/secretary, there were two NewGate teachers on the staff. One was a full-time English and reading instructor, the other taught math and science three days a week. Though both teachers were hired mainly to teach college "prep" courses in their respective fields, each taught some college level courses as well, as did two of the counselors. The NewGate program also had four volunteer teachers on its staff—a dance teacher, two art teachers, and one person who taught social studies, English, and reading.

The college instructors were from the College of Santa Fe and taught in the prison program in addition to their normal teaching loads on campus. On the basis of classroom observation and statements made by participants, the caliber of the instructors was high. However, a generally low level of personal involvement by teachers with individual students was also noticed. Teachers provided little feedback to students about their academic progress. In contrast, the NewGate staff, in their capacity as instructors, were observed spending considerable time in individual sessions with the participants. Involving full-time NewGate staff in teaching seemed to be New Mexico NewGate's way of effectively overcoming a deficiency observed in all other programs. Exclusive reliance on instructors who came into the prison to teach one course typically resulted in a lack of personalized follow-through and little coordination with the counseling efforts in other programs.

Curriculum and Counseling. During the winter 1972, thirteen different college courses were offered in the program, drawn from five different majors, which participants could choose for an associate of arts degree from the College of Santa Fe. The majors were social welfare, general business, education, medical technician, and liberal arts. The primary method of instruction was lecture followed by class discussion. Reading material consisted mainly of textbooks but was often supplemented by outside reading, which was relatively easy for the inmate students to obtain. Preparatory classes were smaller, more informal, and followed the participant's needs rather than a predetermined format.

Counseling. Counseling was an integral part of the NewGate program. Under the second director it was provided on an informal basis. Under the third director, systematic academic counseling was provided to every student on a regular basis. On entering NewGate, a participant was assigned a counselor with whom he developed a detailed program outline. During the term the student could confer with his counselor to discuss his progress or other questions related to the program.

Therapeutic counseling was considered an essential part of the program. The participant could choose whether to participate in therapeutic counseling, and if so, whether to take group, individual, or both. He also had a choice of counselors. There were three counselors; one was too new to evaluate. The two who had been working in the program seemed to strike an effective balance. One was confrontive and directive in his approach, his relationship with the students being friendly but very professional. The other counselor was a middle-aged woman with seven grown children. She had a B.A. in social welfare and three years experience counseling in the prison. Her manner tended to be warm and supportive. Her involvement with each of her students was on a deeply personal level. The students interviewed divided fairly evenly as to which counselor they preferred. The Chicanos and native Americans consistently preferred the non-confrontive approach and actively enlisted the woman therapist's counsel.

The counseling staff also visited the various university sites throughout New Mexico where outside participants attended school to maintain continuity between the inside and outside programs. The counselors had an opportunity to learn the strengths and weaknesses of the students before release and were able to anticipate some of the difficulties on the outside. In addition, the experiences of students in the outside program helped inform the counselors about typical transitional difficulties that might have been prevented by following a different approach in the inside program. Also, counselors were able to share anecdotal information with inside participants about the experiences of students on the outside, providing another type of continuity with the outside.

The New Mexico program was the only program studied where female and male inmates took classes and group counseling together inside the prison. The woman counselor (mentioned above) was the pioneer in bringing women into the main prison. She had previously worked three years in the women's division as a student. At that time there were no education programs for women. She began ABE courses and provided academic counseling and tutoring. The following year, while working for NewGate, she was instrumental in enrolling the first women in the college courses provided by the College of Santa Fe. One year later she was involved in NewGate beginning coeducational counseling groups. These experiments proved successful. Today, the New Mexico penitentiary no longer operates a separate ABE program for the women's division. Women attend ABE classes inside the men's penitentiary daily. ABE classes were taught by male inmates from the college program who had completed more than 20 hours of college class work. It was expected that women college students would soon be teaching in the ABE program.

Two other changes were made during the fall of 1972. Women attending classes in the men's penitentiary had previously been escorted from the women's division; they were now permitted to walk unescorted from the women's division, through the main administration building, to the control center inside the prison. Also, a new therapy group composed of couples was started. The couples consisted of men and their spouses or girlfriends who were incarcerated in the women's division. The group was led by both NewGate's female counselor and a male counselor from the prison.

Many released participants interviewed indicated that they had benefited a great deal from the New Mexico NewGate counseling program. Some were enthusiastic about new insights gained from the structured group setting and the straightforward approach of the therapist. Others emphasized the importance of personal contact with certain staff members and the warmth and concern they found in the relationship. Since all released participants in the sample went through the program before the third director took over, the participants' reaction to the program under the third director came from the inside participant questionnaires. For the most part, the inside participants had positive feelings about their counseling experience. They were particularly favorable toward individual therapy. Many claimed this provided an opportunity to talk about problems they were unwilling to share with a group. New Mexico participants rated their counseling higher than did participants in any other program. Twenty-six percent rated individual counseling very good, and 28 percent rated group counseling very good. The corresponding figures for all other programs combined were 9 percent and 10 percent.

In the fall of 1972 a new LEAA-funded psychological service was set up inside the prison. The new staff was directed by a prominent psychiatrist from the Santa Fe area. Each week a group meeting was held with the new staff and the NewGate counseling staff to discuss their work and to develop improvements in their techniques. Any NewGate participant involved in a group run by the new service was not included in a NewGate group. He could, however, still be seen on an individual basis.

Cultural and Extracurricular Programs. An extensive art project was operated as part of the NewGate program. The New Mexico State Arts Commission funded the project in 1972 with $3,000 for the art program, $2,000 for a drama program, and $2,000 for a summer art show. Inmates who were not NewGate students also participated in this program, giving them exposure to the college program. Since the art program was highly publicized, it also served to acquaint the general public with NewGate.

In addition, there were a variety of other activities and facilities, which were not part of the regular curriculum but which helped create a "college atomsphere" in the NewGate quarters. The education floor had a nonprison atmosphere. There was light and color and a feeling of escaping from the more oppressive surroundings of the drab and barred prison building. There were unlocked classrooms, study quarters, and browsing rooms. There was an extensive collection of books and magazines. Additional material could be ordered from the state library and the Santa Fe Public Library through staff, who picked up the books requested. The prison library also had some additional books, but there was limited use of this facility because access hours were very restricted. In an attempt to expand the supply of contemporary reading materials, two NewGate staff members wrote major publishers requesting free or discounted books, and a Santa Fe drugstore donated paperback books. Also, about 50 books were donated each month to the program by private individuals in the state.

NewGate students could move around the education facilities without restriction. Prison guards no longer appeared on the floor. Former participants who were interviewed emphasized how important the physical environment had been in making them feel freer and more hopeful, even inspired to think beyond their prison stay. They also emphasized that the physical layout had encouraged interaction with their peers. They said one of the most effective ways of learning how to study had been by watching students who had previous college experience. New Mexico NewGate understood the importance of creating an environment conducive to learning better than any other programs visited, except perhaps Pennsylvania. This can be traced directly to the fact that the program was run by educators with a commitment to the academic world, and with little or no negative influence imposed by the prison administration.

One of NewGate's volunteer teachers arranged outside speakers to keep students in touch with events beyond their regular classroom work. The director estimated that there was a visit by one outside speaker every week, on the average. Some of the subjects have been how to buy a used car, renewing and qualifying for driver's licenses, applying for jobs, bachelor cooking, nutrition and balanced diets, purchasing insurance, consumer protection—the mobile homes racket, and recent innovations in electric appliances. Staff members, too, attempted to bring in information from the outside to break down the social and cultural isolation of inmates. Outside volunteers were encouraged to share skills and resources with the NewGate participants and other inmates. It was hoped that the involvement of outside volunteers with the prison program would develop a greater awareness about life inside the prison and lead to a commitment from the volunteers to the NewGate program, to the participants, and to prison

·inmates in general. The NewGate director estimated that 42 hours
of volunteer time was donated to the program each week. ABE and
vocational students were also able to participate in these activities.

Relationship of the Program to the Prison. The NewGate program
under the third director was viewed positively by the prison administration and staff. In fact, the college program in New Mexico was
more thoroughly integrated and accepted than in any other prison
visited. This, of course, did not happen overnight. Initially there
was much resistance. (Of the released participants interviewed, 51
percent viewed the administration as negative toward NewGate, 64
percent viewed the attitude of the guards as negative. In 1972, of the
inside participants 65 percent perceived the administration positively,
and 63 percent perceived the guards as responding positively to New-
Gate.) As discussed above, strategies were followed that overcame
the early resistance. In addition to the project's efforts, other factors
contributed to NewGate's success in establishing good relationships
with the correctional program. An obvious reason for greater acceptance was that NewGate had been around long enough to be accepted
as part of the routine (this alone was not enough, as we can see from
the experiences of other programs in the sample). The second reason
was that NewGate had not caused any serious trouble—in fact, just
the opposite. The publicity NewGate received was usually good, and
this reflected well on the prison administration. Moreover, though
some procedures developed for students caused some extra work for
the prison staff, this was offset by less work in other areas. Some
persons with serious discipline problems calmed down after they
became involved in NewGate. After the prison administration determined that NewGate was "reliable," it permitted long term "hard-
core" inmates in the program. Guards reported that these inmates
became less bored, found something constructive to which they could
devote their time, and began to think better of themselves. Prison
case workers also reported these changes and said that NewGate had
lightened their work load. The prison administrators were of the
opinion that the program reduced the number of discipline problems.
    The third reason for NewGate's wide acceptance was its reputa-
tion as being serious. The guards, as a whole, did not feel the inmates were "getting something for nothing." They believed that inmates had to work once they got into the program. The inmates
believed this too. The warden placed two guards who were highly
respected by their fellows to monitor the college program. This
served two purposes. The other guards were confident that inmates
would not be allowed to get away with anything. Also, the high prestige of the monitors helped dispel the doubts of other guards when
they reported the program was okay.

The fourth reason was the behavior of the NewGate staff. Friendly relations developed between the NewGate and correctional staffs. The NewGate staff had a basketball team, which played NewGate inmates and teams of prison staff. Sometimes the NewGate staff team was short and asked guards to join them. NewGate and prison staff sat together in the lunch room and engaged in frequent exchanges of practical jokes and repartee. NewGate staff attended parties given for staff people, made hospital visits, and engaged in other activities that indicated their personal interest in all the members of the institution.

NewGate staff were also involved with prison staff on a professional basis. As mentioned above, one counselor was extensively involved with the women residents. The director served on treatment committees and the classification committee. Members of the NewGate staff were involved in helping inmates set up a group known as Concerned Convicts for Children. The NewGate office manager helped schedule television interviews for the group and appeared with the inmates on several shows. This same staff member sponsored the prison Jaycees. He was one of the most important forces in solidifying the spirit of trust and cooperation with the prison staff. Moreover, he was a Chicano, as were 95 percent of the prison staff. His knowledge of Spanish and the Chicano culture, coupled with his friendly style, was important in promoting a favorable image for NewGate.

A fifth factor bolstering the position of NewGate at the prison was NewGate's outside power base as a project sponsored and endorsed by Eastern New Mexico University. The program director could draw on the reputation and resources of the university for support. NewGate operated directly out of the university president's office with three interested and committed friends on campus: the director of special programs, the dean of students, and the campus coordinator of NewGate. The university helped build a resource base for NewGate by securing a yearly commitment for state matching funds of $30,000 from the state legislature.

Finally, New Mexico, unlike the other projects in the sample, had an active statewide advisory council, which helped immeasurably in selling the NewGate program to the state legislature. On the executive committee were a representative from Eastern, the only black state legislator, the assistant superintendent of schools in Albuquerque, a well-known Santa Fe civic leader, and a member of the New Mexico State Arts Commission, who was instrumental in creating the NewGate arts program. The publicity and independent backing NewGate received from the committee's activities pictured the prison as an innovative and progressive institution, which helped in solidifying NewGate in the plans of the State Corrections Department.

Relationship Between Participants and Other Inmates. As difficult as
it is to make generalizations about an entire prison population, the
impression was that NewGate students were accepted and respected
by the other inmates. It had not always been this way. At first the
inmates were suspicious that the program was controlled by the prison
administration, and they shunned the program. (Of the released participants interviewed, only 13 percent viewed the other inmates as
cooperative and supportive. However, 30 percent of the inside participants believed other inmates to be cooperative and supportive.)
Early participants were labeled as "snitches" and "sellouts." They
were suspected of trying to avoid their work obligations and of trying
to obtain a quick release. For the first year the NewGate staff did
nothing to dispel these misgivings. When the second director was
appointed, things began to change for at least five reasons.

First, NewGate expanded its recruitment to a broader base of
inmates and deliberately tried to attract inmates who occupied positions of power in the yard. The recruitment of four or five "heavys"
helped legitimize the program. As a result, the participant group
was less homogeneous than when the prison had exclusive jurisdiction
over selection. Heterogeneity prevented nonparticipants and prison
staff from being able to stereotype the NewGate student and the program. The project's open admissions policy reinforced the belief that
there was no exclusionary policy and that any inmate had the opportunity to join if he so chose.

The third and fourth factors that reduced antagonism toward
students were that program participants had few extra privileges to
set them apart and that they were expected to work hard in the education program. Students did not live in separate housing facilities,
which helped keep other inmates in touch with the program and the
participants in touch with the everyday life of the prison. Because
participants had to work hard, they took their role in the program
seriously.

The fifth reason for inmate acceptance of NewGate was that the
program reached out to serve a larger number of inmates. NewGate
in New Mexico had the most effective outreach component of all the
programs in the sample. Its college students taught in the ABE program, bringing the college program into contact with those doing high
school work. The college students tried to involve the ABE students
in the NewGate extracurricular activities. Moreover, NewGate was
designed to help inmates who could not otherwise succeed in a regular
college program, with an emphasis on developing skills such as reading, talking, writing, or arithmetic. Though Chicanos were reluctant
to become involved in the early days of the program, there was
evidence that this had reversed after a few dynamic Chicano students
put out the word that NewGate was a good program.

Involvement in Discipline and Release Procedures. NewGate had considerable influence in study-release decisions. The responsible
classification committee was made up of the classification officer,
the assistant warden for clinical services, a representative for the
state Department of Vocational Rehabilitation, a representative from
the College of Santa Fe program, and a representative from NewGate.
The warden had veto power over all decisions made by the committee.
NewGate influence was greatest in those cases in which the prospec-
tive releasee required financial assistance from NewGate.

It was difficult to assess the repercussions of NewGate's involvement in study-release decisions, since study-release was relatively
new. Initially, NewGate recommended only those inside participants
who were within six months of their scheduled parole board hearing
and who had at least 50 to 60 hours of completed course work. A policy
change made any student who had completed 25 hours eligible to apply.
Study-releasees attended the College of Santa Fe during the day only,
leaving the prison at seven in the morning and returning at seven in
the evening.

Involvement in Parole Decisions. At approximately the same time
NewGate obtained a seat on the Classification Board, the warden permitted the program director to sit in on parole hearings involving
NewGate participants. This was perhaps unparalleled in the history
of prison college education programs and was discontinued when the
second director left the program, making NewGate less directly involved in parole decisions. The program director routinely submitted
a written progress report to the parole board on the student's participation in the program: courses taken, GPA and class attendance
records, and amount of academic and therapeutic counseling. On
occasion, the parole board discussed the report with NewGate staff.

An important factor in parole board decisions was the promise
of NewGate support (financial and counseling) to parolees. With such
support, the parolee had a structured situation in which adjustment
and supervision were anticipated as easier. For this reason, the
parole board rarely turned down someone promised support, according
to the NewGate director.

The NewGate program did not automatically provide financial
support to all students who were released. Only those who had maintained at least a 2.3 GPA, had completed at least 12 hours of course
work, and had taken at least one semester of group counseling and
some individual counseling were eligible. Those not promised outside
support appeared before the board at a disadvantage, since they did
not have such a well-defined parole plan, and they were not treated
as favorably. Students not promised outside support had the option
of asking NewGate not to send its routine report to the parole board,

but the absence of a report also had implications, which may have unfavorably influenced the board.

Outside Program

The New Mexico project's weakest link was its outside program. Originally Eastern New Mexico University was to be the institution that would serve as host to the postrelease students. New Mexico's first students on campus were 19 exconvicts at Eastern. NewGate's supporters on campus were excited about the experiment and worked hard to provide the necessary social and emotional support to these students. The participants were housed in dormitories. Unfortunately, Eastern is located in the small conservative town of Portales, and the exconvict group was very conspicuous in the community. The group was racially mixed and slightly unconventional in its style. The news of their arrival on campus had been publicized in the campus newspaper by their enthusiastic supporters, so the community was aware of what was coming.

The local district attorney opposed introducing such an "unsavory element" into the community. Eastern was located in a county where no alcoholic beverages were served. The district attorney learned that a number of NewGate participants had crossed the county line for a drink in a "border bar." Leaving one's county of residence without the parole officer's formal permission was a violation of parole regulations. This, coupled with a later unsubstantiated accusation by a coed that she was raped by an exconvict led the parole officer to send 13 of the participants back to prison for technical violations. After this, it was decided not to send NewGate students to Eastern.

NewGate concluded the Portales problem resulted from the presence of too many exconvicts in one remote, rural location and from having released some students too soon. It was decided to disperse outside participants among many different college campuses throughout the state. With the exception of the University of New Mexico in Albuquerque with a student population of 15,000, all colleges in the state were small and located in small, isolated rural towns.

Dispersing students all over the state put a tremendous strain on NewGate's follow-up services. The results were obvious in the interviews with the released participants. Many complained they had been dropped on campus without adequate preparation as to what to expect once they arrived. Some said they were forced to drop out of school or had to live under great financial hardship because proper funding arrangements had not been established by NewGate. Many claimed they lost faith in themselves and lost interest in school because they were alone, isolated, and uncomfortable in hostile and prejudiced communities, which they felt were just waiting for them to err. Almost all the participants criticized the NewGate staff for failing to provide systematic support. They never knew when a staff member would be in their town, and when a visit did occur, how long the person would stay.

In retrospect, the decision to disperse outside participants after the incident at Eastern might not have been necessary. One institution, the University of New Mexico in Albuquerque, seemed suitable to serve as the host to the outside program without high visibility. Both the university and the city of Albuquerque are the largest and most diversified in the state. Twenty to 30 exconvicts hardly would have been noticed in this location.

There were several reasons why NewGate did not establish a relationship with the University of New Mexico following the incident at Eastern. The University of New Mexico previously had indicated a lack of interest in NewGate. The university had been slow in developing programs for the poor and the minorities in the state. A second factor was the feeling among some of the NewGate staff that their students would have trouble with the university's academic standards. Finally, Eastern might have been reluctant to involve another academic institution in the NewGate program. Eastern and the College of Santa Fe were already sharing responsibilities, and to involve yet another university might have led to considerable administrative confusion.

The NewGate administration recognized the inadequacy of dispersing students all over the state and have moved to concentrate them on three campuses within 65 miles of the prison: Highlands University in Las Vegas, the College of Santa Fe in Santa Fe, and the University of New Mexico in Albuquerque. Two other developments will affect the outside program in the future. The prison plans to convert an honor farm near Albuquerque to a work- and study-release center, making it easier for NewGate participants on study-release. Also, the University of New Mexico was planning to establish a branch campus in Espinola, about 25 miles from Santa Fe. This campus will probably replace the College of Santa Fe, since tuition for instate residents at the university is $220 a semester, while the College of Santa Fe, which is private, charges $600.

At the time of the evaluation team's last visit, eight students were in study-release at the College of Santa Fe. Four paroled students were provided a full financial package to attend the College of Santa Fe, seven at the University of New Mexico in Albuquerque, and four at Highlands University in Las Vegas. One student was attending New Mexico University in Las Cruces, and one was attending Eastern's branch campus in Roswell. There was one woman on study-release, and one sponsored in school on parole.

Analysis

Did the program offer support structure, personal social space, and challenge to help its students attain their educational goals? In general, the New Mexico NewGate project provided the highest quality inside program in the study. It ranked high on all three dimensions: support structure, personal social space, and challenge. The outside program was deficient in important aspects that are spelled out below. Released participants' responses about the inside program were outdated, since the program had changed significantly since January 1, 1972, the date before which they were all released. However, the overall assessment of the inside college program was supported by the inside participants in their response to the question: How do you rate the college program? Seventy-two percent said it was either excellent or very good. The average response for all programs combined was 47 percent. The second highest was 60 percent for Oregon, followed by 50 percent for Minnesota. The lowest was Illinois, with 5 percent.

Support Structure. One of the most critical features of the program was the counseling provided from the very beginning of a student's participation in the program. (In New Mexico, 74 percent of the inside participants said that the educational counseling was adequate or better, compared with 71 percent in Pennsylvania, 58 percent in Oregon, 48 percent in Ashland, and 46 percent in Minnesota.) On entry, the counselor's evaluation of the student's academic potential and personal development was discussed with each individual, and a program plan for the student was developed. The counselor acquainted the student with the resources available in the program; the requirements for advancement; the necessity for developing objectives, goals, and priorities; and alternative ways the student could work toward them.

Second, the college academic program was designed to maximize support. The A.A. degree could be completed while in the inside program, providing a tangible reward easily within grasp in prison. The A.A. degree also served as an intermediate step along the way to completing a regular four-year academic program. Five different majors were offered, including upper division courses for students who had completed the two-year program. NewGate also attempted to develop a curriculum that met the needs of inmates with a long time still to serve.

The third main support component was psychotherapy, which was regarded as being as important as academics. An effort was made to hire staff with experience and sensitivity in this field. New Mexico NewGate offered several different kinds of group as well as

individual therapy. The director was determined to provide the best
therapy available. The fact that the therapeutic and academic efforts
of the program were designed to complement each other strengthened
the program as a whole. One of the major ways these were integrated
was by having counselors also teach courses.

Fourth, NewGate's commitment to create a supportive framework
through which students could realize their goals was demonstrated
in the program's preparatory component, which recognized that the
prison population was not composed of average college students but
of high school drop-outs needing special enrichment programs, additional skill training, and individual attention and encouragement. In
small classes and on an individual basis, preparatory students were
taught such things as how to write papers, examinations, book reports, outlines, and vitas; how to read quickly and with comprehension;
and how to be logical and to speak convincingly.

Fifth, the fact that NewGate had integrated its program with other
educational efforts in the prison reinforced the effectiveness of each
and formed a total program with maximum ability to accommodate the
interests and needs of students at different levels. From the preparatory component, students were gradually introduced into the college
program. Full-time college students could obtain extra help from the
teaching staff. Persons in the prison's vocational training program
could take preparatory and college courses. NewGate also had systematic contact with the ABE program since college students were
used as ABE teachers, strengthening the college program by providing
a few students with work experience in fields for which they were
training. ABE students, through these teachers, were introduced to
the NewGate program and were encouraged to pursue their education.

The education program as a whole presented a progression of
steps wherein the mastery of one level led logically to the next. A
student could start on his ABE, progress to the NewGate preparatory
component, gradually enter the college program, become a full-time
college student, complete his A.A. degree, move out to the College
of Santa Fe in study-release status, and complete his B.A. degree
on parole. This process was not set up to eliminate students at each
level. Rather, it was designed to move everyone toward completion
by overcoming deficiencies without lowering standards. Educational
institutions in the free society could learn important lessons from the
spirit and effectiveness of the education program in the New Mexico
penitentiary.

The supportive framework in the outside program was deficient.
The widely dispersed students lacked personal contacts on campus to
help them with their academic and emotional problems. The practice
of sending inside counselors out to visit students on campus proved to
be inadequate to compensate for not having a comprehensive aftercare

project at a campus. The experience of the New Mexico NewGate
(when compared with the NewGate programs with a strong outside
component) would suggest that exconvict students generally need the
continuing presence of staff and program resources during the initial
transition to the outside. Otherwise they drop out of school prematurely, thereby wasting much of the positive effect of a high quality
inside program.

Personal Social Space. The New Mexico NewGate program operated
on the premise that prison's most debilitating effect was to deprive
the inmate of the responsibility to make decisions about his daily
life. Routine is so firmly established and rigidly adhered to in prison
that it requires no special effort from the inmate to organize his time.
Life on campus is much different. Students are required to define
their own objectives and to schedule their own time. NewGate attempted to develop the ability to make the kinds of choices needed on
a college campus by establishing a prison program in which participants learned to make choices and to develop their own program. The
student could choose to go or not to go to an academic counselor, and
could choose among several different counselors. He could choose to
take or not to take therapy and with which therapist or group, if he
chose to participate. The student could choose among 13 academic
courses, five majors, and a variety of college preparatory courses.
He even had some choice in teachers. He had a choice as to when and
where to study. He also had a wide assortment of books and research
sources available for use as needed.

The underlying philosophy of the New Mexico NewGate project
was that inmates will change most in a situation where they are provided a variety of experiences and can pick and choose according to
their own interests. This philosophy assumes that inmates, as anyone
else, know what is best for themselves. By contrast, the Minnesota
project started with the premise that inmates do not always know
what is best for them and therefore must be placed, whether they like
it or not, in a context that directs them toward more socially acceptable attitudes and behavior. The idea communicated to the Minnesota
inmate was that there was something wrong with him that he must
deal with if he expects the program to sponsor him. In New Mexico,
the inmate could accept the challenge "to change" when and if he
wanted. The only requirement was that he had to maintain academic
standards.

Challenge. The major distinguishing characteristic of the New Mexico
NewGate project was its deliberate effort to create an inside program
as a catalyst for changing inmates' values, perspectives, and goals by
designing the program to serve, in addition to college-bound students,

segments of the prison population who would not otherwise have attended college without the NewGate experience. The college program had outreach and enrichment components to prepare inmates with academic deficiencies for college work and progressively moved them into higher level and more exacting course work.

Compared with the New Mexico program, non-NewGate programs were at the other end of the continuum. They were not concerned about outreach efforts, nor were they involved with providing assistance to students with academic deficiencies. The other NewGate programs can be placed in between. They attempted to offer the opportunity to go to college to a wider segment of inmates than did non-NewGate programs, mainly by dropping behavioral requirements as prerequisites to admission, providing participants full-time student status, and extending financial assistance to released participants. Despite this emphasis, they did not match New Mexico's ability in developing a student body with such a diversity of interests and abilities. For example, Minnesota's strategy was to focus more intensely on a narrow segment of the inmate population. The Oregon project tried to appeal to just as wide and diverse a segment of the prison population as New Mexico, but provided fewer alternatives and less intensity in those services it did offer. Consequently, fewer were reached in a way that significantly would change their values, perspectives, and goals.

The New Mexico NewGate program saw the staff members with whom the inmates interacted as a primary source of stimulation and challenge. Although Minnesota viewed the inmate's peers as more important than "squares from the free society" as a source of stimulus, New Mexico NewGate saw its staff as role models for the inmates. To provide diverse role models, the staff was picked to represent a variety of different backgrounds and experiences as well as program expertise. The research group was impressed with how well the New Mexico NewGate staff functioned as a team, with each member understanding the program objectives and how his efforts fit in with the efforts of others. The staff members appeared to be caught up in the excitement of the project and brought an unusual amount of energy and commitment to their work. They had high expectations of the participants, accompanied by an understanding of the gaps in the participants' backgrounds and of the pressures facing them in prison and on release.

The extracurricular activities enriched the program. Contact with the world outside the prison was an important stimulus. Interest demonstrated by outsiders also helped to legitimize the program. The New Mexico NewGate program had a good reputation in the state, and there was increasing interest in becoming involved in the program among outside civic associations and prominent individuals. These contacts with outside persons, groups, and institutions served as a further stimulus to the participants.

With respect to the challenge dimension, the New Mexico NewGate program again fell down in its outside program. Due to the absence of a well-defined program on a college campus to which inside students moved after release from prison, the step after the inside program was not as logical and structured as the steps preceding it. Inside students could not count on the future. They could not easily anticipate, and therefore identify with, the role of a college student in the free society, as students could in Pennsylvania, Oregon, or Minnesota. Consequently, many who had begun to experiment with a new identity could have been thwarted by not being integrated into a challenging situation on a campus. In this sense, programs that focused on fewer and more homogeneous students, who could more easily be integrated and supported during the transition to campus life, might produce longer-lasting changes. On the other hand, if New Mexico NewGate is successful in developing a more extensive aftercare unit on one or a few campuses capable of absorbing its diverse student group, the New Mexico project could be a better catalyst for changing values, perspectives, and goals.

Institutional Change. NewGate demonstrated that convicts are educable and convinced people that higher education programs have a legitimate place in the prison. The accomplishments of participants and the efforts by staff were instrumental in selling these ideas to the public and to the correctional authorities.

NewGate caused no public embarrassment to the prison, with the exception of the episode in Portales, and enhanced the public image of the prison through favorable publicity that the program generated. The prison was increasingly willing to accept NewGate on its own terms. A major change in policy was the increasing role NewGate was allowed to play in the recruitment and selection of students. The prison accepted the education experts as competent to select the participants, a good measure of the prison's confidence in the program and a credit to both the prison administration and to the NewGate program.

The practice of bringing women prisoners into the men's prison for coed classes and therapy was another change in the prison practice brought about by NewGate. This was a daring innovation, which began with the hiring of women for the NewGate staff. Their presence in the prison without mishap created the confidence necessary to bring women prisoners into the men's prison.

Perhaps the most recent change in the prison's practice triggered by NewGate was the study-release program hosted by the College of Santa Fe, which was expected to stimulate the development of similar work-release and other community-based treatment programs.

Little change occurred in the universities. The College of Santa Fe, because of its proximity to the prison, and because of its responsibility for the inside academic program, probably experienced the most change. Other campuses throughout the state where NewGate sent participants were almost unaware of these students' presence. Few exconvicts attended at any one time, and they maintained low visibility. As a result, no university took any new or more vigorous interest in corrections and related problems. Even Eastern which saw itself as the primary sponsor of NewGate, did not sponsor research programs at the prison.

A third level at which institutional change could take place was in the power structure level. One way in which the balance of power changed in the New Mexico penitentiary was in its sharing authority with the university in the prison college program. Both the College of Santa Fe and Eastern New Mexico had legitimate roles to play in decision making affecting the program and the leves of inmates. The role NewGate played in the orientation of all incoming inmates and in the selection of program participants was indicative of the extent to which the prison shared power with the program.

There were other changes that, though less tangible, were equally real. The presence of NewGate, with its links to outside institutions, influenced a whole range of activities inside the prison, some of which were only indirectly related to education. Consider, for example, the area of discipline. The presence of staff members who were not part of the traditional corrections system placed the prison increasingly in the position of having to justify practices that outsiders felt were too harsh or unnecessary.

In addition to the university, other outside parties were drawn into the prison operations by the NewGate program. Two of the most important were the state legislature and the New Mexico Arts Commission. The state legislature put up $30,000 as a state matching grant for LEAA funds to help operate NewGate. This appropriation passed because there was interest on the part of many legislators in educational rehabilitation programs. The New Mexico Arts Commission, through its involvement in the NewGate Art Project, also developed a commitment to the program. Some commission members and others who participated in the activities developed a commitment to individual inmates and an interest in their experience while they were incarcerated. This involvement by outsiders can significantly alter the balance of power in some areas of decision making.

Program Survival and Vitality. The inside New Mexico NewGate was found to be a high quality education program. Past and present participants, for the most part, agreed with this finding. The researchers found a program that had integrated itself successfully into its institutional environment without losing its essential features. In tracing the program's development, the program became increasingly comprehensive and ambitious in scope, gained steadily greater control over internal matters, and also became more influential in the prison at large. This trend was contrary to the experience of the other prison college programs observed, where the usual trend was toward a takeover of the program by the prison.

Although many forces were important in accounting for the productive relationship between the college program and the prison, three were especially critical: enlightened leadership, creative and responsible program operation, and the establishment of an external power base. After the first project director, the project leadership implemented a series of steps that interested both convicts and prison staff in the program. A number of steps were taken to integrate the NewGate program into the prison routine, in contrast with the other NewGates, which, in keeping with the "third-force" philosophy, remained more isolated from the prison. At the same time, however, New Mexico NewGate also developed good working relationships with institutions and groups outside the prison that could provide a source of countervailing power when needed.

As of this writing, it appears that the good relationship between prison and program will continue, although it is not inevitable. The critical forces are interdependent. A good program and an active external base of support depends on enlightened direction from the program director.

The interest and commitment of outsiders can promote the hiring of a dynamic director. However, the involvement of outsiders generally is not self-initiated. It has to be cultivated and encouraged. The director, as well as the participating universities, must continue to work to involve the community in treatment programs like NewGate. They must also continue a successful program. A poor reputation might make outsiders reluctant to continue their support.

Ashland

The NewGate Program at the Federal Youth Center in Ashland, Kentucky, was one of the "second generation" NewGate projects. It began operations in 1969, two years after the Oregon project. It was the first to be located in an institution operated by the Federal Bureau of Prisons. Located near the intersection of the Ohio, West Virginia, and Kentucky borders in a rural southern area, Ashland has a population of 29,245. The closest large city is Cincinnati, Ohio, over 150 miles to the west. Ashland's geographic isolation created a serious obstacle for the college program, as will be pointed out below.

Ashland NewGate had several important background features. The first was that it was part of the federal prison system, one of the largest in the country. In 1972 the Federal Bureau of Prisons maintained 21 correctional institutions spread from coast to coast, including United States Penitentiaries, Federal Correctional Institutions, Federal Youth Centers, Federal Prison Camps, and Federal Reformatories. In addition, it had the largest administrative bureaucracy and was the nation's most costly prison system. Two important aspects of the bureau's operation were (1) its independence, and (2) the cumbersomeness of its bureaucratic structure. The federal system enjoys more freedom from local influence and restraints than does any other prison system in the country. Whereas county and state correctional systems come under a variety of pressures from local citizen groups, or state or local politicians, the federal system operates at political and geographic distance from local sources of pressure. Consequently, the federal prison system enjoys a great deal of freedom to establish its operating procedures and standards. A negative aspect of this autonomy is its self-protectiveness. As most large organizations, the federal system attempts to maintain complete authority over its domain. As shall be seen, this had important negative consequences for the NewGate project at the Federal Youth Center.

The cumbersomeness of the federal prison system's bureaucracy results in a high degree of inflexibility. Changes come slowly. The problem is compounded by the division of labor within the correctional bureaucracy. The Federal Bureau of Prisons, the Federal Parole Board, and the Federal Probation Division are all independent entities, though each maintains some degree of jurisdiction over the correctional careers of federal felons. Several special problems for the NewGate project at Ashland were a consequence of the bureaucratic structure of the federal corrections system.

A second and important feature of the Ashland program was that it was a Federal Youth Center, housing prisoners between the ages of 15 to 24, most of whom were in the 19 to 21 age range. Most were sentenced under the Federal Youth Corrections Act to an indeterminate sentence, usually zero to six years. The average length of stay at Ashland was 14 months. Nearly one-half the prisoners at Ashland were sentenced for car theft under the Dyer Act—the interstate transportation of a stolen motor vehicle. This was a special group of prisoners, who were likely to have had weaker and/or fewer ties to stable social organizations, such as families, schools, or occupational organizations, and, therefore, tended to be more transient. Furthermore, they tended to be less sophisticated and more impulsive law breakers. These factors made a relatively high recidivism rate more likely for Ashland's inmates than for other convict populations.

Another important background characteristic was the location of the center. The youth center was not close to any urban setting. It drew its population from all the states east of the Mississippi River, resulting in an inmate population that was culturally heterogeneous, while the institution staff was largely culturally homogeneous.

Another characteristic of the program was a yearly reorganization of program staff, which resulted in confusion about the duties and responsibilities of staff members. This confusion was felt not only by program staff, but also by staff of the host institution and, most important, by program participants. The final important characteristic of the Ashland NewGate program was its failure to establish a successful postrelease phase.

Inside Program

Administrative Staff. The discussion of the Ashland program will focus primarily on the period between fall 1970 and spring 1972, covering the period when the project reached its maximum development and ending when it was taken over by the Federal Bureau of Prisons. First, however, it is necessary to describe the staff changes that took place before and during this period to understand the course of development of events at Ashland.

When the program began in 1969, the project director was the supervisor of education of the youth center. He was named director on an interim basis to legitimize the program to the institutional staff. Morehead State University, the OEO grantee, provided an assistant director, a director of education (NewGate), a director of field services, and a counselor. Six months later, the interim appointment of the director ended, and the assistant director was made project director. The former director of education was made assistant director of inside services and continued to serve as director of education (NewGate). A teacher was hired to assist him. The former director of field services was made assistant director of outside services and continued as director of field services. He, too was, aided by a new employee, the assistant director of field services. By this time, students had been sent to the Morehead State campus; and an office was opened there, staffed by a secretary and a graduate student.

Essentially the same staff structure existed a year later, except for the staff on campus, where a resource coordinator was hired to head the office. This staff position, though not on the same level as the assistant directors, reported directly to the project director and not to the assistant director of outside services, who continued to maintain offices inside the youth center.

The following year, an even more confusing reorganization took place. The assistant director of inside services received a greater degree of responsibility and became the sole assistant director. Under his direction were the director of education (NewGate) (the former teacher), the director of field services (the former assistant director of outside services), and two newly created positions, a prerelease coordinator and postrelease coordinator. The staff outside the youth center remained the same, but with the resource coordinator responsible to both the project director and the assistant director.

These yearly reorganizations took place in part because Ashland was unable to establish an outside program phase. There were problems with the staff structure. First, unlike the other programs, which had two distinct phases with the director overseeing both the inside and outside ones, the Ashland project was divided up in a more complex fashion with the assistant director responsible for some aspects of all phases. This left the director with a more distant and less specific set of tasks. As his responsibilities and duties were described in a "Position Paper" of January 1972, the director was to "coordinate all internal and external NewGate Operations. He maintained an office both at the Federal Youth Center and on the campus of the college or university center in order for him to divide his time equally between the two operations."[4] However, postrelease operations on campus were virtually discontinued in 1971, leaving little need for coordination with the campus. Other aftercare operations were administered from inside Ashland, where the assistant director was in charge, so the director's remaining responsibilities were minimal.

The second problem with the staff structure was that it was awkward. The formal division of responsibilities cut across the various program tasks in a complex fashion. For instance, the director of field services had working under him the prerelease coordinator and the postrelease coordinator. However, the prerelease coordinator's responsibilities were related mostly to the operation inside the prison. The assistant director was in charge of inside operations. This left the director of field services straddled between the inside assistant director's jurisdiction and the outside area, where he had more authority. Also, there was a resource coordinator at the university with formal jurisdiction over some outside operations. Consequently, the formal staff organization had several overlapping spheres of authority. This would not have been as much of a problem if the program had established some on-going procedures, such as regular staff meetings, where conflicts could have been resolved. The lack of such procedures resulted in considerable confusion and resentment among staff members over the division of responsibilities and authority and contributed to the general lack of direction, cohesion, clear purpose, and spirit among the staff.

Another characteristic of the administration of the Ashland program was its "looseness." The program was more permissive, informal, and less rigid and authoritarian than any other studied. Interaction between participants and staff approached "buddy" relationships
rather than the formal relationships typical between superiors and
subordinates. There was little formalization of rules; almost everything was negotiable. The participants felt they had a high degree of
freedom to make suggestions for improving the program, and there
were both positive and negative consequences of this style. On the
positive side, strong rapport was established between the staff and
the participants. Perhaps this was appropriate for persons in this
age group. However, the negative consequences were also important.
Too much information flowing between staff and participants had negative consequences. For instance, the participants knew about the
informal activities of the staff members. They heard of events at
parties among staff and at national NewGate meetings. Of course,
the wildest episodes were the subject of most discussion, giving the
staff a libertine image, which leaked to the prison administration and
damaged the program's chances of survival. Knowledge of the program
budget and of staff travel plans led to resentment among the participants, who felt this money would have been better spent on them than
wasted on trips for the staff.

Academic Staff. Academic instruction was mainly by part-time
teachers hired for particular courses. Most were full-time teachers
at the nearby Ashland Community College. Three of the staff members (the director, the director of education, and the prerelease
coordinator) also taught courses. The instruction seemed to be of
high quality; more participants (97 percent) agreed that the instructors
did a good job teaching than in any other program. The participants
also had a high rate of agreement with the statements "instructors
were sensitive to the problems and capabilities of the convict as a
student" (82 percent), "the instructors showed a personal interest in
the participants" (93 percent), and "the courses stimulated their interest in education" (82 percent). From all indications, instruction
as Ashland was excellent.

Students. Selection began with the treatment team, made up of a case
worker, correctional officer, and educational staff member. Each
inmate was assigned a case worker, who called the team together
periodically to review the convict's program, classification, and
parole. An inmate was considered for NewGate on the request of the
convict, the NewGate program, or the case worker. The criteria
employed by the team seems to have been length of stay, disciplinary
record, and evidence of ability to complete college work. The NewGate

staff then made a final selection based on results of tests—an IQ of
over 95, Stanford Achievement Score in excess of 9.0, completion
of high school or its equivalent, and having no more than 12 nor less
than 4 months expected to serve. In addition, NewGate conducted a
personal interview to evaluate the inmate's ability to "function within
group situations."

Originally, NewGate took persons with less than a high school
education into a GED program. However, after some disappointing
experiences and since the center had a surplus of high school graduates, the GED program was abandoned. This change corresponded
with a shift in the population of Ashland. By 1971 many middle class
youths—draft law violators and new drug offenders—were finding their
way into the federal prison system. This meant a growing number of
youths with a high school education, or even some college. In one
semester the program accepted 12 draft law violators. After dis-
covering this, the Bureau of Prisons suggested the program not accept so many draft law violators because fewer of them were likely
to recidivate and were, therefore, less in need of rehabilitation than
were other segments of the prison population.

The Ashland program's selection procedure operated in favor of
white middle class convicts, although selection was originally random
and stratified by race. Two groups, rural white ("hillbillies") and
blacks, were not represented proportionately in the program. In 1972,
of the prison's population 31 percent was black, but only 18 percent
of the students were black. Ashland was not the only program with a
selection bias, and Ashland's underrepresentation of minority convicts did not seem to be any worse than most other programs.

Program Content. Inside program participants were housed together
in one cell block. At one time they had been moved to a new building
a few yards from the older main building. This new housing unit was
more luxurious and was intended as an honor unit, and the program
participants were moved back into a regular cell block for two reasons. First, the cells in the new building were larger and were
planned to hold several convicts; but there were not enough college
students to fill the entire unit, so many nonstudents were also housed
there, a situation not conducive to studying. In the second place,
there was strong resentment toward the "elitism" of special housing
both from participants and other inmates. The plan was abandoned
and the students were given a cell block in the older building where
no nonstudents were housed and there was enough space for each
student to have a cell of his own. The lights were left on later in
this new location, so the conditions were better for studying.

There was virtually no therapy in the Ashland program. There
was an early attempt to make groups compulsory for NewGate students,

but they walked out during a session and complained to the staff. No systematic counseling or therapy had been attempted since.

The director indicated that counseling and therapeutic needs were served through the informal staff-student relationships characteristic of the Ashland program. It was not clear that this was an accurate evaluation. What was clear was that something close to friendship developed between some staff members and students. However, there were also reports of lack of respect and resentment toward some staff by students. Closeness alone will not ensure constructive relationships. For this type of relationship to be a positive one, the parties who are supposed to be the source of advice, or counseling, must have a clear sense of purpose, some knowledge of effective life strategies, and the ability to convey both. These were lacking in Ashland. However, these impressions might have been due to the timing of the visits to Ashland, which took place when funding by OEO was being reduced and thr future of the program was uncertain.

Each semester the program determined its course needs and submitted them to Ashland Community College. In addition the director of information informally searched out good teachers for the courses. The selection of courses was sufficiently broad. While the program was administered by Morehead State University 17 different courses were offered. After the administration was shifted to the University of Kentucky, 13 courses were offered. All but two courses were repeated at least once.

The style of instruction and the classroom atmosphere insured an intense educational experience. Convicts, if given the opportunity, are more prone to questioning material and ideas than the typical college student. In some settings, such as Lompoc, there was no opportunity for discussion; and the educational experience lost some of its potential. In keeping with the general style of the Ashland program, instruction was open and democratic; consequently, considerable discussion took place and a vast majority of the participants stated that the courses stimulated their interest in education.

The classes were conducted in the education building, which included all the prison's educational programs. The facility included a remedial education room, GED preparation room, and several classrooms used by the college program, including the program office. The learning center and prison library with approximately 5000 non-fiction and reference books were on another floor of the building. All fiction books were kept in the living quarters. The physical facilities were very good; there were sufficient classrooms (14 in all) to contain all educational functions; and the library was larger than that in most of the programs investigated.

Unlike New Mexico, Minnesota, Pennsylvania, and Lompoc, the Ashland education floor was not a highly desirable place to spend nonclassroom hours in informal activities. The library was better, but still not a substitute for an informal lounge, which contributed so much to some of the programs. However, the Ashland NewGate students, all assigned full-time to the college program, had free access to their cell block, where there was a day room on each floor that provided enough physical space for the informal activities necessary for a vigorous academic atmosphere. It was not clear, however, whether the program had achieved as high a level of vitality as was seen in other locations.

There were indications of discontent in the past. As mentioned, the students revolted against group therapy. There were accounts of poor morale due to the group of draft law violators, who were critical of the program and the prison in general and who were highly capable of articulating these criticisms. This discontent was not witnessed firsthand. However, it was clear during the period of observation that a heavy atmosphere of gloom stifled the program's vitality.

Since 1954 the prison had been releasing inmates during the day to attend Ashland Community College. Since 1969 NewGate had been directing this activity, and more than 20 NewGate students had participated. These persons left the institution only to attend class. If there was more than a two-hour free period between classes, the inmate had to return to the institution. To become eligible for this program the individual must have completed satisfactorily one term of NewGate inside the institution, have the recommendation of New-Gate, and the approval of the institutional review committee. There were serious problems with the study-release program, both for the student and the staff. First, there was the difficulty of coordinating transportation schedules. Second was the intense strain on the study-release prisoner, who had to mingle with outside students yet was subject to a stringent time schedule and behavior routine.

The Program's Relationship to the Prison. Although the present and past wardens were strong supporters of NewGate, other segments of the institution's staff were openly hostile. Hostility was directed toward two aspects of the program: the lifestyle and work routine of the NewGate staff, and the special privileges the participants received. In regard to the first, correctional staff were subject to rigid time schedules and behavior rules. Their dress and hours were regulated. They had to obey strict rules of conduct in their relationships with convicts. But they saw the NewGate staff following a more relaxed schedule, dressing in a casual fashion, and behaving in an unprofessional, informal manner toward inmates. Moreover, the staff was generally southern, rural and conservative in beliefs and lifestyle. The NewGate staff, on the other hand, was unconventional, "mod," and "hip" in their attitudes, dress, and leisure activities. The

NewGate staff's image of leading a libertine life away from prison exacerbated these antagonisms. Stories, whether true or not, of parties and NewGate meetings circulated among the students and correctional staff and contributed to the resentment and hostility felt toward some of the NewGate personnel.

The NewGate staff were aware of these problems and made attempts to bridge the gap between themselves and the correctional staff. For instance, one of the younger NewGate staff members joined the prison bowling team. However, due to the differences between the lifestyles of the NewGate staff and the corrections staff, it would have taken a larger systematic effort to reduce hostilities. Nothing of sufficient scope was undertaken. The staff's negative attitudes toward the program might have influenced the course of action pursued by the Federal Bureau of Prisons toward NewGate (discussed below).

The second focus of the correctional staff's hostility was the NewGate students. First it was believed they were being pampered, since they didn't have to work at a regular assignment, were housed in special living quarters, with special privileges (lights on at night), and were given special consideration on parole and disciplinary matters. (The opinions among the staff and students of NewGate were mixed on whether the program reduced the length of sentence, but there seemed to be some agreement that NewGate students received favorable treatment in disciplinary matters because NewGate staff would intervene on their behalf.) Second, correctional staff resented the type of convict who predominated in the NewGate program—the white middle class student, some of whom were "hippies" and generally critical of American society. Probably the major source of aggravation was the fact that these "felons" were receiving advantages that the staff members could not afford for their own children, a criticism that surfaced at almost every site studied but was most intense at Ashland.

Relationship Between Participants and Other Inmates. There were indications that other convicts harbored strong hostility and other negative attitudes toward the program. Over 50 percent of the participants interviewed stated other convicts had negative attitudes toward them as students, higher than for any other program. In informal interviews and the group expert session with nonparticipants, considerable negative feelings toward the program were detected, stemming from two sources. The first was that NewGate students were treated as an elite group and given special privileges. The second was that the program was elitist, excluding blacks and rural whites. Ashland had three main sociocultural groups of inmates: "hippies," "blacks," and "hillbillies." The program drew many persons from the hippie group, some from the black group, but almost none from the hillbilly group.

The absence of hillbillies in the program can be explained partially by the selection criteria, particularly SAT in excess of 9.0 and
completion of high school or its equivalent. In addition, they were the
group most likely to reject the program. They shared few interests
with the hippie "intellectuals" who were in the majority in the program.
In terms of the hillbilly's world view, this may have stigmatized the
program. Though the "hippie" group was the best prepared for and
had the greatest desire to attend school, the program should have
moved away from loading the program with those students most likely
to continue school after release. The program should have made an
effort to recruit more blacks and rural whites, who could have pro-
fited greatly from the experience. The vitality and dynamism of the
New Mexico program, for example, was a result of this type of outreach into the general population.

Role in Prison Release Decisions. From the outset, the program was
deeply involved in the parole function. As indicated earlier, most of
the sentences in Ashland were indeterminate, and the program's release phase constituted the convict's release plan. Typically, the
treatment team in the institution established a treatment strategy for
the individual, and when this was completed he was released. The
treatment team took into consideration the severity of the crime to
determine how much time each person "should" serve according to
an unstated norm. The parole board generally followed the recommendation of the treatment team for all prisoners. The administration established a special NewGate treatment team to handle all the
NewGate students. The recommendations for parole and development
of a pre- and postrelease treatment program were responsibilities of
this team. The implications of the arrangement were recognized by
the convicts. Eighty-three percent of those interviewed indicated that
they had entered NewGate to have a better chance for early release.
However, it was not clear that NewGate students served shorter sentences. The participant sample served an average of 16 months; the
same as the control sample. The average for the institution was 14
months. Apparently, enrolling in NewGate did not lead to an early
parole.
     As mentioned above there was some indication that NewGate
staff were involved in disciplinary proceedings and were somewhat
successful in obtaining decisions in favor of the student. However,
such intervention might have served only to balance the more punitive
attitude guards had toward NewGate students. The students felt they
were more likely to receive a "shot" (disciplinary write-up) than
other convicts. There were no actual figures to determine if this
were true, but both NewGate staff and students in the program believed it to be the case.

Outside Program

Ashland departed from the NewGate model in that it never succeeded in establishing a solid aftercare base. The ideal, which was
approximated in Minnesota, Oregon, and Pennsylvania, showed the
program with a firm link to an outside educational institution where
it had a base of operations, including an office and living quarters for
the exprisoners. For several reasons, Ashland failed to develop a
viable outside program phase.

Ashland's first effort at establishing an outside postrelease program was at Morehead State, the host institution for the Ashland
NewGate. The on-campus study center was set up at the insistence
of OEO, who saw the postrelease activity as an important component
of the NewGate experience, and over some objection from the Bureau
of Prisons, who felt the Ashland population wasn't sufficiently homogeneous to be integrated into a common postrelease program. The
cultural atmosphere at Morehead State and the surrounding community
was small town, rural, southern and not very conducive to the establishment of a prison rehabilitation program.

A NewGate office on campus was set up, but no supervised group
residence was provided. Within a few months of the start of the
Morehead phase, six of the 12 NewGate students had incurred new
felony charges, and only one participant was still enrolled at the
university. NewGate and Morehead came to a mutual agreement that
the on-campus program should be terminated. The university, re-
flecting both its feelings and those of the surrounding community,
decided it really didn't like having exconvicts around, especially after
firearms were discovered in the NewGate facility.

For its part, NewGate didn't like the atmosphere of either the
town or the university and felt the university's commitment to the
project extended only as far as collecting its overhead payments.
Morehead was often slow to pay NewGate's bills, another factor of
concern to the NewGate staff.

Since the inside NewGate instructors came from Ashland Community College, which is part of the University of Kentucky system,
NewGate thought that program administration would be simplified if
the University of Kentucky were made both the host (administering
university) and the location of the postrelease project. The University
of Kentucky seemed a better location for the postrelease project because both the university and the surrounding community, Lexington
(population 108,137) were more cosmopolitan than Morehead. Further,
there was a commitment to the NewGate idea from members of the
University of Kentucky faculty.

In 1971 the program was transferred to the University of Kentucky,
and seven NewGate students were paroled to the new study center in the

fall of 1971. In contrast with Morehead, group living quarters were
provided at the University of Kentucky in a large house on the edge
of the campus. However, there still was no systematic supervision.
The University of Kentucky study center terminated a few months
later following a series of thefts committed by the NewGate students.
For example, a color television stolen from a nearby motel was discovered in the NewGate house. A stolen steer, butchered and ready
to eat, was discovered in the house freezer. One of the students stole
a staff member's credit card.

The director, in analyzing the failure, stated, "The NewGate
House, in my opinion, failed because the mixture of personalities
living there was conducive to any incident snowballing and consequently involving a number of our students rather than one. Also,
supervision was poor for a house of that nature. The alternatives
would obviously be either to spread the men out, allowing them to
live wherever they please, but not together, or institute a stronger
form of supervision, i.e., half-way house."5 The authors must
especially stress the importance of providing adequate supervision
for students drawn from the Ashland Youth Center, whose relative
youthfulness, immaturity, and emotional instability made them poor
risks, especially when they could, for all practical purposes, operate
as a gang formed by the NewGate project.

Another contributing factor to the failure of the University of
Kentucky center was the location of the residence house. In comparison with the Oregon, Minnesota, and Pennsylvania NewGates, the
residence house was far from the campus. This made it difficult for
the students to become involved in campus activities, especially in
the evening. They were more commuting students than campus residential students. Thus, it is not surprising that, lacking supervision
and easily available campus leisure time activities, they returned to
crime.

One of the major sources of difficulty in setting up a postrelease
program at Ashland was the nature of the federal parole system. The
policy of the parole board was to return parolees to the jurisdiction
from where they were sentenced. Not only did this return them to
the supervision of the court of original jurisdiction, but it also returned them to their home and family. As one of the Bureau of Prison's major youth institutions, Ashland received inmates from all
states east of the Mississippi. Therefore, because of the nature of
the population and the parole board's standard operating procedure,
keeping released participants in school near Ashland, or in any other
single location, called for a change in the usual parole procedure.
The Federal Parole Board provided a mechanism for transferring a
parolee out of his home district. To transfer to another district, the
parolee must have the approval of the federal judge who supervises

parole in the district. Judges in general, and the judge whose district covered Kentucky in particular, were reluctant to accept parole
transfers since it meant more work for their staff. The Ashland
judge was also against having state funds (both NewGate aftercare
programs were at state universities) spent on transient criminals
from other states, who would most likely take whatever benefits they
gained from their education back to their home state, leaving little
in Kentucky.

Passage to the Outside. After 1971, the program did not attempt to
establish a base at a university. The aftercare phase was reduced
to aid in gaining admissions to any school the student wanted to attend
and to providing postrelease support (mainly financial aid). The New-
Gate staff advised the student before release about school possibilities
and aided in obtaining admission with phone calls and correspondence
to admissions offices. After a school had been selected and the chances
looked good for admission, an outside coordinator often visited the
campus to facilitate entry and to obtain information about financial
aid, residence possibilities, and other campus or community resources. In addition, contacts were made with the local parole agency
to explain the program to the participant's future parole agent.

On release the parolee was given $300 to pay for his transporta-
tion, initial food and residence expenses, and new civilian clothing.
When possible, a NewGate field worker (the postrelease coordinator
or the director of field services) went to the campus with the releasee
to facilitate the individual's entry into civilian and campus life. Of
course, there were limitations as to the number of persons two staff
members could assist in this transition. Many parolees were entering
school each semester, and these were spread among many different
schools. Of the 40 persons interviewed, 13 were released to either
Morehead State or the University of Kentucky; and the other 27 were
released to 25 different schools spread between California, Florida,
and New York. The difficulties of providing adequate release counseling and aid, as well as aftercare help, are obvious.

Aftercare Support. From 1970-72, the program provided $150 per
month the first five months, $75 per month for the next four, and
$38 for a final three months. The student was expected to find other
means of support after the first year. This money was sent to the
student after it was established that he was still attending school.
Theoretically, the program's director of field services and the postrelease coordinator would visit the man in the field if there were some
special problem or if it were possible to do so. However, with the
students spread far and wide, this was not done to any great extent.
Over two-thirds of those interviewed who had attended school stated

that they did not have any regular contact with the program after
release.

The receipt of financial aid was not always according to plan.
Many students claimed they did not get the checks they were supposed
to receive or that checks were late. Several stated they were forced
to drop out of school because funds failed to arrive. The program
director attributed these delays to several problems: (1) After the
program shifted its administration to the University of Kentucky, the
procedure for administering checks became more complicated; and
requests for checks had to be made three weeks prior to issuance.
(2) There was great difficulty in communication between staff and
students, and it was often difficult to determine if a parolee was still
attending school. (3) During the spring of 1972, the program released
more students than they had support money for, and they had to reduce the size of each monthly payment.

It is clear that the Ashland outside program was its weakest link.
The absence of a single base on a favorable campus, the impossibility
of keeping in contact with persons after they left, and the difficulties
in sending support checks combined to defeat the purpose of the New-
Gate program. There was virtually no contact with peers or staff
who could offer help to the released student. Most were absolutely
alone. Forty-three percent were released to a strange location.
Other than those attending Morehead State and the University of Kentucky, only two persons in the sample attended a school where there
was another NewGate parolee. Less than 10 percent of those interviewed indicated that there was any interest in using the convict as
a resource in classes, departments, or community groups, a much
lower figure than for the other NewGate programs. For instance, in
the Minnesota program, 87 percent indicated that there was some
interest in using them in classes, 67 percent in college departments,
50 percent in civic groups, and 75 percent in discussion groups.

The Ashland exconvict population—younger, more transient, less
attached to stable social organizations—was the group that needed
aftercare support features more than any other group in the sample.
The consequences were clear. Fewer Ashland parolees continued in
school than in any other NewGate program. Only 15 percent were
attending school when interviewed. The averages for the other New-
Gate programs were Pennsylvania, 55 percent; Minnesota, 40 percent;
Oregon, 43 percent; New Mexico, 15 percent. Only Texas, with no
aftercare program, had a lower percentage (8 percent) attending
school among all the programs studied.

Outside Program's Relationship to Other Institutions. As indicated
above, after attempts to establish ties with two different schools on
other than an administrative basis failed, the Ashland program had

no significant ties with academic institutions. The release coordinators attempted to facilitate entry into an institution and aid in ongoing
support, but no lasting or strong link was established with any college.
Also as indicated, there were no formal or informal ties established
at any college by the exconvicts. They attended school as individuals
and remained hidden as exconvicts.

In regard to the parole agency, after the program achieved a
degree of respectability in the eyes of the parole board, it became
a condition of parole that the released participants continue in school.
However, it was discovered that this condition was not met by most
participants; the majority dropped out of school. Their parole was
not terminated for this; however, some strong hostility on the part
of many parole agents toward those students who had received support
from the program and then had not followed through was observed.
This was aggravated in some cases, where drop-outs continued to
receive support after the agent knew they were not in school. Overall,
support for the program by the parole agency was mixed. Parolees
were spread out in as many parole supervisory districts as the different colleges they attended. There was no opportunity for an "official" parole agency posture toward the program. Attitudes toward
the program varied with each individual parole agent.

Analysis

Did the Ashland NewGate program provide its participants enough
support framework, personal social space, and challenge to achieve
their educational goals?

Support Framework. The inside program at Ashland came close to
providing an ideal college atmosphere. As indicated, the classroom
instruction, both in style and content, and the selection of courses
were among the best in the sample. Moreover, the routine and the
physical facilities provided conditions that were conducive to an informal campuslike atmosphere. Where the supportive framework
broke down was in failing to define explicit guidelines for action for
both the participants and for the staff.

Personal Social Space. The inside Ashland program ranked high on
social space. Social space involves freedom to choose and an absence
of interference in participating in the college program. A person
assigned all day to the education program with unrestricted access
to the education floor, the library, his living quarters, and to a full
range of recreational facilities had great freedom of movement and
choice in his daily routine. He had an adequate range of courses to
choose from, and staff members were as accessible to the student to

aid or advise him as in any other program. It is important to note that more persons agreed they could make suggestions and criticisms about the program (90 percent) and that their suggestions would be implemented (88 percent) than in any other program.

Challenge. The challenge was relatively intense in the inside Ashland program. Over 80 percent agreed that the courses stimulated their interest in education. The close, informal contact with the staff contributed to this feeling. There was also a stimulating peer culture. Despite some feelings of discontent observed among the program participants and staff, there was strong evidence of an intense program, which offered a great deal of challenge to the participants.

In the outside program, Ashland fell down on all three dimensions. There was a little support for the student in the initial transition to the outside, but then support faded out. Financial aid was the only form of support the program offered after departure, and this was inconsistent in some cases and was terminated after a year. Continuing support had to be located by the person himself, and this younger population was not the most capable of doing this. As for the other dimensions, social space and challenge, these were beyond the control of the program. The space was limited by the absence of support and the restrictions imposed by the parole system. As indicated, the parole routine varied greatly because each man had a different parole agent. The challenge that existed originated in the college milieu. But if the problems of no support and too much space were too overwhelming, it is doubtful the person could endure in the setting or settle down to the normal university routine.

The most serious failure of the Ashland program was the weaknesses of the aftercare component. However, it must be noted that, to an extent, this situation was beyond the control of the NewGate staff. They were faced with a prison located in an unfavorable setting, a population drawn from half the United States, and a system that mitigated against establishing the kind of base necessary to develop a sound aftercare program.

Institutional Change. The Ashland NewGate project initiated little change. As in many of the prisons, there was some change at the ideational level simply from demonstrating that prisoners could complete college work. However, this was counterbalanced by the general resentment of the program. The image of pampering the students and the catastrophes at Morehead State and the University of Kentucky, in which most of the students were charged with a new crime, brought back to prison, absconded, or quit attending school, demonstrated to the prison staff that the program was not successful. On the programmatic level the impact on the institution's operation was limited. In fact the scope of the operation seemed to be narrowing. However, the program had some impact on policy in the federal prison system. The Washington office, while not supporting all aspects of the program, accepted the concept of college education in prisons and was exploring ways to establish college programs in other federal institutions.

The program's staff and students had extremely limited influence on the decision-making procedures in the prison or the bureau. The furthest penetration in this direction was the inclusion of a program staff member on the treatment team, where decisions pertaining to internal program and parole recommendations were made.

The outside program, with its failures at Morehead State and the University of Kentucky and its extreme dispersion, had negligible positive impact on external institutions.

Program Survival and Vitality. It is in this area that the program suffered its most serious setbacks. The program experienced drastic cutbacks after the 1972 spring semester. At the end of that fiscal year (1971-72), OEO reduced its funding by more than half. As with most programs, Ashland NewGate had been looking for alternate funding. The Federal Bureau of Prisons had indicated some funds would be earmarked for college education, and NewGate would get a portion of that. Ashland NewGate submitted a budget similar to the one on which the program had operated in the past. There was a period of negotiation, during which the bureau indicated the old administrative structure and expenditures were not acceptable. In the ensuing conflict between the bureau and the project director, the bureau took over the operation of the inside program, while the project director conducted the outside phase. The remaining OEO funds paid his salary and provided aftercare support for the students and little more. Administration of the inside program was turned over to the prison education director. Only one NewGate staff person (the former assistant director) was retained on the staff.

The prison eeucation director had a much narrower conception of the program. Many services were discontinued. It appeared that many of the special liberties the students enjoyed were lost. For example, in the past NewGate staff had taken students on field trips to Ashland Community College. These trips were no longer being made because there was no staff to accompany the students. After the 1972-73 fiscal year, OEO funds for the outside aftercare component ceased. All who had been involved in the program—staff and students—felt this seriously injured the program. There was no opportunity to examine the program under the new plan, so this evaluation cannot be confirmed. According to the conception of a model program, however, the Ashland NewGate suffered a serious setback.

The takeover of the Ashland NewGate illustrated the pressures faced by an independent program within the prison setting. Correctional bureaucracies operate with a great deal of autonomy. The Federal Bureau of Prisons has perhaps even more autonomy than most state systems due to its wide geographic spread and the fact that its controlling authority, Congress, is further removed politically from events at a local prison than is a state legislature. One of the latent functions of bureaucracies is protecting their power and autonomy. More negotiation was required to establish NewGate within the federal system than in any state system, due in large part to the Bureau of Prisons' long history of independence and their concern about not having complete control over all activities inside one of their institutions. Among the reasons leading the bureau finally to accept the NewGate program were their interest in correctional innovation, the chance to acquire a new program at no cost for several years, and a desire to protect the bureau's progressive reputation. It was not clear at the beginning how the bureau intended to absorb the program, but such an intent was clear.

Once under way, events at the Ashland NewGate weakened its autonomy and strengthened the bureau's hand. The NewGate staff allowed too much animosity to develop with the Ashland correctional staff. This led to a steady flow of negative feedback about the project, which gave the bureau both motivation and reason for acting against the project.

The failure of the Ashland NewGate to develop a strong link with a university deprived it of a major source of countervailing institutional power for protection from the bureau's power play. By comparison, Pennsylvania, the only other NewGate program to have been taken over by the correctional system, had a strong base in the state's most powerful university; but the Ashland Project Director antagonized both the prison and the university, driving them into an alliance against him.

Special Problems at Ashland. The Ashland program had two major problems, both of which were detailed above. The first was the failure to establish an adequate aftercare program. The natural obstacles to accomplishing this were tremendous. The location of the prison, the characteristics of the convict population, the structure of the aftercare program, and the nature of the federal bureaucracy all mitigated against success in this area.

The second problem was one of public relations. The staff did not recognize how important and sensitive this area was, especially in a federal prison located in a rural southern community. To avoid serious hostilities from the correctional staff and to strengthen the program against them when they do emerge, a program such as

NewGate has to make vigorous efforts to establish good working relationships within the prison. Ashland NewGate not only failed to
develop good relationships but also did things that led to open hostility
toward the program from the correctional staff and that contributed
to the program's loss of independence.

Pennsylvania/New View

The college program at the State Correctional Institution at Rockview (SCIR) in Pennsylvania began in July 1969. Rockview was the
state's only minimum security facility and the only institution to offer
a college program. Rockview is located in the center of the state in
a rural area near Bellefonte, an old mining town, and State College
(population 33,780), the home of the Pennsylvania State University
with about 20,000 students. With its vast agricultural acreage and
supply of cheap labor, the institution has always been self-supporting.
The prison staff at all levels was drawn from nearby communities
and steeped in the traditions of independent Pennsylvania small far-
mers. These people believe in hard work and individual responsibility and have little understanding of or tolerance for the complexities
of today's urban crises and fast growing, automated world. Most of
the inmates were from major metropolitan areas. At least half were
black or Puerto Rican and had grown up in the slums and ghettoes of
the inner cities. The cultural gap between inmates and staff could not
have been wider or more noticeable. Despite these differences, Rockview had the reputation of being a quiet and smooth operation, due in
part, however, to the prison's minimum security status and its ability
to declare trouble-makers "security risks" and transfer them to other
institutions.

The college program at SCIR went through two distinct organizational phases. First it was a NewGate program. The original proposal was submitted to the OEO jointly by Penn State and the Pennsylvania Department of Justice, Bureau of Corrections, with Penn
State's College of Human Development acting as delegate agency. The
administration at Rockview was almost totally uninvolved in the initial
planning stages. It accepted the new college program because it was
imposed from above by the director of the Pennsylvania Department
of Corrections. Following the NewGate model, the program was set
up to operate semiautonomously within Rockview. From the beginning,
however, considerable friction developed between the program and the
prison. The situation became increasingly polarized, with the nearby
communities eventually drawn into public debate over whether Penn
State should continue to operate the program.

In August 1970 a new superintendent took over at SCIR who made it clear that he believed that NewGate should be made a responsibility of the prison, under his authority. His point of view was eventually strengthened in the spring of 1971, when a blue ribbon task force was appointed by the state attorney general to investigate the NewGate controversy. In July it recommended transfer of authority over the program to the prison over a six-month period to provide for an orderly transfer of administrative responsibility.

OEO put the finishing touch on the transfer when it withdrew funding from Penn State's College of Human Development in July 1971. The NewGate project and the superintendent had submitted competing proposals to OEO at the end of fiscal year 1970. By funding the proposal from the superintendent, OEO thereby denied any further role in the program to its originators. Immediately, the superintendent took over as director of the college program, beginning Phase II of the Pennsylvania project. He hired a new deputy director, and the name of NewGate was changed to New View, a symbol of the new orientation and image the college program would take.

In the following discussion of the Pennsylvania program Phase I (NewGate) and Phase II (New View) will be considered separately. Although there were significant continuities, the division is intended to highlight the differences in orientation between two distinct organizational strategies.

Phase I (NewGate)

The first project director conceived of a broader and more comprehensive project than a college program. His plans included vocational training programs, extensive community release facilities, the establishment of a computer center at the prison, and strategies that would have involved persons at Penn State as administrators, students, teachers, and researchers. The project was conceived as (1) a training facility for persons on campus and in the prison, and (2) an experimental laboratory in which new ideas about rehabilitation and training could be tried and tested. OEO funding was a vehicle by which at least part of the plan could be implemented.

One of the basic premises of the Pennsylvania NewGate was the belief that expanded social and educational opportunities would correct criminality. The inmate would seek alternatives to criminal behavior once he was provided viable opportunities in socially respectable sectors of the society. Criminality was not viewed as pathological. Consequently, the program played down the need for a therapeutic component. Persons with deep psychological problems were not encouraged to enter NewGate because the program neither intended to provide nor was capable of providing for such individuals. This orientation made the Pennsylvania program different from the NewGate program in Minnesota, which has always seen itself as a therapeutic program, and from the New Mexico NewGate program, which was designed to serve the educational needs of a broader base of inmates, many of whom were never serious college prospects. From the beginning, care was taken to design the program so the question of whether college education programs were rehabilitation mechanisms could be tested reliably and validly. An experimental and a control group were formed at random from a pool of inmates who NewGate administrators felt were qualified for the college program. Both groups of inmates were to have been studied after release from prison. Unfortunately for research purposes, many members of the control group were admitted into the college program when the prison took over the program and dispensed with the research component.

Students. The first year's final report stated that in recruiting inmates: "preference has been given to those with high potential but poor prior academic records, to those devoid of any substantial economic standing within the community and to those from multi-problem broken homes and urban ghettoes. Care has also been taken to select black inmates based upon their proportioned representation within the (Rockview) institution—approximately 50-50."[6]
The initial student body consisted of 50 male inmates who were selected from correctional institutions and a few county jails throughout the state. Several inmates from the federal penitentiary in nearby Lewisburg were also included. At institutions other than Rockview, inmates had already passed an informal selection process by the time NewGate staff interviewed them. The staff of these prisons had screened their populations and provided NewGate a list of names. The NewGate staff only had access to the inmates on these lists. At Rockview, NewGate interviewed interested inmates and others who, on the basis of information gleaned from prison records, appeared to have the potential to do college work. After these inmates were interviewed by members of the NewGate staff and found acceptable, they had to appear before a prison committee for "staffing." This committee was composed of the deputy superintendent, the work supervisor, the director of treatment, the prison parole representative, the inmate's counselor and two persons from NewGate. Its primary function was to show that the prison had final control, but only a few persons recommended by NewGate were denied entrance.
The first NewGate students included some who were close to completing college, students who had no previous college but were ready to begin, and some who were not yet ready to enter college full-time. This selection was made to experiment with the program's ability to accommodate students at different levels of preparedness. The more

highly advanced were also included because of OEO-NewGate's urging
that it was good political strategy to demonstrate success as quickly
as possible.

Custody or security concerns did not enter heavily into selection
since every man in the institution was considered minimum security.
Prison officials on the selection board deferred to the education experts in determining whether a man would benefit educationally. The
fact that Rockview was a minimum security facility affected the selection of inmates from other institutions. In effect, it served as an
unstated selection criterion by selecting out any inmate considered
to be a discipline problem or one who because his crime could not
be considered for "minimum." NewGate participants from other institutions had to qualify for minimum custody status before they could
be transferred to Rockview.

Many Rockview officials were suspicious that the other prisons
would take advantage of the program and unload their "undesirables"
on Rockview. Some of the Rockview staff indicated to the NewGate
staff that some black inmates they had chosen were not suitable for
such a program.

A student could be removed from the program by the prison if he
lost his "A-rating" from the prison's discipline committee. Although
not used often, this provided a means of control over program participation to the prison; and when it was exercised, decisions appeared
to have been arbitrary and inconsistent.

Staff. The first NewGate staff members were young but experienced
in fields related to prison education: teaching, working with disadvantaged youth, vocational training, work release, and parole. They
were enthusiastic about developing a new program, and their excitement was contagious. Students, consulted regularly about their views
and wishes, were hopeful for the future. Teachers were excited about
teaching, and students became excited about learning.

The students' commitment to NewGate grew naturally out of their
observation of staff dedication, which was enhanced when opposition
between the prison and program developed. The students saw the
staff as in their camp pitted against the common enemy: the prison;
this was similar to the Oregon situation.

Program Content. The college academic program was provided by
Penn State through the Department of Continuing Education. The
deaprtment director on campus maintained a list of professors qualified and willing to teach courses inside the prison. Six or seven
courses were offered each semester. In addition to the regular classroom, programmed learning and informal instruction were provided.
Programmed instruction was used to prepare persons in areas in

which they had an insufficient background to do college work and as
a supplement in some of the college courses. The informal or "transitional" instruction was provided by NewGate instructor/counselors.
These courses were developed when the need for them was suggested
by students. Usually these extra sessions supplemented some of the
programmed materials and were related to the college courses.

These two components were not used as extensively as the
planners had anticipated. Staff members attributed the lack of interest to the low level of prestige associated with these instructional
areas when compared with regular Penn State courses. Former participants agreed with this explanation but added that the stimulus
from classroom dialogue and contact with college professors contributed to the attraction of the regular classes. Another reason for
the lack of interest shown in the programmed learning and remedial
curricula was the behavior modification routine introduced to motivate
students to take advantage of the instructional facilities offered. New-
Gate developed a system where students were rewarded for points
earned. Rewards were given in the form of privileges such as access
to the student lounge, leisure time, access to music, and coffee, or
special commendations such as "student of the week" and "most-
improved student" awards, and cash in lieu of points. Many of the
participants were uncomfortable with this system. Some felt it was
too impersonal; others objected to the intense interpersonal competition it promoted.

The behavior modification system was severely curtailed because
the prison objected that it violated the principle of equal treatment
for all inmates. There was considerable legitimacy in this objection.
The program gave NewGate students privileged access to benefits
that nonparticipants were also anxious to have, but there was no alternative program in the prison which provided a comparable opportunity to nonparticipants.

The NewGate staff capitalized on the prison's close proximity
to the Penn State campus in developing its academic program. The
same courses taught on campus were offered inside the prison with
the same instructors. NewGate also insisted that the same standards
of performance used on campus be imposed on the inmate-students,
so they would not be shocked by differences once they transferred to
campus. The staff felt that if students were to be convinced that they
were capable of making it, they would have to succeed at work comparable with work on campus. NewGate worked closely with the college instructors and encouraged them to simulate a campus atmosphere as much as possible. Instructors were also encouraged to
develop personal relationships with their students and to keep in
contact by prison visits and by telephone.

The education coordinator tried to acquaint instructors with some of the typical educational handicaps of the students. Special emphasis was placed on skill training in areas such as reading, taking notes, speech, logic, writing essays, and taking examinations. NewGate staff worked with the students on study techniques. Special facilities and hours were set aside exclusively for studying.

Counseling. One of the main components of the inside program was its academic counseling. Each student had a counselor at the time he entered the program who advised him as to what program he should follow.

Psychotherapy was a minor part of the program. Most staff members seriously questioned its need and utility. If any therapy were recommended, it was as a by-product of an interpersonal relationship between a student and a staff member, which developed on its own. The success of this approach depends on having serious and sensitive staff members who are able to respond to the students honestly and straightforwardly. The released participants were about equally divided as to whether productive "helping relationships" were developed with the NewGate staff. In the follow-up interviews, in response to the question whether there was adequate psychological preparation provided by the staff, 45 percent responded "yes," 45 percent responded "no." Ten percent had no opinion. This part of the program was neglected during the struggle with the prison. Since more and more time was spent in battle, the staff members found less time to schedule informal discussions with their students.

Outside Program. NewGate was designed to facilitate a smooth and gradual transition to life on the streets. Before some students were granted parole they were transferred to a halfway house situated on the institution grounds, approximately one-quarter mile from the main prison. From there the students were escorted by a NewGate staff member to the Penn State Campus to attend classes. At night they were supervised by an undergraduate student counselor. Students who participated in this education release status were those within several months of a parole date to come during the middle of the school term, or students who had been in the inside program so long that they had completed all the courses offered inside. Once parole was granted, NewGate students could live wherever they wished. NewGate provided money for clothing, tuition, books, room and board, and incidental expenses.

The College of Human Development provided NewGate rent-free office space on campus. An aftercare director, counselors, and a secretary worked with NewGate students in the State College area. They did not function in a supervisory capacity but as a source of

assistance, if requested, in providing information about and referral
to existing university services and help in developing financial assistance for students once their NewGate money was scheduled to run out.

Informal gatherings at the NewGate aftercare office on campus
were used extensively by NewGate students to share experiences and
as a communication network with fellow NewGate students. During
NewGate, the aftercare staff was in constant contact with the inside
operation through visits and staff meetings. Among other benefits,
this allowed for communication between the inside and outside participants.

NewGate students became integrated into the university quickly
and easily. The close proximity of the campus to the prison enabled
students, while they were still inside, to familiarize themselves with
many aspects of life on campus. They were able to remain in contact
with the same professors who had taught courses on the inside. The
college student body was also extremely receptive to NewGate students
and to the idea that Penn State was involved in a prison reform project.
As remote as the town of State College is, the student body is fairly
sophisticated since it draws mainly from metropolitan areas. The
community of State College was also congenial for NewGate students.
It is a college town, largely dependent for its livelihood on the university and its student body. It espouses the same liberal values as
the people at the university. Nearby towns, which are older and more
parochial, were not as accepting of the idea of NewGate and NewGate
students as State College. During the public controversy over whether
authority over NewGate should be shifted from Penn State to SCIR,
these outlying towns were in full support of the prison.

Relationship of the Program to the Prison. From the beginning Pennsylvania NewGate's relationship with the prison administration was
tenuous at best. The lower echelon prison staff was antagonistic to
the idea that inmates should receive a college education. Moreover,
they resented the presence of urban intellectuals running NewGate.
They felt that the NewGate staff did not understand the convict and
the problems of running a prison. The top echelon staff resented the
program having been imposed from above. During much of the first
year, the superintendent was sick and effectively incapacitated. The
deputy superintendent performed essential administrative tasks but
did not have the authority to act on exceptional matters. Therefore,
controversy was often left unresolved.

In addition to the distrust prison personnel had of outsiders and
their jealousy in guarding their own turf, there were other sources
of tension. Some prison staff took a personal dislike to some of the
NewGate students, who the staff felt were devious and capable of out-
smarting the naive NewGate staff. They hated to see convicts "putting

something over" on the prison. The prison staff also was involved in a controversy over what books were to be used by NewGate. They particularly opposed books by black authors, sometimes confiscating books from the inmate-students. Books were no longer an issue when the new superintendent took over with his more liberal policies.

During this period, there was constant harassment of NewGate staff and instructors over hair and dress regulations. There were instances in which persons were prevented entry to the prison because of style of dress and length of hair or beards. Under the new superintendent, this policy, too, was altered.

There were two other issues that served to further exacerbate antagonism between the prison and NewGate staff. As mentioned earlier, the prison had agreed that the behavioral modification routine could be introduced. However, implementation details had to be negotiated, and this developed into a major source of controversy. The NewGate director was particularly aggravated over the difficulties of fully introducing the behavioral modification component and interpreted the problems as deliberate acts of bad faith by the prison.

Finally, the NewGate director looked forward to the day when the other facets of his design would be implemented. He not only pushed for it inside Rockview, but he made reference to the project and began mobilizing resources and interest for it both at the university and in offices in the state Department of Corrections. The Rockview administration was opposed to more involvement by outsiders.

When the new superintendent took over, relationships did not improve. The battle lines had been drawn, tension continued to mount, and NewGate became increasingly isolated. The new superintendent began to centralize control over prison operations to ensure that his plans for the prison were carried out. His predecessor had been ill, and the authority of the position of superintendent had diffused during this period. This, coupled with the presence of a prison staff that had been at Rockview a long time and was resistant to change, made it essential for a new superintendent to consolidate his power if he ever hoped to make changes. Opposition to an independent NewGate might have been the new superintendent's way of compensating the opposition forces, which developed internally in response to other changes he had made.

Phase II (New View)

Despite the intensity of the struggle between NewGate and the prison and the suddenness of the transfer of authority, the programmatic changes subsequently made were neither abrupt nor dramatic

Students. NewGate, during its last stages, made a decreasing effort to recruit students from other state institutions. It is not clear whether this was due to the conflict between the prison and the college program, which might have upset the complicated and delicately co-ordinated administrative machinery set up for these purposes. Whatever the reason, when NewGate became New View the practice of bringing inmates from other institutions to attend college at Rockview was discontinued altogether. New View thus became exclusively a program of the Rockview institution until January 1973, when the program staff once again began to schedule visits at other institutions.

One result of the shift away from external recruitment was a change in the quality of the program participants. The program had more slots for Rockview residents and thus for a broader base of inmates. It no longer had an opportunity to select only the most qualified through the state. The second result was to put the Rockview prison administration in a more central role in the selection process. Because Rockview inmates had to be reassigned to the college program by the Rockview prison staff, the Rockview officials had the final authority over the composition of the participant group.

New View, as NewGate, considered college level educational training to be its principal goal, in contrast with some programs in the sample that had, to varying degrees, a commitment to promoting personality changes among the participants. New View, as its predecessor, saw an inmate's potential to do college work as the primary qualification for admission.

The admission procedure began with the interested student contacting the college program staff at the beginning of the term. The case was reviewed by a New View committee consisting of the deputy director, the director of the four-year program, the director of the two-year program, and the director of the aftercare program. To be considered, the applicant must:

(1) have an A-rating (instructional behavioral standard);
(2) have a high school diploma or GED;
(3) be able to achieve minimum custody status (which permitted him to leave the institution under conditions of limited super-vision) by the time he had completed two semesters of college work (an inmate was eligible for minimum custody after having served half his minimum sentence);
(4) be close enough to his release date (expiration of minimum sentence) to be paroled within six to eight semesters, or one and a half to two years;
(5) attend a personal interview with the New View staff before the beginning of each semester;

(6) and score 35 percent or better on the <u>Analysis of Learning</u>
<u>Potential</u>, a test administered by the program staff at the time
of the personal interview, which was said to be similar to an IQ
test but not culturally biased.

After the New View committee screened an applicant, its recommendations were referred for "staffing" to another committee including
his counselor, his work supervisor, and a representative from the
custody staff. According to the New View deputy director, this committee approved New View's suggestions automatically, unless there
were unusual circumstances.

Although the procedures and criteria for admissions appeared to
be straightforward and fair, an unusual amount of suspicion about
them among the inmates was in evidence during the inside panel of
experts interview and in the responses on the inside participant questionnaires. In response to the question: "Does the student admissions
process have clear standards?", 75 percent of the inside participants
stated that it did not, highest of all the programs. Closest was Oregon,
with 58 percent of the participants answering in the negative. Another
question—"Is the selection process open and fair to all applicants?"—
showed similar results. Sixty-one percent of the inside Pennsylvania
participants said that it was not, again higher than any other program.

The reason for this suspicion of arbitrariness was not immediately
obvious. However, two explanations appear possible. First, despite
the formalized and seemingly objective procedure, many exceptions
to the general rules appear to have been made. The following are
some examples: (1) the four-year program also admitted inmates who
had more than the usual maximum of two years left to be served before
the expiration of their minimum sentence if these inmates were reasonably sure of being assigned to one of the state's new community
treatment facilities within two years; (2) some inmates were assigned
to the New View halfway house before they were within six months of
the expiration of their minimum sentence if they were "saturated
students," that is, students who had taken all the courses offered
inside (they could attend classes during the day on campus); and (3)
there were also some students without minimum custody status and
no minimum sentence dates (such as those serving life sentences)
who were permitted in the college program. Furthermore, three of
the "life" students were saturated and were escorted to campus three
days each week to attend class. Which inmates would be made exceptions to the rules was not determined by uniform and objective
criteria, causing confusion and forming the basis of much of the suspicion of arbitrariness and unfairness that the inside participant questionnaires revealed.

The second reason is more general. The study revealed that the
NewGate and New View participants distrusted the prison staff. It
follows that every aspect of the New View program in which the prison
administration was heavily involved, such as the admissions and
selection procedure, was influenced by the inmate's hostility toward
the prison. The distrust of the Rockview staff was revealed dramatically in contrast with responses of participants from other programs.

Perhaps the question that revealed most dramatically the student's
skepticism about the prison administration's commitment to the program was the one which asked whether the students thought "the primary motive behind having it is to improve the prison's image or to
provide a quality education." Thirty-nine percent of the inside participants in the Pennsylvania program felt the program was primarily
intended to bolster the prison's public image. The only higher response was Illinois, with 62 percent. In contrast, NewGate programs
with some autonomy uniformly demonstrated that their students had
greater faith in the program's (and prison's) earnestness: Ashland
11 percent, Minnesota 12 percent, New Mexico 14 percent, and Oregon
17 percent.

Staff. Probably the most abrupt change occurred in the authority
accorded program staff. All New View staff were hired by and directly
answerable to the prison administration. They had explicit instructions to act only in the educational areas of the inmate's life and to
leave other matters (therapy, custody, discipline, or release) to the
appropriate departments of the prison. Though on paper this seems
greatly to circumscribe the New View staff's role, in practice it
served as a warning to handle matters in other areas with delicacy
and finesse.

After the superintendent took over the program there was less
deliberate and arbitrary harassment of college students by lower
level prison staff. This meant less need for the college staff to act
as advocates for the students. Another benefit of having the superintendent as the college program director was that the New View staff
had privileged access to the prison's chief executive.

Staff composition changed significantly. But here too, change did
not have any dramatic impact on programmatic emphasis. Generally,
the New View inside personnel were younger and less experienced
than the NewGate staff. The former NewGate staff members were
transferred to the aftercare program at Penn State.

The superintendent hand picked a new deputy director, a man
who was familiar with Penn State operations, having received his
B.A., M.A., and Ph.D. in educational administration from Penn
State as well as having served on the university faculty. Under New

View, the deputy director's role was not one of policy making. Rather, he served as the executor of the superintendent's (director's) plans.

In addition to the deputy director, a director of the four-year degree program (the former position of NewGate's education coordinator) and three counselor-tutors (formerly instructor-counselors) were hired.

Also as part of New View, a director of a two-year vocational training program and one counselor were hired. This was a new addition based on the first director's original plan. The first vocational program was in landscape design and ornamental horticulture, operated in cooperation with Penn State's College of Arts and Architecture and College of Agriculture. On completion of the curriculum requirements, the student would receive an A.A. certificate. The program was intended to provide long termers an educational-vocational experience that could be completed on the inside. Initially, the new program did not appear to be successful. Of the original 18 participants, nine dropped out by the time data collection was completed.

The director of the four-year program in the fall of 1972 had a background in philosophy and sociology of knowledge. He was replaced by a man completing work on a Ph.D. in chemistry. Under the second director one counselor had a B.A. in law enforcement and corrections, another in chemistry, and another was working on his B.A. in political science. All received their academic training at Penn State and, therefore, were able to provide firsthand knowledge about the nearby campus. This appeared to be important to the academic counseling and prerelease planning. Pennsylvania was the only program where the staff was so closely involved with the host university.

Program Content. New View made no significant departure from NewGate's primary emphasis on academics. From the time the student entered the program, he was encouraged to concentrate on preparing himself academically for attending college. New View was a college preparation program designed to channel students into a four-year program on a college campus. For admission to Penn State, applicants need to have completed fifteen Carnegie units, courses usually taken in high school. Some students entered New View with this requirement unmet. Counselors helped these students make up their deficiencies in math, English, and science. New View could arrange for participants to fulfill the requirements by examination.

Little use was made of the programmed learning materials left by NewGate. Rather than convening small informal classes, the counselors provided individual tutoring in their fields. Groups of students met together as the need arose to work together on class-related work.

The behavioral modification routines were abandoned. The student lounge that had been created as part of the system of rewards was opened to all the New View students for study breaks where they could listen to music, read the newspaper, drink coffee, play chess or checkers, and engage in private discussions at their leisure.

The curriculum was basically the same as before. Courses were intended to acclimate the student to college work and to help him meet Penn State's general requirements. Inside courses were still taught by instructors from the Penn State campus. One noticeable difference was the presence of fewer full professors and of more graduate students among the prison faculty. However, the classes visited were well taught and enthusiastically received by the students. Class discussion was uninhibited. The instructors observed were imaginative and challenging in their approach. Ninety-seven percent of the inside participants found that the courses stimulated their interest in education.

Counseling. New View provided no psychotherapy in addition to what was available to the general inmate population. As NewGate, New View counselors envisioned personal growth taking place in the classroom or in the course of a student's studies. The counselor's primary function was to advise students about their academic program, what remedial courses they should take, and what department requirements were on campus and to discuss their academic progress while in the inside program.

The counseling component appeared to be lacking in direction and coherence—one of the biggest differences between NewGate and New View. The deputy director was reluctant to give the director of the four-year program specific instructions. The latter, in turn, seemed to exert almost no supervisional control over the activities of his counseling staff who appeared to be relatively uninspired. Over the period of the evaluation, the director of the four-year program resigned and was later replaced. Perhaps under new direction the counseling staff will be more dynamic and systematic in carrying out its prescribed functions.

Relation to the Prison Staff. Under New View the relationship between the college program and the prison staff was overtly cordial. For the prison staff to be otherwise would be construed as insubordination to the superintendent-director. Despite this surface improvement, a strong undercurrent of resentment and hostility toward college students and to the very idea of college for convicts was observed during site visits. The Pennsylvania inmates documented this in no uncertain terms. In response to the question "What were the attitudes of the guards?", 79 percent of the released participants said they were

negative (cynical and hostile). The only program that was higher was
Illinois, with 95 percent of the released participants saying the
guards' attitudes were negative. In response to the question on the
inside participant questionnaire, "What are the attitudes of the guards
toward you?", 42 percent said the attitudes were negative, higher than
in any other program in the sample. The closest were Texas with
37 percent, Illinois with 36 percent, and Oregon with 32 percent of
the inside participants indicating that the guards' attitudes were negative. In response to the question on the follow-up interview, "What
was the attitude of the prison administration toward program and
program participants?", 70 percent of the released participants reported it was negative (cynical and hostile). The closest in comparison
was Illinois, with 61 percent of the released participants reporting
that it was negative. The released participants were referring mainly
to a period in which there was a struggle between the prison and the
college program (then NewGate). Since then, there appeared to be
relatively less antagonism at this level. In response to the question
on the inside participant questionnaire, "What was the attitude of the
administration toward you in prison?", responses were about average
compared with the other programs.

It was clear that the superintendent was faced with a continuing
problem of selling New View to the custodial officers. This was no
small matter. The superintendent set out deliberately to undercut the
usual objections to this type of program by providing classes to correctional personnel whereby they could earn credits and pay increases.
These classes were provided free, participants were given time off
from work, and they were held on the college floor. Innovations such
as these eventually could make New View more acceptable to the
prison staff.

Relationship Between New View Students and Other Inmates. Inmates
interviewed from the general prison population appeared to be supportive of the New View students, particularly older inmates who considered themselves too old to take advantage of the academic program.
They encouraged the present students to work hard and to help improve
conditions for all inmates. These inmates claimed that the guards
were especially hard on the college students and that the prison administration kept the student in a constant state of anxiety by con-
struing his participation in the program as a privilege he was continually required to prove he deserved. Younger inmates from the
general population were concerned about the New View admissions
criteria and sometimes felt that decision making was capricious and
arbitrary. Consequently, there was some resentment and suspicion
of the New View program, but not of participants who had managed
to "slip through."

The college program participants confirmed the high degree of cooperation between the participants and the other inmates. Forty-eight percent of the released participants reported that other inmates were "cooperative and supportive." The closest of the other programs was Lompoc, with 27 percent of the released participants finding other inmates "cooperative and supportive." In response to the question posed in the inside participant questionnaire, "What is the attitude of other inmates toward you since you are in the program?", 81 percent of the Pennsylvania participants said it was positive. Closest was the Texas program in which 74 percent of the inside participants reported that nonstudent inmates' attitudes toward them were positive. The average was about 65 percent for the other programs.

The unusually close relationship between program participants and the rest of the inmate population at Rockview can be explained in a number of ways. Perhaps most important was that college participants were not provided any benefits other inmates considered unjust. The most critical of these was earlier release. At Rockview, almost all inmates (not just program participants) were paroled at the expiration of their minimum sentence. In addition, college students were expected to live by the same rules as everyone else. The second reason for the cooperation could have been the prison's deliberate attempt to keep the ethnic ratios of its college students evenly balanced, removing a possible source of antagonism between the participant group and outside groups, who might have felt they had been arbitrarily excluded. Indian and black inmates in the St. Cloud Reformatory in Minnesota were antagonistic toward their NewGate program because they felt there was an inadequate representation of minorities in the program. A third factor that might account for the cooperation in Rockview was the unusual antagonism between the students and guards. This polarization might have worked to strengthen the bonds among the entire inmate population.

Program's Relationship to the Release Function. In Pennsylvania, prisoners are assigned a minimum and maximum date at the time of sentencing, except for murder convictions. Parole is granted, except under unusual circumstances, at the expiration of the minimum date. Since there is no such thing as "good time" (which effectively reduces time to be served) in the Pennsylvania system, the date of parole is fairly well established. This not only eliminates indeterminacy, which creates anxiety among inmates, but also limits the discretionary authority of the parole board. It permits a program such as NewGate or New View to outline a step-by-step release procedure, which participants are reasonably certain to follow as they approach their minimum dates. Six months before parole students are transferred to the halfway house and later to the community residence house during their last semester prior to parole. Because all NewGate and New View students are paroled at their minimum date, there is never any need or occasion for the college program to become involved in negotiating individual participant's release dates, as so often happens in other programs.

Inmates with murder convictions are not paroled unless their sentences are commuted by the governor. Since there were some inmates with life sentences in the college program, the staff became, to a limited extent, involved in some release questions. Staff suggested that saturated lifers be allowed to attend classes on campus and spoke on behalf of certain individuals with the prison administration. It also wrote to the governor's office asking that several be considered for commutation.

Outside Program. No major changes were made in the aftercare program. New View students in the outside program were in one of the following three statuses: (1) Having taken all the courses available inside or within six months of parole, they could be assigned to the halfway house on the prison grounds and commute to the Penn State campus. These students ate breakfast and dinner at the house. (2) Three months prior to parole, students could be assigned to the community residence house in State College under minimum supervision. Here they shared three apartments, each of which had separate social and kitchen facilities. Once students were paroled they could live anywhere they wanted while attending school. During the fall term 1972, there were six students in the halfway house, seven at the community residence, and 23 on parole on the Penn State campus. Seventeen students were attending other schools. (3) New View made special provisions for inmates serving life sentences at Rockview. If they had taken all the courses offered in the inside program, they were permitted to attend classes on campus three days a week, as long as they were escorted at all times by a custodial officer. Since the New View staff was hired by the prison administration, its members were qualified to perform this security function.

Both the halfway house and the community residence house were assigned an outside New View staff member as supervisor. In addition, there was an undergraduate who lived in rent-free and served as a counselor.

The Pennsylvania project did more than any other college program studied to smooth the transition to the outside. In the first place, the closeness of the campus enabled the student to feel very much a part of Penn State while still inside. The lifers who commuted to classes on campus provided constant feedback about events on campus. In addition, New View attempted to prepare the student even before he left the prison by providing a one-day visit to the campus to meet his academic advisor and to get a feel for the campus. Each student received a home furlough for seven days before he was released. Finally, the aftercare staff continued to ease the student into the normal social and academic life of a student on campus. The thoroughness of this effort on the outside, particularly the range of services provided by the aftercare staff, was impressive.

In addition to supporting parolees on the Penn State campus, New View provided financial assistance to some students who went to another university. NewGate-New View had an impressive number of students still attending college; they have done well. One served as undergraduate student body president at Penn State. Another served as undergraduate study body president at Washington Technical Institute. Another joined the New View staff.

Analysis

Did the Pennsylvania college program offer sufficient supportive framework, personal social space, and challenge to make an improvement in an inmate's life chances after release from prison? Compared with the other programs in the sample, the Pennsylvania program ranked "high" on all three variables.

Supportive Framework. The most important support feature of the Pennsylvania program was its close proximity to the Penn State campus, which cannot be emphasized enough. This provided a quality academic curriculum, strong continuities between inside and outside efforts, the development of a good transition program to the campus, and an authentic college experience inside prison, which enabled inmates to become familiar with a student identity while still in prison. No other program in the sample had this strong a link with a university.

Second in importance to the academic program was the counseling component. Students who were unfamiliar with college life required advice and direction. NewGate provided competent academic counseling. Staff members were for the most part mature, understanding, and familiar with the requirements at Penn State. One area in which NewGate counselors demonstrated their commitment to the students was in the coordination of academic classes with the counseling effort. The NewGate counselors saw themselves as part-time instructors and deliberately attempted to create intellectual excitement among students by engaging them in related activities outside the regular classroom. New View counselors did not exhibit this commitment, and the effort became haphazard and lacked direction and coordination. Penn State instructors who had taught courses inside the prison

from the beginning indicated that there had been a significant loss in
the vitality of the program staff, and consequently in the program as a
whole. It is predictable that the initial excitement of a new program
will wear off. However, there are compensating strategies a program can adopt. The New View staff did not appear to have been
effective in this. They were thwarted by the structure of New View,
which encouraged them less than their predecessors to take a role
in innovation and developing the program. Another reason may have
been a lack of ambition on their part. The limited role they had would
have discouraged anyone with ambition from staying with the job very
long.

The third most critical support feature in the Pennsylvania program was the spirit of the participant group. During NewGate, students were encouraged to work together cooperatively. The success
of any student was seen by all as strengthening the entire program.
Under New View there was still some evidence that the students were
mutually supportive inside and outside the classroom, but much of
this was due to those students who were participants during NewGate.
They commanded a great deal of respect among the other students
and helped set a tone of seriousness and hard work for the program.
Cooperation among students was facilitated also by the absence of the
indeterminate sentence. Participants knew when they would be released. They did not have to "con" program staff or compete with
fellow students to get a favorable release recommendation. They could
plan their program and concentrate totally on using the time to better
prepare themselves for life outside.

The fourth most important support features were the physical
facilities provided the college program. Spacious, light, modern,
well ventilated, and comfortable, they helped provide an atmosphere
conducive to learning. The education building in which New View
was located, Prasse Educational Center, was new and separate from
other prison buildings. It contained the prison's library, and in the
New View section, a large classroom area, a special room reserved
for typing, a comfortable student lounge, and a section in which 50
individual study carrels were located.

There were two features missing in the supportive framework.
First, the library facilities inside the prison were limited. This was
a common problem in all programs in the study. The New Mexico
NewGate program was the only one that compensated for it by establishing its own library. It has been emphasized elsewhere how crucial
a library containing relevant books is to a college program. Students
must be able to obtain books they need and that interest them. The
seriousness of this issue was somewhat mitigated in the Pennsylvania
program by the possibilities for students to order books of their own
from the local college bookstore and to depend on instructors and

program staff to bring in books. What was lacking, nevertheless, was the opportunity for students to browse and sample literature from choices in front of them.

The second support feature missing at Pennsylvania was a formal therapy component. In the course of the study it became evident that programs should make therapy available for those who want it. Therapy can complement a student's efforts in the classroom by helping him sort out his experiences with the new student identity. It can also help the student anticipate some of the difficulties ahead in his transition to life in the free society. In the New View program there was no group therapy and only some individual, nonacademic, counseling. Only 25 percent of the students reported participating in individual counseling. The prison provided group counseling, but the inmates indicated there were serious problems with it. In the inmate panel of experts discussion, inmates complained that group leaders were untrained and that participants were either dishonest or superficial because of the lack of confidentiality and fear of reprisals by the prison authorities. Forty-five percent of the inside participants took advantage of the group counseling provided by the prison.

Personal Social Space. The program set out to create an atmosphere similar to that of a college campus. Once an inmate set foot on the education floor, he was to be treated as a college student, not as a prisoner. He could move around freely and schedule his time and work. Within the classroom, topics for discussion were unrestricted. New View should have had a wider range of choice in course offerings; only six to seven courses were offered each semester, and students had little say in course selection. Some inside participants complained about the lack of cultural courses such as music, art, drama, creative writing, speech, black history and literature. Others complained about the absence of minority and women instructors who would bring different perspectives to the classroom. These criticisms apply almost universally to every program in the sample. Only Oregon and New Mexico had women instructors, and only New Mexico provided courses in drama and art.

As mentioned above, the New View student, as the NewGate student before him, had no choice in type of therapy and therapists. The student could choose a counselor for help with his academic program or choose whether to consult a counselor, one of his professors, or another student for help with his studies. When he began to make plans for release, he could again choose among several sources of advice and assistance, such as written materials (catalogues and brochures), staff personnel or other students, and persons on campus who could write, telephone, and even sometimes meet with him personally.

It was difficult to determine whether a NewGate student had less or more personal social space than did a New View student. The fact that there was less harassment by prison officials provided the student more leeway. However, under NewGate, the programmed materials allowed the student to proceed at his own pace. The New View program was more standardized. In the final analysis, both NewGate and New View recognized there would be students at different levels of preparedness who would require different kinds of programs. Considerable flexibility was built into the program to adjust to individual needs.

Challenge. The strongest stimulation in the Pennsylvania program came from the classroom, from the college instructors, and the students. It is mainly from this context that new ideas, values, perspectives, ideas, and goals emerge. The classroom was complemented by the availability of reading and research materials. Students could buy almost any book desired, and staff members would pick up additional materials from the Penn State library.

The importance of the proximity of the Penn State campus as a support feature was discussed above. This proximity also served as a major source of challenge. The campus was a lure to the inside students. Because of the links between the program and the campus such as professors, the campus aftercare program, local and student body newspapers, inside commuting students, the telephone, visits to prison by persons from university admissions and financial aid offices, and campus visits by participants, the campus became a realistic goal to the inside student. No other program in the sample made college a more realistic possibility than did Rockview.

Proximity to the Penn State campus also facilitated the operation of New View's graduated three-step release strategy. Breaking down the transition to the outside into three discrete stages meant the student would not have to cope with too much too soon. It also provided new opportunities to which one could strive. The challenge was evident. Each new liberty extended to the New View student required the assumption of greater personal responsibility.

One source of stimulation that New View made little use of was extracurricular and cultural activities, which could bring inmates in touch with the outside world. During NewGate this was a stronger component, and the staff made deliberate efforts to create a climate of intellectual inquiry and social and political concern.

Despite the apparent decrease in initiative and enthusiasm on the part of the New View staff, the students still experienced a high degree of challenge. Compared with the other programs in the sample, New View ranked very high on this variable.

Institutional Change. NewGate-New View made the idea of college
education for prison inmates acceptable to a wide audience. The publicity generated during the NewGate-Rockview struggle and the state
investigation was an important event in institutionalizing the idea.
In the process the public became familiar with the program and some
of its implications. The fact that the central question was not whether
to have a college program but how best to administer it, was clear
acknowledgment that the program should have a permanent place in
the correctional system. The prison publicly committed itself to the
essential features of the NewGate program.

The well-publicized successes of NewGate-New View students
were a boost to nonparticipating inmates of Rockview and throughout
the Pennsylvania system. Some of their kind had "made it." This
made inmates proud and bolstered their self-confidence. The existence
of the program also assured them there were some alternatives,
however limited, available to the convict. Rockview inmates interviewed said as much. They also indicated that the college program
might have increased the respectability of "brains" in the inmate
culture.

The NewGate-New View success encouraged the Pennsylvania
corrections system to develop similar treatment programs. Rockview developed a number of new ideas. The success of New View provided credibility to embark on other experimental ventures. Projects
were being considered in community treatment and vocational and
technical training, which resembled the original NewGate model but
which provided opportunities to inmates who were not college material.

NewGate-New View failed to involve outside institutions in the
correctional enterprise. During NewGate, the university, especially
the College of Human Development, was instrumental in some planning
and operational decisions; but by 1972 this was no longer true. In fact,
people at the college knew little about the current activities of the
program. The superintendent was so dominant and had such comprehensive plans of his own that he appeared to outsiders to monopolize
totally the initiative in prison innovation and reform.

Program Survival and Vitality. The NewGate program administered
by Penn State did not survive. The controversy was described above.
It still, however, is not clear that the outcome was inevitable. Most
of the programs in the study experienced similar problems, but they
were resolved differently.

The transfer of authority was officially justified as something that
had been planned from the beginning. The superintendent argued that
NewGate was set up as a research and demonstration project; and
once it had proved its success, it was to become a permanent part of
the prison operation. He further contended that for the program to

survive it had to be put on firm financial footing. What could be firmer than having the corrections system responsible for financing it? The administration of the College of Human Development more or less agreed with the superintendent. It had little tolerance for conflict and was more interested in getting the college involved in corrections research than in operating a social project. The NewGate project coordinator at OEO's federal headquarters eventually favored the prison over the NewGate director at the college. She did not support the project director, with whom she had strong differences of opinion regarding NewGate's research component. She felt that it interfered with the delivery of services to the inmates and did not appreciate the benefits of the effort to set up reliable testing of the project's effectiveness.

The main issue, however, was not the relative emphasis on research, or even personalities. It was power. To assert full authority to develop other innovations at Rockview, the Superintendent had little choice but to begin consolidating his authority by taking over the NewGate project.

Although there were no dramatic changes from NewGate to New View, there are at least two danger signals that need to be highlighted. The centralization of initiative in the superintendent's office limited the role of the inside staff, which could lead to discouragement and frustration of the more energetic, independent, and imaginative staff members. There was some evidence that the inside program was losing vitality. Centralization also led to the isolation of the aftercare office and shut out input from it's staff. If New View is seen as primarily a prison project run by the superintendent, the follow-up components will play a less important role. There was evidence that the continuity between inside and outside staff had been broken. The inside staff did not relate to the outside, and contributions from the outside were largely ignored. Third, the centralization of initiative in the superintendent's office led to an emphasis on the prison aspects, away from the higher education aspects of the program. Penn State is a critical source of educational resources, facilities, manpower, ideas, and expertise. To have Penn State participate in New View only in response to initiative from Rockview is to limit its potential contribution. There was evidence that Penn State participated only in this reduced fashion.

The second major danger is the heavy dependence on a progressive superintendent for the quality of the college program. It was because of the unusual qualities of the superintendent, who had a Ph.D. in psychology, who taught courses at Penn State, and who understood what constituted a college atmosphere that the NewGate model was left largely undisturbed. What will happen when he is succeeded? There were no structural features to ensure that the

college program would not be reduced in effectiveness, as happened
at Illinois when there was a change of wardens. New View was wholly
dependent on one man for its preservation. This appears to be a major
defect in long term planning. Penn State should be provided a permanent, institutionalized role in the college program at Rockview
to help establish structural continuity.

NON-NEWGATE

Menard

The Illinois Prison originally was built as a facility for con-
federate prisoners of war during the Civil War. It now serves as
one of the major correctional institutions for the state of Illinois.
With a rated capacity of 2,600, it is second in size only to the Joliet-
Statesville branch.

Menard is a maximum security institution with a conservative
approach toward its inmate population. It is geographically located
on the banks of the Mississippi River, 50 minutes from the closet
"urban centers," of Murphysboro and Carbondale. Most of the correctional officers live in the small rural town of Chester, seven miles
from the prison. The rest of the prison staff commute from Carbondale or Murphysboro.

Menard's isolation is furthered by its geographical separation
from the central state correctional office. A general attitude of the
central and local administration at the time of the study was that
innovations at Menard had low priority. The state's Department of
Corrections seemed to be concentrating on those institutions where
work-release, furlough, and study-release programs were more
feasible because of their immediate proximity to essential outside
facilities. In contrast, Menard was remote from any urban center
where resources could be tapped for delivering these more sophisticated services to inmates.

The prison routine seems to have been established in the interest
of efficient and effective control of inmates. The first counselors the
prison had were introduced in 1969, a skeletal staff of four or five
to serve 1,624 inmates; there were no case workers. At about the
same time women were permitted to work in other than the front
office for the first time in the prison's history. Both these innovations
reluctantly were adopted at the urging of officials of the state's Department of Corrections.

At the time of our visits, one still saw inmates marching in double lines to their work detail and to the mess hall for meals. In- mater could not gather informally or spend more than five minutes passing from one location to another. While in transit they could not be anywhere not expressly authorized by the "pass" they had to carry. The only inmates who could walk about freely were clerks with special assignments. Not surprisingly, these were highly coveted positions. All outgoing and incoming inmate correspondence was censored, and persons could be removed from an inmate's correspondence list with- out explanation to the inmate. Books were also censored, which was a source of continuous debate between conservative and more pro- gressive elements inside the prison. At the time of the site visit, some members of the custody staff were questioning several books using profanity that had been authorized by the superintendent of education. Visitors were permitted no physical contact with inmates and sat in a long row to speak with the inmate sitting across from them on the other side of a wide table. If a large number of inmates were being visited at the same time, this seating arrangement made it difficult to hear without speaking loudly and provided no atmosphere of privacy. Completing the picture of a rigid and disciplined institu- tion were frequent body shakedowns of all inmates when leaving or entering a building. Menard was the only institution visited where members of the research team were searched routinely when they moved from one building to another.

Inside Program

Since 1957, college level instruction had been provided at the Illinois State Penitentiary, Menard Branch, by Southern Illinois Uni- versity (SIU), Carbondale, Illinois. The first classes were introduced with the support and encouragement of the warden, thereby laying the groundwork for a long term cooperative enterprise between the two institutions. This was a daring innovation in the field of corrections at the time. The provision of quality higher education for convicts was taken seriously. The basic point of departure from previous efforts elsewhere was the planners' attempt to create a college atmos- phere. They felt the provision of a few classes consisting of only classroom instruction was a shallow gesture. Second, the "partner- ship" established between the prison and SIU was tacit acknowledgment that a prison could, and should, create working arrangements with outside institutions to tap resources not available within the prison.

The reputation of the college program in Menard and the close working agreement between the prison and an academic institution was one of the reasons Menard was included in this study. Another reason was that, since this program had been in existence since 1957, it could be expected to have reached a degree of sophistication and refinement newer programs were striving to attain. Being a program with a history of educating convicts inside prison, it was felt Menard could provide clues to the solution of problems typical in this type of program. Another reason for this program's inclusion was the hope that something could be learned about long term relationships between prisons and academic institutions. Had SIU effectively entered the domain of the prison and made significant contributions to its educational and other programs? Or, conversely, had it become dominated by the prison's custody and security concerns and rendered impotent?

The research team found the Illinois program to be far different from what had been anticipated based upon its reputation; it appeared to have undergone dramatic changes since its inception. At the time of the site visit, it was most unimpressive. Some college courses were offered by instructors from the SIU campus, but there was no attempt to develop a college atmosphere. The program was dominated by custody and security concerns. Contact between inmate students and program personnel was formal and limited. The students were cynical, skeptical, and afraid. The program personnel avoided taking risks and were reluctant to do anything not formally required of them. The present administration seemed to value the program essentially as "window dressing" to make the prison look "better" to the outside. (Sixty-three percent of the inside participants at Menard saw the program as one intended to improve the image of the prison, rather than to provide a quality education program. A distant second was Pennsylvania at 39 percent.) The discussion that follows will attempt to describe and account for the changes the program has undergone in hopes that future college programs can learn from the mistakes of their predecessors.

Students. At the time of this study, 68 inmates out of a total population of 1,624 attended college courses at Menard. Fifteen of these were considered full-time students and constituted what was called the "college gang." The other 53 took one or two courses and had a regular work assignment in prison. According to the superintendent of education, about 115 inmates had enrolled at the start of the semester, indicating that about 46 had dropped out for one reason or another.

In theory, all inmates had an equal opportunity to enroll for college courses. There were only two requirements. Students had to have a high school diploma or its equivalent GED certificate. Second, they had to take the SCAT and score at least in the 45th percentile. The SCAT test was given four times a year by a representative of SIU, who served as liaison between the division of continuing education at SIU and Menard. As an agent for the university, he interviewed all applicants and, on the basis of their SCAT scores and background, decided whether to admit them to the college courses as full- or part-time students. In effect, the liaison man alone decided who would be admitted into the program, which was known as SIU's Residence Attendance Center at Menard. Inmates taking college courses at Menard earned regular university credits.

Although, theoretically, admission to the program was open, an inmate who could pay his own way had a clear advantage. Veterans eligible for GI benefits received preferential admission consideration because they were required to pay for their own tuition and books with VA educational benefits, which greatly reduced costs to the prison in the operation of the program. At the time of the site visit to Menard, 30 of the 68 students were receiving GI benefits.

There were two ways inmates could be dropped from the college program. If an inmate failed to complete a course, he was not permitted to reenroll until one term had elapsed. The second reason for being dropped from the college program was a bad discipline record. The superintendent of education implied the education program was reluctant to allow behavior records to interfere with an inmate's education, recognizing the pettiness of some punishment at Menard (for example, "talking too loud in line will get a guy in isolation"). Generally, if an inmate was in isolation and unable to attend class, he was given an excused absence.

The superintendent felt the strict rules gave his department "college students who were regular attenders and good students, and therefore a better college program." It is questionable whether this fact alone made the program better. The number of participants was small. Moreover, many inmates who were interested and eligible chose not to participate because they did not want to give the prison anything to "hold over their heads" (that is, the power to deprive them of some extra benefits).

The Board of Trustees of SIU in 1962 made special tuition provisions for penitentiary residents. Menard was required to pay only one-fourth the regular $10 a quarter-hour tuition plus $1.05 a course for book rental. Menard paid tuition out of the Inmate Benefit Fund from profits from the commissary. Inmates eligible for GI benefits received $175 per month if attending college full-time. They could keep the entire stipend after paying book rental and tuition.

Staff. Not unlike the other non-NewGate programs, the entire education program at Menard was understaffed. There was one superintendent of education, one director of secondary education, and a staff position. In addition a person paid by a new federal program was added to the education staff. The noncollege education program relied heavily on 22 inmate instructors. The superintendent of education estimated he was able to spend only one-third of his time on the college program, the rest being distributed among ABE, GED, Title III, programmed methods (by which inmate-tutors followed programmed schedules for instructing other inmates on a one-to-one basis), art, and library programs. Four inmate clerks worked on the education floor to assist with clerical and administrative tasks. The superintendent of education reported to the assistant warden of treatment and was on the same level as the director of counseling and the director of vocational training programs.

The superintendent of education began working at Menard as a secondary teacher in 1963. He had been in the public school system for 30 years, 21 of which were spent as a principal. He received his B.A. in history and his M.A. in school administration from SIU in Carbondale while it was still a small teacher's college. The superintendent of education was hindered in developing a quality education program by a prison administration reluctant to devote the resources or autonomy needed for the task. The assistant warden of treatment did not advocate a more liberal atmosphere for the education program because he accepted the preeminence of custody interests.

All instructors in the college program came from the SIU campus in Carbondale. Whereas teaching at Menard was considered a privilege in the early years, instructors on the SIU campus were much less interested at the time of our visit. The majority were graduate students, and consequently they had little long range commitment to the development of the program or to a personal involvement with the convicts or the prison staff. The instructors' efforts each term had almost no cumulative effect because few instructors taught in Menard on an on-going basis.

The academic program was coordinated with the prison by the liaison man. He determined the courses needed and submitted his projection, four terms in advance, to the dean of continuing education. The offering of courses at Menard depended on the availability of instructors. During the term visited (summer 1972), there was no math course given because no instructor was available. During the fall term, nine courses were offered. However, SIU only offered five courses out of nine requested during the winter term because of problems of scheduling and a shortage of funds to pay instructors.

The liaison man also taught classes at Menard and seemed satisfied with the college program and was willing to aggravate the prison administration by pressing for change. He rarely attempted to exert influence on the prison administrator through SIU's institutional power.

An interview with the dean of the Division of Continuing Education revealed the difficulty of attracting top-flight, regular faculty to the Menard program. At the inception of the program, full-time faculty taught at Menard as a part of their regular campus teaching load, but this practice was later halted. The dean reported that he had made an agreement with various departmental heads on campus whereby full-time faculty would again be made available for the Menard program. It is hoped that this development will provide the program with vitality; a stronger link with the university campus; an on-going relationship, which will provide more encouragement for the convicts to continue their education on the campus; and the development of personal contacts with members of the faculty on campus who will be able to assist the men during the transition period following release.

Program Content. The course offerings were primarily those that met general liberal arts requirements for the first two years of college. During the term visited, the following courses were offered: business statistics and economics, western tradition-history, American political economy, biology, English composition, conservation, and two art appreciation courses. No A.A. or B.A. degree was offered.

Black students, as well as several white students, reported they had requested the inclusion of black studies courses, but these requests were denied by both the liaison man and the prison administration. The racial composition of the population would seem to warrant such a course. The general prison population was 35 percent white and 65 percent black. The prison administration also opposed black instructors coming into the institution to teach, consistent with the conservatism of the prison and of the area. Out of a total of 289 guards, only two were black. As late as 1964, schools in the Carbondale area were still racially segregated. At the time of the site visit, the education floor was one of the least racially segregated areas of the prison. Eleven of the 19 full-time college students were black. Thirteen of the 24 full-time high school students were black, three Spanish-speaking, and eight white. Out of the 22 inmate teachers, 16 were black and six were white. In the vocational training programs, the ethnic ratio was significantly different: 43 were white, but only 11 were black. It was implied that some of the vocational instructors were prejudiced and that blacks gravitated toward the academic programs because of the education superintendent's reputation for fairness. There might have been another factor involved in the ethnic distribution. Most of the white inmates talked to preferred working as clerks, a position that had greater privileges than attending school full-time. If white inmates had easier access to these clerk positions, the black inmates' only real alternative was the education program. But black inmates might have been more interested in education than white inmates since the majority of whites were from rural areas in the southern part of the state. The blacks were from the larger northern cities, where education is more emphasized.

Most of the college classes were taught in a traditional style.
Instructors lectured; students listened and took notes. Quizzes and
examinations were given, and some written papers were assigned.
On the whole, the quality of the instruction was good. However,
dialogue between instructors and students was conspicuously absent.
Establishment of a dialogue was hampered by at least two factors.
Instructors were told to limit discussions to class subject matter.
Therefore, topics for discussion were circumscribed by the instructor. This was reinforced by stationing guards where they could over-
hear classroom discussions. Students were apprehensive about raising
certain subjects. Second, students could not stay after class to talk
with their instructors since they were expected to proceed immediately
to their next assignment after the class period formally ended. For
the same reason, they rarely arrived at class before the official
starting time.

Other than the interview that students had with the university
liaison man prior to enrollment, no academic counseling was provided. There was no staff person to help convicts pick courses,
choose a major, or plan a career. There was no one well-informed
about outside opportunities or requirements to guide an inmate's
efforts. As a result, most inmates followed a general studies program
with no firm notion of to what their present efforts would lead in the
future. The superintendent of education regarded this as one of the
most serious deficiencies of the program.

No therapeutic counseling was provided as part of the education
program. The four counselors the prison hired provided only a meager counseling service since they were too few and functioned primarily as caseworkers to answer special requests, for example,
helping the inmates obtain permission to have a new name on his
approved correspondence list, to get a different work assignment,
or to obtain a cell change. The supervisor of the counseling services
suggested some other reasons why the counseling program was not
more successful. He indicated that many inmates who came to his
program were insincere and were motivated only by how good it might
look on their record. The fact that counselors also wrote reports to
the parole board put them in the role of being evaluators and not just
counselors. This, he suspected, might also interfere with an inmate's
sincerity. Menard had one part-time psychiatrist. The supervisor
indicated that such people were hard to find, since professional people
did not want to live in southern Illinois or work in a prison.

There were few other activities or facilities to enhance the educational experience of the students. In an article appearing in the
Nebraska Law Review in 1966, entitled "The University's Role in
Prison Education," Delyte Morris, the former president of SIU,
stressed the importance of producing a full and enriching program.

He described what we have called a "college atmosphere." He suggested that cultural and extracurricular programs needed to be created deliberately to compensate for the lack of stimulation normally available to the average college student on campus. He suggested newspapers, magazines, special radio and television programs, pocket books, paperbacks, field trips, concerts, exhibits, performances, and a visiting program whereby students from campus take classes inside with the inside students. [7]

None of these were available in the Menard program. An adequate, up to date library, perhaps among the most important stimulants was conspicuous in its absence. Apparently, several thousand books had been donated to the library by SIU. However, most of these were dated, and SIU made no attempt to continue to develop the facility. Compounding the problem were prison rules, which made access to the library extremely difficult. Catalogues of books were prohibited in the institution. Personal books could be ordered if an inmate knew what he wanted and where to obtain it. However, there was a chance that the prison might prohibit its entry once it arrived. There were no book or magazine racks on the education floor. There was little opportunity for students to discuss subject matter or pertinent literature with their fellow students.

Relationship of the Program to the Prison. It has been emphasized that custody concerns dominated every facet of prison life. Some ways this interfered with the development of a college program already have been suggested. Other examples are that students were not permitted to move about the education floor. Nor could students be in a room without supervision. Students could not smoke or use profanity in the classroom. Guards entered the classroom to take students out at their discretion. Inmates were required to take three showers a week. These were taken in the middle of the day and therefore required taking students out of class. Although evening showers would have been more in the interest of the education program, it was claimed that they would have presented a security problem.

Relationship Between Program Participants and Other Inmates. No antagonism was detected between college participants and nonparticipants. The latter seemed to respect the former for their hard work but were not envious of their position. The only extra privilege afforded full-time students was to permit them to keep their lights on all night. They were all housed together in the same cellblock for this purpose.

Most of the nonparticipants were emphatic about preferring not to participate in the college program. They could see no payoff after release and felt it made more sense to seek prison jobs that gave access to greater liberty and more comfort inside the prison. The inmates attending college courses did not do so because the college program was engaging or exciting or because the felt that they were preparing themselves for more effective transition to life on the streets. (Only 34 percent of the inside participants viewed the program as one designed for men planning to continue their education. This was the lowest rating among programs in the study. They were principally taking courses to keep from becoming bored with prison life. They did not see their role as one of forming an intellectual cadre who might arouse the intellectual curiosity and development of convicts not going to school.

Relationship of the Program to Other Correctional Functions. Everyone on the prison staff was a security officer and obliged to take action in the case of any rule infraction. The education staff was no exception. Once an inmate had been cited no other staff member on the same hierarchical level could intervene.

The college education program at Menard had no substantial effect on parole decisions. Program staff members were not permitted to make statements on behalf of inmates. The program did, however, submit an inmate's college record to the parole board when he came up for consideration. Although the corrections department promoted the idea that what an inmate did with his time in prison had a bearing on release decisions, inmates and officials interviewed doubted it happened in practice. The superintendent of education thought that inmates probably believed their school record in prison carried more weight with the parole board than it actually did.

Outside Program

As noted earlier, the Menard college program was affiliated with Southern Illinois University, but there was no outside program for participants after release from prison. Though SIU did not host a formal outside program on its campus, roughly 20 percent of the follow-up sample had enrolled in SIU after release.

The SIU liaison man was instrumental in this phase too. He provided all interested students with applications to a committee that reviewed all applications from correctional institutions. Except for unusual circumstances, one person made the admissions decisions for the committee. His judgment was based on the inmate's application plus a written report from the prison sociologist, psychologist, and department of education. If the record showed the inmate was motivated and had made a "satisfactory adjustment," he was recommended for university admission.

An admitted exconvict student was eligible for financial assistance from the DVR to pay room and board and tuition and student fees, though not all actually received this aid. In addition, the liaison man said there was a standing agreement with the Office of Student Work and Financial Assistance that any student he recommended would be provided an on-campus job. He also reported he had been able to obtain off-campus jobs for students from time to time through personal contacts. According to interviews with released participants on the SIU campus, the liaison man provided other types of assistance and was an invaluable source of assistance during the transition to life on campus. Among the reasons why many released participants did not enroll at SIU were difficulty in obtaining DVR support and the participants' dislike of the conservatism of the Carbondale area.

Analysis

Did the college program offer supportive framework, personal social space, and challenge sufficient to help its students attain their educational goals? In comparison with the other college programs in the sample, the Menard program ranked "low" on supportive framework, personal social space, and challenge. Responses of inside participants were consistent with this ranking. In fact, they rated their program the lowest of the entire sample on the questions designed to measure these three variables.

Support Structure. The Menard college program ranked low on support structure. First, there was no effort to promote the program inside the prison or to inform new entrants into the prison that there was a college program. Second, once an inmate was in the program, he was provided no systematic counseling either to choose a vocational goal or academic program or to provide feedback about his progress. There was no significant psychotherapy. Nor did support come from close personal contact with professors who typically serve as positive role models for college students. Participants in the panel of experts convened at Menard were aware of the lack of support. Although most of the lower division courses the participants needed during their first two years of college were provided, many upper division courses requested by the students were not. Inmates serving long prison terms were quickly saturated and had no choice but to drop out of the college program.

Personal Social Space. Menard participants had limited freedom of choice, particularly in not being able to structure their time to fit their own needs. Guided by custody and security concerns, the prison administration left little room for individual initiative. It was administratively efficient to treat everyone exactly alike and in groups, and this undermined the education program.

Freedom to choose what to study was also limited. The university liaison man was the final authority about the number and kinds of courses an individual could take. Since the courses offered were limited and repetitious, a participant after some time had to skip a term until a course he had not taken was offered. In class there was little encouragement or opportunity to investigate a subject beyond the regular syllabus. Few research materials were available in the prison. Finally, the students had no role in developing a curriculum or choosing instructors to fit their interests. Menard participants saw themselves as having the least amount of freedom to make suggestions for improving the program in the entire sample. Less than 20 percent of both interviewed released participants and inside participants felt they had any voice in improving the quality of the program. Menard students were first and foremost inmates, and they were never allowed to forget this.

Inmates at Menard were more tense and afraid of doing something that could be construed as a rule infraction than at any other prison visited, with the possible exception of Eastham (Texas). Three persons invited to participate on the panel of experts refused to enter the room. The only relatively relaxed inmates were men serving long sentences and working at good jobs in the prison. The panel of experts interview was taped by the research team, as it had been in several of the other institutions visited. After the session, the assistant warden of treatments insisted that the tape be censored before it would be allowed to leave the prison. The research team had it erased so the confidentiality promised the participants would not be violated. The close ties between the program and the unusually rigid prison routine made it unavoidable that fear and tension could not be prevented from permeating the college program.

Challenge. The Menard college program was particularly low on the dimension of challenge. Classroom activities were circumscribed, and access to outside materials and activities was discouraged by prison officials and instructors. There was practically no program at all outside the classroom.

Moreover, students had no extended contact with instructors, program staff, or fellow students. The panel of experts emphasized the importance of such contact as a source of stimulation. Several inmates who had been involved in the college program four years before but currently were not enrolled, indicated that they had been inspired by their contact with professionals in the Mental Health Department. About ten clerks working in this department had become involved in the college program together. Not only did they receive reinforcement from the professionals, but also the inmates developed a dialogue among themselves and had access to typewriters, books, newspapers, space to study, and reference sources.

Inside participants had no idea what former students did after release, nor were they aware of opportunities to continue their studies or obtain financial assistance and where they should inquire. The college program participants had no college catalogues or counselors to advise them, and they received little cooperation from the prison administration in their attempts to set up a release program. They were not permitted to write anyone not on their approved mailing list, even if only requestion information about a release job or application for college entrance. This lack of contact with the outside undermined student's motivation because of the difficulty of seeing the relevance of present efforts.

Institutional Change. From all indications the college program at Menard, as compared with other prison college programs in the sample, had relatively little positive impact on its students. This is not to say that it had no impact at all. Those who participated developed academically and also personally to some extent. However, more could have been accomplished if the program had been struc- tured differently. Although a substantial number of released Menard participants enrolled in college after they left prison, this cannot be attributed to the program's impact. These individuals either had college experience prior to incarceration or, according to the inter- views, intended to go to college before entering the Menard program. It appears their intentions to continue college after release, instead of being precipitated by their participation in the program, accounted for their perseverance to continue in the program despite the many obstacles placed in their way by a prison administration primarily committed to custody and security. The college program had little impact on the prison staff. The inside program was of such low visibility that persons working in the prison had little information to change their attitudes toward convicts and convict students.

No significant rule changes were made in the prison routine to accommodate the needs of the college program. In fact, the opposite happened; the program bent to fit the needs of custody and security. As a result no college atmosphere developed in which students had a fair chance to participate in a full educational experience.

SIU, on the other hand, did make significant changes in its rules and procedures to accommodate the Menard program and exconvict students. In addition, its initiatives had an effect on other institutions of higher learning. Shawnee Junior College near the Vienna Correc- tional Institution began a junior college program inside Vienna. Johnny Logan Junior College set up a similar program at the Federal

Correctional Institution at Marion. Both these programs were initiated by SIU.

Since about 1970 SIU's commitment to the Menard program
gradually dwindled. This was apparent in the decreasing time and
money it was willing to devote to its operation.

It was said that during the prior warden's tenure treatment took
precedence over, or at least stood equal with, custody; but that clearly
was due to the personality and priorities of the warden. At the time
of the site visit, it was vastly different. The college program had no
bargaining power. Nor did the university, which had many political
resources at its disposal and thus considerable potential leverage.

Program Survival and Vitality. The Menard college program did not
maintain its essential features. On the basis of close scrutiny of the
Menard experience and the experiences of other prison college programs, it can be suggested that the deterioration of the Menard program was a result of one major oversight: the failure to create an
institutional structure, which would have combined the wisdom and
protected the interests of representatives from both the prison and
university. As it was created, it depended too much on particular
personalities at both institutions. Once they left their respective
posts, which happened almost concurrently, there was no mechanism
to sustain the vitality of the college program.

The warden from 1953-65 was sincerely committed to education
and fully supportive of the college program. In contrast, the man
who was warden during this study was a hard-line custody-oriented
administrator with little commitment to education. His interest in
treatment did not extend beyond teaching convicts a trade. But even
in this area, he did little to provide more sophisticated vocational
and technical training programs in the institution.

The personalities involved at SIU were also important. The college program was initiated in 1957 and developed into a full program
in 1962 by three individuals on the SIU campus: an associate dean of
the graduate school; the chancellor of SIU; and Morris, the dynamic
and ambitious president of the university. While these three were at
SIU, the university experienced tremendous growth. It was a time of
excitement and possibility. The faculty was young, enthusiastic, and
adventurous. Interest in the college program at Menard was at its
greatest. There was a waiting list of regular faculty members wanting
to teach classes in the prison. In 1968 this began to change. Expan-
sion stopped, and many dynamic people left for better opportunities.
There was a funding cutback in 1970, and the Republican governor
elected in 1968 was less supportive of higher education programs
than his predecessor. Eventually the responsibility for the college
program at Menard was given to the division of continuing education.

The division saw its new responsibility as of no special importance. Moreover, remote from the university's academic departments and the centers of power at the university, the division lacked power to gain influence with the prison.

Lompoc

The Federal Correctional Institution at Lompoc, California, sits in an isolated small coastal valley 150 miles north of Los Angeles, adjacent to the town of Lompoc (25,000 population) and Vandenburg Air Force Base. The warden has been active in the nationwide trend of introducing innovations into the prison enterprise. Several major programs have been developed. One of these is Project Breakthrough, a program of exdrug addicts lecturing to groups outside the prison. This program grew up somewhat spontaneously inside, but was given approval and space to grow by the prison administration.

The college program took shape similarly. At first, it was no more than a couple of courses offered by instructors from the Allan Hancock Community College. Since this small beginning in 1968, it grew slowly. In 1972 there were seven courses offered to 150 students. It grew as much from pressures within as from planning and initiative from above. The administration regulated and guided the internal momentum, allowing it to go in certain directions and at prescribed speeds. Some involved (mainly convicts) argued that the progress had been too slow, but there was steady growth and there were plans for a more ambitious program in the future.

Inside Program

Facilities. The most impressive aspect of the Lompoc program was its newly refurbished facilities. The education wing of the prison, which was approximately 170 feet by 120 feet was renovated into an "open education" space at an expense of over $100,000. The overall appearance was modern, pleasant, and cheerful. The education wing was renovated in conformance with two education principles. The first is that of the open classroom, where a variety of educational activities take place in the same general area without definite separation. Though this might result in some distraction, it creates a mood of dynamism and vitality. The second principle is the flexible use of space. There were many movable partitions that were used to close off areas. Some of these partitions were equipped with file cabinets, desks, and shelves to form an office. The areas along the sides were partially closed off for classrooms, an area in the corner had been

made into an office space, and the middle of the room, which had
tables and chairs, was left relatively open for study and other purposes. A "pit" formed by the circular wall near the entrance had
become a lounge with brightly colored chairs and small tables and
was probably the most pleasant and comfortable spot to which the
convicts had access.

The Lompoc program's greatest weakness was its lack of books.
The prison itself had no library. The federal prisons in 1967 had
moved toward "programmed learning" and felt no need for a library.
Most of the books at Lompoc were stored away or burned. There
were several shelves of paperback books in the "inmate activities
room," which was open in the evening; but these were mostly popular
novels. In the education wing there were approximately 150 text and
reference books. In addition, the prison had accumulated several
hundred texts for the regularly offered courses. An individual convict
could keep up to ten books in his cell, but books were difficult to acquire. If he had money, he had to go through a slow process of obtaining approval to purchase books. A book might not be approved if
it were considered subversive, leading to violence, or pornographic
(the criteria used to classify books according to these attributes were
not spelled out, so judgment was arbitrary). At Christmas he could
receive one book from a person outside.

The impact of this shortage of reading material on the educational
enterprise was obvious. There simply weren't enough books or reference materials to support college education. The prison suggested
that this was a temporary state of affairs and that a new library was
being planned. On the other hand, the convicts argued that they had
been complaining about this problem for three years and nothing had
been done.

Staff. The educational department had several functions, each with
an individual staff member in charge. In addition to the director of
education, there were persons in charge of remedial reading, related trade training, the programmed learning center, the teaching
machines, and evening school. All these, as well as the college activities, took place in the open education room. However, there was
not a particular staff person assigned to the college program. By and
large, the coordination of the college program was accomplished by
different people, but mainly through the efforts of the director of
education and the evening school coordinator. The latter set up the
class schedules and assigned convicts to them. At the time of the
last site visit (December 1972), a new staff position had finally been
assigned to the college program.

It was clear by the staff assignments, the use of space, and the
investment in books, that the college program did not have priority

in the prison's educational efforts. The related trades instruction, the teaching machines, and the remedial reading program, all of which were directed toward less educationally advantaged persons, received much more attention. The college education program grew with little investment of the prison's resources or staff time. The instruction was offered by the local community college. Space and some minimal administrative efforts were all that the prison supplied.

However, this historic pattern seemed to be changing. Several students indicated that an associate warden had been sensitive to their requests, some of which he succeeded in implementing. Most of these were not related directly to the education program, but one innovation in this area was the offering of a course in transcendental meditation. Moreover, a discussion with the warden indicated a shift to greater support for the college program.

Students. The convict population from which the college program drew was not a typical one. There was the usual heavy representation of minority persons—mainly Chicanos and blacks—a few Indians, and large numbers of white middle class young adults because of the position of this prison in the federal system. Lompoc is for less serious young adult offenders. This meant it housed a large number of drug-related offenders, especially persons connected with smuggling narcotics across the border. For instance, in the interviewed college sample, 21 percent were "heads" or persons whose criminal behavior was related to the use of psychedelic drugs. As indicators of the atypicality of the prison population, of the 1,020 inmates over 500 had completed high school, and 345 had IQs of over 120. These are extremely high proportions for a prison population. The above figures indicate at least 500 persons were potentially eligible for college courses; but only 150 were enrolled. Selection was first come, first served from among those inmates who had completed high school or whose academic achievement test scores were high enough to indicate they could complete college work.

Because of the surplus of potential students and shortage of classes, and because the college program was not considered an essential component in the educational enterprise, there were no outreach activities. The result was predictable; the college classes were filled primarily with white convicts. In fact, of the 148 enrollment in the fall of 1972, only 9 were black and 12 were Chicano. Moreover, of the 33 persons interviewed, 30 percent had attended some college before imprisonment. The Lompoc program, by default, catered to middle class whites and failed to extend its services to other segments.

Instructors and Courses. The instructors supplied by Allan Hancock
Community College were not typical college instructors. Many of the
instructors worked at some other occupation and taught part-time for
extra money. Several were retired servicemen returning to school
to earn an advanced degree. The instructors were more conservative
and not as up with innovations in their fields as would be a more
typical college faculty. Courses tended to be uninspiring; and did not
provide as good an alternative role model for the inmates as did the
instructors at other programs, who were generally liberal and who
could interact better with young nonconformists.

A total of 40 courses had been taught in the prison since the
inception of the program in the fall of 1968. There were 24 in history,
English, math, art, and business. The range of courses offered
made it difficult to meet the requirements for an A.A. degree through
Allan Hancock. The student was allowed to take only two courses per
quarter; and though the number of courses offered each quarter had
grown (7 for the last two quarters in 1972), it was still difficult to
plan an academic program because of the small range of courses.

In addition to the difficulty of fulfilling the requirements for an
A.A. degree, the narrowness of the offerings contributed to the program's failure to be academically challenging, inspiring, or exciting.
Some of the vital areas of contemporary education, such as sociology,
political science, humanities, and philosophy were not represented.
There had been one introductory course in psychology (repeated once)
since the beginning of the program. The lowest percentage of participants (52 percent) of any program agreed that the courses stimulated their interest in education.

Other Activities. The education floor hosted other activities that
influenced the prison atmosphere and the college education program,
if only indirectly. The warden, in attempting to recognize and control the growing organizational propensities of convicts, allowed
convict "clubs." To form a club, a group of convicts had to find a
sponsor from the staff and produce a constitution and by-laws to be
approved by the administration. Then they were given a cubicle in
the activities wing and the privilege of holding weekly meetings.
Approved persons from the outside community (but no more than 15
at one time) could attend every other meeting. The organizations
and clubs recognized by the prison included: The Hawaii's Sons, Auto
Club, Cultural Forum, Nordic-Celtic, 7 Steps, JayCees, Alcoholics
Anonymous Pathfinder, Afro-American Society, Gavel Club, Tribe
of Five Feathers, Operation Success.

The impact of these clubs on the college education program was
twofold. First, many of the meetings of these clubs were held in the
education room and could interfere with educational activities. Second,

they competed for attention with the college program and thereby drained off energy and ideas, which could have benefited the college program. For instance, the need for ethnic history classes lessened when there was an ethnic-centered club. Some of the clubs requested ethnic consciousness courses, but these efforts were unsuccessful.

Program's Relationship to the Prison. The college program was not very important in the prison's overall plan. It began as a perfunctory gesture, without a great deal of planning, and grew somewhat more from pressures from the students than from any commitment from the prison administration. The warden implied that college education was suitable only for a small segment of the prison population and that other forms of education, such as remedial and vocational education, were much more important. However, this argument did not seem valid for Lompoc, where over half the population had a high school diploma and over one-third had an IQ score of 120 or more.

With the opening of the education open room, the commitment to the college program seemed to strengthen. Course offerings were increased, and there were plans to expand the outside phase. Perhaps the slow, less ambitious planning that took place will result in a more stable program in the long run.

There was little conflict between the program and the correctional staff. There was no separate college education staff. Administrative tasks were carried out by the prison education department as a part of the ongoing correctional enterprise. There was some indication that past attempts to push the college program too fast resulted in opposition from both the education administrators and the central administration.

One source of resentment toward the program was the supervisory staff in some of the prison industries. All convicts had to have a full-time work assignment. Taking education courses did not relieve one of this requirement. When an inmate signed up for courses during the day (most courses were at night) he was permitted to leave his job for class, but for no longer. Many students had jobs where there was little conflict with their work assignment; but some, especially those in the "industries," indicated that their job supervisors resented their going to class. It was related that if they attended too many classes, some supervisors would transfer them to the kitchen detail (a form of punishment, since this work was considered undesirable).

The relationship between the college students and other convicts seemed to be cooperative or neutral. There was little cause for antagonism since attending the college program did not earn the student any extra privileges, such as extended time off work or a full- or part-time assignment to education, or access to a reading or study area. The education floor, one of the more pleasant spots in the prison, was open to everyone.

Santa Barbara Component. In 1971 a convict from the Lompoc honor
camp was admitted to the University of California at Santa Barbara.
He obtained approval to attend from the Bureau of Prisons central
offices in Washington. He arranged to be picked up by a student (an
exconvict) who was attending the college. The camp supervisor later
allowed four students to travel the 60 miles to the Santa Barbara
campus each morning and return at night.

There was disorganized, decentralized support on the Santa
Barbara campus for this and other facets of Lompoc's program. The
Education Opportunity Program (EOP) gave financial support to the
four students from the camp. An EOP staff member traveled 60 miles
to Lompoc to pick up the students at 6:30 a.m. each weekday. Other
individuals and campus organizations offered to conduct classes or
other activities at Lompoc. However, there was no official university
policy on these activities. Recently, a dean was assigned to coordinate
prison activities and to formulate policy in this area.

In the past, the prison administration has been reluctant to become involved with the university because of the lack of official posture and because of Santa Barbara's libertine, permissive, and
"radical" image. Once the university started forming a policy, the
prison offered a plan to expand the scope of the Santa Barbara program. The prison was willing to allow convicts to travel to the campus on Monday, stay in campus dorms during the week and return to
the prison on Friday. This would reduce two problems the prison
administrators saw in the present setup—the troublesome and expensive travel, and "contamination." It was believed that convicts
on the campus were likely to engage in sexual activities, to use drugs
and to take on radical viewpoints. This in itself was a problem, but
the main concern was with their return to the prison each night to
"contaminate" others with stories and rhetoric related to these activities.

Irvine Component. Since 1969 a professor at the University of California at Irvine had been visiting Lompoc to encourage inmates to
apply for admissions to the Irvine campus. He attempted to facilitate
admissions, secure financial support, and locate housing. He did
this as a volunteer with no formal program, official ties with the
prison, or official capacity at the university. There appeared to be
no special program other than the admissions and financial aid aspects. This instructor made himself available for informal counseling
whenever it was requested by the men, but carefully avoided for-
malizing the program in any way. In fact, he refused to list the students he had helped because he wanted to protect their anonymity.

The Irvine program was limited by its distance from the prison
and from the former residences of most of the convicts in Lompoc.

Irvine is about 40 miles south of Los Angeles in a sparsely populated
area. There is no residential area around the campus. The students
either live in campus dorms or commute several miles. There is
no bus service. There were some housing tracts being built, but it
would be several years before there was adequate off-campus student
housing in the area.

The cultural and social climate was extremely conservative.
Irvine is in Orange County, the heartland of the John Birch Society
in California. This is far from the ideal setting for an exconvict
program. In the first place, there was a lack of community facilities,
such as jobs, residences, and urban activities, to sustain and absorb
them. The community was conservative and intolerant, and there
was no community heterogeneity to protect the citizens and the convicts from each other. As can be seen from other case studies, this
is a situation ripe for disaster. This is probably an important reason
why the professor in charge insisted on anonymity and secrecy for the
program.

This atmosphere discouraged many students from considering the
university. Several released participants stated that they had considered Irvine and decided against it. Only 12 percent of the released
sample attended Irvine.

Analysis

Did the college program offer supportive framewlrk, personal
social space, and challenge sufficient to help its students attain their
educational goals? Lompoc had only one of the ingredients required
for a vital college atmosphere, the comfortable education room. That
room and the club activities, where groups of persons with shared
interests came together for informal discussions, gave rise to many
of the informal activities that help make up college ambience. However, the college atmosphere stopped here. The other ingredients,
such as adequate reading material, excellence of instruction, and
variety in course offerings, were seriously lacking and prevented the
inside Lompoc program from achieving excellence.

Support Structure. Support in the college program was almost totally
absent. There was no counseling or advising system. There was a
shortage of materials, especially reading materials. Administrators
offered virtually no encouragement to pursue an academic career,
nor did they supply information about outside college possibilities.
The support that did exist came in two forms: the knowledge and
skills one acquires in the classroom, which may facilitate future
educational progress, and support from peers in informal relationships. As indicated earlier, Lompoc had an especially large number

of middle class youths who had some college. These inmates were
a source of knowledge about outside opportunities.

Personal Social Space. The prisoner could make plans without un-
reasonable restriction from rules or subtle pressures, such as trying
to please a parole board. However, the social space was limited by
the range of choice in the college program. One could participate in
classes if he could get in or could come and hang around the education
room or join in a discussion with other students. That was about all
the educational choice he had. Few succeeded in obtaining minimum
custody and transfer to the honor camp, which would have expanded
alternatives to include the Vandenburg Air Force Base and Santa
Barbara programs.

Challenge. What challenge to acquire new values, perspectives,
ideas, and goals that existed at Lompoc also came mainly from informal interaction. The new education floor, the freedom to move
about the prison and the education room, the club activities, and the
level of sophistication of the inmates generated some informal intellectual activities. It is regrettable that these activities were not
supplemented or enhanced by more stimulating academic content and
instruction as well as other activities such as more contact with
outside cultural and intellectually stimulating programs.

Outside Program. The Allan Hancock program was entirely too restrictive and narrow to be considered an outside program that is
supportive, challenging, and giving of social space. The student had
virtually no space in which to operate on campus. This was especially
disturbing because the range of alternatives at the school was considerably broader than in the prison.

The support and challenge in this atmosphere was also poor. As
a branch of a community college on an Air Force base it lacked most
of the stimulating and supportive aspects of a typical college campus.
There was no student culture, few high quality stimulating courses,
no tutoring or counseling services. Its only strength was in wider
course offerings than in the prison.

The program at Santa Barbara had the potential for becoming
first rate. The Santa Barbara campus had many qualities that made
it an ideal campus for prisoners or exprisoners. As with all the
large and "wealthier" University of California branches, it had a
variety of counseling, tutoring, and financial aid services. The academic program was both stimulating and practical. There was a
spirit of support for disadvantaged persons among the students and
the faculty. The campus was heterogenous and located next to Santa
Barbara, a city with a somewhat liberal atmosphere. In fact, the

heterogeneity of Santa Barbara probably worried the prison administrators. Finally, the intellectual stimulation was excellent. The
university was becoming a first rate school, student activities were
intense, and all the ingredients for a stimulating college experience
for the prisoner or exprisoner were present.

The Irvine program did not have the potential of Santa Barbara.
In the first place it lacked the range of alternatives available in Santa
Barbara. The campus was smaller, more isolated. It had a less
heterogeneous and more conservative student body. The choice in
friends and lifestyles, and the potential moral support for exconvicts
were all lacking. The surrounding community had less to offer. It
was a high quality university, but stimulation was less intense because
the school was new, smaller, and more isolated. This, coupled with
its distance from the prison, seemed to limit its future role in Lompoc's program.

Institutional Change. Changes were occurring at Lompoc: the educational program was growing, there were new convict organizations,
and the general atmosphere in the prison had become less tense and
disciplinarian (convicts could grow mustaches and hair down to the
collar). The college program was only a minor cause of these
changes. A major influence was the convicts' newly broadened consciousness, which included new conceptions of themselves, their
capabilities, and their rights and which led to a steady push to be
allowed to participate in a variety of activities that formerly had not
been open to them. This new consciousness would not have developed
as it did if the administration had not allowed it. The warden allowed,
in fact encouraged, new activities. So a second major factor was the
administration's response to the new pressures from the inmates.

The college program and the other organizational activities
altered the prevailing ideas about prisoners. The staff saw that
prisoners were capable of undertakings that would not have been
allowed in former years.

In the area of policy or program changes, the students were
inventive. They initiated the program at Santa Barbara. They suggested a tutorial program, which became a regular part of the educational operation. The students and other convicts, with the support
of the administration, initiated a wide variety of organizational activities. Some of the new directions emerging from these efforts
were: (1) convicts leaving the prison during the day to attend class,
(2) convicts leaving the prison to speak to the public on drug and related problems, and (3) convicts remaining on a college campus during
the week to return to the prison on the weekend. These changes in
turn had the potential of opening up other new directions.

Program Survival and Vitality. Lompoc's problem was how to grow
into a vital program. As indicated, an ideal physical location and
relaxed routine existed in Lompoc. Add an adequate library, richer
and higher quality course offerings, and a more secure link with an
appropriate outside academic institution and Lompoc could become
one of the best education programs. Establishing an adequate library
is mainly a matter of dollar investment. Issues such as access to the
reading material and scope of material require some care in planning.
However, these are relatively easy matters to solve. The most
promising links to a university seems to be with the University of
California at Santa Barbara, which has the resources to offer the
type of inside academic courses and instruction that are essential
and has the facilities for an adequate outside program.

Why did the Lompoc program fail to realize its potential? No
doubt partly because the program developed without preplanning or
effort in shaping its direction. It was allowed to develop, but without
the strong backing or interest of anyone in the administration. That
was changing, but there were gaps to be filled such as the shortage
of books. It is possible that with the new education floor and growing
interest in the program from within and without, Lompoc will move
to achieve a high degree of excellence.

A contributory cause of the slow growth was the obstacles to
innovative programs present in any prison, resulting from the need
for the prison (1) to maintain control over convicts, (2) to accomplish
the work of the prison with the least amount of effort, (3) to maintain
as much sovereignty as possible over one's domain, and (4) to avoid
unfavorable outside commentary on the prison. These produce stubborn forces, which must be countered before there can be change. In
other locations, programs came into being or remained vital because
of the vigorous efforts of committed individuals or through the influence of an outside countervailing force, for example, a government
bureaucracy with funds or an outside college structure. These were
not present at Lompoc.

Offers to aid the growth of the program from individuals with no
formal affiliation with the institution were refused. The motive might
not have been stubborn, selfish, or petty obstructionism but a concern to move "slow and steady" and to avoid reckless, ill-conceived,
or irresponsible ventures. After the University of California at Santa
Barbara finally made a formal institutional commitment, Lompoc
expressed a willingness to explore some startling innovations, such
as the release to campus of convicts during the week to be returned
on the weekend. The proof will be in how the program develops in
the future. If it becomes an excellent program, the remarkable thing
will be that it did so with little investment.

Special Problems at Lompoc. Mention was made earlier of the desire
to avoid unfavorable public comment and its counterpart, the desire
to receive favorable comment. Many prison programs are undertaken
for this unstated motive as well as for official reasons. In other
words, a great many innovations in prisons are no more than window
dressing. This could be a basic problem at Lompoc. There was a
very large investment in the new education room, which to the casual
observer looks impressive. However, once one looks beyond this
room, he finds a lack of substance in the program. It could be only
a question of time before the rest of the program is filled in. However, the desire to provide window dressing and nothing more might
be a problem at Lompoc.

Texas: The Eastham Unit

The Texas Department of Corrections maintains a complex of
14 adult prisons located within a hundred mile radius of Houston.
The separate units, which vary in inmate population from 500 to
2,000, house a total of approximately 16,000 inmates, varying in
inmate characteristics and function. For instance, there are units
designated for younger first-timers, younger recidivists, older first-
timers, older recidivists, and "malcontents." In addition, there is
a women's unit, a diagnostic unit, a prerelease unit, and a unit for
persons charged with nonviolent crimes.

All but the diagnostic, women's, and prerelease unit have a
heavy emphasis on agricultural production, and slightly less emphasis
on industrial operations. Besides these revenue earning activities,
most of them have educational and vocational training or other rehabilitative enterprises. These, however, are subordinate to the
cash enterprises.

The Eastham unit is one of the largest institutions, with a capacity of 1,750 inmates. It is a maximum security prison for middle
range prisoners (not the younger, less serious or older, more
serious offenders).

Inside Program

In what was certainly the largest effort to provide college in
prison in the nation, 12 of the Texas facilities offered college courses.
In the fall semester of 1971, approximately 1,300 students completed
at least one course. Five community colleges were involved in this
program. The apparent ambitiousness of this effort was the principal
reason for this study of one of the Texas projects. A second reason

was that it was planned and implemented by the Department of Corrections, and it could be compared with NewGate programs that were initiated by people outside the system. Eastham was selected because it appeared to be representative of the Texas programs.

The college education program was one of the last steps the Texas Department of Corrections made to move from one of the most backward and punitive systems in the nation to one of the most modern. In 1947, Austin MacCormick, invited to survey the Texas prison system, found it to be one of the most inefficient and cruel systems in the country. As an example, he noted that in 1947, there were 80 inmates who cut their heelstrings to avoid the arduous daily work routine, and more prisoners escaped in one month than in the federal prison system in an entire year. The Texas Department of Corrections in the 1950s made a giant leap to catch up with the nation's other prison systems, which themselves were experiencing rapid changes. In terms of building new modern facilities, increasing prison industries, and removing egregiously punitive practices, they did extremely well. Moreover, some progress was made in instituting rehabilitative programs. The college program was first introduced as an experiment in 1965 at the Ramsey Unit in cooperation with nearby Alvin Junior College, which sent three instructors to teach English, algebra, and history. Lee Junior College joined the program the next year, and by 1967 there were 700 inmates participating in the college program.

Two characteristics of the Texas prison system, which were reflected in its college programs, must be emphasized. The first was its large size. It is more than just a well-worn cliche that everything in Texas is big. Its college program, once begun, grew to grand scale and became the largest in the country. However, in emphasizing large scale the importance of other essential qualities often is missed. To a great extent, this was a problem in the Texas college programs. Another overriding characteristic of the Texas prison system was its basic conservatism. Texans embrace a conservative philosophy of rugged individualism, individual responsibility, and initiative and a public policy of laissez-faire rather than the welfare policies that have emerged in other large industrial states. In the prison system this meant that programs and routines were more disciplinarian, authoritarian, and austere, if not punitive. This had considerable impact on the development of the college program.

Students. In outward appearance the selection process in the Eastham program was clear-cut, fair and nondiscriminatory. Formally, the college program was open to all who (1) possessed a high school diploma or its equivalent and (2) had a clean conduct record in the prison. An inmate could take one course his first semester. Upon satisfactory completion, he could return the following semester and take two courses, and the following, three. Three courses a term was the maximum.

The inside participants reported that program selection procedures used clear standards. Of those responding to the question, 78 percent answered in the affirmative. The only program that was slightly higher was the New Mexico NewGate—79 percent—which was open to everyone who could meet minimum academic standards.

A clean record meant 80 points on the trimonthly conduct sheet. However, according to the inmates interviewed, discrimination and arbitrariness found their way into the selection process through the method of determining points. Points were awarded by several staff members, such as one's work supervisor. It was possible to earn 60 points from the work assignment alone, and a person could earn 15 points from the chaplain, as well as points for participating in other voluntary programs. An inmate could earn 20 points for school. It seems that it should be easy to achieve the 80 level, but the discretionary factor could bar a person from the education program.

There was also an unintended selection process operating in the programs in that they perpetuated the bias in educational opportunity that began long before prison. Once begun, unequal educational opportunities are perpetuated because admission to higher levels is predicated upon completion of lower levels. Once a person falls behind, the likelihood that he will catch up is small. If there is not a vigorous outreach operation, directed to finding and encouraging the educationally handicapped to attempt higher education, and a compensatory program, directed at overcoming student deficiencies, the bias is perpetuated passively. The Eastham education program, though it concentrated on basic elementary education and made it possible for persons to earn a GED if they desired, did not engage in any outreach activities or in college preparatory instruction.

Finally, the program attracted some who were not educationally motivated. In the Texas prison system every person had a work assignment; most were assigned to agricultural work, which was hard and deemed undesirable by many. If assigned to agricultural or other hard work, one way to avoid a few hours work was to receive "lay-ins"—temporary permission to miss a day or a half day's work. There was no full-time or half-time school assignment, but a person would receive half-day lay-ins to attend class. Many signed up for courses to receive lay-ins rather than from a desire to seek the benefits of education. This is not necessarily a serious problem. In fact in some ways it is desirable, since many men who began for this insincere reason later developed a sincere interest in education. Several ex-program participants indicated that this had happened to them.

Staff. The Texas program, though large, was streamlined administratively. There were three staff members involved in the administration of the program at the state level, none of whom devoted full-time to the Eastham College program. At the top was the director of education of the Texas Department of Corrections, who was in charge of all education in all units. His role was mainly one of setting broad policy and plans. He was also involved in promoting college education and evaluating the success of the college programs. Immediately under the director in the administrative hierarchy were two college education coordinators, one for the southern units and the other for the northern units. They planned the actual course offerings, oversaw the central record-keeping, and coordinated the activities between the prison and the community colleges. Their main impact on the local programs was determining what courses would be offered. They were also the liaison between the individual programs and the central prison administration. They were stationed in the central office but made frequent trips to each of the units under their jurisdiction.

At the unit level itself there was a supervisor of education and recreation, who was in charge of remedial education, the high school program, hobby and sports activities, as well as the college program. His office was located adjacent to the library on the education floor of the prison. His main functions relative to the college program were (1) selecting applicants for the programs; (2) supervising the library; (3) supervising the education staff (the instructors and inmate clerks); (4) supervising inmate conduct on the education floor; and (5) communicating program needs to the local and central prison administration.

The program had approximately 15 instructors, most of whom were full-time employees of Lee College. They taught one or two courses each semester at Eastham, which was over 100 miles from Lee College. One of the major motivations for teaching at Eastham was salary augmentation. It was possible to carry a full-time teaching load at Lee College and earn extra money teaching in one of the prisons.

The quality of instruction at Eastham was high. The full-time Lee College instructors were better than many of the teachers in other programs in the sample. Moreover, they simultaneously taught courses inside and outside, which promoted a better perspective on standards and facilitated their staying abreast with their field. Inside and released participants reported that the quality of instruction was high and was the major source of support and challenge in the program. Of the inside participants, 97 percent agreed or strongly agreed that instructors taught well. The only program higher on this question was the New Mexico NewGate. The Texas program was

also among the most highly rated in response to the question whether
courses stimulated an interest in education. In response to the question, "Are instructors sensitive to the convict as a student?", the
Texas respondents again ranked the Lee College instructors high—
75 percent agreed or strongly agreed, higher than the other programs
in the study.

Facilities. The facilities of the college program at Eastham consisted of a library with approximately 13,000 books and two 15-feet
by 24-feet classrooms. The library and the rooms were clean, light,
and cheerful. There was no special study space provided for students,
so, other than the classrooms, there was no place where students
could congregate. The classrooms were small, however, and were
crowded and stuffy when more than 25 students occupied them. Moreover, they had no air conditioning and in the summer months become
extremely hot and humid. The college program was initiated after the
prison was built and there were only four classrooms on the education
floor. Also on the same floor was a large open hall called the
"piddling" room, where convicts worked on crafts. The piddling
room was as large as all the classrooms put together. There were
plans to convert some of this space to educational use; but as it was,
there was more space for a dozen or so men to while away hours on
a craft (from which they usually earned a small income) than there
was for 200 men engaged in college activities.

Program Content. The program consisted of approximately 12
courses, each of which met for one three-hour period one day a week.
In the spring of 1972 the offering consisted of a course in business
administration, two in history, two in English, one in psychology,
one in economics, one in government, two in math, one in sociology,
and two in physiology. Seven of these were core courses in the associate arts curriculum at Lee College. The other five were electives
that also applied toward the A.A. degree.

There was no program beyond the college courses. There were
no extra classroom educational activities of any kind. The available
space and time schedule discouraged this. Moreover, there was no
movement generated within the program to expand the scope of the
program. The convict culture in the Texas system seemed to be rife
with suspicion and atomism, which the administration did not oppose
since group activities were considered threats to the stability of the
system. The education program was conceived in the narrowest
sense. The broader dimensions of education including extracurricular
activities, which make up a vital college education, were either not
recognized or not allowed to develop.

Many of the college programs studied viewed counseling as an important component of their program. In the Eastham program there was no formal counseling. Some informal counseling took place, but for the most part this was advice and concrete help, for example, contacts to outside schools, which only could be gleaned by the students from the instructors in the few available minutes after class before leaving the education floor. During the semester, or over several semesters, a few students might get to know one or two instructors well enough to develop stronger ties. In these cases more advice, information, and help could be obtained. But that was not typical. More students in the Texas program than in any other program stated that they received no help in their outside plans and indicated that there was not enough information about outside education programs available.

Relationship of the Program to the Prison Administration and Staff. The administrators of the college program were firmly a part of the correctional system. There was no ideological conflict between them and the prison administration, other staff members, or guards. The local program supervisor performed custodial functions along with his other supervisory tasks and, therefore, was not seen as too permissive or liberal. His views on crime and corrections were little different from the prison administration. Both suggested that criminal behavior, to a great extent, was a problem of deficient personal values and lack of education and vocational skills. Moreover, all agreed that the opportunity to better one's self through discipline and work was the right correctional strategy. Consequently, there was none of the strain stemming from different ideologies between prison and program staff that existed in many other programs.

There was the potential for conflict between prison staff and the instructors. The instructors, by and large, were more liberal; that is, they were more likely to see criminal behavior as a sociological or psychological problem and to relate to prisoners in a less disciplinarian manner. Moreover, their interests and lifestyles were somewhat more urban than those of the prison staff. This potential was not allowed to develop into actual conflict because of the program's structural arrangements and routines. The functions of the instructors were defined in the narrowest sense; they only conducted classes in the prison. They had no counseling, decision making, or other duties. In fact, even class behavior standards were set and enforced by the prison. This, and the fact that they had to travel so far to the prison, meant they did not spend any unnecessary time there. They held their classes and left. Consequently, they were not in contact with most facets of the prison routine; therefore, there was no conflict.

For all intents and purposes the program had no relationship beyond providing classes to the prison or the correctional system. Unlike other programs, it had not penetrated other parts of the penal enterprise. For example, the program staff played no role in classification, disciplinary, or release functions. The supervisor did evaluate the students' conduct and awarded points, which had some bearing on earning "good time" credits and could have some influence on parole decisions. But there was no direct communication in the form of special written reports or personal appearances before the parole board, as was the case in some programs.

One covert function that the education program served in Eastham was that of maintaining control, which in all prison systems is the dominant concern. It was obvious how this was accomplished: To get into the program, an inmate had to conform to prison regulations and receive favorable conduct reports. The positive consequences to the prison system of this relationship were offset somewhat by at least two losses to the college program. First, persons who were capable of completing college work, who could benefit from it, and who, in fact, might become the best candidates for future educational endeavors, were excluded because they were seen as trouble makers, nuisances, or nonconformists. A second loss was that the necessity of conforming to rather rigid standards dampened the potential vitality of the program. To promote a free and vital ambiance, universities on the outside generally have created a tolerant setting, where a considerable amount of deviant behavior is overlooked. Some have argued that this has promoted, or at least permitted, campus turmoil. However, the tolerance has been maintained to generate vigorous and challenging activities. This was not the spirit of the Texas program, where the atmosphere was dominated by conformity, mistrust, and discipline.

Relationship Between Program Participants and Other Inmates. The relationship between the program participants and other inmates was neutral or harmonious because the program lacked distinctiveness and high visibility. Students were not removed from regular work assignments. They were not housed apart, and they did not spend large amounts of their time, other than classroom hours, in a special location. Other convicts either ignored the program or were mildly favorable to it.

There were, however, indications that the program was affected by racial prejudice against black inmates in the prison. Black inmates were somewhat antagonistic towards the program, believing that they were unfairly excluded through deliberate manipulations of their conduct records. Those black inmates who did enter the program maintained that they had had to overcome the obstacle of being regarded by other prisoners and some staff as inferior because of their race.

Role of the Program in Prison Release Decision. Texas was moving toward more use of parole as a release procedure. As this occurs, it is reasonable to believe that many additional prison personnel will be pulled into parole decisions in an advisory capacity. The education supervisors, as well as work and housing unit supervisors, will be asked to write recommendations to the parole board. Then some of the problems related to involvement in the parole process that exist at other sites will emerge in Texas. But so far this had not happened. For instance, only 42 percent of the Texas participants stated that obtaining an early release was an important reason for participating in the program. The percentage for all program participants was 58 percent.

Relationship of the Program to Outside Colleges. One of the most surprising aspects of the Texas program was the thinness of its tie with outside colleges, even though the community colleges (especially Lee College) were involved so thoroughly in the education of prisoners. Fully one-third of Lee College's students were prisoners in the Texas system. This was financially beneficial to the college because the state Department of Corrections payed $8.33 a student-unit to Lee College. However, out of 46 released participants interviewed or followed through indirect contacts, only three had attended Lee College on release. There was virtually no effort to establish a conduit from the prison to Lee College.

It was possible for a realeased prisoner to attend Lee, or other colleges for that matter. Their failure to do so stemmed from the total lack of effort to encourage them to attend and to facilitate their entry into college. This would require, at a minimum, taking available information about outside college opportunities, supplying postrelease aid in securing admissions, and offering at least some financial aid or part-time jobs. As it was, instructors on their own supplied information to the student. Informally, some helped students make contacts at the college, but nothing of any scope nor any organized system was offered.

Outside Program

There were no transitional postprison efforts made by the Department of Corrections or any college. Lee College, which serviced most of the units including Eastham, had no postrelease program beyond offering admission to exconvicts. Sam Houston College in Huntsville (the hub of the Texas Department of Corrections) had a heavy emphasis on penology and other related subjects and made use of Huntsville for on the job training and research in corrections. But the college not only made no effort to establish a postrelease program for exconvicts; they, in fact, would not admit an exconvict to the school.

Legislation and administrative policy permitted the Texas Department of Vocational Rehabilitation to support some exprisoners attending school. Very few (only two in the sample) took advantage of this because (1) they had no knowledge of this opportunity, (2) there was too much difficulty experienced in trying to secure aid, and (3) they had been refused aid by some local offices. The few who did take advantage of this funding source all attended school in the Houston area. Persons who resided in other parts of Texas upon release had no success in their attempts to obtain DVR aid.

The Texas Department of Corrections had established one unit—the Jester Unit—whose sole function was prerelease preparation. It had systematic involvement with organizations from the private and public sectors. Persons from these organizations served as guest speakers in the prerelease education program, which covered a series of topics related to the release problems of convicts. The unit also provided counseling (including job counseling) and had a work-release program. The department claimed considerable success with the prerelease effort. However, this program had little relationship with the college program at Eastham. None of the participants passed through the Jester Unit before release. So, although Jester might have been laying the ground work for a transitional program, there had been no progress in the college programs in this direction.

Analysis

Did the program offer sufficient supportive framework, personal social space, and challenge to help its students attain their goals? The Eastham program did not stand up too well on the variables thought to be important for providing an atmosphere for change. In comparison with the other programs in the sample, it ranked "low" on supportive framework, personal social space, and challenge.

Supportive Framework. The minimum physical facilities for creating a college atmosphere were not present at Eastham. There should be an adequate library with up to date references, texts, and journals in the major fields; a study room preferably in or close to the library; and an area where students can participate in informal student activities, as a minimum.

The library in Eastham (which had the largest collection of the 12 units) was inadequate in several ways. Though the history and

literature collection was large, there was a shortage of up to date
references and texts; and there were no journals. The library grew
mainly through donations and to become adequate would require a
large expenditure by the department. A possible alternative would
be a program to borrow books from the community college library
system. The space allocated to the college program was inadequate.
The large "piddling" room could have been available, but there was
no inclination to convert it to educational use.

Programmatically, a college atmosphere requires at least three
features: (1) time for students to comingle in a setting related to the
college enterprise, (2) some after-class contact with instructors, and
(3) information about outside colleges including requirements, offerings, supportive resources, and informal campus life. None of
these was present at Eastham, where the education program was
narrowly conceived.

Education was individualistic. There was no student or intellectual
culture. College education was nothing more than taking college
courses. There was a remarkable lack of informal ties among students, much more so than in the other programs. For example, few
exprisoners who were classmates knew the whereabouts of any other
classmates or, for that matter, could even remember who other students in the program were. It was very different in the other programs, where lasting friendships and postrelease contact were common.

If there was a single most important feature contributing to a
program's supportive framework it was the establishment of an outside
aftercare program located on a college campus. Texas had no relationship with a college that would enable its participants to capitalize
on the education they received on the inside. Whereas the majority of
the students desired to continue their college education, only five of
the 46 (11 percent) in the sample completed one semester outside.
This compared with an overall percentage of 62 percent for all programs.

Personal Social Space. The Texas program offered as little personal
social space as the Illinois college program. Both institutions constantly reminded the inmate that he was a prisoner and thus prevented
him from experimenting with a student identity. The rehabilitation
of convicts seems unlikely unless they are given the opportunity to
develop new, more socially desirable roles to escape from the criminal life. Participation in the college program was not encouraged
by the prison and was viewed suspiciously. Inmates were accused of
wanting to attend college classes to avoid work or to learn how to be
better criminals.

The student had little control over his daily routine, his personal contacts, or the substance and scheduling of the college courses. Rules governing classroom behavior were rigid, smoking was prohibited, and time spent in the library was allocated carefully and supervised at all times. Certain subjects were not discussed in the classroom. Prison guards stood outside the classrooms and, occasionally, even remained inside. Students were reluctant to expose their own values and perspectives lest they be branded as troublemakers.

Challenge. The college program at Eastham was somewhat challenging, due, first, to the power of ideas to challenge. Exparticipants stated their perspective, and their beliefs and values were changed because of the ideas presented in the courses. The following are quotes from exparticipants in response to, "What was the most important part of the program that helps you in your life today?": "It stimulated my interest in ideas;" "It gave me a desire to learn;" "Three courses contributed to my awakening: business law, psychology, and economics;" "It gave me a broader view of the world."

The second challenge factor was the discovery by prisoners that they could successfully complete college courses. This fact alone shattered some of their more degenerating views of themselves and led them to adopt more favorable self-conceptions. Indicative of some degree of challenge, a majority of persons in the program (89 percent) indicated they intended to continue their college education when released. As indicated above, however, few actually did enroll after release; though most released participants interviewed desired to return to school and expressed disappointment at being unable to do so.

Institutional Impact. The Eastham program precipitated change only on the ideational level, mainly among actors in the setting. Many convicts changed their views of themselves by witnessing convicts successfully earning college credits. Some discovered they could handle the world of ideas. Black and Chicano students, who suffered from stereotyping, saw that they, too, could succeed in this prestigious endeavor.

In similar fashion, many on the correctional staff had to readjust their thinking about convicts. Stereotypes of worthlessness and stupidity have been changed by convicts earning A.A. degrees. In addition, the teachers at the community colleges, especially Lee College, discovered that many convicts are qualified students. The instructors indicated the convict students were just as bright, slightly less prepared, but more motivated than their outside students.

As for the broader community, it is hard to say if the college program precipitated any change in ideas about prisons and prisoners. Community participation in the Jester prerelease program indicated considerable support for the new rehabilitative directions the department had taken. However, the community colleges did not embark on any postprison program.

Nothing changed in policy or procedure, or in the power structure. The prison routine, even for the students, remained basically the same. Moreover, there were no new inputs into the decision-making process in the department, either from within (staff or convicts) or without (college personnel or community figures) because of the college program. Whether the changes on the ideational level eventually will lead to other changes is not clear.

Program Survival and Vitality. The other prison college programs, especially the NewGates, were introduced by outside interests and then experienced a period of grace during which they were allowed to exist with a high degree of vigor. In some cases, the forces opposed to the program eventually took control in one of two ways: (1) the prison established narrow limits within which the program had to operate, or (2) the prison actually took over the program.

The experience in the case of Texas was different in that the program was introduced on the initiative of the state Department of Corrections. It was never vital or dynamic because it was compromised from its inception. The problem now becomes one of implementing strategies that have been found essential to establishing a meaningful college program.

It seems clear that under the present structural arrangement not much will be changed. Failure in the past to develop the college program beyond the offering of college courses was due to the absence of a person willing and able to take the responsibility. The state level staff were part of the Department of Corrections bureaucracy. They saw themselves pursuing a career within the department, not as persons particularly involved in college education. Even if they had had a commitment to increasing program quality, they would have been thwarted by their remoteness to the local operation and by their obligations to the other institutions and programs. Also, the superintendent of education at Eastham should have been involved in developing a higher quality program, but he had other responsibilities and no staff to assist him. Even had he more time and help, however, he would need encouragement and cooperation from the Eastham administration. But it is unlikely that he would receive it, since the top staff has never been committed to the college program but merely has gone along with it because it was imposed from above by the state corrections department.

The only other source of vitality and further enrichment of the program was the Lee College teaching staff, who were limited by the structural arrangement between the prison and instructors. They taught solely upon the invitation of the prison and were cautioned about their behavior in the classroom, that certain topics relating to the prison were to be avoided in classroom discussions, and close personal relationships with inmates were to be discouraged. These limitations, plus the fact that instructors usually came and went after a short time, meant they could not be relied on to develop a college atmosphere as a way of compensating for the lack of prison staff interest.

Large bureaucracies are inherently conservative. Correctional bureaucracies are particularly so. Because of the nature of their task and the perceived nature of their client—the convict—there is a dominant emphasis on control and security. It does not seem likely that any internal changes are going to come about that will themselves result in significant forward steps in the college program. What must occur for this to take place is for some outside force to take an interest in the prison college educational enterprise.

NOTES

1. "Corrections in Service of Justice: Biennial Report", Oregon State Corrections Division Biennial Report (Salem: Division of Corrections, 1970), p. 5.

2. "Oregon State Penitentiary—A Historical Survey and a Description of the Agency's Functions and Objectives," Oregon State Corrections Division Biennial Report (Salem: Division of Corrections, 1968), p. 225.

3. Oregon State Corrections Biennial Report, 1970, op. cit., p. 12.

4. Kentucky NewGate Project Position Paper, Paramus, New Jersey, National Council on Crime and Delinquency, January 25, 1972.

5. Personal communication with the author.

6. "Project NewGate (Pennsylvania) Final Report, First Year," (State College: Pennsylvania State College, College of Human Development, May 1970), p. 1.

7. Delyte Morris, "The University's Role in Prison Education," Nebraska Law Review 45, no. 3 (May 1966).

Adams, Stuart. "College-Level Instruction in U.S. Prisons."
Mimeographed. Berkeley: University of California, School of
Criminology, 1968.

_____. "Is Corrections Ready for Cost-Benefit Analysis?" Revised
version of paper presented at the 98th Congress of Corrections,
San Francisco, August 1968.

American Correctional Association. Proceedings of 1870 Congress
of Corrections. New York: American Correctional Association,
1870.

Baker, Keith, J. Irwin, S. Haberfeld, M. Seashore, and D. Leonard.
"Summary Report: Project NewGate and Other Prison College
Education Programs." Washington, D.C.: U.S. Office of Eco-
nomic Opportunity, 1973.

Brockway, Zebulon. Fifty Years of Prison Service. New York:
Charities Publication, 1912.

Clemmer, Donald. The Prison Community. New York: Holt, Rinehart and Winston, Inc., 1940.

Cremin, Lawrence H. The Transformation of the School. New York:
Vintage Books, 1964.

Cressey, Donald, ed. The Prison. New York: Holt, Rinehart and
Winston, Inc.

Education Commission of the States. "Legal Considerations Involved."
Appendix II to unpublished concept paper. Denver, Colo. : Correctional Education Project, July 1975.

Glaser, Daniel. Effectiveness of a Prison and Parole System. New
York: Bobbs-Merrill Company, 1964.

Goffman, Erving. Asylums. Garden City, N.Y.: Anchor Books, 1961.

Gottfredson, Don M., and J. Bonds. A Manual for Intake Base Expectancy Scoring (Form CDC-BE-61A). Sacramento, Calif.:
Research Division, California Department of Corrections, 1961.

_____, et al. A National Uniform Parole Reporting System. Davis,
     Calif.: National Council on Crime and Delinquency, December
     1970.

Haberfeld, Steven, M. Seashore, and J. Irwin. "Additional Data
     Analysis and Evaluation of 'Project Newgate' and Other Prison
     College Programs," prepared by Marshall Kaplan, Gans, and
     Kahn, San Francisco, as final report to U.S. Department of
     Health, Education, and Welfare, Office of the Secretary, contract
     HEW-OS-74-168, 1975.

Hansen, W. Lee, and Burton A. Weisbrod. Benefits, Costs and
     Finance of Public Higher Education. Chicago: Markham Pub-
     lishing Co., 1969.

Hentzel, David. "The Cost of Crime: An Alternative Model," unpub-
     lished manuscript, University of Missouri, 1972.

Irwin, John. The Felon. Englewood Cliffs, N.J.: Prentice Hall, 1970.

_____, S. Haberfeld, M. Seashore, and D. Leonard. "An Evaluation
     of 'NewGate' and Other Prison Education Programs," prepared
     by Marshall Kaplan, Gans, and Kahn, San Francisco, as final
     report to U.S. Office of Economic Opportunity, contract B2C5322,
     1973.

Kassebaum, G., D. Ward, and D. Wilner. Prison Treatment and
     Parole Survival. New York: J. Wiley and Sons, 1971.

MacCormick, Austin H. The Education of Adult Prisoners. New
     York: National Society of Penal Information, 1931.

Martinson, Robert. The Effectiveness of Correctional Treatment.
     New York: Praeger, 1975.

Morris, Delyte. "The University's Role in Prison Education."
     Nebraska Law Review 45, 3 (May 1966): 542-564.

Neithercutt, M.G. "Consequences of 'Guilty'." Crime and Delin-
     quency. 15 (October 1969): 459-462.

President's Commission on Law Enforcement and Administration of
     Justice. Task Force Report: Corrections. Washington, D.C.:
     U.S. Government Printing Office, 1967.

Rootman, Irving. "Voluntary Withdrawal from a Total Adult Socializing Organization: A Model." Sociology of Education 45, 3
(Summer 1972): 258-270.

Saleeby, George. Hidden Closets, report to the California Youth
Authority. Sacramento, Calif.: California Youth Authority,
March 1975.

Seckel, Joachim P. Employment and Employability Among California
Youth Authority Wards, Research Report no. 30. Sacramento,
Calif.: Department of the Youth Authority, August 31, 1962.

Sewell, William. "Community of Residence and College Plans."
American Sociological Review 29, 1 (February 1964): 24-38.

Sizer, Theodore R. Secondary Schools of the Turn of the Century.
New Haven, Conn., and London: Yale University Press, 1964.

Spady, William G. "Dropouts from Higher Education: Toward an
Empirical Model." Interchange 2, 3 (1971): 38-62.

Sutherland, E., and D. Cressey. Criminology. Philadelphia, New
York, and Toronto: J.B. Lippincott Company, 1974.

Syracuse University Research Corporation. School Behind Bars.
Syracuse, N.Y.: Syracuse University Research Corporation,
1973.

Takagi, Paul. "Evaluation and Adaptations in a Formal Organization," unpublished manuscript. Berkeley: University of California, School of Criminology, 1965.

Thompson, Victor A. "How Scientific Management Thwarts Innovation." Trans-Action 5, 7 (June 1968): 51-55.

Tinto, Vincent, and John Cullen. "Dropout in Higher Education: A
Review and Theoretical Synthesis of Recent Research," report
for the Office of Planning, Budgeting, and Evaluation. Washington, D.C.: U.S. Office of Education, 1973.

U.S. Bureau of the Census. Statistical Abstracts of the United
States. Washington, D.C.: U.S. Government Printing Office
(1974): 120.

Vanderbilt Law School, "The Collateral Consequences of Criminal
Conviction." Vanderbilt Law Review 23, 5 (October 1970): 929-
1241.

Wilkins, Leslie. Evolution of Penal Measures. New York: Random House, 1968.

Wiseman, Jacqueline. Stations of the Lost. Englewood Cliffs, N.J.: Prentice Hall, 1970.

ABOUT THE AUTHORS

MARJORIE SEASHORE is currently Associate Professor and Chairperson of the Sociology Department at San Francisco State University. She is a highly skilled specialist in research methods and design, evaluation methodology, and computer applications for statistical analysis.

Dr. Seashore has served as the primary Research Methodologist on the study of NewGate and other prison college programs and on the Department of Health, Education, and Welfare's supplementary analysis of this earlier study. In addition to her work with the social research and planning firm of Marshall Kaplan, Gans, and Kahn, she has since 1968 worked as a Research Associate in the Department of Psychiatry, Stanford University School of Medicine. Dr. Seashore is presently engaged, with Drs. Haberfeld and Irwin, in a major two-year study of the impact of Alaska's experimental prison, the Eagle River Correctional Center. Dr. Seashore holds a B.A. in Psychology and an M.A. and Ph.D. in Sociology from Stanford University.

STEVEN HABERFELD is currently an Associate Member of Marshall Kaplan, Gans, and Kahn. In this capacity he has directed numerous research studies concerned with reforming federal, state, and local prisons for adults and juveniles. As Deputy Director of the original NewGate study, Director of the HEW NewGate Study, and Director of the HEW study of federal education programs in state and local institutions for delinquent and neglected children, he has become recognized as a specialist on correctional education.

Dr. Haberfeld has served as a Lecturer in the Department of Behavioral Sciences at the University of California, Davis. He earned his B.A. in Economics at Reed College, Portland, Oregon, and his M.A. and Ph.D. in Public Law and Government at Columbia University in New York.

JOHN IRWIN is currently an Associate Professor of Sociology at San Francisco State University and a Consulting Associate with Marshall Kaplan, Gans, and Kahn.

Dr. Irwin is a criminologist of national standing and has published widely. As author of The Felon, co-author of Struggle for Justice, and author of numerous articles in professional journals, he has been a major discussant in the current national debate on urgent criminal justice issues. He served as Project Director of the original study of "Project New Gate and Other Prison College Programs."

Dr. Irwin earned his B.A., M.A., and Ph.D. in Sociology from the University of California.

KEITH BAKER is a Social Science Analyst in the Office of the Deputy Assistant Secretary for Planning and Evaluation/Education at the Department of Health, Education, and Welfare.

Dr. Baker has directed numerous national studies of the effectiveness of education programs in correctional institutions, including the original and supplementary analyses of "Project NewGate and Other Prison College Programs."

Dr. Baker has in the past served as Assistant Professor in the Department of Community Development at Pennsylvania State University. He earned his B.A. in Sociology from the University of Miami and his M.A. and Ph.D. in Sociology from the University of Wisconsin. He has published a number of professional journals.

CRIME AND DELINQUENCY: Dimensions of
Deviance

edited by Marc Riedel and
Terence P. Thornberry

CRIME PREVENTION AND SOCIAL CONTROL

edited by Ronald L. Akers and
Edward Sagarin

THE EFFECTIVENESS OF CORRECTIONAL
TREATMENT: A Survey of Treatment Evaluation
Studies

Douglas Lipton
Robert Martinson
Judith Wilks

IMAGES OF CRIME: OFFENDERS AND VICTIMS

edited by Terence P. Thornberry and
Edward Sagarin

ISSUES IN CRIMINAL JUSTICE: Planning and
Evaluation

edited by Marc Riedel and
Duncan Chappell

POLICE: PERSPECTIVES, PROBLEMS, PROSPECTS

edited by Donal E. J. MacNamara and
Marc Riedel

POLITICS AND CRIME

edited by Sawyer F. Sylvester, Jr.,
and Edward Sagarin

PRISON WITHOUT WALLS: Report on New York
Parole
Citizens' Inquiry on Parole and
Criminal Justice, Inc.

TREATING THE OFFENDER: Problems and Issues
edited by Marc Riedel and
Pedro Vales